Treasured Recipes for Family & Friends

With Love from Darling's Kitchen

by Renny Darling

Other Simply Delicious Cookbooks
by Renny Darling

The Joy of Eating
The Love of Eating
The Joy of Entertaining
The Joy of Eating French Food
Great Beginnings & Happy Endings
Easiest & Best Coffee Cakes & Quick Breads
Entertaining Fast & Fancy

8th Printing

Published by Royal House Publishing Co., Inc.
        P.O. Box 5027
        Beverly Hills, CA 90210
Printed in the United States of America
Library of Congress Catalog Card Number: 82-60913
ISBN: 0-930440-17-X

The Introduction

The world of food is the world of love. For me, it is a wonderful world . . . and full of wonders, too. How fortunate, I feel, to be a part of it. The gentle art of cooking for family and friends is truly a labor of love. It is the most unselfish and giving art I know. It is a world of caring and bringing pleasure to others. Rarely (if ever) would we prepare a multi-course dinner for only ourselves. But, if we invite just one other person, out comes the silver and crystal and candles . . . out comes our favorite recipes . . . and it all seems so worthwhile. That is the loving magic of food and it never fails to amaze me. It is a quiet way of saying, "I like you." in just another way.

So often, childhood memories are associated with food. I look back with fondness to when we were growing up. What a joy it was to awaken to the aroma of fresh bread baking in the oven. The five of us would run into the kitchen to claim our favorite parts of the loaf. After much negotiating, ("I want the heel." "You had it last time.") we settled into the pure pleasure of homemade bread, watching the sweet creamy butter melting into each of its little pores.

When the weather was raging outside, how comforting it was to sip a thick and delicious soup, just bursting with flavor and goodness. And when we trudged home, after a hard day at school, the fragrance of freshly baked cookies would greet us half way down the street, and we would race the rest of the way, for the happiness that awaited us. How long and lasting are the simple pleasures of childhood.

This is a cookbook for family and friends. It is a cookbook that can be used and enjoyed every day, for the recipes are amazingly easy and joyously delicious. However, if you serve these on formal china and silver platters, they will enhance the most discriminating dinner party. The recipes are exceedingly glamorous, even though the ingredients used are basic to most kitchens.

As always, I have kept technique to a minimum, so that the most novice cook can be assured of success. And seasoned and accomplished gourmets will find it exciting to be able to produce such astonishing results, in so little time. This is a cookbook for everyone.

So, I am offering you, here, my little "treasures" and sincerely hope they become yours, as well. They will help transform an average day into a celebration. And what is a celebration without sharing a glorious bite or two? (mostly two).

As always, enjoy with love.

Renny Darling

A FEW SUGGESTIONS BEFORE YOU BEGIN . . .

— Always read a recipe over very carefully. Then assemble all your ingredients before you start the preparation.

— Always preheat your oven.

— Cooking times are always approximate due to slight variations in oven temperatures, the size pan you are using, etc. Look for the description in the recipe to guide you, such as . . . "until a cake tester inserted in center comes out clean" or "until custard is set" or "until top is lightly browned."

— The number of people served is also approximate, depending on appetites, the number of courses and the size of the portions you are serving.

— Powdered sugar and cocoa should always be sifted to remove any unsightly lumps.

— The amounts of salt to use have been left to your personal preference. Very little salt was used in preparation of these recipes.

— Always use unsalted butter where "butter" is called for.

— Always use heavy or whipping cream where "cream" is called for. "Half and Half" is a combination of equal quantities of cream and milk.

— Whenever possible, use freshly ground pepper. White pepper is preferred for delicate cream sauces.

— As a general rule, unless it is specifically noted, it is not necessary to sift flour. Sifted flour is lighter and appropriate in certain recipes.

— Shallots are recommended wherever the recipe calls for these. However, you can substitute the bulbs of green onions (scallions), but results will be slightly altered.

— Always use the very finest ingredients available for maximum flavor . . . the best quality meats, the freshest produce and the highest quality of herbs and spices.

The Contents

Thank You

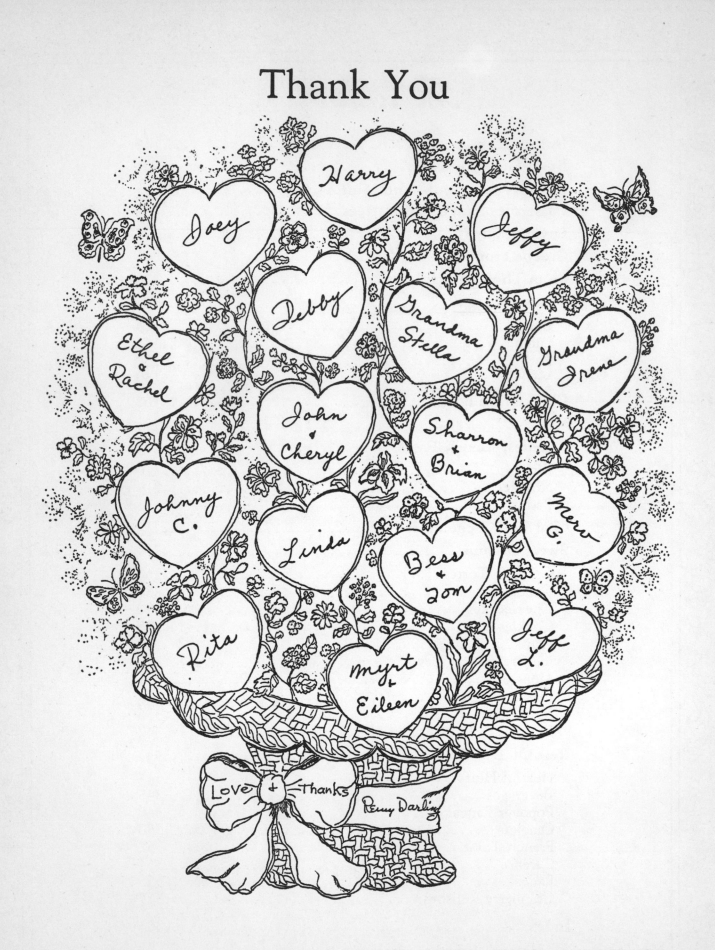

Bread is Beautiful

and Muffins, too

Bread IS beautiful . . . and baking bread is one of the true joys of the culinary experience. Bread has a magic all its own. Starting with the simplest of ingredients and watching them transform into a majestic loaf or joyous muffins or fluffy biscuits, is little short of a miracle.

The aroma of bread, baking in the oven, fills a home with love and warmth. It amazes me how much joy a homemade loaf of bread can bring to family and friends dining together.

So many people are intimidated by yeast doughs and feel they need a fund of patience and endurance to produce a single loaf. Not so. You simply mix a few ingredients and the dough does all the work for you, growing and expanding on its own, while you are free to do other things.

And sweet breads and muffins are the essence of simplicity to prepare. In fact, they literally need to be stirred, the less, the better. The recipes that follow are my absolute favorites and I couldn't wait to share them with you. All of the muffins are deep and rich and flavorful, sparkled with oranges and strawberries and blueberries and cranberries. They are further enhanced with a variety of glazes that add the perfect finishing touch.

The sweet breads are homey, tender loaves, bursting with flavor and goodness. They are grand accompaniments to breakfast or brunch. Everybody loves them. You will find a variety of shapes . . . large loaves, mini-loaves, squares and rings . . . all adding interest and excitement.

And my Best Butter Egg Bread, is simply the finest bread I have ever made. It is a little more work, braiding the dough, but the results are worth every bit of effort. If you had to buy the book for this one recipe alone, it would be worth it. It is simply that good.

And lots of holiday breads to add love to the celebration. How I hope you enjoy these as much as we do.

Yes, bread is beautiful and the stuff legends are made of.

Dark & Delicious Sticky Bran Muffins with Orange & Walnuts

Pure and simple best describes these marvellously flavored bran muffins. They are recklessly delicious, and one would hardly guess that they are filled with such good things.

1 1/2 cups 100% bran
   1 cup milk

   1 egg
   1 medium orange, grated
1/2 cup sour cream
1/3 cup oil
   1 cup brown sugar
   1 cup chopped walnuts

1 1/4 cups flour
   1 tablespoon baking powder
1/2 teaspoon salt
   1 teaspoon cinnamon

In a bowl, soak bran with milk until softened, about 10 minutes. In the large bowl of an electric mixer, beat together next 6 ingredients until blended. Beat in the soaked bran mixture until blended. Add the remaining ingredients and beat just until moistened. (Do not overbeat!)

Divide batter between 12 paper-lined muffin cups and bake in a 400° oven for about 22 to 25 minutes or until muffins are beginning to color and a cake tester, inserted in center, comes out clean. Allow to cool for 10 minutes, remove muffins from pan, and continue cooling on a rack. Brush tops with Raisin Cream Glaze and serve with love. Yields 12 muffins.

Raisin Cream Glaze

1 1/2 tablespoons cream
1/4 cup powdered sugar, sifted
   2 teaspoons finely grated orange peel
   1 tablespoon finely chopped yellow raisins

Stir together all the ingredients until blended.

Note: - Be certain not to overbeat the batter when you add the flour. Simply beat for about 30 seconds or until the dry ingredients are moistened.

Buttermilk Date Nut Muffins with Orange & Pecans

        1   egg
        1   cup buttermilk
      1/3   cup melted butter
      3/4   cup sugar
        1   cup chopped pecans
        1   cup snipped dates (cut with scissors into
              small pieces)
        1   medium orange, grated

    2 1/4   cups flour
        2   teaspoons baking powder
        1   teaspoon baking soda
      1/2   teaspoon salt
        1   teaspoon cinnamon

In the large bowl of an electric mixer, beat first 7 ingredients until blended, about 30 to 45 seconds. Add the remaining ingredients and beat just until dry ingredients are moistened. (Do not overbeat!)

Divide batter between 12 paper-lined muffin cups and bake in a 400° oven for about 22 to 25 minutes or until muffins are lightly browned and a cake tester, inserted in center, comes out clean. Allow to cool for 10 minutes, remove muffins from pan, and continue cooling on a rack. Serve warm with Whipped Orange Pecan Butter. Yields 12 muffins.

Whipped Orange Pecan Butter

      1/2   cup (1 stick) butter, softened
        2   tablespoons honey
        1   tablespoon grated orange peel
        2   tablespoons finely chopped pecans

Beat butter until creamy. Beat in the remaining ingredients until blended.

Note: - Please be certain not to overbeat the batter when you add the flour mixture. Simply beat for about 30 seconds, or until the dry ingredients are moistened. To be safe, you can stir batter by hand.

Sour Cream Orange Muffins with Orange Glaze

Tender, gossamer muffins, so full of flavor and goodness, these tasty morsels will thrill the most jaded appetites. One bite, and I promise you, you will have to control yourself from squealing out loud. The Orange Glaze is optional, but a lovely addition, for a brunch or luncheon buffet.

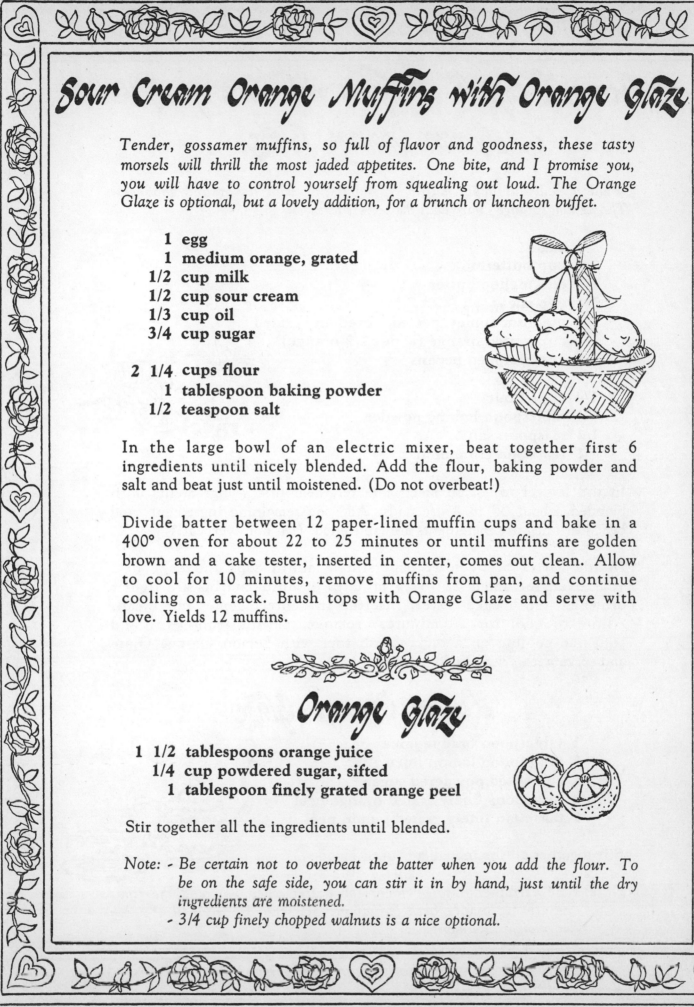

    1 egg
    1 medium orange, grated
  1/2 cup milk
  1/2 cup sour cream
  1/3 cup oil
  3/4 cup sugar

2 1/4 cups flour
    1 tablespoon baking powder
  1/2 teaspoon salt

In the large bowl of an electric mixer, beat together first 6 ingredients until nicely blended. Add the flour, baking powder and salt and beat just until moistened. (Do not overbeat!)

Divide batter between 12 paper-lined muffin cups and bake in a 400° oven for about 22 to 25 minutes or until muffins are golden brown and a cake tester, inserted in center, comes out clean. Allow to cool for 10 minutes, remove muffins from pan, and continue cooling on a rack. Brush tops with Orange Glaze and serve with love. Yields 12 muffins.

Orange Glaze

1 1/2 tablespoons orange juice
  1/4 cup powdered sugar, sifted
    1 tablespoon fincly grated orange peel

Stir together all the ingredients until blended.

Note: - Be certain not to overbeat the batter when you add the flour. To be on the safe side, you can stir it in by hand, just until the dry ingredients are moistened.
- 3/4 cup finely chopped walnuts is a nice optional.

Buttermilk Apple Muffins with Orange, Pecans & Lemon Orange Glaze

What a delicious apple muffin, just bursting with flavor and goodness. The Lemon Orange Glaze adds the perfect tartness.

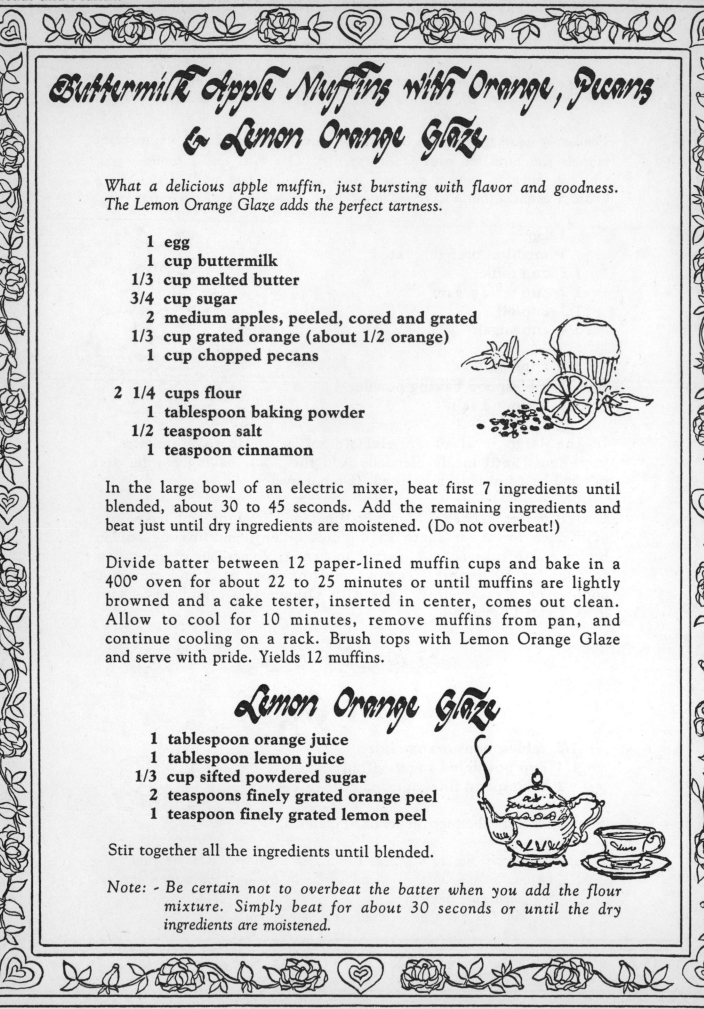

- 1 egg
- 1 cup buttermilk
- 1/3 cup melted butter
- 3/4 cup sugar
- 2 medium apples, peeled, cored and grated
- 1/3 cup grated orange (about 1/2 orange)
- 1 cup chopped pecans

- 2 1/4 cups flour
- 1 tablespoon baking powder
- 1/2 teaspoon salt
- 1 teaspoon cinnamon

In the large bowl of an electric mixer, beat first 7 ingredients until blended, about 30 to 45 seconds. Add the remaining ingredients and beat just until dry ingredients are moistened. (Do not overbeat!)

Divide batter between 12 paper-lined muffin cups and bake in a 400° oven for about 22 to 25 minutes or until muffins are lightly browned and a cake tester, inserted in center, comes out clean. Allow to cool for 10 minutes, remove muffins from pan, and continue cooling on a rack. Brush tops with Lemon Orange Glaze and serve with pride. Yields 12 muffins.

Lemon Orange Glaze

- 1 tablespoon orange juice
- 1 tablespoon lemon juice
- 1/3 cup sifted powdered sugar
- 2 teaspoons finely grated orange peel
- 1 teaspoon finely grated lemon peel

Stir together all the ingredients until blended.

Note: - Be certain not to overbeat the batter when you add the flour mixture. Simply beat for about 30 seconds or until the dry ingredients are moistened.

Strawberry Orange Muffins with Walnuts
Strawberry Orange Glaze

Gloriously flavored and joyously delicious are these superb muffins. Sparkled with strawberries and orange and walnuts, they can become a favorite at your house. If strawberries are not in season, you can substitute frozen strawberries (not in syrup.)

    1   egg
    1   small orange, grated
    1   cup sliced strawberries, fresh or frozen
  1/2 cup milk
  1/2 cup sour cream
  1/3 cup oil
  3/4 cup sugar
    1   cup chopped walnuts

2 1/4 cups flour
    1   tablespoon baking powder
  1/2 teaspoon salt

In the large bowl of an electric mixer, beat first 8 ingredients until blended, about 30 to 45 seconds. Add the remaining ingredients and beat just until dry ingredients are moistened. (Do not overbeat!)

Divide batter between 18 paper-lined muffin cups and bake in a 400° oven for about 22 to 25 minutes or until muffins are lightly browned and a cake tester, inserted in center, comes out clean. Allow to cool for 10 minutes, remove muffins from pans, and continue cooling on a rack. Brush tops with Strawberry Orange Glaze for a lovely touch. Yields 18 muffins.

Strawberry Orange Glaze

    2 tablespoons orange juice
  1/3 cup sifted powdered sugar
    1 tablespoon finely grated orange peel
    1 tablespoon mashed strawberries

Stir together all the ingredients until blended.

Note: - Be certain not to overbeat the batter when you add the flour. Simply beat for about 30 seconds or until the dry ingredients are moistened.

Cranberry Orange Muffins with Apples & Walnuts

Oh, what a delicious muffin. Cranberries with orange and apples and walnuts, all add a distinct flavor, making these totally irresistible.

        1   egg
      1/2   cup sour cream
      1/2   cup milk
      1/3   cup oil
      3/4   cup sugar
        1   cup chopped walnuts
        1   apple, peeled, cored and grated
      1/2   medium orange, grated
        1   cup cranberries, coarsely chopped. (This can
              be done in a food processor.)
    2 1/4   cups flour
        1   tablespoon baking powder
      1/2   teaspoon salt
        1   teaspoon cinnamon

In the large bowl of an electric mixer, beat first 9 ingredients until blended, about 30 to 35 seconds. Add the remaining ingredients and beat just until dry ingredients are moistened. (Do not overbeat!)

Divide batter between 12 paper-lined muffin cups and bake in a 400° oven for about 22 to 25 minutes or until muffins are lightly browned and a cake tester, inserted in center, comes out clean. Allow to cool for 10 minutes, remove muffins from pan, and continue cooling on a rack. Serve warm with Whipped Sweet Orange Butter. Yields 12 muffins.

Whipped Sweet Orange Butter

      1/2   cup (1 stick) butter, softened
        2   tablespoons honey (or more to taste)
        1   tablespoon grated orange peel

Beat butter until creamy. Beat in the remaining ingredients until blended.

Note: - Please be certain not to overbeat the batter when you add the flour mixture. Simply beat for about 30 seconds, or until the dry ingredients are moistened. To be safe, you can stir by hand.

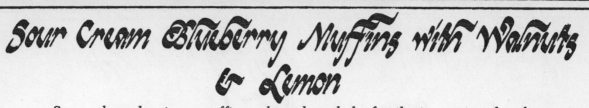

Sour Cream Blueberry Muffins with Walnuts & Lemon

Serve these luscious muffins when the whole family is coming for dinner. What could be a nicer accompaniment to roast chicken than these warm, delectable blueberry muffins with just a hint of lemon?

- 1 **egg**
- 1 **cup sour cream**
- 1/3 **cup melted butter**
- 3/4 **cup sugar**
- 1 **cup chopped walnuts**
- 2 **tablespoons grated lemon, (use peel, juice and fruit)**

- 2 1/4 **cups flour**
- 1 **tablespoon baking powder**
- 1/2 **teaspoon salt**

- 1 1/2 **cups firm ripe blueberries, fresh or frozen**

In the large bowl of an electric mixer, beat first 6 ingredients until blended, about 30 to 35 seconds. Add the flour, baking powder and salt and beat just until dry ingredients are moistened. (Do not overbeat!) Stir in the blueberries.

Divide batter between 12 paper-lined muffin cups and bake in a 400° oven for about 22 to 25 minutes or until muffins are lightly browned and a cake tester, inserted in center, comes out clean. Allow to cool for 10 minutes, remove muffins from pan, and continue cooling on a rack. Brush tops with Lemon Glaze and serve with sweet, creamy butter. Yields 12 muffins.

Lemon Glaze

- 1 **tablespoon lemon juice**
- 1 **tablespoon cream**
- 1/3 **cup sifted powdered sugar**
- 1 **teaspoon finely grated lemon peel**

Stir together all the ingredients until blended.

Note: - Please be certain not to overbeat the batter when you add the flour mixture. Simply beat for about 30 seconds, or until the dry ingredients are moistened. To be safe, you can stir by hand.

Peasant Sweet Potato Muffins with Apples, Orange & Walnuts

I hesitated to share this recipe with you. The muffins are on the hardy side (perish the word, "heavy"), but everyone enjoyed them, so here they are. These muffins should be prepared 2 days before serving, so that the flavors mellow.

- 1 **cup sugar**
- 1 **cup canned sweet potatoes (or yams)**
- 1/2 **cup (1 stick) butter**
- 2 **eggs**
- 1 **cup sour cream**

- 1 1/2 **cups flour**
- 3 **teaspoons baking powder**
- 2 **teaspoons pumpkin pie spice**
- 1/2 **teaspoon cinnamon**

- 1 **apple, peeled, cored and grated**
- 1/2 **cup yellow raisins**
- 1 **cup chopped walnuts**
- 2 **tablespoons grated orange peel**

Beat together sugar, sweet potatoes, butter, eggs and sour cream until mixture is blended.

Combine flour, baking powder, pumpkin pie spice and cinnamon and add all at once to egg mixture. Stir by hand until flour mixture is blended. Do not overmix. Stir in the remaining ingredients.

Divide dough between 24 paper-lined muffin cups and bake in a 375° oven for about 40 to 45 minutes or until a cake tester, inserted in center, comes out clean. Tops should be browned. Allow to cool in pan. Store muffins in double plastic bags and store in the refrigerator. Reheat before serving. Serve with whipped sweet butter. Yields 24 muffins.

Note: - Store these for 2 days before serving. The fruit flavors intensify and muffins are quite moist.

Royal Buttermilk Bread with Orange & Poppyseeds

This bread is a special delight, fragrant and moist and joyously delicious. It is especially easy to prepare and you will enjoy the fact that it is also economical.

      2   eggs
    1/2   cup oil
    3/4   cup buttermilk
    1/2   orange, grated. Use peel, juice and fruit.
      1   teaspoon vanilla

  1 3/4   cups flour
      1   cup sugar
      2   teaspoons baking powder
      2   tablespoons poppy seeds

In the large bowl of an electric mixer, beat together first 5 ingredients until blended. Add the remaining ingredients and beat for 1 or 2 minutes until batter is nicely blended. Do not overbeat.

Pour batter into 3 mini-loaf pans, 5x3-inches, that have been greased and lightly floured. Bake in a 350° oven for about 35 minutes, or until a cake tester, inserted in center, comes out clean. Allow to cool in pans for about 10 minutes and turn out on a rack to continue cooling. Yields 3 mini-loaves.

Note: - As an extra touch, you can glaze the breads with a thin coating of Buttermilk Orange Glaze.

Buttermilk Orange Glaze

    1   tablespoon buttermilk
    1   tablespoon grated orange peel
  3/4   cup sifted powdered sugar

Stir together all the ingredients and brush lightly on cooled breads.

Apple Walnut Bread Ring
with Brown Sugar Cinnamon Topping

This delicious bread will grace a brunch table with taste and style. It is lovely to look at and delicious, too. It is also a treat at snack time.

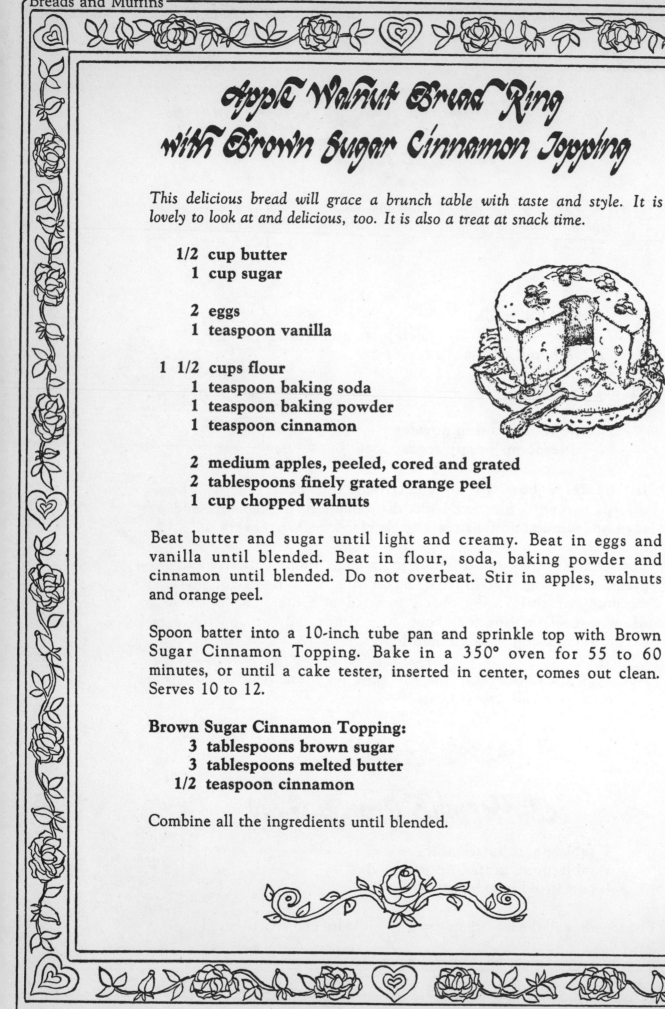

    1/2 cup butter
      1 cup sugar

      2 eggs
      1 teaspoon vanilla

  1 1/2 cups flour
      1 teaspoon baking soda
      1 teaspoon baking powder
      1 teaspoon cinnamon

      2 medium apples, peeled, cored and grated
      2 tablespoons finely grated orange peel
      1 cup chopped walnuts

Beat butter and sugar until light and creamy. Beat in eggs and vanilla until blended. Beat in flour, soda, baking powder and cinnamon until blended. Do not overbeat. Stir in apples, walnuts and orange peel.

Spoon batter into a 10-inch tube pan and sprinkle top with Brown Sugar Cinnamon Topping. Bake in a 350° oven for 55 to 60 minutes, or until a cake tester, inserted in center, comes out clean. Serves 10 to 12.

Brown Sugar Cinnamon Topping:
      3 tablespoons brown sugar
      3 tablespoons melted butter
    1/2 teaspoon cinnamon

Combine all the ingredients until blended.

Super-Moist Spiced Banana Bread with Chocolate & Walnuts

This is a somewhat unusual bread and a nice change from the usual spiced pumpkin. It is a nice accompaniment to a glass of milk or a cup of coffee.

1 1/2	cups sugar
2	eggs
2	medium ripe bananas, mashed
1/2	cup oil
1 3/4	cups flour
1	teaspoon baking soda
1/2	teaspoon baking powder
1 1/2	teaspoons pumpkin pie spice
1	teaspoon cinnamon
1	package (6 ounces) chocolate chips
1	cup chopped walnuts
1/2	teaspoon vanilla

Beat together, sugar, eggs and bananas until blended. Beat in the oil. Beat in the remaining ingredients just until blended. Do not overbeat. (Stir by hand, if you want to be sure.)

Pour batter into 4 3x5-inch greased foil loaf pans and bake in a 350° oven for 45 to 50 minutes or until a cake tester, inserted in center, comes out clean. Cool for 10 minutes and then remove breads from pans and continue cooling on a rack. Place breads back into pans for storing. Yields 4 mini-loaves.

Note: - These breads freeze beautifully. Wrap in double thicknesses of plastic wrap and then foil. Remove wrappers when defrosting.
- If you are planning this as a gift from your kitchen, then glaze the top. To make glaze, stir together 1 tablespoon cream, 1 teaspoon banana liqueur, and enough sifted powdered sugar to make glaze a drizzling consistency, about 1 cup.

Holiday Spiced Pumpkin Bread Ring with Orange & Walnuts

2 cups sugar
2 eggs
2/3 cup oil
1/2 orange, grated (use fruit, juice and peel)
1 teaspoon vanilla
2 cups flour
1 teaspoon baking powder
1/2 teaspoon baking soda
3 teaspoons pumpkin pie spice
1 cup canned pumpkin
1 cup chopped walnuts
1/2 cup yellow raisins

In the large bowl of an electric mixer, combine all the ingredients and beat until blended. Do not overbeat. Place batter into a 10-inch angel tube pan that has been greased and lightly floured. Bake in a 350° oven for about 1 hour 10 minutes or until a cake tester, inserted in center, comes out clean. Allow to cool in pan.

Remove from pan and drizzle top with Orange Glaze. Serves 12.

Orange Glaze

1 tablespoon orange juice
1 tablespoon grated orange peel
2 tablespoons finely chopped walnuts
3/4 cup sifted powdered sugar (about)

Combine all the ingredients and stir until blended. Add a little sugar or orange juice until glaze is a drizzling consistency.

Note: - Do not glaze the bread if you are planning to freeze it. Defrost and then glaze.

Sour Cream Banana Bread with Chocolate, Walnuts & Sour Cream Glaze

1/4 cup butter, softened
1/2 cup sugar
  1 egg
1/2 cup sour cream
1/2 teaspoon vanilla

  1 cup flour
1/2 teaspoon baking powder
1/2 teaspoon baking soda
    pinch of salt

  1 banana, mashed
1/2 cup semi-sweet chocolate chips
1/2 cup chopped walnuts

In the large bowl of an electric mixer, beat together first 5 ingredients until mixture is blended. Add the flour, baking powder, baking soda and salt, all at once, and beat until blended. Do not overbeat. Stir in the banana, chocolate and walnuts.

Divide mixture between 2 greased 6½x3½-inch loaf pans. Place pans on a cookie sheet and bake in a 350° oven for 30 to 35 minutes or until a cake tester, inserted in center, comes out clean. Allow to cool in pan for 10 minutes, remove loaves from pan and continue cooling on a rack. Brush tops lightly with Sour Cream Glaze. Yields 2 loaves.

Sour Cream Glaze

  1 tablespoon sour cream
1/4 cup sifted powdered sugar
1/4 teaspoon vanilla
  2 tablespoons finely chopped walnuts

Stir together all the ingredients until blended.

Note: - Recipe can be doubled, yielding 4 loaves.
- Bread freezes beautifully. Wrap in double thicknesses of plastic wrap and then, foil. Remove wrappers while defrosting.

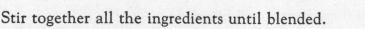

Farmhouse Buttermilk Date Nut Bread with Creamy Orange Glaze

1/2 cup sugar
1/4 cup butter (1/2 stick), softened
1 egg
1/2 cup buttermilk
1/2 teaspoon vanilla

1 cup flour
1/2 teaspoon baking soda
1/2 teaspoon baking powder
   pinch of salt

1/2 cup chopped dates
1/2 cup chopped walnuts
1 tablespoon grated orange peel

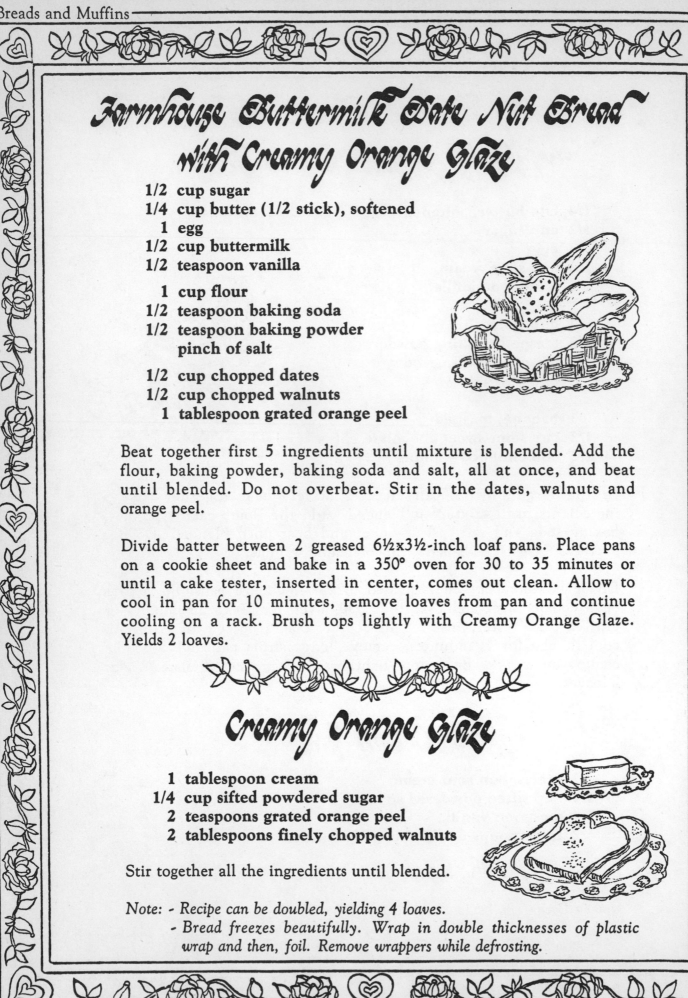

Beat together first 5 ingredients until mixture is blended. Add the flour, baking powder, baking soda and salt, all at once, and beat until blended. Do not overbeat. Stir in the dates, walnuts and orange peel.

Divide batter between 2 greased 6½x3½-inch loaf pans. Place pans on a cookie sheet and bake in a 350° oven for 30 to 35 minutes or until a cake tester, inserted in center, comes out clean. Allow to cool in pan for 10 minutes, remove loaves from pan and continue cooling on a rack. Brush tops lightly with Creamy Orange Glaze. Yields 2 loaves.

Creamy Orange Glaze

1 tablespoon cream
1/4 cup sifted powdered sugar
2 teaspoons grated orange peel
2 tablespoons finely chopped walnuts

Stir together all the ingredients until blended.

Note: - Recipe can be doubled, yielding 4 loaves.
- Bread freezes beautifully. Wrap in double thicknesses of plastic wrap and then, foil. Remove wrappers while defrosting.

Super-Moist Apple & Carrot Cinnamon Bread

This is an irresistible loaf with deep, satisfying character. It is marvellously flavored with fruit and spice and everything nice.

1 egg
1/2 cup buttermilk
1/3 cup oil

2 cups flour
1 cup brown sugar
1 tablespoon baking powder
2 teaspoons cinnamon
1/4 teaspoon salt

1 small apple, peeled, cored and grated
3/4 cup grated carrots
1/3 cup chopped walnuts

Combine all the ingredients in a large bowl and beat just until blended. Do not overbeat. Place batter in a 9x5-inch loaf pan that has been buttered and lightly floured. Bake in a 350° oven for about 1 hour or until a cake tester, inserted in center, comes out clean.

Allow to cool for 10 minutes and then remove from pan and continue cooling on a rack. Drizzle top with Buttermilk Glaze when cool. Yields 1 loaf.

Buttermilk Glaze

1 tablespoon buttermilk
1/2 teaspoon vanilla
1 cup sifted powdered sugar

Stir together all the ingredients until blended. Add a little sugar or buttermilk to make glaze a drizzling consistency.

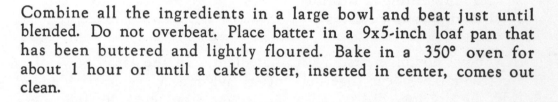

The Best Pumpkin Bread with Apples, Raisins & Walnuts

2 cups flour
1 teaspoon baking powder
1 teaspoon baking soda
1 teaspoon pumpkin pie spice
1/8 teaspoon salt

1/2 cup melted butter
3/4 cup sugar
1 egg

1 cup canned pumpkin puree
1 apple, peeled and grated
1 cup chopped walnuts
1/2 cup yellow raisins

In a bowl combine first 5 dry ingredients. In the large bowl of an electric mixer, beat together butter, sugar and egg until blended. Add the dry ingredients, all at once, and beat until dry ingredients are nicely moistened. Do not overbeat.

Place batter into a 9x5-inch greased loaf pan and bake in a 350° oven for 1 hour or until a cake tester, inserted in center comes out clean. Allow bread to cool about 10 minutes and then turn out on a rack to finish cooling. When bread is cool, drizzle with Vanilla Cream Glaze. Yields 1 loaf.

Vanilla Cream Glaze: Stir together 1 tablespoon cream, 1/2 teaspoon vanilla and about 1 cup sifted powdered sugar until mixture is a drizzling consistency.

Best Butter Egg Bread with Poppy Seeds

Oh! what a divine loaf. Making it is so satisfying and enjoying it with sweet butter is the stuff poetry is made of. It is a little more work, but worth every bit of it, I promise you.

- 1 **package dry yeast**
- 1 **cup warm water (105°)**
- 2 **heaping tablespoons sugar**

- 2 **cups flour**
- 3/4 **teaspoon salt**

- 3/4 **cup butter, softened**
- 4 **eggs**

- 3 **cups flour**

- 1 **egg yolk mixed with 1 teaspoon water for egg wash**
  poppy seeds

In the large bowl of an electric mixer, place yeast, water and sugar. Allow to rest for 10 minutes or until yeast is dissolved and starts bubbling. Add the 2 cups flour and salt and beat for 30 seconds. Add the butter, and the eggs, beating well after each addition. Beat for 3 minutes using the paddle beater.

Beat in 2 cups of the remaining flour and beat another 3 minutes. Add the remaining 1 cup flour and beat another 3 minutes. Place dough in an oiled bowl and turn, so that it is oiled on top. Cover with a towel and allow to rest in a warm place until it is doubled in bulk, about 1 hour. Punch dough down and break off 1/4 of it. Now, separate each piece into 3 sections. Roll each piece into a rope, 12-inches long.

Braid the 3 larger pieces, tuck in the ends and place on a greased cookie sheet. Braid the 3 smaller pieces and place on top of the larger braid. Baste the top and sides with the egg wash and sprinkle generously with poppy seeds. Allow to rest again, for about 1 hour or until almost doubled in bulk.* Bake in a 400° oven for 35 minutes or until top is golden brown and bread sounds hollow when thumped. If bread is browning too quickly, tent loosely with foil. Allow to cool in pan and cut into slices with a serrated knife. Yields 1 large 12-inch loaf.

*Note: - *During the second resting, place 3 long sandwich-type toothpicks in the dough, and tent it with plastic wrap. If the plastic wrap touches the dough, it will stick and be a little tricky to remove.*
- You must use a paddle beater, or a dough hook. The rotary beaters will not work for this method.

2~Minute Hot Pepper Bread with Onions & Cheese

What a wonderful bread to serve with Moroccan or Mexican food. Let me say, at the outset, that I do not relish food that is too hot and where the flavor of the dish is overpowered. Not so with this delightful bread. It has a light bite, but delicately balanced with the onions and cheese.

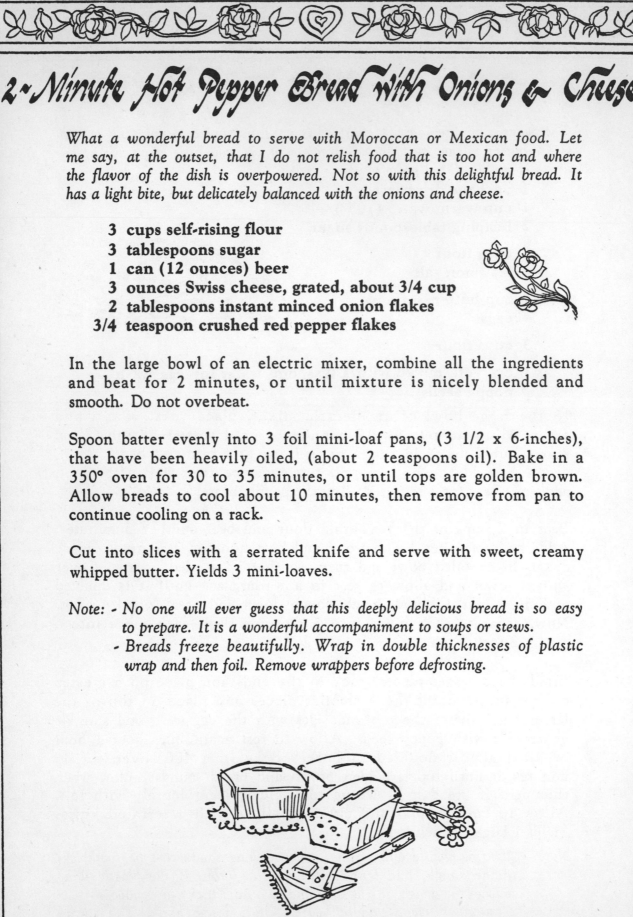

> 3 cups self-rising flour
> 3 tablespoons sugar
> 1 can (12 ounces) beer
> 3 ounces Swiss cheese, grated, about 3/4 cup
> 2 tablespoons instant minced onion flakes
> 3/4 teaspoon crushed red pepper flakes

In the large bowl of an electric mixer, combine all the ingredients and beat for 2 minutes, or until mixture is nicely blended and smooth. Do not overbeat.

Spoon batter evenly into 3 foil mini-loaf pans, (3 1/2 x 6-inches), that have been heavily oiled, (about 2 teaspoons oil). Bake in a 350° oven for 30 to 35 minutes, or until tops are golden brown. Allow breads to cool about 10 minutes, then remove from pan to continue cooling on a rack.

Cut into slices with a serrated knife and serve with sweet, creamy whipped butter. Yields 3 mini-loaves.

Note: - No one will ever guess that this deeply delicious bread is so easy to prepare. It is a wonderful accompaniment to soups or stews.
- Breads freeze beautifully. Wrap in double thicknesses of plastic wrap and then foil. Remove wrappers before defrosting.

2-Minute Green Onion Flat Bread with Cheese & Herbs

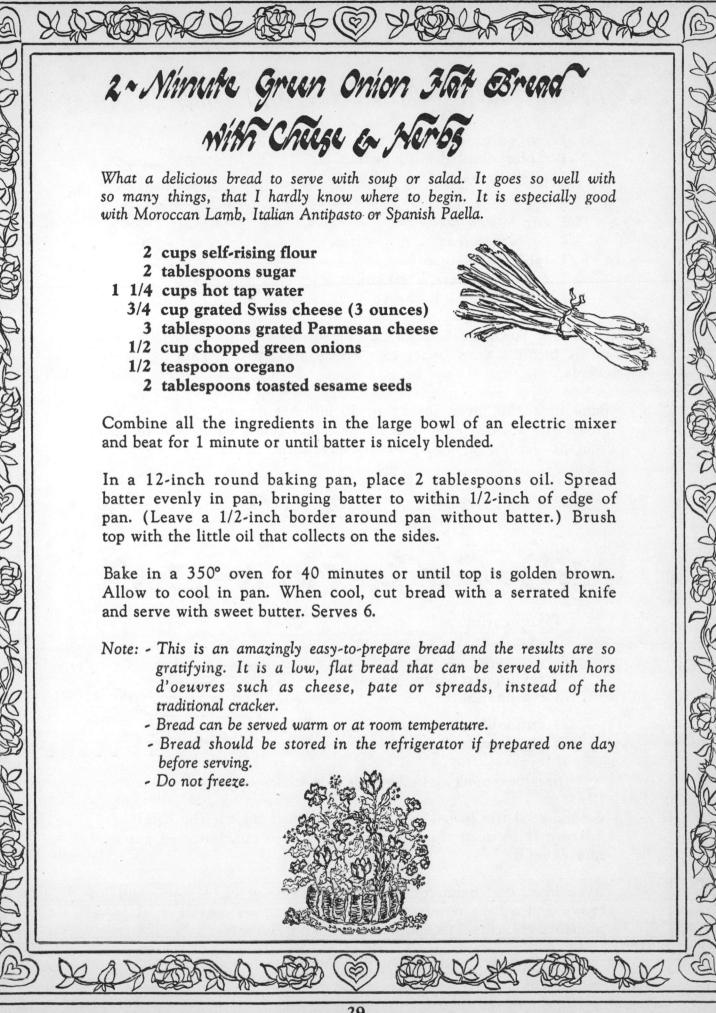

What a delicious bread to serve with soup or salad. It goes so well with so many things, that I hardly know where to begin. It is especially good with Moroccan Lamb, Italian Antipasto or Spanish Paella.

- 2 cups self-rising flour
- 2 tablespoons sugar
- 1 1/4 cups hot tap water
- 3/4 cup grated Swiss cheese (3 ounces)
- 3 tablespoons grated Parmesan cheese
- 1/2 cup chopped green onions
- 1/2 teaspoon oregano
- 2 tablespoons toasted sesame seeds

Combine all the ingredients in the large bowl of an electric mixer and beat for 1 minute or until batter is nicely blended.

In a 12-inch round baking pan, place 2 tablespoons oil. Spread batter evenly in pan, bringing batter to within 1/2-inch of edge of pan. (Leave a 1/2-inch border around pan without batter.) Brush top with the little oil that collects on the sides.

Bake in a 350° oven for 40 minutes or until top is golden brown. Allow to cool in pan. When cool, cut bread with a serrated knife and serve with sweet butter. Serves 6.

Note: - This is an amazingly easy-to-prepare bread and the results are so gratifying. It is a low, flat bread that can be served with hors d'oeuvres such as cheese, pate or spreads, instead of the traditional cracker.
- Bread can be served warm or at room temperature.
- Bread should be stored in the refrigerator if prepared one day before serving.
- Do not freeze.

Easiest & Best Corn Bread with Chiles & Cheese

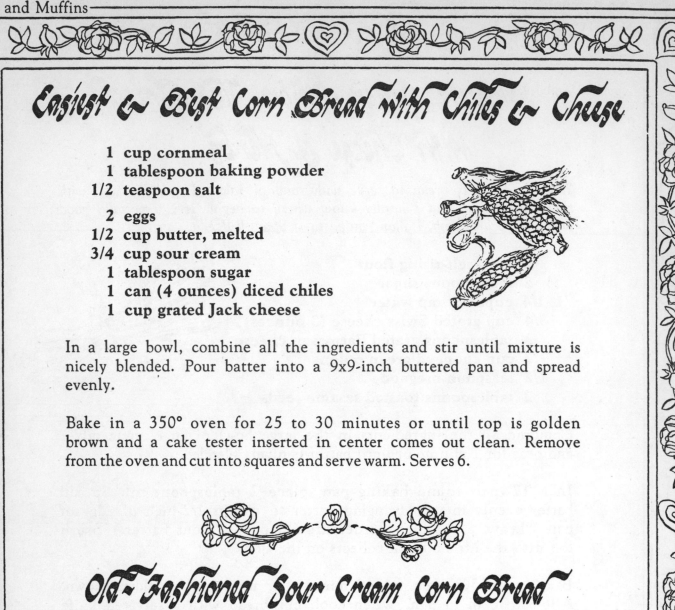

    1   cup cornmeal
    1   tablespoon baking powder
    1/2 teaspoon salt

    2   eggs
    1/2 cup butter, melted
    3/4 cup sour cream
    1   tablespoon sugar
    1   can (4 ounces) diced chiles
    1   cup grated Jack cheese

In a large bowl, combine all the ingredients and stir until mixture is nicely blended. Pour batter into a 9x9-inch buttered pan and spread evenly.

Bake in a 350° oven for 25 to 30 minutes or until top is golden brown and a cake tester inserted in center comes out clean. Remove from the oven and cut into squares and serve warm. Serves 6.

Old-Fashioned Sour Cream Corn Bread

    1   cup cornmeal
    1   cup flour
    1/4 cup sugar
    1   tablespoon baking powder
    1/2 teaspoon salt

    3/4 cup milk
    1/2 cup sour cream
    2   eggs
    6   tablespoons melted butter (3/4 stick)

Combine all the ingredients in a large bowl and stir (by hand) until mixture is blended. Pour batter into a 9x9-inch buttered pan and spread evenly.

Bake in a 350° oven for 25 to 30 minutes or until top is golden brown and a cake tester inserted in center comes out clean. Remove from the oven, cut into squares and serve warm. Serves 6.

French Herbed Cheese Bread with Onions & Bacon

This is an incredibly delicious pastry. When you serve it with cheese or pate and a glass of wine . . . what a fine beginning to a meal. It will feel like a party.

1 **cup milk**
4 **tablespoons butter (1/2 stick)**

1 **cup flour**
1 **tablespoon dried onion flakes**
1 **teaspoon oregano flakes**

4 **eggs, at room temperature**
pinch of salt

3 **tablespoons grated Parmesan cheese**
4 **slices bacon, cooked crisp, drained and crumbled**

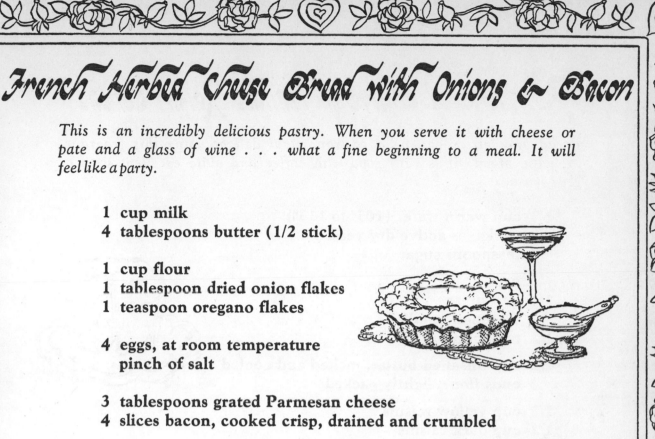

In a saucepan, heat milk and butter until mixture comes to a boil. Add the flour, onion flakes and oregano, and cook and stir until a dough forms and leaves the side of the pan, about 2 minutes. Place dough in large bowl of electric mixer and beat in eggs, one at a time, beating well after each addition. Beat in remaining ingredients until thoroughly blended.

Grease a 10-inch porcelain quiche baker and spoon dough along the edge of the pan to form a 1 1/2-inch ring. Bake in a 400° oven for 15 minutes. Lower heat to 350° and continue baking for about 30 minutes or until pastry is puffed and golden brown. Serve warm with cheese or pate.

Note: - Batter can be prepared earlier in the day, spooned into the porcelain baker and refrigerated until ready to bake. Add a few minutes to baking time.
- Pastry can be baked earlier in the day and reheated before serving. Heat in a 350° oven for 15 minutes. However, it is best made at serving time.

Panettone - A Buttery Italian Raisin Bread

Bread and butter can be a gastronomical delight using this fragrant aromatic bread. It is very good with coffee and quite excellent with a glass of wine.

  1/3 **cup warm water (105° to 115°)**
    3 **packages active dry yeast**
    3 **teaspoons sugar**

    3 **eggs**
  1/4 **cup sugar**
    1 **teaspoon vanilla**
  1/2 **teaspoon salt**

  1/2 **cup unsalted butter, melted and cooled**
    3 **cups flour, lightly packed**

  1/2 **cup yellow raisins**
  1/2 **cup dark raisins**

In a glass measuring cup, stir together warm water, yeast and sugar. Allow to stand until doubled in volume. This is called "proofing the yeast" and if it does not foam, yeast is not active and should be discarded.

In a large mixer bowl, beat eggs, sugar, vanilla and salt. Add yeast and beat until blended. Beat in melted butter and flour. If you have a dough hook, use it at this time. If not, then you must knead the dough until it is smooth and satiny, about 5 minutes. Shape into a ball and turn into a greased bowl. Cover and let rise in a warm place (85°) until double in volume. Punch down dough and knead in the raisins. Shape into a ball and place into a 1 1/2-quart souffle dish that is lightly greased and floured. Cover and let rise again until dough is doubled in volume.

With a knife, indent a cross on the top of the dough. Brush top with melted butter and bake in a 400° oven for 10 minutes. Reduce heat to 350° and continue baking for about 30 minutes or until top is a deep golden brown. A lovely crown will have formed and it will be studded with raisins. Allow to cool in baking dish on a rack. Slice with a serrated knife and serve 12 with grand ceremony.

Note: - Read this very detailed recipe carefully before you start. This is a beautiful bread and well worth the little extra work. Good luck!

Country Easter Bread with Cherries & Almonds

This is an incredibly delicious bread to serve with your Easter meal. Buttery and sweet, it is further enhanced with the addition of fruits and nuts. You can use a sugar glaze to decorate the top but that is optional.

1/4 cup warm water (105° to 115°)
2 packages active dry yeast
1 tablespoon sugar

3 eggs, beaten
3/4 cup melted butter
1 cup scalded milk
1/3 cup sugar
1 teaspoon vanilla
3/4 teaspoon salt

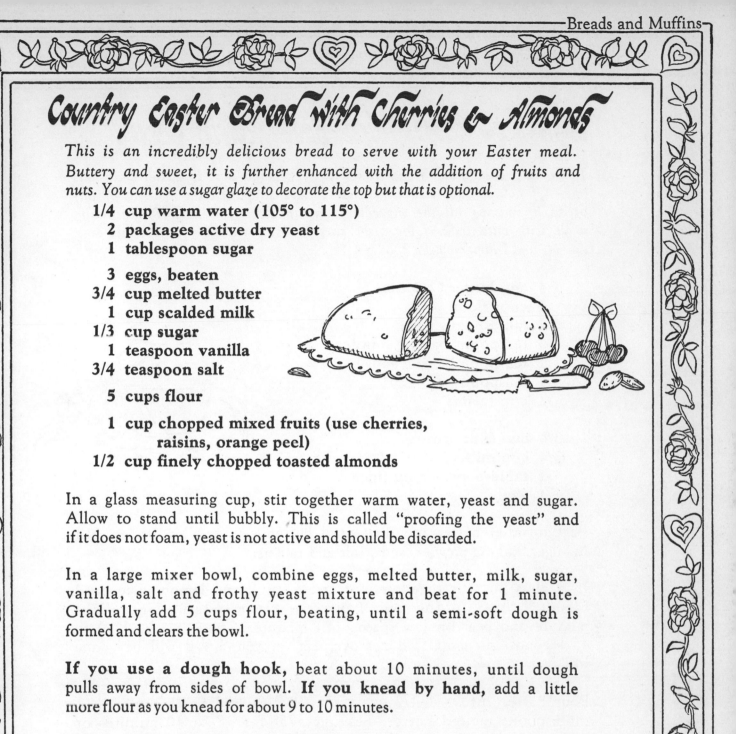

5 cups flour

1 cup chopped mixed fruits (use cherries, raisins, orange peel)
1/2 cup finely chopped toasted almonds

In a glass measuring cup, stir together warm water, yeast and sugar. Allow to stand until bubbly. This is called "proofing the yeast" and if it does not foam, yeast is not active and should be discarded.

In a large mixer bowl, combine eggs, melted butter, milk, sugar, vanilla, salt and frothy yeast mixture and beat for 1 minute. Gradually add 5 cups flour, beating, until a semi-soft dough is formed and clears the bowl.

If you use a dough hook, beat about 10 minutes, until dough pulls away from sides of bowl. **If you knead by hand,** add a little more flour as you knead for about 9 to 10 minutes.

Lightly oil a large bowl and turn dough into it to oil the top. Cover bowl with plastic wrap and place in a warm place (85°) until double in volume. Punch dough down and knead in the fruits and nuts. Shape into a ball and place on a sheet of parchment paper. Let rise in a warm place until double in volume. Brush top with beaten egg and place parchment paper with bread on a baking sheet. Bake at 350° for about 30 minutes or until loaf is nicely browned. Cool on a rack. Glaze is optional, but if you do, decorate top with additional cherries and slivered almonds.

Glaze:
Beat together 1 cup sifted powdered sugar with 2 tablespoons cream and 1/8 teaspoon vanilla. Drizzle over cooled bread.

Easiest & Best Irish Soda Raisin Bread

There is probably no bread you will ever make that is easier than this one. Of course, no need to knead. I have simplified the making of this bread by mixing all the ingredients in an electric mixer. Traditionally made with buttermilk, I loved the way it tasted made with milk and sour cream, and I hope you do, too.

- 1/4 **cup butter (1/2 stick)**
- 3 **cups flour**
- 2 **tablespoons sugar**
- 3 **teaspoons baking powder**
- 1 **teaspoon baking soda**
- 1 **teaspoon salt**
- 1 **cup raisins**

- 3/4 **cup sour cream**
- 3/4 **cup milk**
- 1 **tablespoon lemon juice**
- 1 **egg**

Beat together butter and flour until butter is in small particles. Stir in sugar, baking powder, soda, salt and raisins.

In a glass jar, stir together sour cream, milk and lemon juice until blended. Beat in the egg. Pour sour cream mixture into flour mixture and beat on low speed until mixture is smooth, about 30 to 45 seconds, no more. Do not overbeat, or your bread will be "done in."

Pour batter into a 1 1/2-quart souffle dish and baste top with 2 tablespoons melted butter. Bake at 375° for 35 to 40 minutes or until top is golden brown and bread sounds hollow when rapped (like "knocking.") If a cake tester inserted in center comes out clean, then bread is finished baking. Remove bread from pan and cool on a rack. Slice and serve warm with lots of creamy butter.

Note: - There are many opinions as to how thick Irish Soda Bread should be sliced. Some adamantly feel that soda bread should be cut into paper thin slices and others believe it should be cut into thick slices or wedges. However, try both and find what suits you best.

Country Cottage Bread with Onions, Dill & Cheese

This bread is so delicious you will want to make it often. It is excellent for a luncheon with soup or salad and baking it in an 8-inch round pan makes it easy to slice and serve. Serve it warm with whipped sweet butter . . . delicious!

- 1 **package dry yeast**
- 1/4 **cup warm water (105°)**
- 2 **tablespoons sugar**

- 1 **cup small curd cottage cheese**
- 3 **tablespoons butter**
- 2 **tablespoons dried onion flakes**
- 1/2 **cup grated Parmesan cheese**
- 1 **egg**
- 1 **teaspoon dried dill weed**

- 2 1/4 **cups flour**

In the large bowl of an electric mixer, stir together yeast, water and sugar and allow to stand for 5 to 10 minutes, or until yeast starts to foam up. If yeast does not foam, it is not active and should be discarded.

Add the next 6 ingredients to the mixer bowl and beat for 2 minutes or until everything is nicely blended. Add the flour and beat for 4 minutes. (This takes the place of kneading.)

Place batter into an 8x2-inch round baking pan that has been generously oiled and cover with plastic wrap. Leave in a warm place, and allow to rise until doubled, about 45 minutes.

Bake in a 350° oven for about 50 minutes or until top is browned and bread sounds hollow when thumped. Allow to cool for about 30 minutes, remove from pan, and continue cooling on a rack. Yields 1 loaf and serves 6 to 8.

Note: - Bread freezes well. Wrap in double thicknesses of plastic wrap and then foil. Remove wrappers to defrost.
- If you are planning an Italian dinner, substitute the dill weed with 1 teaspoon oregano flakes. Similarly, if you are planning a French meal, substitute the dill with 1 teaspoon thyme flakes. Everything else remains the same.

Easy No-Knead Country Bran Bread with Raisins & Orange

No one will ever guess that this honorable loaf did not take more than a few minutes to prepare. It is a sturdy bread with good honest character and a wonderful accompaniment for soups and salads. Serving it with sweet butter and honey will have everyone chirping like birds.

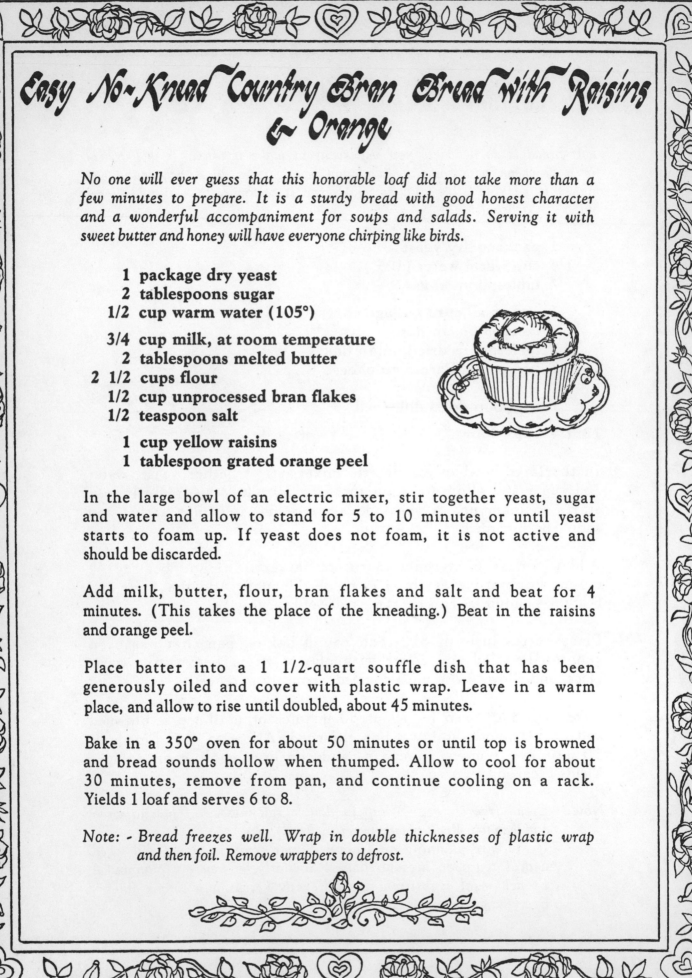

   1 **package dry yeast**
   2 **tablespoons sugar**
 1/2 **cup warm water (105°)**

 3/4 **cup milk, at room temperature**
   2 **tablespoons melted butter**
2 1/2 **cups flour**
 1/2 **cup unprocessed bran flakes**
 1/2 **teaspoon salt**

   1 **cup yellow raisins**
   1 **tablespoon grated orange peel**

In the large bowl of an electric mixer, stir together yeast, sugar and water and allow to stand for 5 to 10 minutes or until yeast starts to foam up. If yeast does not foam, it is not active and should be discarded.

Add milk, butter, flour, bran flakes and salt and beat for 4 minutes. (This takes the place of the kneading.) Beat in the raisins and orange peel.

Place batter into a 1 1/2-quart souffle dish that has been generously oiled and cover with plastic wrap. Leave in a warm place, and allow to rise until doubled, about 45 minutes.

Bake in a 350° oven for about 50 minutes or until top is browned and bread sounds hollow when thumped. Allow to cool for about 30 minutes, remove from pan, and continue cooling on a rack. Yields 1 loaf and serves 6 to 8.

Note: - Bread freezes well. Wrap in double thicknesses of plastic wrap and then foil. Remove wrappers to defrost.

Fluffy Brunch Biscuits with Bacon & Onions

       2 cups cake flour
       3 teaspoons baking powder
     1/2 teaspoon salt
     1/4 cup butter
     1/4 cup shortening
       1 cup milk
       3 strips bacon, cooked crisp, drained and crumbled
       1 tablespoon dried onion flakes

In a bowl, place flour, baking powder, salt, butter and shortening. With a pastry blender, cut butter and shortening in flour until mixture resembles coarse meal. Add the milk and stir until blended. Stir in bacon and onions. Do not overmix.

Roll a spoonful of dough in cake flour to lightly coat, and place biscuits on a greased cookie sheet. Bake in a 450° oven for about 10 minutes or until biscuits are golden brown. Yields about 16 biscuits.

Note: - Biscuits can be brushed with melted butter for a nice touch.

Giant Herbed Popovers with Cheese & Onions

       3 eggs
       1 cup milk
       1 cup flour
          pinch of salt
     1/4 teaspoon dried dill weed
     1/2 tablespoon dried onion flakes
       2 tablespoons grated Parmesan cheese

Combine all the ingredients and beat until blended. Heavily butter 12 muffin molds. (Use the regular size muffin pan.) Divide batter evenly between the muffin molds and bake in a 400° oven for 25 to 30 minutes or until popovers are puffed and golden brown. Serve immediately. Yields 12 popovers.

Note: - Batter can be made earlier in the day and stored in the refrigerator. Add a few minutes to baking time.

Family ~ Style Poppyseed Onion Rolls

This is a delicious and unusual roll. What it actually is, is a cream puff dough made with matzoh meal instead of flour. It is leavened with eggs and excellent any time of year.

1/2 cup margarine
1 cup water
2 tablespoons dried onion flakes

2 cups matzoh meal
1/2 teaspoon salt
1 tablespoon sugar

4 eggs
1 teaspoon poppy seeds

In a saucepan, bring margarine, water and onion flakes to a boil. Stir in matzoh meal, salt and sugar until blended.

Place dough into large bowl of electric mixer and beat in eggs, one at a time until nicely blended. Beat in poppy seeds.

With moistened hands, shape dough into 12 rolls and place on a greased cookie sheet. Cut a cross on the top of each roll. Bake in a 350° oven for about 50 minutes to 1 hour or until top is golden brown. Yields 12 rolls.

Note: - These rolls can freeze.

Casseroles & Small Entrees

Pate Mousseline with Onions, Bacon & Cream Cheese

This is an unusual pate but delicious and interesting. It is lovely and light. Serve it with a Gougere (Burgundian Pastry) and a glass of wine and it becomes a celebration.

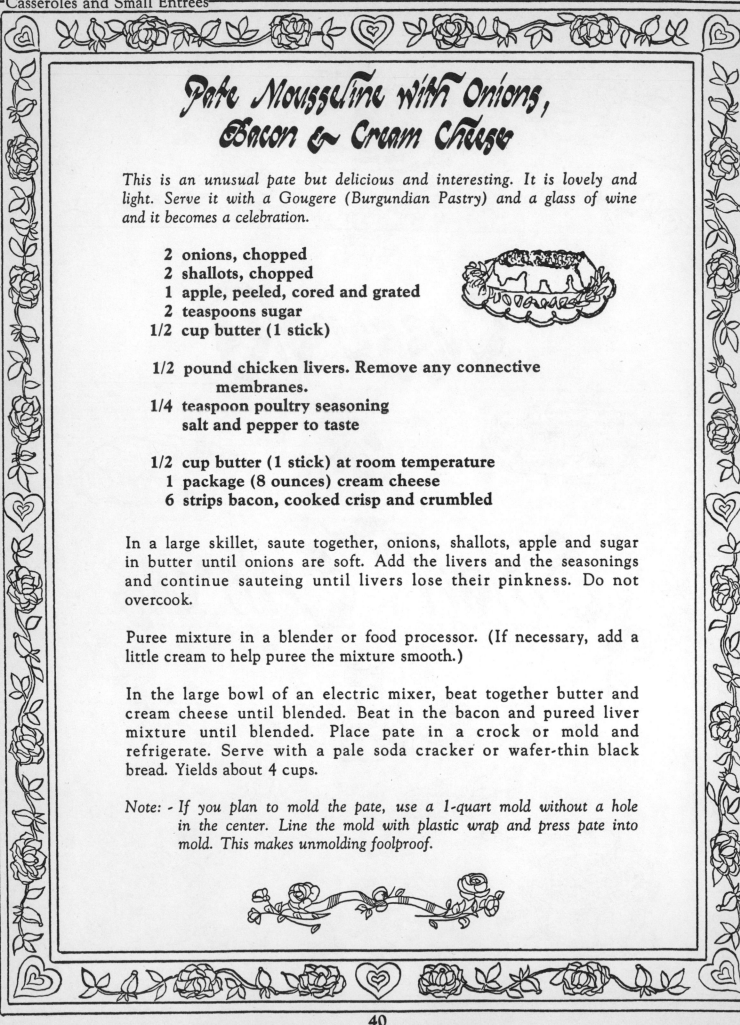

- **2 onions, chopped**
- **2 shallots, chopped**
- **1 apple, peeled, cored and grated**
- **2 teaspoons sugar**
- **1/2 cup butter (1 stick)**

- **1/2 pound chicken livers. Remove any connective membranes.**
- **1/4 teaspoon poultry seasoning**
  salt and pepper to taste

- **1/2 cup butter (1 stick) at room temperature**
- **1 package (8 ounces) cream cheese**
- **6 strips bacon, cooked crisp and crumbled**

In a large skillet, saute together, onions, shallots, apple and sugar in butter until onions are soft. Add the livers and the seasonings and continue sauteing until livers lose their pinkness. Do not overcook.

Puree mixture in a blender or food processor. (If necessary, add a little cream to help puree the mixture smooth.)

In the large bowl of an electric mixer, beat together butter and cream cheese until blended. Beat in the bacon and pureed liver mixture until blended. Place pate in a crock or mold and refrigerate. Serve with a pale soda cracker or wafer-thin black bread. Yields about 4 cups.

Note: - If you plan to mold the pate, use a 1-quart mold without a hole in the center. Line the mold with plastic wrap and press pate into mold. This makes unmolding foolproof.

California Pizza • Calzones ~ with Beef, Tomatoes & Cheese

This is an exciting adaptation of Calzones, gaining in popularity in the Southern California area. It's basically a pizza-style pie with a double crust. Traditionally made with bread dough, I enjoy making it with puff pastry. I find it lighter, crisper and frankly, much more delicious.

> **2** packages frozen patty shells (12 shells), thawed
> **1** egg, beaten
> **4** tablespoons grated Parmesan cheese

Stack 2 patty shells together and roll out to measure an 8-inch circle. Place 1/6 of the Beef, Tomato & Cheese Filling in the center. Moisten the edge with water and fold over. Press the edge down with the tines of a fork, and scallop it.

Brush top with beaten egg and sprinkle with grated Parmesan cheese. Place Calzone on a greased cookie sheet. Repeat with the remaining patty shells. (Can be held at this point, in the refrigerator.)

Bake in a 400° oven for 25 to 30 minutes or until pastry is puffed and top is a deep golden brown. Serve with an Italian-style salad. Yields 6 Calzones and serves 6.

Beef, Tomato & Cheese Filling :

> **2** onions, chopped
> **2** cloves garlic, minced
> **2** tablespoons oil
>
> **1** pound lean ground beef
>
> **1** can (1 pound) stewed tomatoes, drained. Reserve juice for another use.
> **1** teaspoon Italian Herb Seasoning
> **1** teaspoon sweet basil flakes
> **1** package (8 ounces) Mozzarella cheese, grated
> **1/2** cup grated Parmesan cheese
> **1/4** teaspoon red pepper flakes
> salt and pepper to taste

In a skillet, saute onions and garlic in oil until onions are soft. Add the ground beef and saute until meat loses its pinkness, breaking up the large pieces of meat. Drain off any oil or fat.

Place meat mixture in a bowl and stir in the remaining ingredients. Will fill 6 Calzones. Delicious! and enjoy.

Veal & Pork Dumplings with Bearnaise Mayonnaise

1/2 pound ground veal
1/2 pound ground lean pork
2 eggs
3 slices egg bread, crusts removed, moistened
    with water and squeezed dry
1/4 cup chopped chives
2 tablespoons finely chopped parsley
1/4 cup grated Parmesan cheese
1/8 teaspoon garlic powder
    salt and pepper to taste

flour for coating

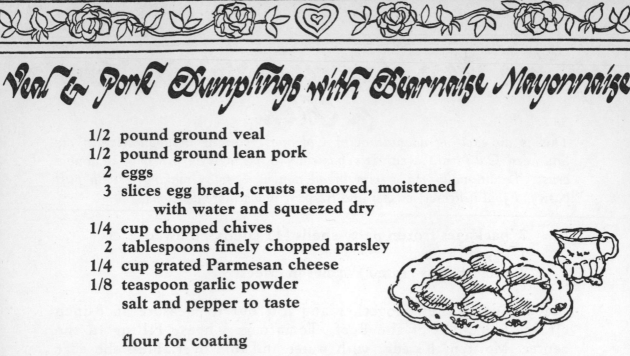

In a large bowl, combine first 9 ingredients and mix until thoroughly blended. Shape mixture into 3/4-inch balls and roll in flour. Saute meatballs in a large skillet, in batches, shaking pan, so that the meatballs brown on all sides. Drain.

Place meatballs in a porcelain baker. When ready to serve, heat through in a 350° oven. Serve with Bearnaise Mayonnaise on the side for dipping. Yields about 30 meatballs.

Bearnaise Mayonnaise

3 egg yolks
1 1/2 tablespoons lemon juice
1 tablespoon tarragon vinegar
1 teaspoon chopped parsley
1 tablespoon chopped chives
1/8 teaspoon dried tarragon
    salt and white pepper to taste

3/4 cup oil

In a blender container, combine first 7 ingredients and blend for 10 seconds. Add the oil, very slowly, and in a thin, steady stream, while the blender continues running at high speed. When the oil is completely incorporated, place sauce in a serving bowl, cover with plastic wrap, and refrigerate until serving time. Yields about 1 cup sauce.

Note: - Meatballs and Bearnaise Mayonnaise can be prepared earlier in the day and stored in the refrigerator.

Buffalo Wings with Red Hot Honey Glaze

There is a lot of commotion lately about "Buffalo Wings." I had some recently and they were very good, indeed. This is my adaptation of these, as the recipe is the biggest secret. Traditionally deep-fried, I have chosen to bake these, thus reducing calories. Also, they are served with a Blue Cheese Dressing, which I am sharing, for the purists. I personally, did not find that it enhanced the dish, so I am not recommending it.

    3 pounds chicken wings, tips removed and split at the joint. Sprinkle with salt, pepper and garlic powder. Baste with a little butter.

Buffalo Red Hot Honey Barbecue Glaze:
    1 cup good quality barbecue sauce
    1/2 cup honey
    2 tablespoons vinegar
    1/2 teaspoon cayenne pepper

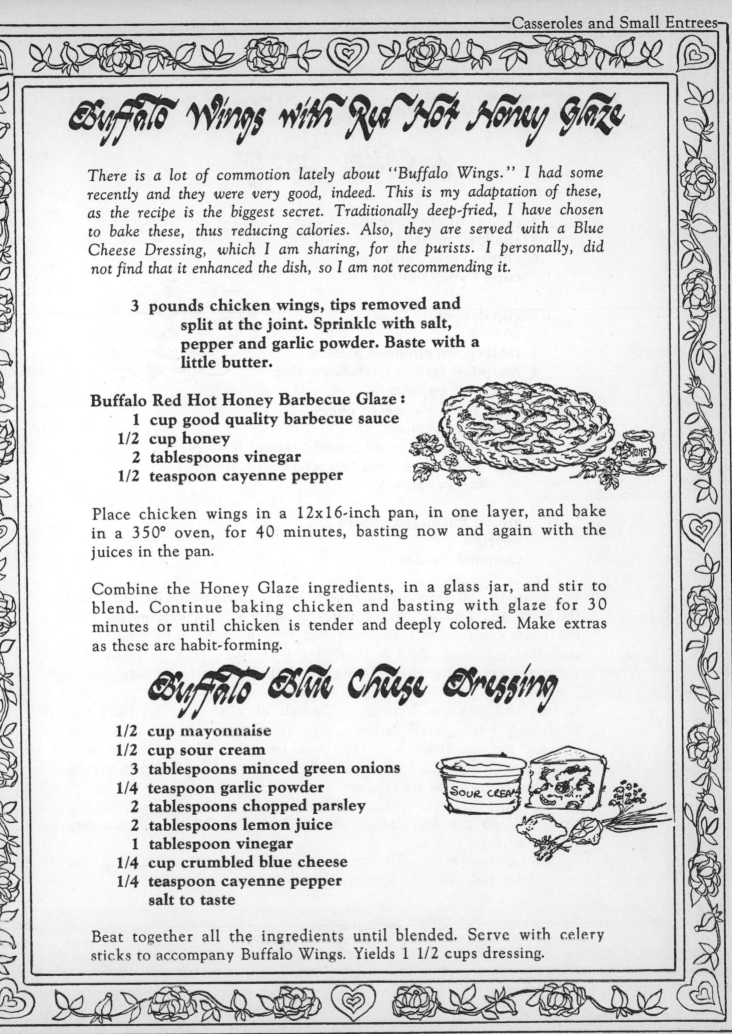

Place chicken wings in a 12x16-inch pan, in one layer, and bake in a 350° oven, for 40 minutes, basting now and again with the juices in the pan.

Combine the Honey Glaze ingredients, in a glass jar, and stir to blend. Continue baking chicken and basting with glaze for 30 minutes or until chicken is tender and deeply colored. Make extras as these are habit-forming.

Buffalo Blue Cheese Dressing

    1/2 cup mayonnaise
    1/2 cup sour cream
    3 tablespoons minced green onions
    1/4 teaspoon garlic powder
    2 tablespoons chopped parsley
    2 tablespoons lemon juice
    1 tablespoon vinegar
    1/4 cup crumbled blue cheese
    1/4 teaspoon cayenne pepper
    salt to taste

Beat together all the ingredients until blended. Serve with celery sticks to accompany Buffalo Wings. Yields 1 1/2 cups dressing.

Stuffed Clams Oreganata with Garlic & Herbs & Cheese Topping

1 onion, finely chopped
3 shallots, minced
6 cloves garlic, minced
1/2 cup (1 stick) butter

1/3 cup dry white wine

1 tablespoon chopped parsley
1 teaspoon Italian Herb Seasoning
1 teaspoon paprika
1/4 cup grated Parmesan cheese
pinch of cayenne
3 cups fresh egg bread crumbs (about 6 slices)
2 cans (7 ounces, each) minced clams, drained.
    Reserve juice.

grated Parmesan cheese
paprika
chopped parsley

Saute onion, shallots and garlic in butter until onion is soft. Add the wine and simmer for 2 minutes or until wine is evaporated. Add the next 7 ingredients and toss and turn mixture until crumbs are completely coated. Add a little of the reserved clam juice so that the stuffing binds together. (Do not allow the stuffing to get soggy).

Divide the mixture between 12 small clam shells. Sprinkle top generously with grated Parmesan cheese. Sprinkle with paprika and chopped parsley. Bake in a 350° oven for about 20 minutes or until piping hot. Yields 12 stuffed clam shells. Serve 1 or 2 depending on the other courses you are serving.

Note: - Clams can be filled and stored in the refrigerator 1 day before serving.
      - Can be frozen. Wrap in double thicknesses of plastic wrap and then foil. Allow to defrost in the refrigerator.

Clam Puffs with Chili Horseradish Sauce

This savory hors d'oeuvre, sparkled with cheese, is just delicious with the chili sauce. It has a little "bite" with the addition of horseradish. The sauce is fine to use with shrimp or crabmeat.

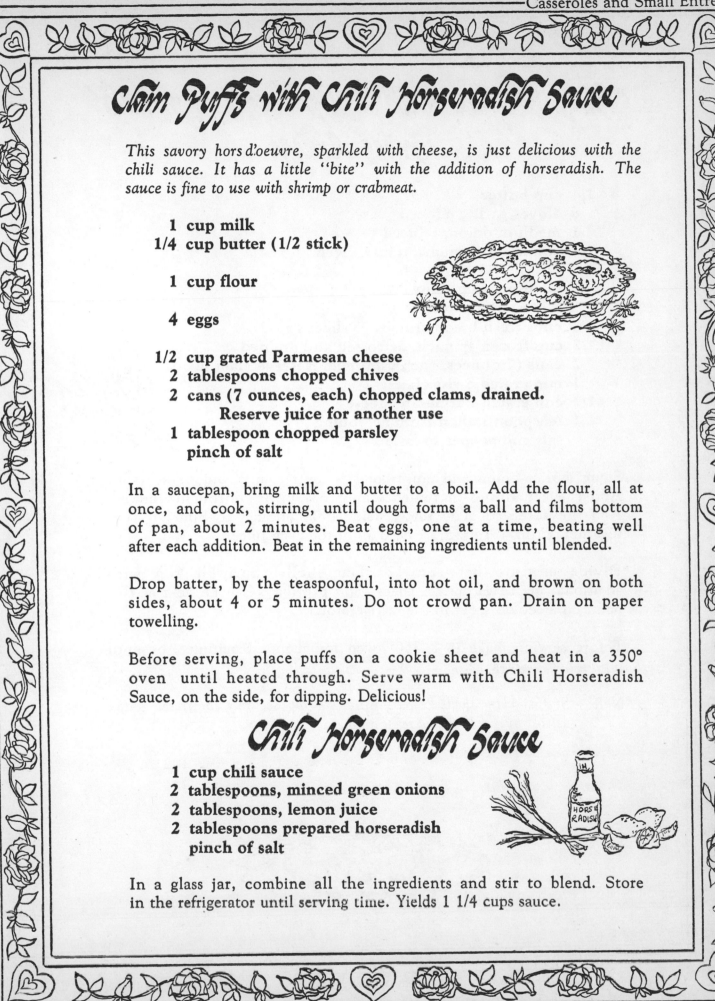

- 1 cup milk
- 1/4 cup butter (1/2 stick)
- 1 cup flour
- 4 eggs

- 1/2 cup grated Parmesan cheese
- 2 tablespoons chopped chives
- 2 cans (7 ounces, each) chopped clams, drained. Reserve juice for another use
- 1 tablespoon chopped parsley
- pinch of salt

In a saucepan, bring milk and butter to a boil. Add the flour, all at once, and cook, stirring, until dough forms a ball and films bottom of pan, about 2 minutes. Beat eggs, one at a time, beating well after each addition. Beat in the remaining ingredients until blended.

Drop batter, by the teaspoonful, into hot oil, and brown on both sides, about 4 or 5 minutes. Do not crowd pan. Drain on paper towelling.

Before serving, place puffs on a cookie sheet and heat in a 350° oven until heated through. Serve warm with Chili Horseradish Sauce, on the side, for dipping. Delicious!

Chili Horseradish Sauce

- 1 cup chili sauce
- 2 tablespoons, minced green onions
- 2 tablespoons, lemon juice
- 2 tablespoons prepared horseradish
- pinch of salt

In a glass jar, combine all the ingredients and stir to blend. Store in the refrigerator until serving time. Yields 1 1/4 cups sauce.

Clams Stuffed with Mushrooms, Spinach & Swiss Cheese

1/4 cup butter
6 cloves garlic, minced
1 medium onion, minced
1/4 pound mushrooms, thinly sliced

2 tablespoons parsley
1 tablespoon paprika
3 cups fresh bread crumbs (6 slices bread)
1/2 cup frozen spinach, defrosted and drained
2 cans (7 ounces, each), drained. Reserve clam juice.
1 cup grated Swiss cheese
1/2 cup grated Parmesan cheese
1 teaspoon Italian Herb Seasoning
salt and pepper to taste

Saute garlic, onion and mushrooms in butter until onions are soft. Add the remaining ingredients and toss until thoroughly mixed. Add the reserved clam juice, using only enough to bind mixture together. (You will probably need all of the clam juice.)

Divide mixture between 12 clam shells. Sprinkle top with additional grated Parmesan cheese and paprika. (Can be held at this point on a cookie sheet in the refrigerator.)

Before serving, bake in a 350° oven for about 30 minutes, or until piping hot. Serves 12.

Note: - Stuffed clam shells can be frozen. Wrap securely for freezing and defrost overnight in the refrigerator.

Roulade of Herbed Mushrooms in Mushroom Wine Sauce

There are few small entrees that are more exciting or more delicious than this one. It is an excellent main course for lunch and a lovely small entree before dinner. The dough is one of my favorites, easy to prepare, easy to handle and incredibly delicious.

- 1 cup butter (2 sticks)
- 1 package (8 ounces) cream cheese
- 2 cups flour
  pinch of salt

- 1 egg, beaten
  grated Parmesan cheese

Beat together butter and cream cheese until blended. Add flour and salt and beat until mixture is smooth. Form dough into a 6-inch circle and wrap in floured wax paper. Refrigerate for several hours or overnight.

Divide dough into 4 parts. Roll out, one part at a time, on a floured pastry cloth, until dough measures about 9x9-inches. Spread 1/4 of the Herbed Mushroom Filling along the center of the dough. Bring up one side of the dough and cover the filling. Repeat with the other side, ending with a roulade measuring about 3x9-inches.

Place roulade, seam side down, on a lightly greased 12x16-inch pan. Repeat with the remaining 3 parts of dough. Pierce tops with the tines of a fork, brush with beaten egg and sprinkle generously with grated Parmesan cheese. Bake in a 350° oven for 30 to 35 minutes or until tops are golden. Cut into slices and serve hot. Yields about 24 slices.

Roulade of Herbed Mushrooms (continued)
Mushroom Wine Sauce

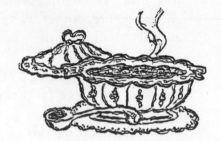

1 large onion, minced
3 shallots, minced
3 cloves garlic, minced
4 tablespoons butter

1 pound mushrooms, thinly sliced
1/4 cup dry white wine
2 tablespoons flour
1/2 teaspoon poultry seasoning
1 cup sour cream
  salt to taste

Saute onion, shallots and garlic in butter until onion is soft. Add mushrooms and saute until mushrooms are tender. Add wine and cook until liquid is almost evaporated. Add flour and poultry seasonings and cook and stir for 2 minutes. Stir in sour cream and salt and cook and stir for 2 minutes.

Red Hot Barbecued Chicken Wings with Honey & Mustard Glaze

3 pounds chicken wings (tips removed), sprinkle
    with salt, pepper and garlic powder
1 cup barbecue sauce
1/2 cup brown sugar
1/2 cup honey
1/2 cup vinegar
2 tablespoons Dijon mustard
1/4 cup butter, melted
1/2 teaspoon cayenne pepper

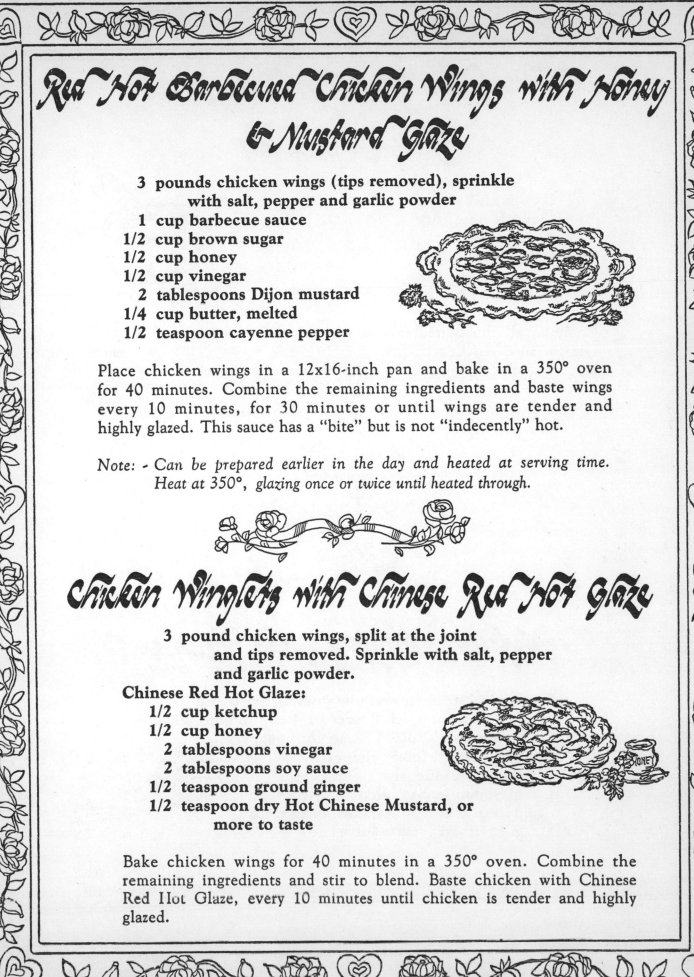

Place chicken wings in a 12x16-inch pan and bake in a 350° oven for 40 minutes. Combine the remaining ingredients and baste wings every 10 minutes, for 30 minutes or until wings are tender and highly glazed. This sauce has a "bite" but is not "indecently" hot.

Note: - Can be prepared earlier in the day and heated at serving time. Heat at 350°, glazing once or twice until heated through.

Chicken Winglets with Chinese Red Hot Glaze

3 pound chicken wings, split at the joint
    and tips removed. Sprinkle with salt, pepper
    and garlic powder.

Chinese Red Hot Glaze:
1/2 cup ketchup
1/2 cup honey
2 tablespoons vinegar
2 tablespoons soy sauce
1/2 teaspoon ground ginger
1/2 teaspoon dry Hot Chinese Mustard, or
    more to taste

Bake chicken wings for 40 minutes in a 350° oven. Combine the remaining ingredients and stir to blend. Baste chicken with Chinese Red Hot Glaze, every 10 minutes until chicken is tender and highly glazed.

Honey Plum Jam Barbecue Sauce for Ribs & Chicken

- 2 cups chili sauce
- 1/3 cup lemon juice
- 1/4 cup honey
- 1/4 cup plum jam
- 1 teaspoon paprika
- 1 teaspoon hot pepper sauce

Combine all the ingredients in a saucepan and heat until blended. Use on ribs, chicken or pork roasts. Yields about 2 1/2 cups sauce. Unused sauce can be stored in the refrigerator for 2 weeks.

Mexican Dipping Salsa Picante

- 1 can (1 pound) stewed tomatoes, drained and finely chopped. Reserve 1/4 cup tomato juice.
- 1 can (4 ounces) diced green chili peppers
- 4 green onions, finely chopped
- 1 tablespoon vinegar
- 1 tablespoon lemon juice
  pinch of red pepper flakes, or to taste
- 1/4 cup reserved tomato juice

Combine all the ingredients in a jar with a tight-fitting lid and stir to blend. Refrigerate overnight. Serve with chips or on tostadas or tacos.

Spinach Dip for Raw Vegetables, Fish or Shellfish ~ Salsa Verte ~

This recipe is one of my sister's favorites. It is basically a form of Sauce Verte with the difference of the Leek Soup Mix. It is a good choice for a party dip as it should be made 1 day earlier.

- 3/4 cup sour cream
- 3/4 cup mayonnaise
- 1/4 cup chopped parsley
- 1/2 cup chopped onion
- 1/2 teaspoon dill weed
- 1/2 teaspoon garlic powder
- 1/2 package Knorr's Leek Soup
  salt and pepper
- 2 packages (10 ounces, each) frozen chopped spinach, thawed and drained

Place first 8 ingredients in blender or food processor and blend for about 1 minute. Stir in the chopped spinach. Place in a glass bowl, and store in the refrigerator overnight. Serve with raw vegetables for dipping. Yields about 3 cups sauce.

Cucumber Yogurt Dip with Green Onions & Lemon

- 1 cup plain low-fat yogurt
- 1/3 cup finely chopped green onion
- 1/4 cup cucumber, peeled, seeded and grated
- 2 tablespoons lemon juice
- 1 tablespoon chopped parsley
- 1/8 teaspoon garlic powder
  salt and pepper to taste

In a glass bowl, stir together all the ingredients until blended. Refrigerate for several hours. Serve with raw vegetables for dipping. Yields about 1 3/4 cups sauce.

Petite Mushroom Crostinis with Herbed Cheese & Chives

This is a charming canape, that is an excellent hors d'oeuvre, and a lovely accompaniment to soup or salad.

8 slices of white bread. Remove crusts and flatten slightly with a rolling pin.

3/4 pound mushrooms, thinly sliced
1 onion, minced
3 cloves garlic, minced
1/4 cup (1/2 stick) butter

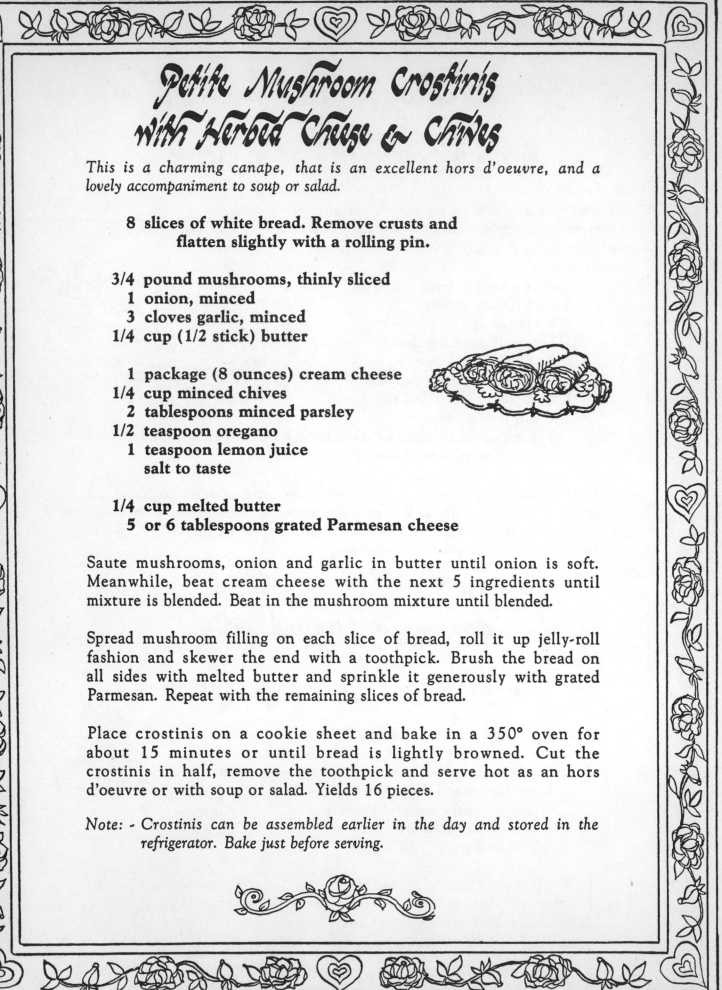

1 package (8 ounces) cream cheese
1/4 cup minced chives
2 tablespoons minced parsley
1/2 teaspoon oregano
1 teaspoon lemon juice
salt to taste

1/4 cup melted butter
5 or 6 tablespoons grated Parmesan cheese

Saute mushrooms, onion and garlic in butter until onion is soft. Meanwhile, beat cream cheese with the next 5 ingredients until mixture is blended. Beat in the mushroom mixture until blended.

Spread mushroom filling on each slice of bread, roll it up jelly-roll fashion and skewer the end with a toothpick. Brush the bread on all sides with melted butter and sprinkle it generously with grated Parmesan. Repeat with the remaining slices of bread.

Place crostinis on a cookie sheet and bake in a 350° oven for about 15 minutes or until bread is lightly browned. Cut the crostinis in half, remove the toothpick and serve hot as an hors d'oeuvre or with soup or salad. Yields 16 pieces.

Note: - Crostinis can be assembled earlier in the day and stored in the refrigerator. Bake just before serving.

Smoked Salmon Quiche with Tomatoes, Chives & Dill

This is a marvellous pie to serve as an hors d'oeuvre or as a main course for brunch. The combination of salmon and chives with a hint of lemon and dill is simply delicious.

1 9-inch deep dish frozen pie shell, baked in a 400° oven for about 10 minutes or until just beginning to take on color

3 eggs
1 cup cream
4 ounces cream cheese
1/4 cup chopped chives
2 tablespoons lemon juice
1/2 teaspoon dried dill weed

1/4 pound smoked salmon, cut into 1/2-inch pieces

1 medium tomato, peeled, seeded and cut into paper-thin slices. Drain on paper towelling. (Important! or they will render liquid.)

Prepare pie shell. Beat next 6 ingredients together until blended. Stir in the smoked salmon. Pour mixture into prepared pie shell and place drained tomatoes on top in a decorative fashion. Sprinkle top with additional chopped chives.

Place quiche on a cookie sheet and bake in a 350° oven for about 40 minutes or until custard is set. Can be served warm or chilled. Serves 6.

Creamy Broccoli Quiche with Onions & Cheese

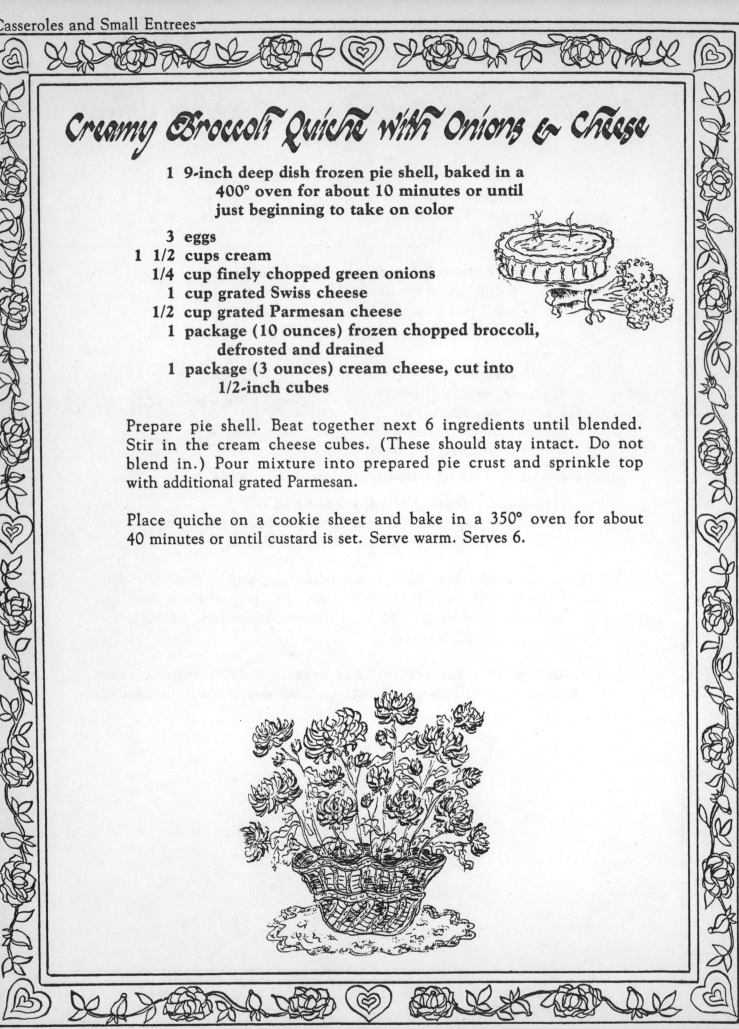

1 9-inch deep dish frozen pie shell, baked in a
400° oven for about 10 minutes or until
just beginning to take on color

3 eggs
1 1/2 cups cream
1/4 cup finely chopped green onions
1 cup grated Swiss cheese
1/2 cup grated Parmesan cheese
1 package (10 ounces) frozen chopped broccoli,
defrosted and drained
1 package (3 ounces) cream cheese, cut into
1/2-inch cubes

Prepare pie shell. Beat together next 6 ingredients until blended. Stir in the cream cheese cubes. (These should stay intact. Do not blend in.) Pour mixture into prepared pie crust and sprinkle top with additional grated Parmesan.

Place quiche on a cookie sheet and bake in a 350° oven for about 40 minutes or until custard is set. Serve warm. Serves 6.

Cheese Lover's Pie
with Cheese Crumb Butter Crust

This lovely quiche is an excellent choice for lunch. The cheese crumb crust is outstanding and harmonizes splendidly with the cheesy filling. And to add to its virtues, it can be prepared earlier in the day.

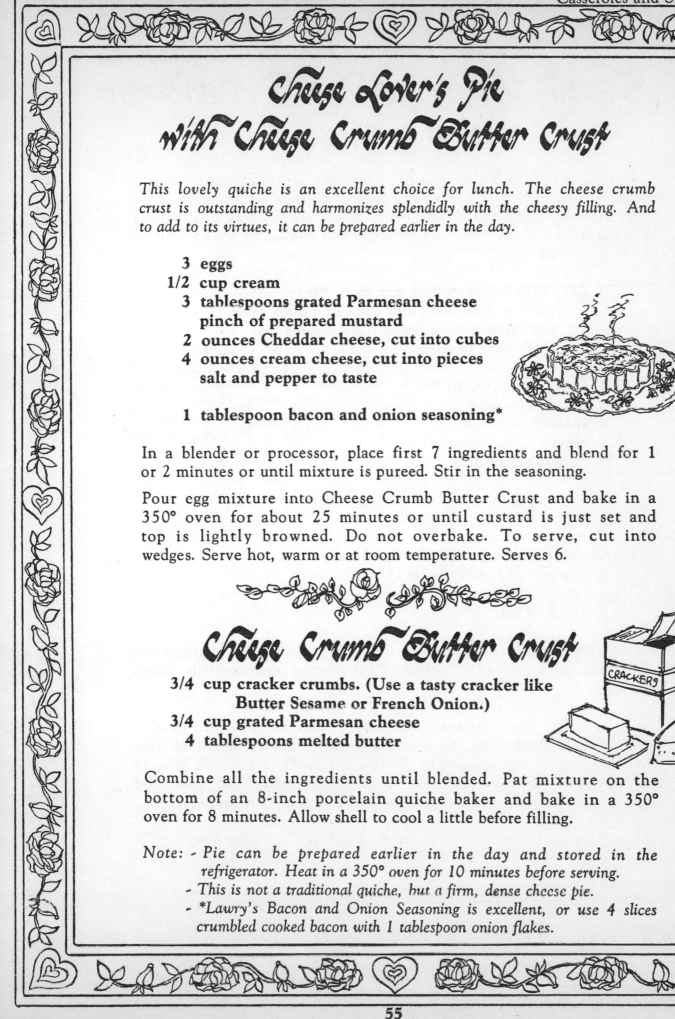

    3 eggs
    1/2 cup cream
    3 tablespoons grated Parmesan cheese
       pinch of prepared mustard
    2 ounces Cheddar cheese, cut into cubes
    4 ounces cream cheese, cut into pieces
       salt and pepper to taste

    1 tablespoon bacon and onion seasoning*

In a blender or processor, place first 7 ingredients and blend for 1 or 2 minutes or until mixture is pureed. Stir in the seasoning.

Pour egg mixture into Cheese Crumb Butter Crust and bake in a 350° oven for about 25 minutes or until custard is just set and top is lightly browned. Do not overbake. To serve, cut into wedges. Serve hot, warm or at room temperature. Serves 6.

Cheese Crumb Butter Crust

    3/4 cup cracker crumbs. (Use a tasty cracker like
         Butter Sesame or French Onion.)
    3/4 cup grated Parmesan cheese
    4 tablespoons melted butter

Combine all the ingredients until blended. Pat mixture on the bottom of an 8-inch porcelain quiche baker and bake in a 350° oven for 8 minutes. Allow shell to cool a little before filling.

Note: - Pie can be prepared earlier in the day and stored in the refrigerator. Heat in a 350° oven for 10 minutes before serving.
*   - This is not a traditional quiche, but a firm, dense cheese pie.*
*   - *Lawry's Bacon and Onion Seasoning is excellent, or use 4 slices crumbled cooked bacon with 1 tablespoon onion flakes.*

Heavenly Chicken Quiche with Mushrooms, Onions & Cheese

Oh! what a glorious pie to serve for a luncheon or a light supper. It is a beautiful combination of flavors and texture. Chicken breasts are best for this. However, keep this dish in mind, if you are planning to glamorize some leftover chicken. Add a vegetable salad and warm spiced fruit as lovely accompaniments.

1 **deep dish frozen 9-inch pie shell. Place on a cookie sheet and bake in a 400° oven for about 8 minutes or until shell is just beginning to color.**

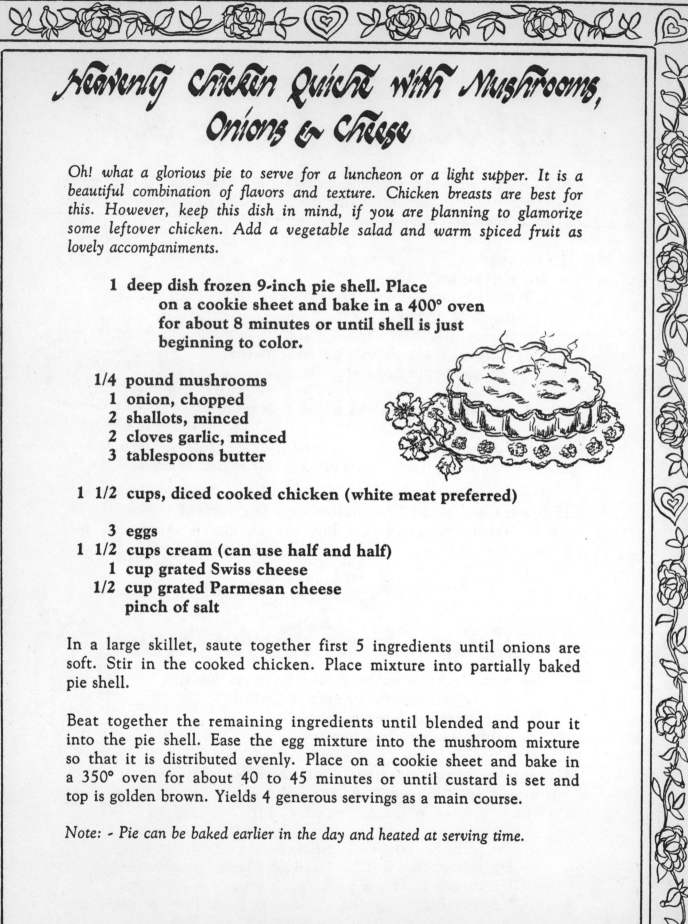

1/4 **pound mushrooms**
1 **onion, chopped**
2 **shallots, minced**
2 **cloves garlic, minced**
3 **tablespoons butter**

1 1/2 **cups, diced cooked chicken (white meat preferred)**

3 **eggs**
1 1/2 **cups cream (can use half and half)**
1 **cup grated Swiss cheese**
1/2 **cup grated Parmesan cheese**
pinch of salt

In a large skillet, saute together first 5 ingredients until onions are soft. Stir in the cooked chicken. Place mixture into partially baked pie shell.

Beat together the remaining ingredients until blended and pour it into the pie shell. Ease the egg mixture into the mushroom mixture so that it is distributed evenly. Place on a cookie sheet and bake in a 350° oven for about 40 to 45 minutes or until custard is set and top is golden brown. Yields 4 generous servings as a main course.

Note: - Pie can be baked earlier in the day and heated at serving time.

Red Hot Texas Chili with Pork & Beans

2 pounds coarsely ground pork (chili grind)
1 pound coarsely ground beef (chili grind)
4 cloves garlic, minced
2 onions, finely chopped
4 tablespoons oil

1 can (1 pound 12 ounces) crushed tomatoes in
    tomato puree
1 can (6 ounces) tomato paste
1 can (7 ounces) diced green chiles
1 can (1 pound) kidney beans, rinsed and drained
1/2 teaspoon red pepper flakes
    salt and pepper to taste
4 tablespoons chili powder
1 teaspoon cumin
1 teaspoon oregano

2 cups grated Cheddar cheese

In a Dutch oven casserole, place first 5 ingredients and saute mixture until meat loses its pinkness. Add the remaining ingredients (except the cheese) and cook mixture, partially covered, for about 45 minutes, or until it is very thick. Stir in the grated Cheddar. Serve chili in bowls with finely chopped onion on top. Crusty French Bread with Bubbly Cheese & Garlic is a grand accompaniment. Serves 8.

French Bread with Bubbly Cheese & Garlic

- 1 loaf French Bread, cut into 1-inch slices
- 1 cup mayonnaise
- 1 egg, beaten
- 2 cloves garlic, finely minced
- 2 cups grated Cheddar cheese
- 1/2 cup grated Parmesan cheese
  paprika

Combine all the ingredients (except the paprika) and stir until blended. Spread mixture on one side of each bread slice and sprinkle with paprika. Place on a cookie sheet and broil for a few minutes until top is bubbly and lightly browned. Serve at once. Serves 8.

Note: - Bread can be assembled earlier in the day and stored in the refrigerator. Broil before serving.

Cannelloni Firenzi with Cheese in an Instant Cheese & Chive Sauce

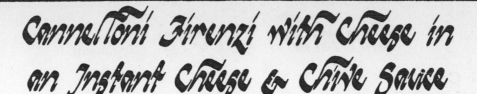

The inspiration for this dish came from a small restaurant we happily enjoyed in Florence. The dish was presented in a classic Mornay Sauce that was very good. I think you will find the Instant Cheese Sauce just a little quicker and especially good, too.

16 7-inch Herb Crepes

Filling:

    1 **cup cottage cheese**
    1 **package (8 ounces) cream cheese, softened**
    2 **eggs**
1/2 **cup fresh bread crumbs**
    1 **cup grated Swiss cheese**
1/2 **cup grated Parmesan cheese**
    1 **teaspoon Italian Herb Seasoning**
        salt and white pepper to taste

Combine all the filling ingredients and beat until blended. Divide the filling between the crepes, (about 2 heaping tablespoons on each.) Roll and place filled crepes, seam side down, and in one layer, in a 12x16-inch pan. (You can also arrange 2 filled crepes in 8 individual au gratin dishes.)

Spread Instant Cheese & Chive Sauce over the crepes and bake in a 350° oven until heated through. Broil for a few seconds to brown top. Serves 8.

Instant Cheese & Chive Sauce

  1 **cup sour cream**
  1 **cup cream**
  1 **cup grated Swiss cheese**
1/2 **cup grated Parmesan cheese**
  1 **tablespoon chopped parsley**
  1 **tablespoon chopped chives**

In a bowl, stir all the ingredients together until well blended.

Note: - Entire dish can be made earlier in the day and refrigerated. Before serving, heat in a 350° oven for 25 minutes or until bubbling hot.

Cannelloni Firenzi (continued)

Herb Crepes:
- 1 1/2 cups flour
- 1 1/2 cups milk
- 1/4 cup water
- 5 eggs
- 2 tablespoons oil
- 1 tablespoon minced parsley
- 2 tablespoons minced chives
- pinch of salt

In a large bowl, combine all the ingredients and with a whisk or hand beater, beat until mixture is blended and smooth.

Heat a small omelet-type pan with rounded sides, (7 to 8-inches) and butter bottom with a paper napkin or paper towel. When pan is very hot, but butter is not browned, pour about 1/8 cup batter into the pan. Tilt and turn pan immediately to evenly coat the bottom with a thin layer of batter. Pour out any excess batter.

Cook on one side for about 45 seconds or until bottom is golden and top is dry. Turn and cook other side for about 15 seconds. Makes about 16 to 20 crepes.

Cannelloni Firenzi with Cheese in an Instant Marinara Sauce

16 cannelloni filled with cheese (see previous recipe)

Place cannelloni in one layer in a 12x16-inch pan or arrange 2 cannelloni in 8 individual au gratin dishes. Pour Marinara Sauce over the top. Sprinkle top with

8 ounces Mozzarella cheese, grated
1/2 cup Parmesan cheese, grated

Heat cannelloni in a 350° oven for about 20 to 30 minutes or until piping hot. Broil for a few seconds to brown top. Serves 8.

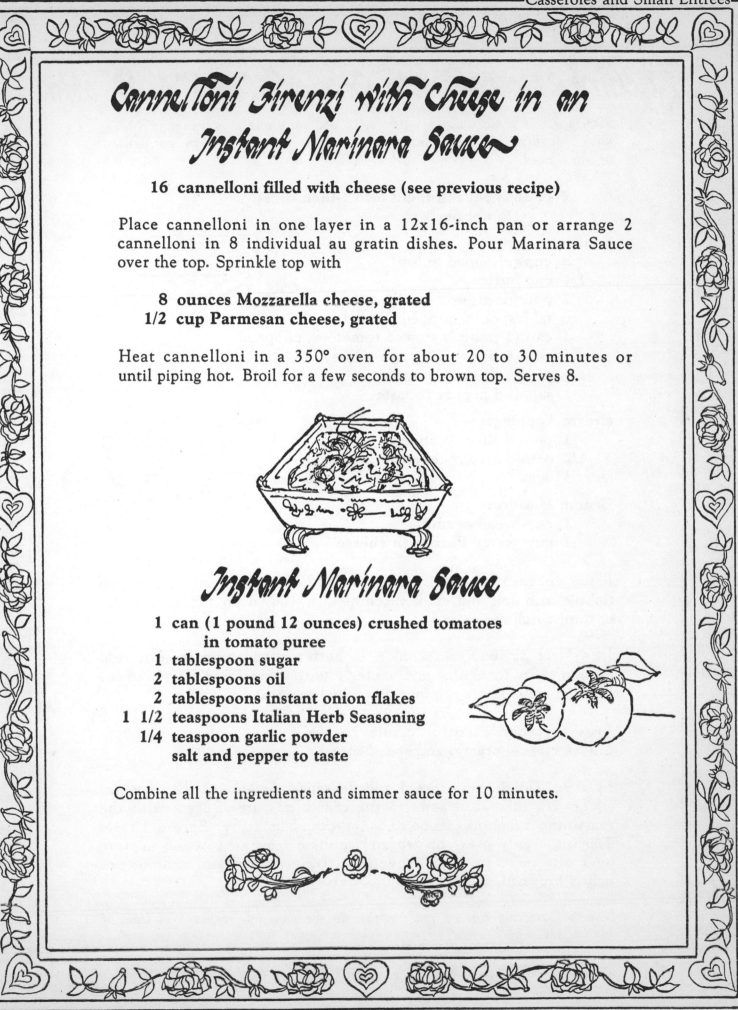

Instant Marinara Sauce

1 can (1 pound 12 ounces) crushed tomatoes
**   in tomato puree**
1 tablespoon sugar
2 tablespoons oil
2 tablespoons instant onion flakes
1 1/2 teaspoons Italian Herb Seasoning
1/4 teaspoon garlic powder
**   salt and pepper to taste**

Combine all the ingredients and simmer sauce for 10 minutes.

Zucchini Casserole with Ground Lamb & Ricotta

Moussaka is traditionally made with eggplant but is very good indeed with zucchini. Exceptionally delicious, it is also a very convenient one-dish meal.

2 pounds zucchini, cut into 1-inch slices. Do not peel.

Sauce:
- **3 cups chopped onions**
- **1/4 cup butter**
- **2 pounds ground lamb**
- **6 tablespoons minced parsley**
- **1 can (1 pound) stewed tomatoes, chopped**
- **1 can (8 ounces) tomato sauce**
- **1/4 teaspoon garlic powder**
- **salt and pepper to taste**

Cream Topping:
- **1 pound Ricotto cheese**
- **1/2 pound cream cheese**
- **3 eggs**

Crumb Mixture:
- **1 cup bread crumbs**
- **1 cup grated Parmesan cheese**

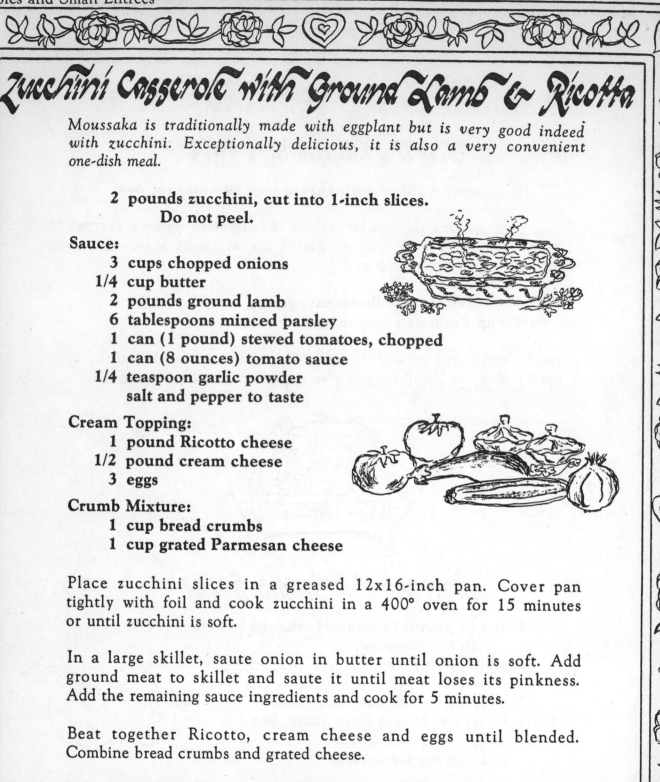

Place zucchini slices in a greased 12x16-inch pan. Cover pan tightly with foil and cook zucchini in a 400° oven for 15 minutes or until zucchini is soft.

In a large skillet, saute onion in butter until onion is soft. Add ground meat to skillet and saute it until meat loses its pinkness. Add the remaining sauce ingredients and cook for 5 minutes.

Beat together Ricotto, cream cheese and eggs until blended. Combine bread crumbs and grated cheese.

In a 9x13-inch pan, spread a little sauce. Layer 1/2 the zucchini slices, 1/2 the sauce and 1/3 the crumb mixture. Repeat with the remaining zucchini, sauce and 1/3 crumb mixture. Spread Cream Topping evenly over the top and sprinkle remaining crumb mixture over all. Bake in a 350° oven until piping hot and crumbs are lightly browned, about 35 minutes. Serves 8.

Note: - Casserole can be made earlier in the day and reheated at time of serving.

Old West Tamale Casserole with Sour Cream, Chili & Cheese

There is probably no dish that you can make that is easier than this one or more fun to eat. Everybody loves it. Serve it with some hot corn tortillas, generously spread with sweet butter.

- 8 prepared tamales (about 3 ounces, each) from the refrigerated section in your market. Cut tamales into 1-inch slices.
- 1 chili brick (1 pound) from the refrigerated section in your market
- 1 can (1 pound) stewed tomatoes, chopped. Do not drain.

- 1 cup sour cream
- 8 ounces medium sharp Cheddar cheese, grated
- 1/2 cup chopped green onions

In a 12-inch porcelain baker, place tamale slices evenly. Heat together the chili brick and stewed tomatoes until mixture is blended. (If chili is very thick, dilute with 1/2 cup beef broth.)

Spread chili mixture over the tamale slices. Spread sour cream on top and sprinkle with grated cheese and green onions. Heat in a 350° oven for about 30 to 40 minutes or until casserole is heated through and cheese is thoroughly melted. Serve with pink rice. Serves 6.

Note: - Entire casserole can be assembled earlier in the day and stored in the refrigerator. Heat before serving.
To the basic recipe, you can add 1 can (12 ounces) kernel corn, drained, or 1 can (1 pound) kidney beans, drained and mashed.

Casserole of Rice & Peas with Onions, Bacon & Tomatoes

While in Italy, we had a wonderful dish that resembled this one. Rice and peas, sometimes called "Risi e Bisi" is a delightful casserole. The addition of onions, bacon and tomatoes adds a certain depth to this dish. Add 2 cups cooked and shredded chicken and it will do quite well for a light supper.

- **1 cup rice**
- **1 can (10 1/2 ounces) chicken broth**
- **3/4 cup water**
- **1 medium tomato, peeled, seeded and chopped**
- **4 tablespoons butter**

- **1 large onion, chopped**
- **1 tablespoon butter**

- **1 package (10 ounces) frozen peas**
- **1/4 cup grated Parmesan cheese (or more to taste)**
- **6 strips bacon, cooked crisp, drained and crumbled**
- **salt and pepper to taste**

In a saucepan, place first 5 ingredients, cover pan and simmer mixture until liquid is absorbed and rice is tender.

Meanwhile, saute onion in butter until onion is soft. Add the peas and saute for several minutes or until peas are tender. In the pan with rice, add the onion mixture, cheese, bacon and seasonings and heat through. Serves 4 as a main dish or 6 as an accompaniment.

Note: - Casserole can be prepared earlier in the day and stored in the refrigerator. Add a few drops of water when reheating, and stir, now and then, to prevent scorching.

Old World Cheese Blintzes with Strawberries

1 cup small curd cottage cheese
1 package (8 ounces) cream cheese
2 tablespoons sour cream
1/2 cup sugar
1 tablespoon grated lemon peel
1/2 cup yellow raisins

Beat together cottage cheese and cream cheese until blended. Add the remaining ingredients and beat until blended.

Divide mixture between 16 crepes. Roll crepes up, jelly roll fashion, and place in one layer, seam side down, in a greased baking pan. (If you do not own a 12x16-inch pan, you will have to use 2 smaller ones.)

Bake in a 350° oven for about 15 minutes or until heated through. Serve with a dollup of sour cream and a tablespoonful of strawberries in syrup. Yields 16 crepes.

Basic Crepes

1 cup flour
1 cup milk
3 eggs
4 tablespoons melted butter
1/4 cup water
pinch of salt

Combine all the ingredients in a bowl and beat until blended. Heat a 7-inch skillet and butter it with a paper towel. Pan should be hot, but butter should not brown. A drop of water, splashed in pan, should skitter around.

Pour about 1/8 cup batter into pan. Quickly tilt and turn the pan so that the bottom is completely covered with batter. Pour out any excess batter. Place pan back on the heat and continue cooking the crepe for about 45 seconds or until top is dry. Turn and cook other side for about 15 seconds. Remove crepe onto a platter.

Heat pan and start again. As the batter contains butter, you do not have to butter the pan after each crepe. Yields about 16 7-inch crepes.

Shrimp & Rice Casserole with Peppers, Onion & Tomatoes

3 tablespoons butter
2 cups chicken broth (homemade or canned)
   salt to taste
1 cup long-grain rice

1 small green pepper, cut into strips
1 small red pepper, cut into strips
1 large onion, chopped
2 cloves garlic, minced
3 tablespoons butter

1/2 cup tomato sauce
1/2 pound cooked baby shrimp
1/3 cup grated Parmesan cheese (optional)

In a saucepan, place butter, broth, salt and rice, cover pan and simmer mixture until rice is tender and liquid is absorbed, about 25 to 30 minutes.

Meanwhile, in a large skillet, saute together the peppers, onion and garlic in butter until vegetables are soft. Add the tomato sauce and cook for 2 or 3 minutes, stirring.

Combine cooked rice, vegetables and shrimp and heat through. Stir in the optional Parmesan cheese and serve at once. Serves 6.

Note - *If you are planning to prepare this earlier in the day, then, cook the rice and vegetables and combine them in a casserole. Add the shrimp before reheating. The cheese is optional, but an excellent addition.*
   - If you have leftover turkey, substitute it for the shrimp. Use about 2 cups of cooked shredded turkey.

Broccoli & Cauliflower Crustless Quiche with Onions, Cheese & Bacon

If it is your turn for a luncheon meeting, this is a lovely dish for the buffet. It is delicious and filled with all good things.

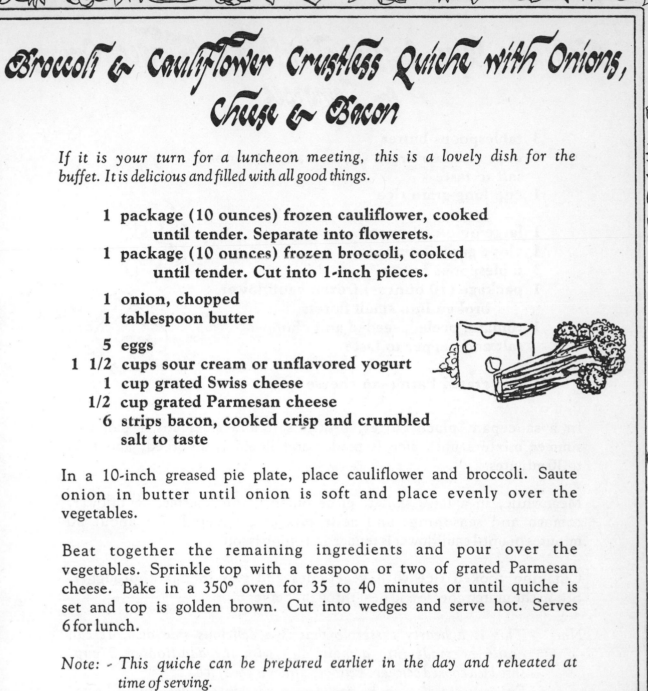

- **1 package (10 ounces) frozen cauliflower, cooked until tender. Separate into flowerets.**
- **1 package (10 ounces) frozen broccoli, cooked until tender. Cut into 1-inch pieces.**

- **1 onion, chopped**
- **1 tablespoon butter**

- **5 eggs**
- **1 1/2 cups sour cream or unflavored yogurt**
- **1 cup grated Swiss cheese**
- **1/2 cup grated Parmesan cheese**
- **6 strips bacon, cooked crisp and crumbled**
- **salt to taste**

In a 10-inch greased pie plate, place cauliflower and broccoli. Saute onion in butter until onion is soft and place evenly over the vegetables.

Beat together the remaining ingredients and pour over the vegetables. Sprinkle top with a teaspoon or two of grated Parmesan cheese. Bake in a 350° oven for 35 to 40 minutes or until quiche is set and top is golden brown. Cut into wedges and serve hot. Serves 6 for lunch.

Note: - This quiche can be prepared earlier in the day and reheated at time of serving.
- Do not freeze.

Delicious Rice Casserole with Cauliflower, Onions & Tomatoes

3 tablespoons butter
2 cups chicken broth (homemade or canned)
    salt to taste
1 cup long-grain rice

1 large onion, chopped
1 clove garlic, minced
3 tablespoons butter
1 package (10 ounces) frozen cauliflower,
       broken into small florets
1 tomato, peeled, seeded and chopped
    salt and pepper to taste

1/3 cup grated Parmesan cheese

In a saucepan, place butter, broth, salt and rice, cover pan and simmer mixture until rice is tender and liquid is absorbed, about 25 to 30 minutes.

Meanwhile, in a large skillet, place onion, garlic, butter, cauliflower, tomato and seasonings and cook mixture, covered, for about 20 minutes or until cauliflower is tender and onion is soft.

Combine cooked rice with vegetables and toss to mix thoroughly. Stir in the grated cheese and heat through. Serves 6.

Note: - This is a hearty casserole that is a delicious side dish. It can easily be made into a main dish with the addition of 2 cups shredded cooked chicken. Leftover turkey is good, too.
- Entire casserole can be prepared earlier in the day and reheated before serving.

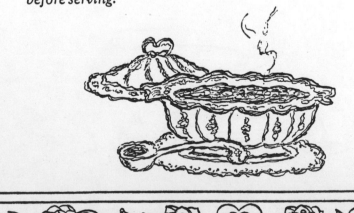

Heavenly Casserole with Shrimps, Mushrooms & Lemon Wine Sauce

If you're looking for elegance in a one-dish meal, this casserole is ultimate in taste and presentation. It serves well for lunch or dinner. The taste is glorious and just bursting with flavor.

- 1/2 pound mushrooms, sliced
- 1 small onion, chopped (about 1/2 cup)
- 2 cloves garlic, minced
- 1 shallot, minced
- 2 tablespoons butter

- 1/4 cup dry white wine

- 1/4 cup flour
- 3/4 cup cream

- 1 pound cooked shrimp, medium-size
- 1 jar (8 ounces) marinated artichoke hearts,
  Discard dressing.
- 1/4 teaspoon dried dill weed
- 1 1/2 cups grated Swiss cheese
- 2 tablespoons lemon juice
  salt and pepper to taste

In a large skillet, saute together first 5 ingredients until onion is soft. Add wine and cook for 2 minutes until wine has evaporated. Stir in the flour and cook and stir for 2 minutes. Stir in the cream and cook for 2 minutes or until sauce is very thick. Stir in the remaining ingredients.

Transfer mixture to an oval au gratin porcelain baker and sprinkle top with Buttered Cheese & Crumb Topping. (Can be held at this point, in the refrigerator.)

Before serving, heat in a 350° oven until heated through. Serve with a simple pilaf and a Compote of Mixed Berries. Serves 6.

Buttered Cheese & Crumb Topping:
- 1/4 cup grated Parmesan cheese
- 1/4 cup dry bread crumbs
- 2 tablespoons melted butter

Combine all the ingredients until blended.

Note: - Crabmeat or scallops can be substituted for the shrimp.

Picante Guacamole Mold with Tomatoes, Onions & Chiles

1 package unflavored gelatin
1/2 cup water

4 avocados, mashed
1 cup sour cream
1 can (4 ounces) chopped green chiles
4 tablespoons lemon juice, or more to taste
1 small onion, grated
1 tomato, peeled, seeded and chopped
2 tabasco peppers, finely minced (or more
    if you are stout of heart)

In a metal measuring cup, soften gelatin in water. Place in a pan of simmering water until dissolved.

In a large bowl, stir together the remaining ingredients until well mixed. Stir in the dissolved gelatin. Spoon mixture into a 6-cup mold and refrigerate until firm.

Unmold onto a lovely platter and decorate with green leaves and scored lemon slices. Serve with toasted flour tortillas as an accompaniment.

Note: - To toast flour tortillas, place in a toaster oven (not a pop-up toaster) and toast for about 1 or 2 minutes or until tortillas are crispened. Bubbles will form (this is normal).

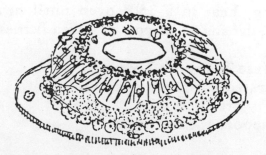

Some like it hot ...

Loving Soups

Some like it cold ...

Soup is the stuff memories are made of. I cannot recall ever having met a single person who did not love soup. Often, I wonder what it is about that magical brew that can stir the hearts of poets and the minds of men.

Soup nourishes and comforts. It exudes of love and caring. When the weather is roaring outside, cuddling by the fire with family and friends, sipping a hearty, robust soup is sheer poetry.

When I summon up remembrances of things past, the memory of Mamma's soup kettle, simmering on the stove for hours on end, fill me with nostalgia. The aroma of soup, drifting out of the kitchen, assures you that love is very close by.

The soups I am sharing with you have a deep and solid character. They are filled with all manner of good things. They are thick and glorious. The garnitures range from the delicate Batonettes of Cheese, made with puff pastry to the hefty Black Pumpernickel with Raisin Butter. The Crispettes and Croustades are lovely accompaniments and add pleasure to the total experience. I do hope you try the Feather Cream Biscuits soon. They are as light as a cloud, and served warm with sweet butter and honey . . . heavenly. And Dumplings. Who doesn't love these fluffy little balls of dough?

There are no rules for making good soup, except the balancing of ingredients to produce maximum depth and flavor. Throwing in tidbits and leftovers will not produce the subtle harmony that makes soups memorable.

Soups make you feel good and warm—all over.

Potage of Zucchini & Tomatoes with Batonettes of Cheese

What a sublime soup, marvellously flavored with onions and garlic and herbs. The Batonettes are incredibly good, and exceptionally easy, starting, as they do, with frozen puff pastry.

6 medium zucchini, scrubbed, but do not peel. Cut into thin slices.
2 large onions, chopped
4 cloves garlic, minced
2 shallots, chopped
3 tablespoons butter

1 can (1 pound) stewed tomatoes, chopped. Do not drain.
2 cans (10 1/2 ounces, each) chicken broth
2 teaspoons lemon juice
1/2 teaspoon sugar
1 tablespoon chopped parsley
1/2 teaspoon dill weed
    salt to taste

1/2 cup cream
1/2 cup sour cream

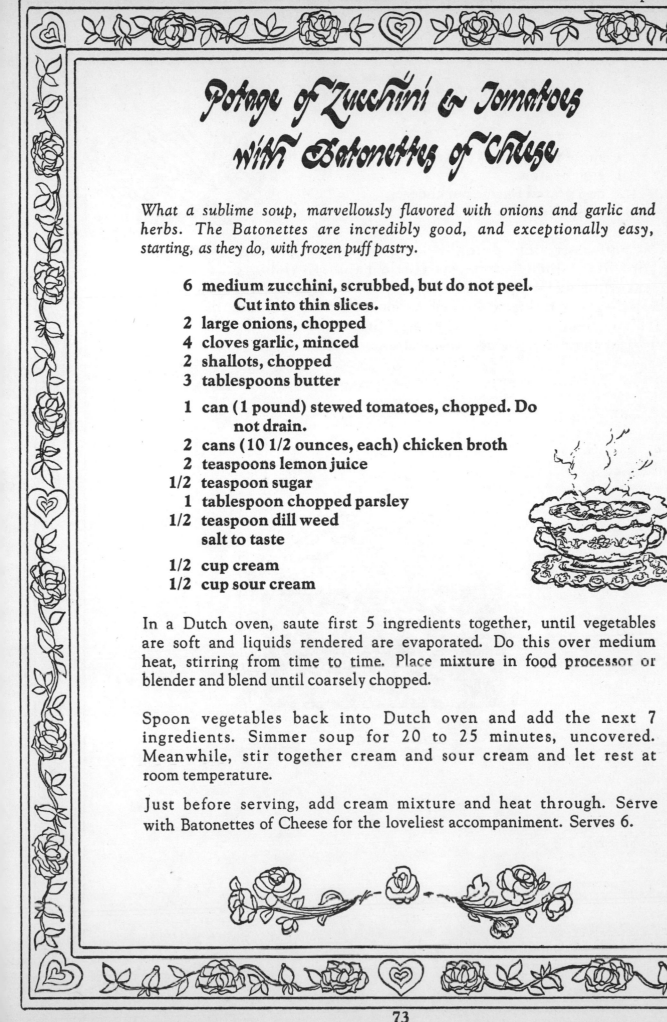

In a Dutch oven, saute first 5 ingredients together, until vegetables are soft and liquids rendered are evaporated. Do this over medium heat, stirring from time to time. Place mixture in food processor or blender and blend until coarsely chopped.

Spoon vegetables back into Dutch oven and add the next 7 ingredients. Simmer soup for 20 to 25 minutes, uncovered. Meanwhile, stir together cream and sour cream and let rest at room temperature.

Just before serving, add cream mixture and heat through. Serve with Batonettes of Cheese for the loveliest accompaniment. Serves 6.

Batonettes of Cheese

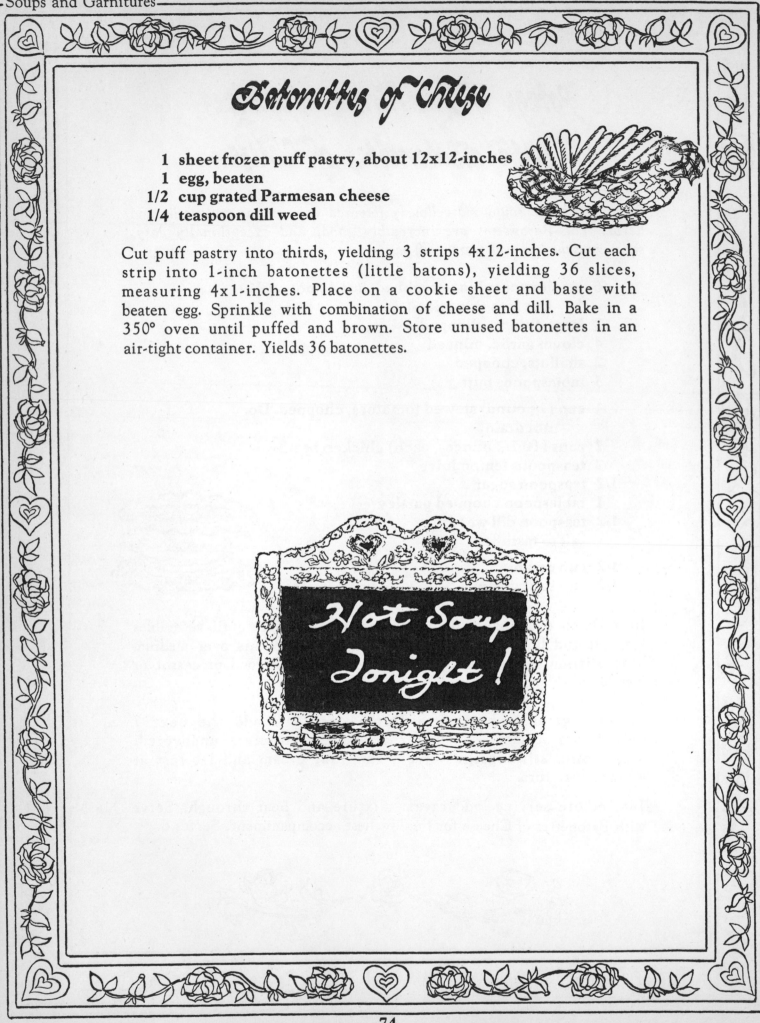

1   sheet frozen puff pastry, about 12x12-inches
1   egg, beaten
1/2 cup grated Parmesan cheese
1/4 teaspoon dill weed

Cut puff pastry into thirds, yielding 3 strips 4x12-inches. Cut each strip into 1-inch batonettes (little batons), yielding 36 slices, measuring 4x1-inches. Place on a cookie sheet and baste with beaten egg. Sprinkle with combination of cheese and dill. Bake in a 350° oven until puffed and brown. Store unused batonettes in an air-tight container. Yields 36 batonettes.

Hot Soup Tonight!

Royal Cream of Zucchini, Mushroom & Onion Soup with Feather Cream Biscuits

If, perchance, you are entertaining an impressive group, this soup will earn you a standing ovation. It has a deep and significant taste, beautifully blended with all manner of good things. The Feather Biscuits are delicate and light and a lovely accompaniment.

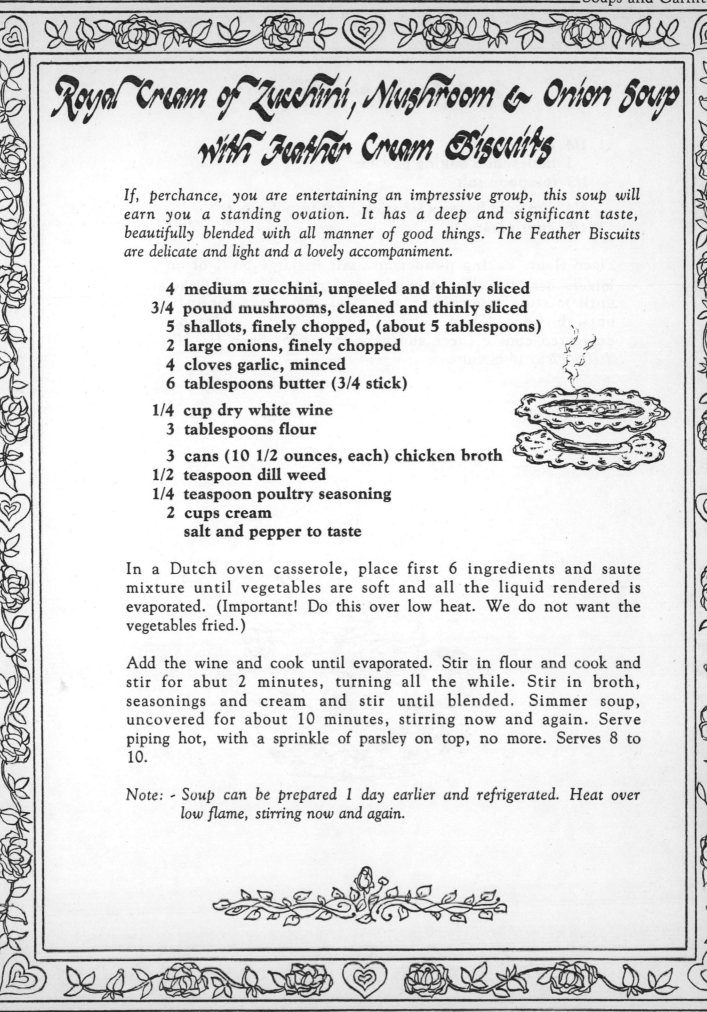

- 4 medium zucchini, unpeeled and thinly sliced
- 3/4 pound mushrooms, cleaned and thinly sliced
- 5 shallots, finely chopped, (about 5 tablespoons)
- 2 large onions, finely chopped
- 4 cloves garlic, minced
- 6 tablespoons butter (3/4 stick)

- 1/4 cup dry white wine
- 3 tablespoons flour

- 3 cans (10 1/2 ounces, each) chicken broth
- 1/2 teaspoon dill weed
- 1/4 teaspoon poultry seasoning
- 2 cups cream
- salt and pepper to taste

In a Dutch oven casserole, place first 6 ingredients and saute mixture until vegetables are soft and all the liquid rendered is evaporated. (Important! Do this over low heat. We do not want the vegetables fried.)

Add the wine and cook until evaporated. Stir in flour and cook and stir for abut 2 minutes, turning all the while. Stir in broth, seasonings and cream and stir until blended. Simmer soup, uncovered for about 10 minutes, stirring now and again. Serve piping hot, with a sprinkle of parsley on top, no more. Serves 8 to 10.

Note: - Soup can be prepared 1 day earlier and refrigerated. Heat over low flame, stirring now and again.

Feather Cream Biscuits

1 1/4 cups flour
   1 tablespoon baking powder
1/3 teaspoon salt

  1/4 cup cold butter (1/2 stick,) cut into 4 pieces
1 1/8 cups cream

Place flour, baking powder and salt in large bowl of an electric mixer. Beat for a few seconds to blend. Add the butter and beat until mixture resembles coarse meal. By hand, stir in the cream until blended. Drop batter by the heaping tablespoon on an ungreased cookie sheet and bake in a 425° oven for 20 minutes. Yields 12 to 14 biscuits.

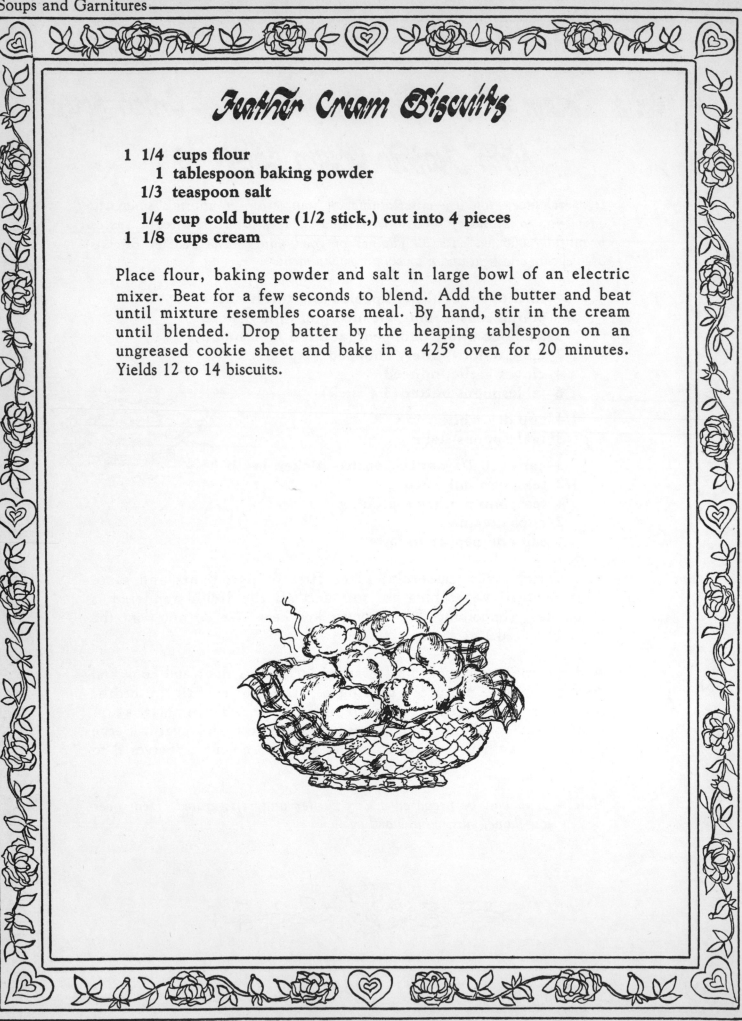

Old-Fashioned Clam Chowder with Red Hot French Cheese Bread

2 tablespoons oil
2 onions, finely chopped
3 cloves garlic, minced
1 can (1 pound) stewed tomatoes, chopped. Do not drain.
2 cups bottled clam juice
2 cups tomato juice
2 tablespoons tomato paste
2 potatoes, peeled and diced
2 cans (7 ounces, each) minced clams
1 carrot, grated
1 stalk celery, thinly sliced
1 tablespoon chopped parsley
1 teaspoon thyme flakes
2 teaspoons sugar
1/4 teaspoon tumeric
1/2 teaspoon red pepper flakes

Combine all the ingredients in a Dutch oven casserole and simmer mixture for 45 minutes or until vegetables are soft. Serve with Red Hot French Cheese Bread as a wonderful accompaniment. Serves 6.

Red Hot French Cheese Bread

12 slices French bread, cut about 1/2-inch thick

1/2 cup (1 stick) butter, at room temperature
1/4 teaspoon garlic powder
1/4 teaspoon paprika
1/2 cup grated Parmesan cheese
1/4 teaspoon cayenne pepper

Place French bread slices on a cookie sheet. Beat together the remaining ingredients until blended. Spread butter mixture on each slice of bread. (Can be held at this point.) Just before serving, broil for 1 minute or so, until tops are just beginning to brown. Watch carefully or bread will burn. Serves 6.

Note: - Soup and bread have a wonderful bite. Not too hot, but just enough to give it character.
      - Soup can be made earlier in the day and stored in the refrigerator. Heat before serving.

Farmhouse Beef & Cabbage Tomato Soup with Black Bread & Raisin Butter

This is a very thick soup, much like a stew. It is deeply satisfying on a frosty night when the weather is raging outside. The black bread slices are the perfect accompaniment to this peasant-style soup.

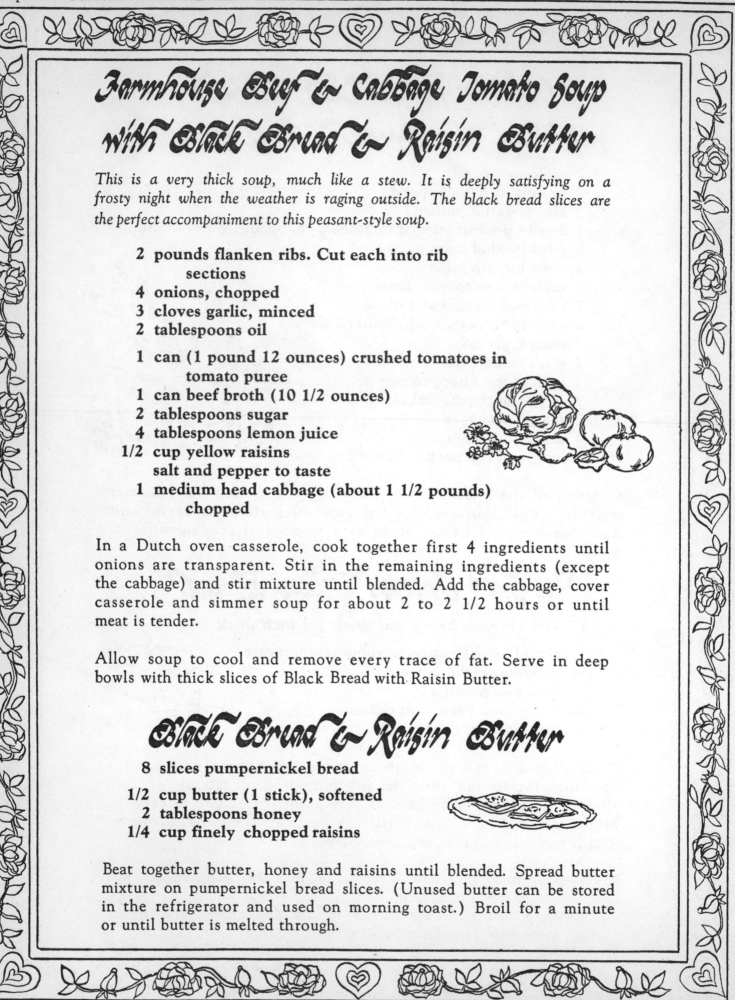

- **2 pounds flanken ribs. Cut each into rib sections**
- **4 onions, chopped**
- **3 cloves garlic, minced**
- **2 tablespoons oil**

- **1 can (1 pound 12 ounces) crushed tomatoes in tomato puree**
- **1 can beef broth (10 1/2 ounces)**
- **2 tablespoons sugar**
- **4 tablespoons lemon juice**
- **1/2 cup yellow raisins**
- **salt and pepper to taste**
- **1 medium head cabbage (about 1 1/2 pounds) chopped**

In a Dutch oven casserole, cook together first 4 ingredients until onions are transparent. Stir in the remaining ingredients (except the cabbage) and stir mixture until blended. Add the cabbage, cover casserole and simmer soup for about 2 to 2 1/2 hours or until meat is tender.

Allow soup to cool and remove every trace of fat. Serve in deep bowls with thick slices of Black Bread with Raisin Butter.

Black Bread & Raisin Butter

- **8 slices pumpernickel bread**

- **1/2 cup butter (1 stick), softened**
- **2 tablespoons honey**
- **1/4 cup finely chopped raisins**

Beat together butter, honey and raisins until blended. Spread butter mixture on pumpernickel bread slices. (Unused butter can be stored in the refrigerator and used on morning toast.) Broil for a minute or until butter is melted through.

Minestrone di la Piazza Navonna di Roma made easy

During our stay in Rome, we enjoyed many versions of the classic Italian Minestrone. The variations were many, but the following includes most of the basics. It is a thick and hearty soup and just right for sipping by the fire. Add an antipasto salad and it is a complete meal.

- 1 pound boneless beef chuck, cut into 1/2-inch cubes
- 2 onions, chopped
- 2 cloves garlic, minced
- 1 teaspoon oil

- 4 carrots, thinly sliced
- 1 stalk celery, thinly sliced
- 1 can (1 pound) stewed tomatoes, undrained and chopped
- 1 cup chopped cabbage
- 2 cans (10 1/2 ounces, each) beef broth
- 2 cans (10 1/2 ounces, each) chicken broth
- 2 cups water
- 1 bay leaf
- 1 teaspoon oregano
  salt and pepper to taste

- 1 can (8 ounces) chick peas, drained (or 3/4 cup)
- 1 can (8 ounces) red kidney beans (or 3/4 cup), drained
- 1 package (10 ounces) frozen cut green beans
- 1 package (10 ounces) frozen peas
- 1 cup spaghetti, broken in small pieces

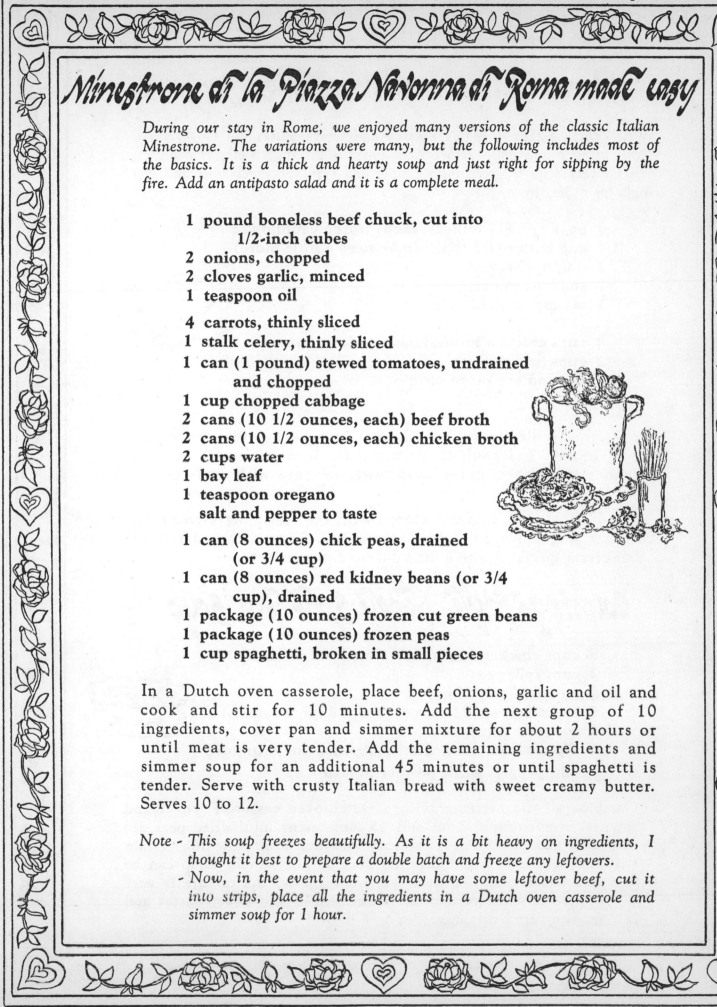

In a Dutch oven casserole, place beef, onions, garlic and oil and cook and stir for 10 minutes. Add the next group of 10 ingredients, cover pan and simmer mixture for about 2 hours or until meat is very tender. Add the remaining ingredients and simmer soup for an additional 45 minutes or until spaghetti is tender. Serve with crusty Italian bread with sweet creamy butter. Serves 10 to 12.

Note - This soup freezes beautifully. As it is a bit heavy on ingredients, I thought it best to prepare a double batch and freeze any leftovers.

- Now, in the event that you may have some leftover beef, cut it into strips, place all the ingredients in a Dutch oven casserole and simmer soup for 1 hour.

Puree of Cream of Cauliflower Soup

When the weather is raging outside and temperatures dip to frosty, a bowl of soup and some freshly-baked bread is the stuff poetry is made of. This lovely soup is exceedingly simple and very, very delicious and just right for sipping by the fire.

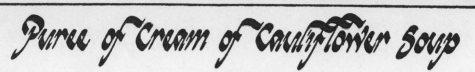

2 packages (10 ounces, each) frozen cauliflower
1/4 cup butter (1/2 stick) (may need a little more)
1 onion, chopped
2 shallots, minced
1 tablespoon lemon juice

4 cups chicken broth, home-made or canned
2 cups half and half
salt and pepper to taste
pinch of dill

In a large skillet, saute cauliflower, onion and shallots in butter until onions and cauliflower are soft. In a processor or in a blender in batches, puree cauliflower mixture with some of the broth.

Pour blended soup into a saucepan with the remaining ingredients. Simmer soup for about 10 or 15 minutes. Serve with a dollup of sour cream sprinkled with a little dill weed. Serves 6.

Country-Style Hardy Split Pea Soup

8 cups chicken broth, home-made or canned
2 cups split peas
2 onions, finely chopped
1 cup thinly sliced carrots (about 2 large carrots)
1/4 teaspoon paprika
6 slices bacon, cooked crisp, drained and crumbled
salt, pepper, garlic powder to taste

Combine all the ingredients in a Dutch-oven casserole, cover and simmer mixture for 1 hour and 15 minutes or until dried peas are very soft and fall apart. Stir every now and again, making certain that the heat is low and that the peas do not scorch. Soup can be put in a blender, if you wish, but in this case, the texture is very nice. Serve it with some freshly-baked bread and sweet butter and it is really a very hardy meal. Serves 6 to 8.

Old-Fashioned Cabbage Soup with Crispettes of Herb & Cheese

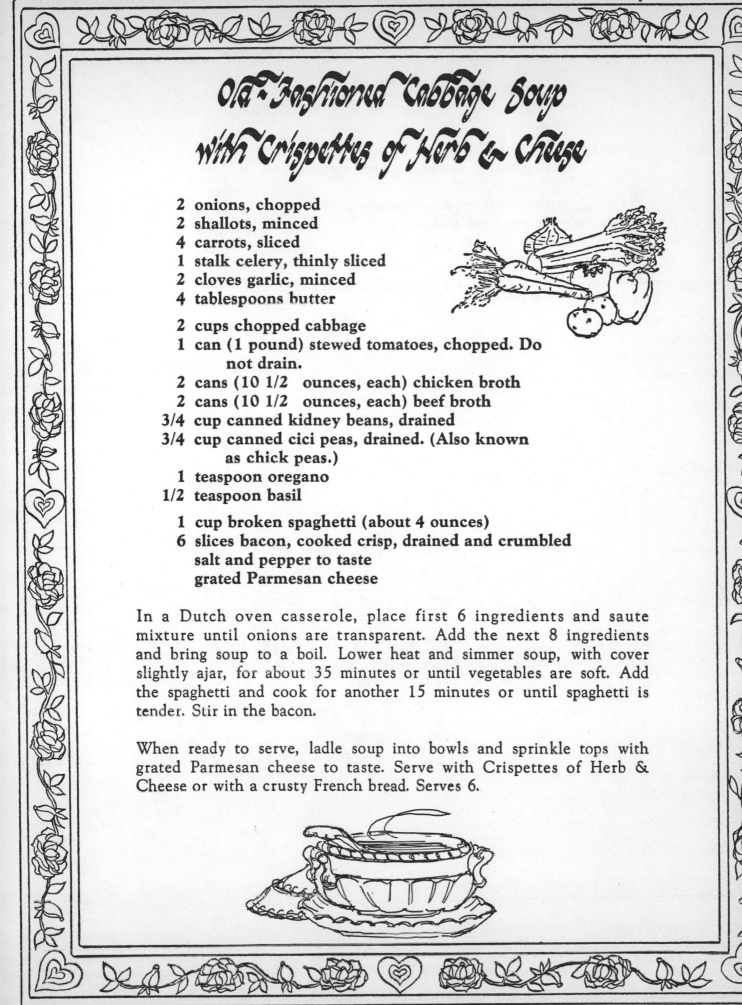

2 onions, chopped
2 shallots, minced
4 carrots, sliced
1 stalk celery, thinly sliced
2 cloves garlic, minced
4 tablespoons butter

2 cups chopped cabbage
1 can (1 pound) stewed tomatoes, chopped. Do
    not drain.
2 cans (10 1/2 ounces, each) chicken broth
2 cans (10 1/2 ounces, each) beef broth
3/4 cup canned kidney beans, drained
3/4 cup canned cici peas, drained. (Also known
    as chick peas.)
1 teaspoon oregano
1/2 teaspoon basil

1 cup broken spaghetti (about 4 ounces)
6 slices bacon, cooked crisp, drained and crumbled
    salt and pepper to taste
    grated Parmesan cheese

In a Dutch oven casserole, place first 6 ingredients and saute mixture until onions are transparent. Add the next 8 ingredients and bring soup to a boil. Lower heat and simmer soup, with cover slightly ajar, for about 35 minutes or until vegetables are soft. Add the spaghetti and cook for another 15 minutes or until spaghetti is tender. Stir in the bacon.

When ready to serve, ladle soup into bowls and sprinkle tops with grated Parmesan cheese to taste. Serve with Crispettes of Herb & Cheese or with a crusty French bread. Serves 6.

Crispettes of Herb & Cheese

6 slices Westphalian pumpernickel bread (from the
    refrigerated section in your market)
4 tablespoons butter
4 tablespoons grated Parmesan cheese
1/2 teaspoon oregano flakes

Place bread on a cookie sheet. Mix together the remaining
ingredients and spread it on the bread. Toast bread in a 350° oven
until bread is crisped and tops are beginning to brown, about 8
minutes. Serve warm or at room temperature.

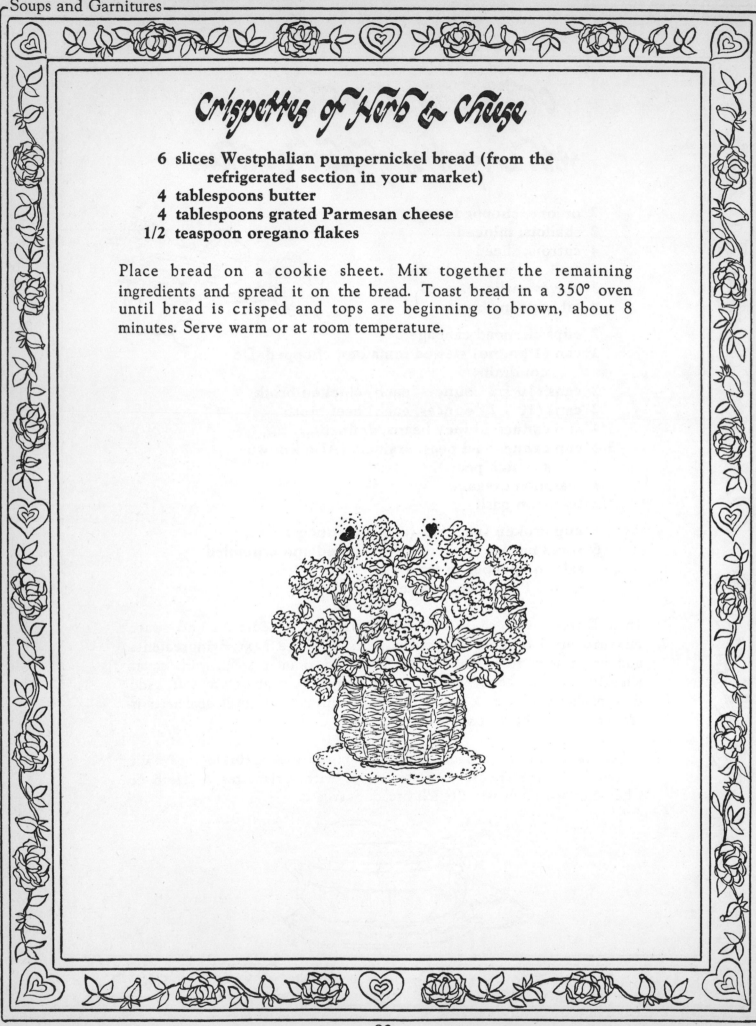

Peasant Vegetable Soup with Basil Garlic Pesto & Onion Cheese Points

Oh! What a soup. It has deep solid character and is brimful with flavor and goodness. The Onion Cheese Points are a wonderful accompaniment.

- 2 cans (10 1/2 ounces, each) beef broth
- 2 cans (10 1/2 ounces, each) chicken broth
- 1 can (1 pound) stewed tomatoes, chopped. Do not drain.
- 2 large onions, finely chopped
- 3 carrots, sliced
- 1 stalk celery, thinly sliced
- 1 package (10 ounces) frozen cut green beans
- 2 potatoes, peeled and cubed
- 1 cup broken spaghetti
- 1 teaspoon oregano
  salt and pepper to taste

- 3 cloves garlic, mashed
- 1 tablespoon dried basil (or 3 tablespoons fresh basil)
- 2 tablespoons olive oil

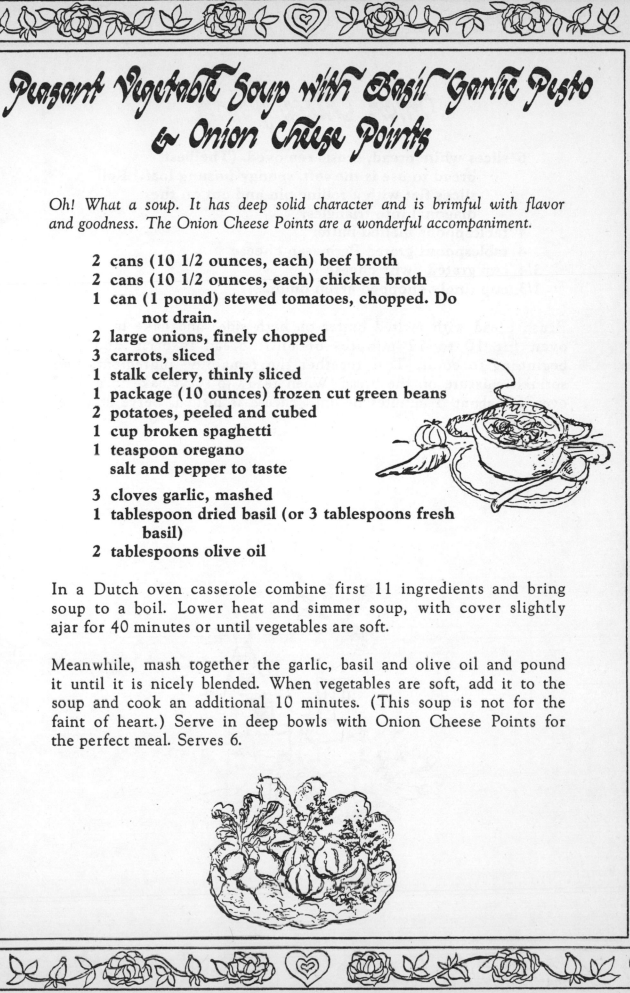

In a Dutch oven casserole combine first 11 ingredients and bring soup to a boil. Lower heat and simmer soup, with cover slightly ajar for 40 minutes or until vegetables are soft.

Meanwhile, mash together the garlic, basil and olive oil and pound it until it is nicely blended. When vegetables are soft, add it to the soup and cook an additional 10 minutes. (This soup is not for the faint of heart.) Serve in deep bowls with Onion Cheese Points for the perfect meal. Serves 6.

Onion Cheese Points

6 slices white bread, crusts removed. (The best
      bread to use is the soft, spongy unsung loaf.) Roll
      slices flat with a rolling pin and cut on the
      diagonal into triangles.
4 tablespoons melted butter
4 tablespoons grated Parmesan cheese
3/4 cup grated Swiss cheese
1/3 cup finely chopped green onions

Brush bread with melted butter on both sides and bake in a 350°
oven for 10 to 12 minutes or until bread is crisp and just
beginning to color. Toss together the remaining ingredients and
sprinkle mixture on the bread. When ready to serve bake in a 350°
oven for about 5 minutes or until cheese is melted. Serve at once.
Serves 6.

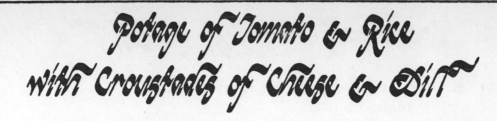

Potage of Tomato & Rice with Croustades of Cheese & Dill

This is a memorable soup and very easy to prepare. Don't feel that because it is made from kitchen staples that it doesn't have real solid character. It is infinitely delicious and the croustades are the perfect accompaniments.

- 2 onions, chopped
- 2 shallots, chopped
- 2 cloves garlic, minced
- 1 teaspoon sugar
- 4 tablespoons butter

- 2 cans (1 pound, each) stewed tomatoes, very finely chopped. (This can be done in a blender or food processor.) Do not drain.

- 2 tablespoons tomato paste
- 3 cans (10 1/2 ounces, each) chicken broth
- 1/4 teaspoon thyme
- 1/4 teaspoon basil
- 1/4 teaspoon dill weed
-     salt and pepper to taste
- 1/2 cup rice

In a Dutch oven, saute together first 5 ingredients until onions are transparent. Add the remaining ingredients and simmer soup for 30 minutes or until rice is tender. Serve with Croustades of Cheese & Dill. Serves 8.

Croustades of Cheese & Dill

8 slices of sourdough bread, brush with
melted butter
1 1/2 cups grated Swiss cheese
6 tablespoons sour cream
3 tablespoons chopped chives
1/2 teaspoon dill weed

Combine Swiss cheese, sour cream, chives and dill until blended. Spread mixture on bread slices and broil for a minute or so, or until cheese is melted. Serve with soup or salad.

Note: - Soup can be prepared earlier in the day and stored in the refrigerator. Heat before serving. Bread can be assembled earlier in the day, but broil before serving.

Cream of Spinach Soup with Onions & Mushrooms

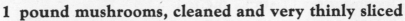

        1 **pound mushrooms, cleaned and very thinly sliced**
        4 **shallots, finely chopped**
        2 **large onions, finely chopped**
        3 **cloves garlic, minced**
        6 **tablespoons butter**

    1/4 **cup dry white wine**

        3 **tablespoons flour**

        3 **cans (10 1/2 ounces, each) chicken broth**
        1 **package (10 ounces) frozen chopped spinach**
    1 1/2 **cups cream**
        pinch of nutmeg
        salt to taste

In a large saucepan or Dutch oven, place first 5 ingredients and saute mixture, over low heat, until mushrooms and onions are soft and all the liquid rendered, is evaporated. Add wine and cook until evaporated. Stir in flour and cook and stir for about 2 minutes, turning all the while.

Stir in broth, and spinach and simmer soup for 2 minutes. Add cream and simmer soup for 10 minutes, uncovered. Add seasonings to taste. Serve with Garlic Crisps with Herbs and Cheese. Serves 8 to 10.

Garlic Crisps with Herbs & Cheese

1/2 cup butter (1 stick) melted
1/2 teaspoon garlic powder
  1 tablespoon lemon juice

1/2 teaspoon Italian Herb Seasoning
  2 tablespoons chopped chives
1/2 cup grated Parmesan cheese

 12 slices egg bread, crusts removed. Roll bread
    flat with a rolling pin. Cut into decorative
    shapes; triangles, fingers, circles, rectangles — or
    use decorative cookie cutters

In a saucepan, melt butter with garlic powder and lemon juice. In a flat pan or dish, combine seasoning, chives and cheese.

Spread butter mixture on both sides of the bread, coating generously. Dip bread, on one side, in cheese mixture and place on a buttered cookie sheet (or teflon pan). Bake in a 350° oven until bread is crisped and tops are beginning to color. Allow to cool and store in an air-tight cannister. Yields about 24 Crisps. (Can be prepared several days before serving).

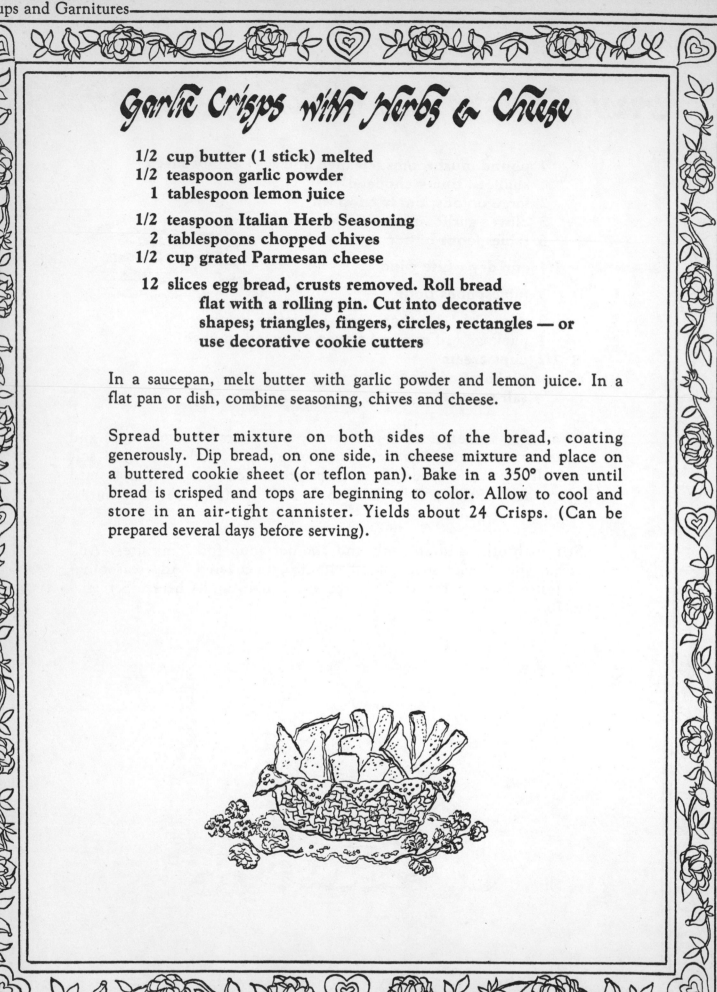

Peasant Bean Soup with Bacon & Cheese & Honey Pumpernickel

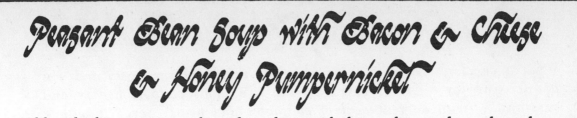

Although this soup is made with undistinguished ingredients, the end result is bursting with flavor. This is a hardy soup and serving it with black bread and honey is practically a complete meal.

3 onions, chopped
1 carrot, grated
1 stalk celery, thinly sliced
3 cloves garlic, minced
4 tablespoons butter

1 can (1 pound) stewed tomatoes, chopped. Do not drain.
2 cans (10 1/2 ounces, each) beef broth
1 can (10 1/2 ounces) chicken broth
1 can (1 pound) kidney beans, rinsed and drained
1 can (1 pound) cici peas (chick peas) rinsed and drained
1 teaspoon Italian Herb Seasoning
salt and pepper to taste

6 strips bacon, cooked crisp, drained and crumbled
1/2 cup grated Parmesan cheese

In a Dutch oven, saute onions, carrot, celery and garlic in butter, until onions are transparent. Add the next 7 ingredients and simmer soup, with cover slightly ajar, for 40 minutes. Stir in the bacon and cheese and simmer soup an additional 5 minutes. Serve with Honey Pumpernickel and additional grated cheese to taste. Serves 6 to 8.

Honey Pumpernickel

8 slices pumpernickel bread with raisins
3 ounces (3/4 stick) butter
3 tablespoons honey

Place bread on cookie sheet. Beat together butter and honey until blended. Spread mixture on bread slices and broil bread for 1 or 2 minutes, or until butter is melted and bubbling. Serve at once.

Note: - Soup can be prepared earlier in the day and reheated before serving.

Old Fashioned Beef & Sauerkraut Soup

What a wonderful soup to serve when the weather turns frosty and you are looking for a bit of magic by the fire. This soup is hearty and substantial, with a great deal of character and heart. Serve it with a dollup of sour cream and lots of black bread with sweet butter.

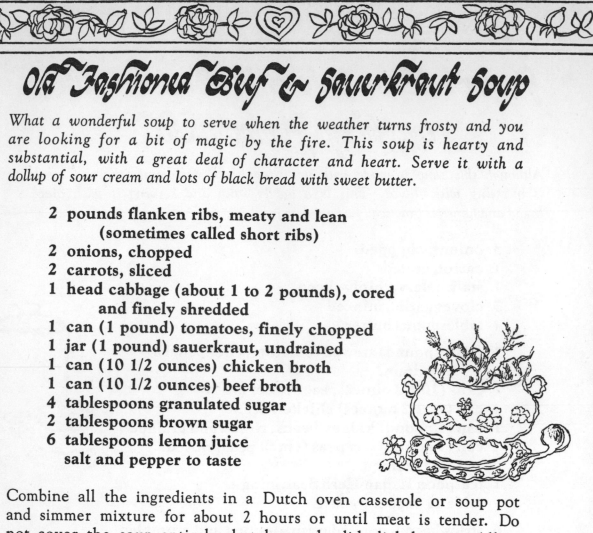

2 pounds flanken ribs, meaty and lean
    (sometimes called short ribs)
2 onions, chopped
2 carrots, sliced
1 head cabbage (about 1 to 2 pounds), cored
    and finely shredded
1 can (1 pound) tomatoes, finely chopped
1 jar (1 pound) sauerkraut, undrained
1 can (10 1/2 ounces) chicken broth
1 can (10 1/2 ounces) beef broth
4 tablespoons granulated sugar
2 tablespoons brown sugar
6 tablespoons lemon juice
  salt and pepper to taste

Combine all the ingredients in a Dutch oven casserole or soup pot and simmer mixture for about 2 hours or until meat is tender. Do not cover the soup entirely, but leave the lid slightly ajar. Allow soup to chill and remove every trace of fat. When ready to serve, heat through and serve with a dollup of sour cream and thick slices of black bread with creamy butter. Serves 6.

Note: - If you like the soup a little thinner, then add 1 can (10 1/2 ounces) beef broth.

Crispettes of Pumpernickel & Cheese

6 slices Westphalian thinly sliced
    pumpernickel
3 tablespoons butter
6 tablespoons grated Parmesan cheese

Spread each slice of bread with 1/2 tablespoon butter and sprinkle with 1 tablespoon grated Parmesan cheese. Broil for about 1 minute or until cheese begins to color and bread is crisp. Cut into rectangles or triangles and serve with soup or salad.

Strawberry Banana Soup served in Melon Halves

*These are two cool, refreshing fruit soups that will transform an ordinary luncheon into a scrumptious repast. Both soups are served cold. A wonderful accompaniment is spicy gingerbread, spread with cream cheese, strawberries and pecans. And, if you really want it to look like a party, serve the soup in sawtooth cut melon halves. ***

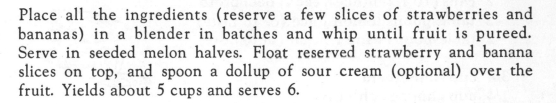

    1 **basket (1 pint) strawberries, hulled**
    2 **bananas**
1 1/2 **cups milk**
    3 **cups strawberry ice cream**
    2 **tablespoons lemon juice**
    1 **teaspoon grated lemon peel**

Place all the ingredients (reserve a few slices of strawberries and bananas) in a blender in batches and whip until fruit is pureed. Serve in seeded melon halves. Float reserved strawberry and banana slices on top, and spoon a dollup of sour cream (optional) over the fruit. Yields about 5 cups and serves 6.

Strawberry Orange Soup with Yogurt & Cinnamon

    2 **baskets (2 pints) strawberries, hulled**
    1 **cup orange juice**
1/4 **cup sugar (or to taste)**
    2 **tablespoons lemon juice**
    1 **teaspoon grated lemon peel**
    2 **cups strawberry-flavored yogurt,**
         (reserve 1/2 cup for garnish)
cinnamon for sprinkling on top

In a blender in batches, puree strawberries with orange juice and sugar, (reserve a few slices of strawberries). Pour mixture in a bowl with the remaining ingredients and stir until blended. Stir in the reserved strawberries. Serve in pretty glass soup bowls with a dollup of yogurt on top and sprinkle with a dash of cinnamon. Serves 5 or 6.

*Note: - *To prepare cantaloupe, cut melons in half in a zig-zag or saw-tooth fashion. Remove seeds. Scoop out about 1/2-inch of fruit and chop it. Add chopped melon to soup.*

Cold Russian Beet Soup with Cucumber & Sour Cream

This is a simplified version of the classic "borscht." While I realize that beets is not a "national" food, this will do well for a change. Serve it with hot piroshkis and it will be a feast. Black pumpernickel with raisins and sweet butter is really very good, too.

1 jar (16 ounces) pickled beets (whole or sliced) and do not drain.

2 cans (10 1/2 ounces, each) beef broth
2 tablespoons lemon juice (or to taste)
2 tablespoons wine vinegar (or to taste)

3/4 cup sour cream
1/4 cup chopped chives
1 medium cucumber, peeled and thinly sliced
dill weed

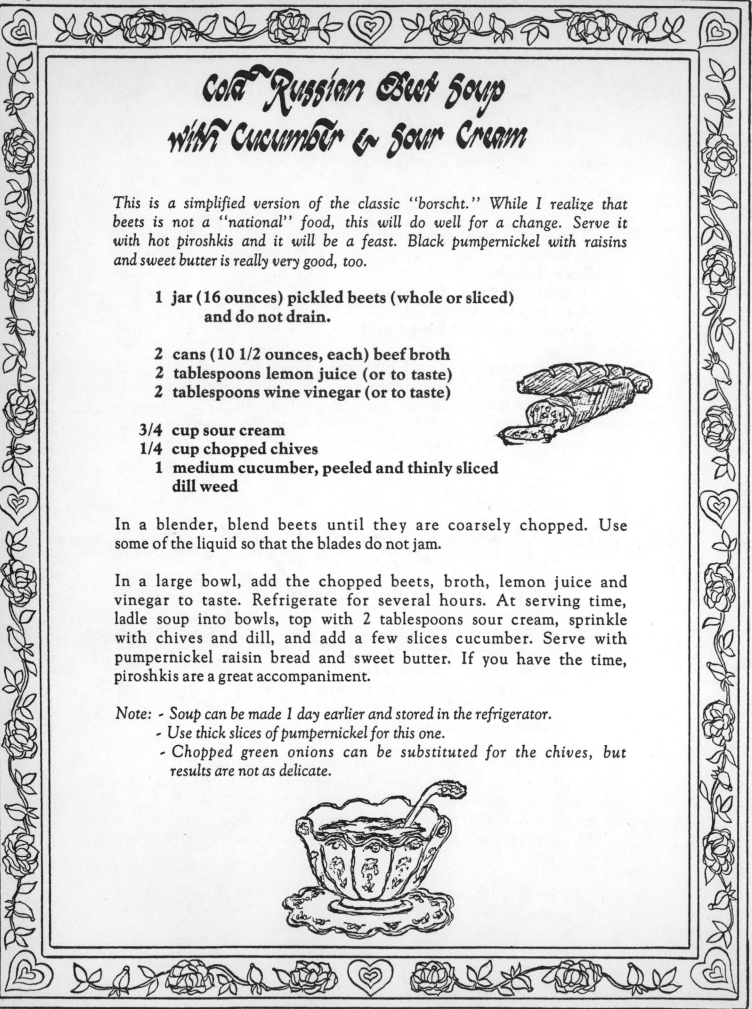

In a blender, blend beets until they are coarsely chopped. Use some of the liquid so that the blades do not jam.

In a large bowl, add the chopped beets, broth, lemon juice and vinegar to taste. Refrigerate for several hours. At serving time, ladle soup into bowls, top with 2 tablespoons sour cream, sprinkle with chives and dill, and add a few slices cucumber. Serve with pumpernickel raisin bread and sweet butter. If you have the time, piroshkis are a great accompaniment.

Note: - Soup can be made 1 day earlier and stored in the refrigerator.
- Use thick slices of pumpernickel for this one.
- Chopped green onions can be substituted for the chives, but results are not as delicate.

Dumplings

I don't know what it is about dumplings that summon such sweet, nostalgic memories. These chubby, fluffy little balls of dough, floating in a rich and fragrant soup or stew, call to mind wintry nights with the weather raging outside. And inside, the house was filled with the aroma of chicken bubbling on the stove. Somehow, it felt so good, so satisfying.

Dumplings take seconds to assemble, so they can really be enjoyed often. However, these fluffy little darlings can somehow turn out as if they were dipped in cement or so soggy and heavy they are no fun to eat at all. There are a few simple precautions to keep in mind and you will be assured of perfect results every time.

** Stir batter with a fork until blended and smooth. Do not beat.

1. Use a pan large enough to allow dumplings room to expand. Dumplings should be steamed in one layer.
2. Liquid should be at a steady simmer. Stew or soup should not boil rapidly or the dumplings will fall apart.
3. If dumplings are being dropped into broth, then cook them for about 10 minutes uncovered or until they float to the top. Then cover and simmer them for another ten minutes.
4. If dumplings are to be dropped on top of a simmering stew, then cover the pot immediately and simmer them for about 20 minutes, undisturbed.
5. Once you cover the pan, do not peak or remove the lid. If you do, you will allow the steam to escape and the dumplings will boil instead of steam.
6. Use a good pan with a tight-fitting lid.

Foolproof Jiffy Herbed Dumplings

The following is a foolproof way of making dumplings if you own a spaghetti cooker. After the dumplings are made, they can be transferred to the soup or stew and they will pick up the flavor of the rich and glorious broth.

- **2 cups biscuit mix**
- **2 teaspoons parsley**
- **1 teaspoon dried onion flakes**

- **1 egg**
- **2/3 cup milk**

Place biscuit mix, parsley and onion flakes in a bowl. Beat together egg and milk until blended. Pour egg mixture into flour mixture and stir, with a fork, until blended.

In a spaghetti cooker, add water to reach 1/4-inch above the level of the strainer. Bring water to a simmer. Place heaping tablespoons of dumpling batter onto strainer, cover pan and simmer for 20 minutes, undisturbed. Test for doneness with a cake tester. If dumplings appear too soft in center, simmer for an additional 5 minutes. Transfer dumplings to soup or stew. Yields 10 dumplings.

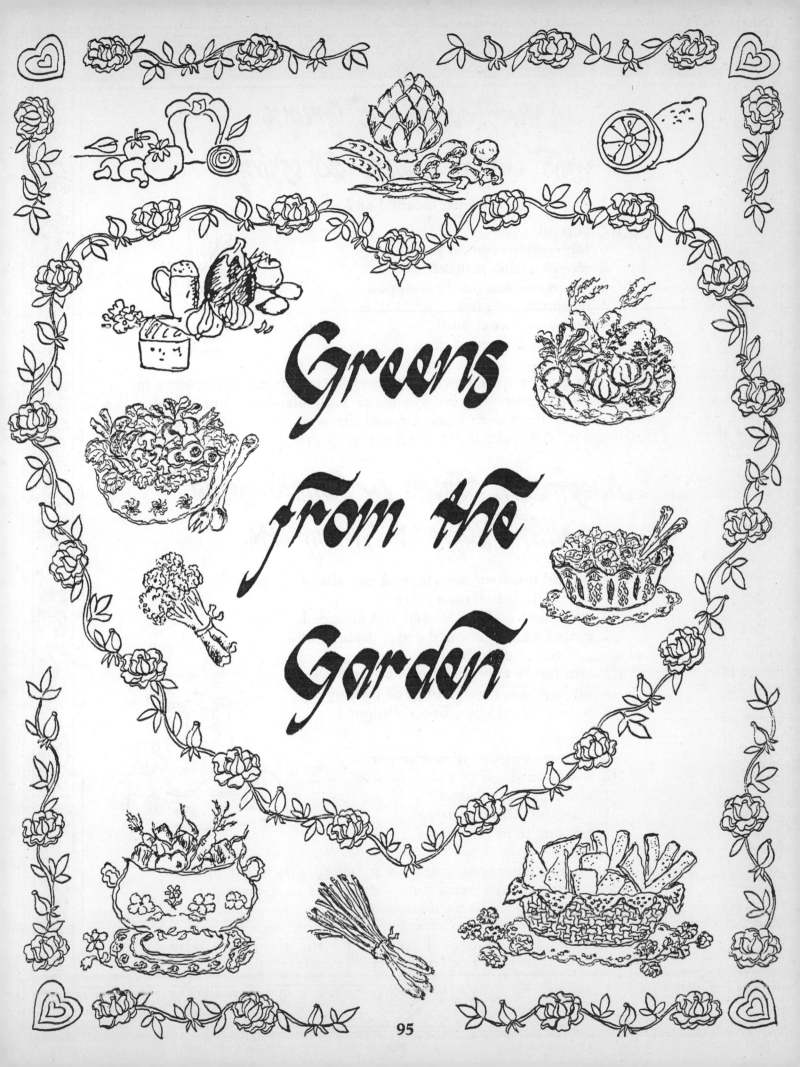

Greens from the Garden

Mushrooms a la Grique with Garlic Lemon Dressing

1 pound mushrooms, cleaned and sliced

1/2 cup oil
6 tablespoons lemon juice
2 cloves garlic, minced
2 green onions, finely chopped
1/2 teaspoon oregano
1/4 teaspoon sweet basil
salt and pepper to taste

Place mushrooms in a bowl. Combine the remaining ingredients in a jar with a tight-fitting lid and shake until blended. Pour dressing to taste over the mushrooms. Unused dressing can be stored in the refrigerator. Yields about 3/4 cup dressing. Serves 4 to 5.

Mushroom, Bacon & Tomato Salad with Mustard Vinaigrette

1 pound mushrooms, cleaned and sliced. Toss
    with 3 T. lemon juice
4 tomatoes, peeled, seeded and chopped
1/2 pound bacon, cooked crisp, drained and
    finely crumbled
1/2 cup finely chopped green onions
2 tablespoons finely chopped parsley
2 hard cooked eggs, finely chopped

1/2 cup oil
4 tablespoons red wine vinegar
1/2 teaspoon sugar
1 clove garlic, minced
1 teaspoon Dijon mustard
salt and pepper to taste

In a bowl toss together the first 6 ingredients until mixture is blended. Combine the remaining ingredients in a glass jar with a tight-fitting lid and shake until blended.

Pour dressing to taste over the vegetables and refrigerate salad for several hours. Serve on a bed of lettuce. Serves 6.

Pasta Primavera in a Creamy Lemon Garlic Dressing

1 pound spiral pasta, cooked firm but tender
   and drained

1 package (1 pound) frozen broccoli, cauliflower
   and carrots mixed vegetables, cooked according to
   the directions on the package and drained. (If your
   market does not carry these mixed vegetables, then
   use 1/2 of a 10-ounce package of each vegetable.)

3 green onions, finely chopped
2 teaspoons lemon juice
   salt and pepper to taste

Creamy Lemon Garlic Dressing

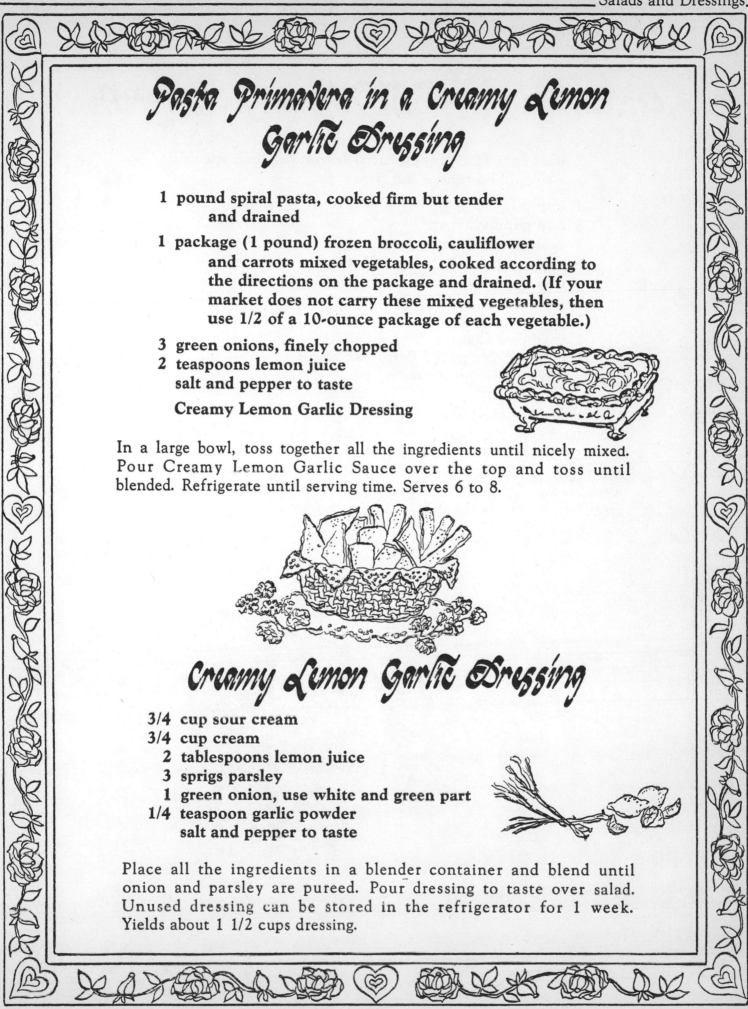

In a large bowl, toss together all the ingredients until nicely mixed.
Pour Creamy Lemon Garlic Sauce over the top and toss until
blended. Refrigerate until serving time. Serves 6 to 8.

Creamy Lemon Garlic Dressing

3/4 cup sour cream
3/4 cup cream
  2 tablespoons lemon juice
  3 sprigs parsley
  1 green onion, use white and green part
1/4 teaspoon garlic powder
    salt and pepper to taste

Place all the ingredients in a blender container and blend until
onion and parsley are pureed. Pour dressing to taste over salad.
Unused dressing can be stored in the refrigerator for 1 week.
Yields about 1 1/2 cups dressing.

Broccoli in an Herbed Dijonnaise Vinaigrette

2 packages (10 ounces, each) frozen broccoli spears,
    cooked tender but firm

1 cup oil
1/3 cup wine vinegar
1 tablespoon Dijon mustard
1 clove garlic, cut into 4 pieces
1 tablespoon minced parsley
2 tablespoons chopped chives
1/2 teaspoon oregano
1 teaspoon sugar
2 tablespoons grated Parmesan cheese
salt and pepper to taste

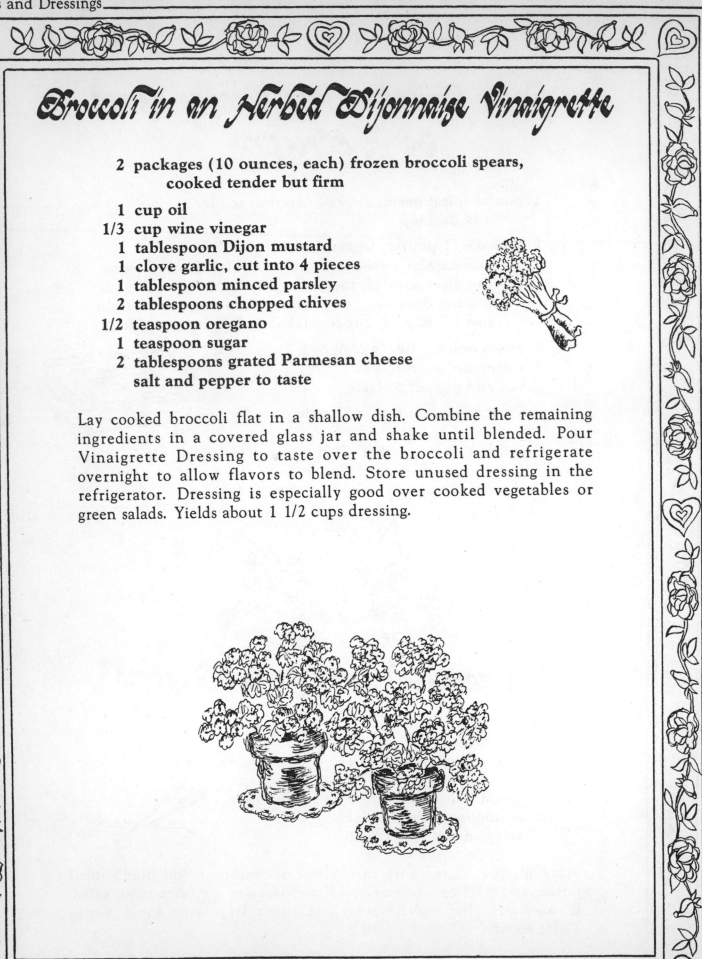

Lay cooked broccoli flat in a shallow dish. Combine the remaining ingredients in a covered glass jar and shake until blended. Pour Vinaigrette Dressing to taste over the broccoli and refrigerate overnight to allow flavors to blend. Store unused dressing in the refrigerator. Dressing is especially good over cooked vegetables or green salads. Yields about 1 1/2 cups dressing.

Eggplant & Mozzarella Salad with Peppers & Tomatoes

1 can (1 pound) stewed tomatoes, finely chopped
1 eggplant, peeled and sliced
1 green pepper, cut into strips
1 red pepper, cut into strips
2 tablespoons oil

1 package (8 ounces) Mozzarella cheese, grated
6 green onions, finely chopped

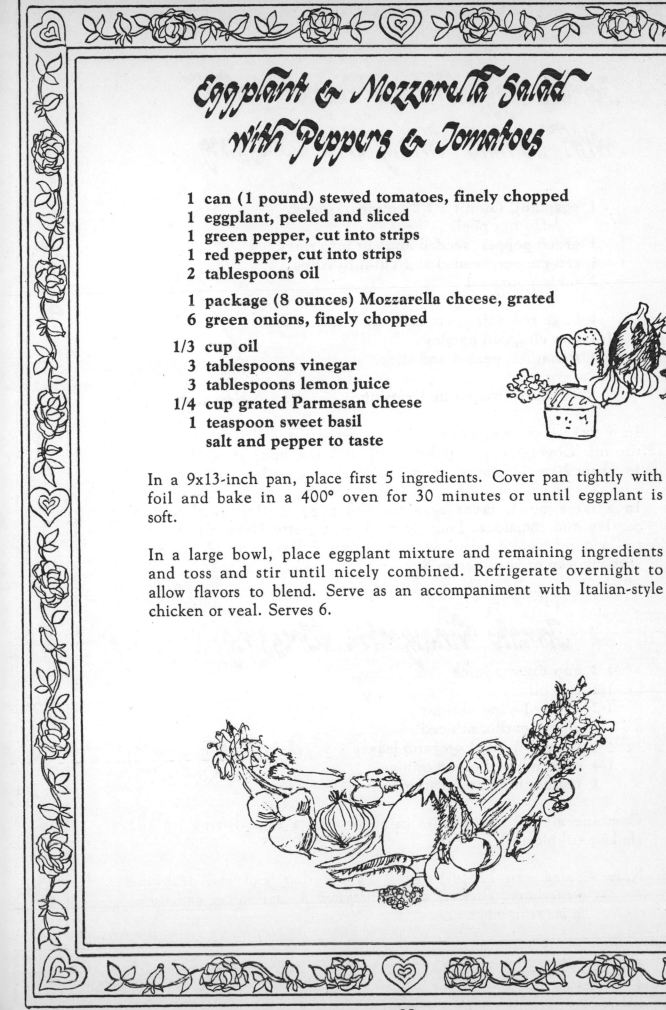

1/3 cup oil
3 tablespoons vinegar
3 tablespoons lemon juice
1/4 cup grated Parmesan cheese
1 teaspoon sweet basil
 salt and pepper to taste

In a 9x13-inch pan, place first 5 ingredients. Cover pan tightly with foil and bake in a 400° oven for 30 minutes or until eggplant is soft.

In a large bowl, place eggplant mixture and remaining ingredients and toss and stir until nicely combined. Refrigerate overnight to allow flavors to blend. Serve as an accompaniment with Italian-style chicken or veal. Serves 6.

Tomato Eggplant & Pepper Salad with Tomato Vinaigrette Dressing

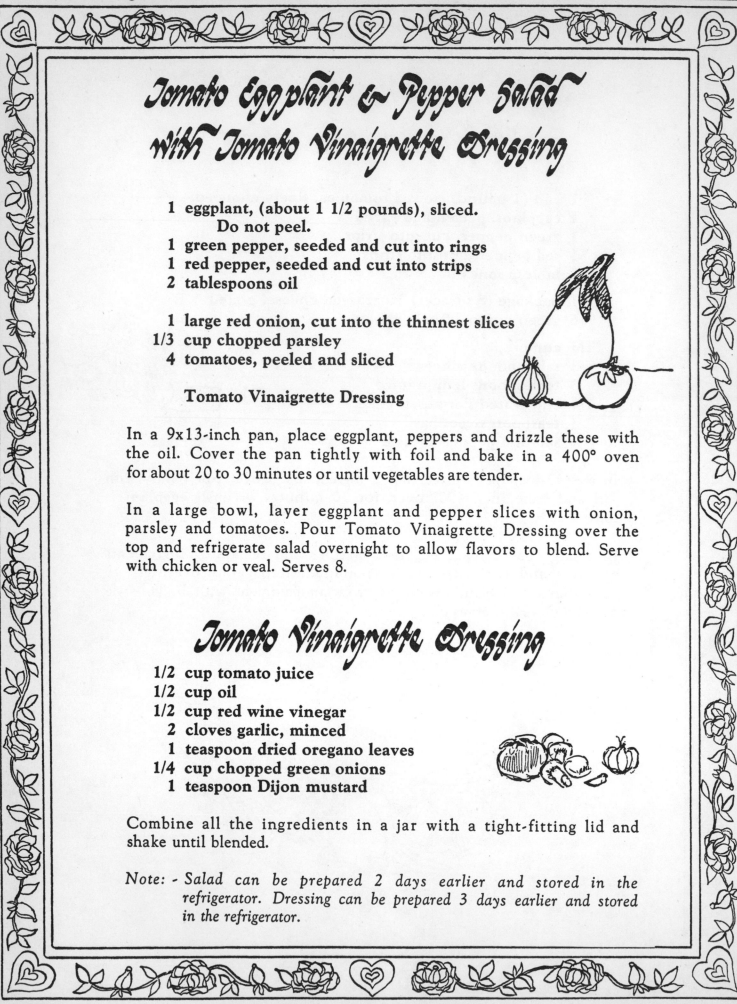

1 eggplant, (about 1 1/2 pounds), sliced.
    Do not peel.
1 green pepper, seeded and cut into rings
1 red pepper, seeded and cut into strips
2 tablespoons oil

1 large red onion, cut into the thinnest slices
1/3 cup chopped parsley
4 tomatoes, peeled and sliced

Tomato Vinaigrette Dressing

In a 9x13-inch pan, place eggplant, peppers and drizzle these with the oil. Cover the pan tightly with foil and bake in a 400° oven for about 20 to 30 minutes or until vegetables are tender.

In a large bowl, layer eggplant and pepper slices with onion, parsley and tomatoes. Pour Tomato Vinaigrette Dressing over the top and refrigerate salad overnight to allow flavors to blend. Serve with chicken or veal. Serves 8.

Tomato Vinaigrette Dressing

1/2 cup tomato juice
1/2 cup oil
1/2 cup red wine vinegar
2 cloves garlic, minced
1 teaspoon dried oregano leaves
1/4 cup chopped green onions
1 teaspoon Dijon mustard

Combine all the ingredients in a jar with a tight-fitting lid and shake until blended.

Note: - Salad can be prepared 2 days earlier and stored in the refrigerator. Dressing can be prepared 3 days earlier and stored in the refrigerator.

Chinese Chicken Salad with Pea Pods & Ginger Honey Dressing

4 cups shredded cooked chicken
3/4 cup chopped green onion
1/2 cup sliced water chestnuts

1 package (8 ounces) frozen Chinese pea pods
1 small head lettuce, shredded
3 tablespoons lightly toasted sesame seeds

In a bowl, toss together all the ingredients. Pour Ginger Honey Dressing to taste, over the salad and toss until blended. Serve with Honey Sesame Points as a lovely accompaniment. Serves 4.

Ginger Honey Dressing:

1/2 cup salad oil
1/2 cup rice vinegar
2 tablespoons sesame oil
1/2 teaspoon dry mustard
4 tablespoons honey
1/4 teaspoon ground ginger
2 teaspoons soy sauce

Combine all the ingredients in a jar with a tight-fitting lid and shake until blended. Yields about 1 1/2 cups sauce. Unused dressing can be stored in the refrigerator.

Honey Sesame Points

4 slices egg bread, crusts removed. Roll flat with
   a rolling pin and cut diagonally into 2 triangles.
2 tablespoons butter, melted
2 tablespoons honey
4 teaspoons sesame seeds

Place rolled bread slices on a buttered cookie sheet. Stir together butter, honey and sesame seeds until blended. Spread mixture on each bread slice. Bake in a 350° oven until bread is crisped and sesame seeds are lightly toasted. Serves 4. (Make extras, for these disappear quickly.)

Red Cabbage Salad with Apples, Raisins & Honey Dressing

This delicious salad is excellent when served either hot or cold. It is a lovely accompaniment to roast pork or braised beef.

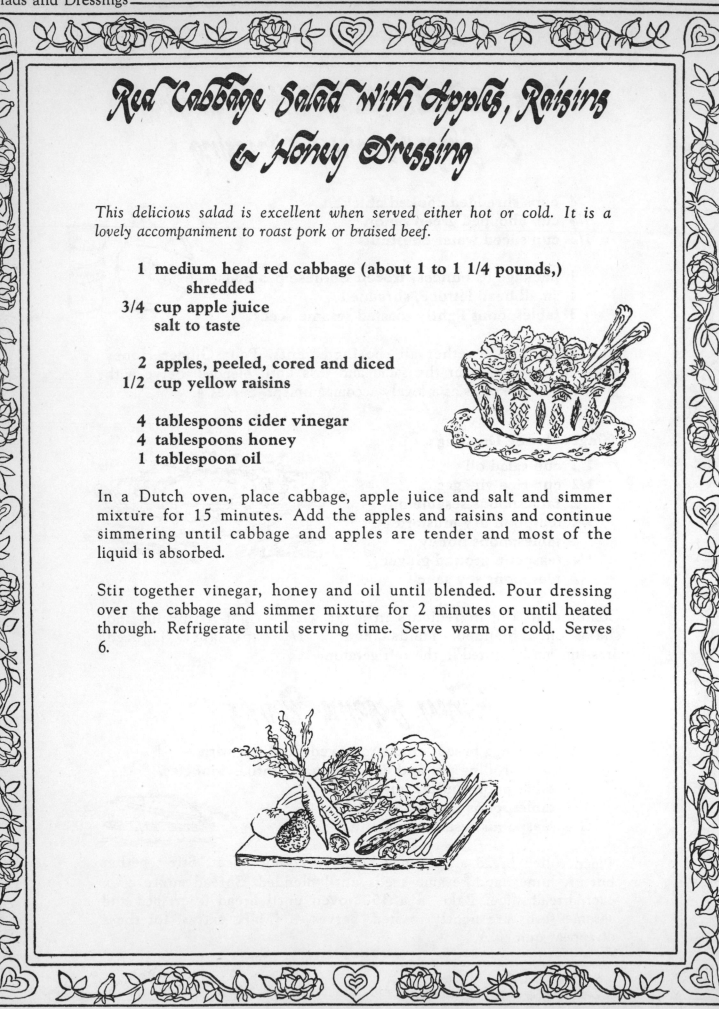

- **1 medium head red cabbage (about 1 to 1 1/4 pounds,) shredded**
- **3/4 cup apple juice**
  salt to taste

- **2 apples, peeled, cored and diced**
- **1/2 cup yellow raisins**

- **4 tablespoons cider vinegar**
- **4 tablespoons honey**
- **1 tablespoon oil**

In a Dutch oven, place cabbage, apple juice and salt and simmer mixture for 15 minutes. Add the apples and raisins and continue simmering until cabbage and apples are tender and most of the liquid is absorbed.

Stir together vinegar, honey and oil until blended. Pour dressing over the cabbage and simmer mixture for 2 minutes or until heated through. Refrigerate until serving time. Serve warm or cold. Serves 6.

Green Peas Salad with Mushrooms, Onions & Pimientos with Lemon Mustard Vinaigrette

2 packages (10 ounces, each) frozen green peas, cooked according to the directions on the package or steamed in a little water, for 5 minutes and drained.

1/2 cup chopped green onions
1 jar (2 ounces) chopped pimientos
1/4 pound mushrooms, thinly sliced

Lemon Mustard Vinaigrette:
1/3 cup oil
2 tablespoons vinegar
3 tablespoons lemon juice
1/2 teaspoon Dijon mustard
1/4 teaspoon sugar
1 tablespoon chopped parsley
1/4 teaspoon basil flakes
1/4 teaspoon thyme flakes
1/4 teaspoon garlic powder
salt and pepper to taste

In a large bowl, toss together peas, onion, pimientos and mushrooms.

Combine the Vinaigrette ingredients in a jar with a tight-fitting lid and shake until blended. Pour dressing over the vegetables and toss until blended. Refrigerate for several hours.

Serve as a cold vegetable accompaniment. Excellent with quiches, giant piroshkis or broiled chicken or fish. Serves 6.

Light Italian Dressing with Herbs & Cheese

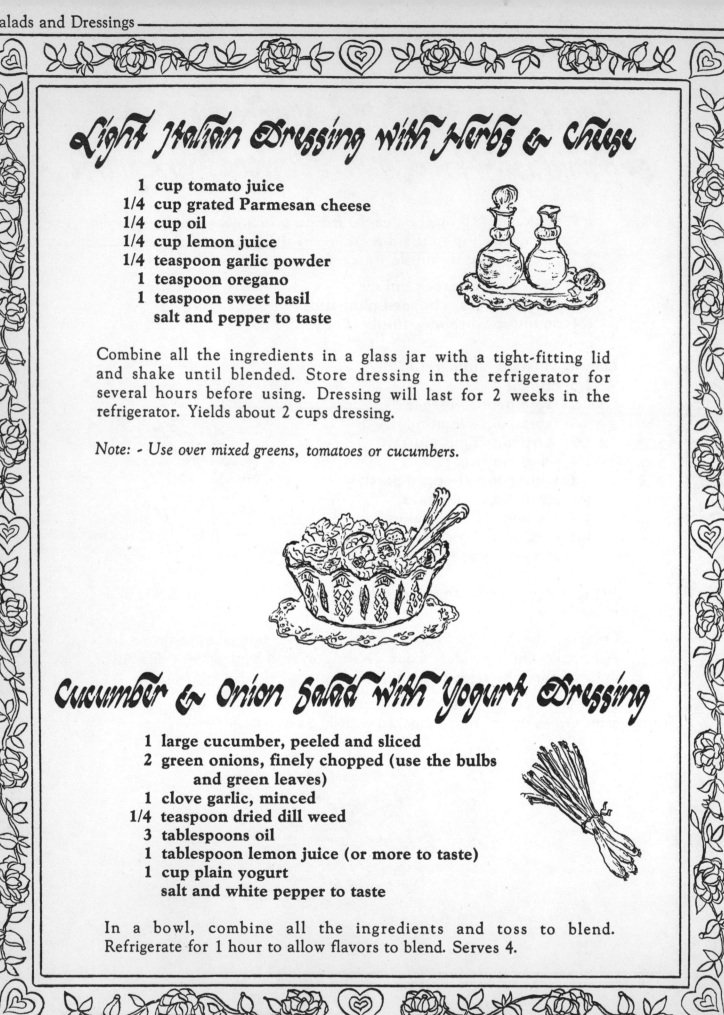

1 cup tomato juice
1/4 cup grated Parmesan cheese
1/4 cup oil
1/4 cup lemon juice
1/4 teaspoon garlic powder
1 teaspoon oregano
1 teaspoon sweet basil
salt and pepper to taste

Combine all the ingredients in a glass jar with a tight-fitting lid and shake until blended. Store dressing in the refrigerator for several hours before using. Dressing will last for 2 weeks in the refrigerator. Yields about 2 cups dressing.

Note: - Use over mixed greens, tomatoes or cucumbers.

Cucumber & Onion Salad with Yogurt Dressing

1 large cucumber, peeled and sliced
2 green onions, finely chopped (use the bulbs
    and green leaves)
1 clove garlic, minced
1/4 teaspoon dried dill weed
3 tablespoons oil
1 tablespoon lemon juice (or more to taste)
1 cup plain yogurt
salt and white pepper to taste

In a bowl, combine all the ingredients and toss to blend. Refrigerate for 1 hour to allow flavors to blend. Serves 4.

Chicken Salad with Pineapple, Raisins & Almonds

6 cups cooked, boned and cubed chicken
1 can (1 pound 4 ounces) crushed pineapple,
  drained. Reserve juice for another use.
3/4 cup yellow raisins, plumped in orange juice
1 cup toasted slivered almonds
2 tablespoons chopped parsley

1 cup mayonnaise
1 cup sour cream
3 tablespoons lemon juice
1 tablespoon honey

In a large bowl, toss together chicken, pineapple, raisins, almonds and parsley until mixture is even. In a jar with a tight-fitting lid, stir together mayonnaise, sour cream, lemon juice and honey until blended.

Toss chicken salad with dressing to taste. Store unused dressing in the refrigerator. Serve on a bed of lettuce. Serves 10.

Note: - A nice addition would be to include 1 teaspoon curry powder to the dressing.

Yogurt Cucumber Salad with Green Onions, Lemon & Dill

2 large cucumbers, peeled. Run a fork from top
  to bottom to score and thinly slice.
1/2 cup yogurt
1/2 cup sour cream
1/3 cup chopped green onions
3 tablespoons lemon juice
1/2 teaspoon dill weed

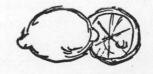

Place the cucumbers in a bowl. Stir together the remaining ingredients until blended. Toss cucumbers with dressing to taste. Store unused dressing in the refrigerator. Serves 6.

Note: - This can be made earlier in the day and stored in the refrigerator.

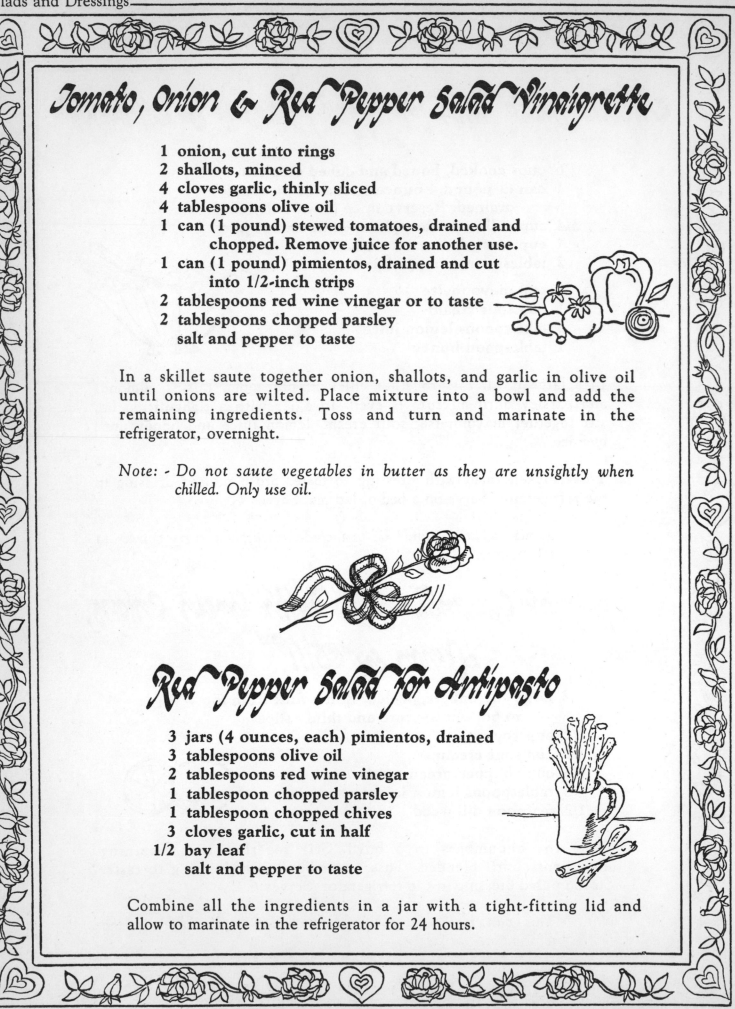

Tomato, Onion & Red Pepper Salad Vinaigrette

1   onion, cut into rings
2   shallots, minced
4   cloves garlic, thinly sliced
4   tablespoons olive oil
1   can (1 pound) stewed tomatoes, drained and
      chopped. Remove juice for another use.
1   can (1 pound) pimientos, drained and cut
      into 1/2-inch strips
2   tablespoons red wine vinegar or to taste
2   tablespoons chopped parsley
    salt and pepper to taste

In a skillet saute together onion, shallots, and garlic in olive oil until onions are wilted. Place mixture into a bowl and add the remaining ingredients. Toss and turn and marinate in the refrigerator, overnight.

Note: - Do not saute vegetables in butter as they are unsightly when chilled. Only use oil.

Red Pepper Salad for Antipasto

3   jars (4 ounces, each) pimientos, drained
3   tablespoons olive oil
2   tablespoons red wine vinegar
1   tablespoon chopped parsley
1   tablespoon chopped chives
3   cloves garlic, cut in half
1/2 bay leaf
    salt and pepper to taste

Combine all the ingredients in a jar with a tight-fitting lid and allow to marinate in the refrigerator for 24 hours.

Antipasto Salad with Artichokes, Salami & Cheese

1   package (10 ounces) frozen artichoke hearts,
     cooked and drained
1/2 pound mushrooms, sliced
1/4 pound Italian salami, sliced and cut
     into pieces
1/4 pound Provolone cheese, sliced and cut
     into pieces
1/4 cup black olives, pitted and sliced
1   tomato, thinly sliced
1/2 cup thinly sliced red onions (about 1/2
     large red onion)
1   jar, (2 ounces) pimiento strips
1/4 cup chick peas, drained
1/4 cup kidney beans, drained

In a large bowl, place all the ingredients and toss to blend.
Amounts are suggestions and feel free to add sweet bell peppers
vinaigrette or proscuitto ham.

Pour Lemon Vinaigrette Dressing to taste and toss to blend. Allow
to marinate in the refrigerator for 2 to 3 hours. Serve on a thick
bed of shredded lettuce. Serves 6 to 8.

Lemon Vinaigrette Dressing

1   cup oil
1/3 cup lemon juice
2   tablespoons cider vinegar
1/4 teaspoon oregano
1/4 teaspoon basil
1   clove garlic, minced
1/4 cup minced green onions
1   tablespoon minced parsley
1/4 teaspoon sugar
     salt and lots of freshly ground pepper to taste

Combine all the ingredients in a jar with a tight-fitting lid and
shake to blend. Yields about 1 1/2 cups sauce. Store unused
dressing in the refrigerator.

Marinated Shrimp Vinaigrette for Antipasto

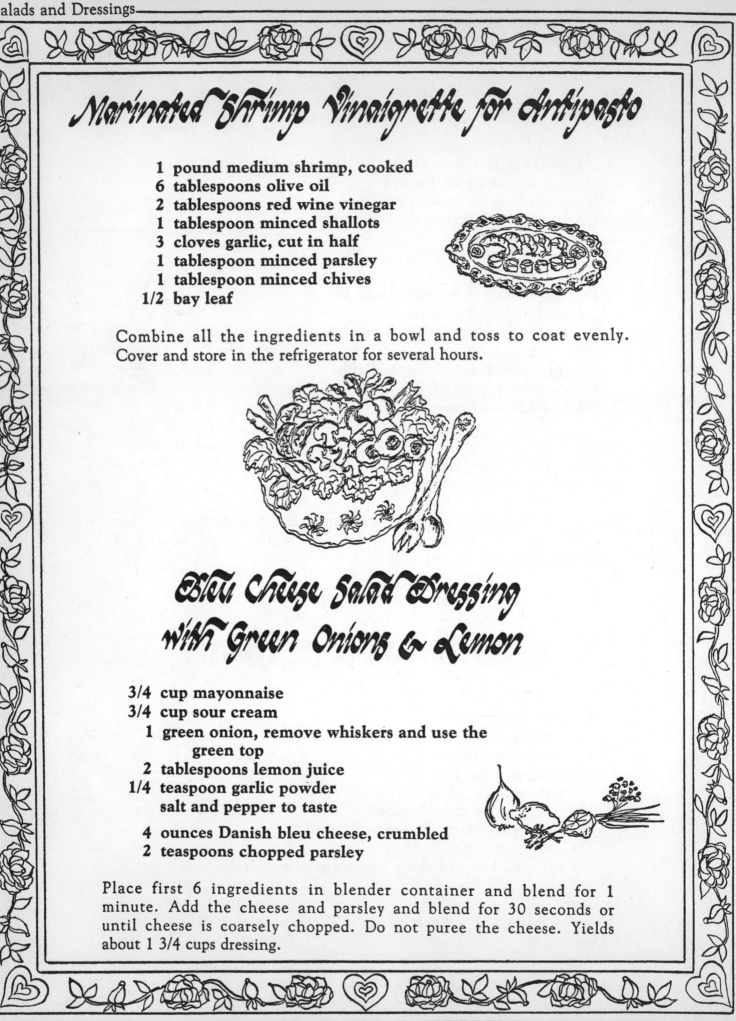

  1 pound medium shrimp, cooked
  6 tablespoons olive oil
  2 tablespoons red wine vinegar
  1 tablespoon minced shallots
  3 cloves garlic, cut in half
  1 tablespoon minced parsley
  1 tablespoon minced chives
1/2 bay leaf

Combine all the ingredients in a bowl and toss to coat evenly. Cover and store in the refrigerator for several hours.

Bleu Cheese Salad Dressing with Green Onions & Lemon

3/4 cup mayonnaise
3/4 cup sour cream
  1 green onion, remove whiskers and use the green top
  2 tablespoons lemon juice
1/4 teaspoon garlic powder
     salt and pepper to taste

  4 ounces Danish bleu cheese, crumbled
  2 teaspoons chopped parsley

Place first 6 ingredients in blender container and blend for 1 minute. Add the cheese and parsley and blend for 30 seconds or until cheese is coarsely chopped. Do not puree the cheese. Yields about 1 3/4 cups dressing.

Royal Louis Dressing for Fish & Shellfish

- 1 cup mayonnaise
- 1/2 cup sour cream
- 1/2 cup chili sauce
- 2 tablespoons grated onion
- 2 tablespoons chopped chives
- 1 tablespoon lemon juice
- 1 teaspoon chopped parsley

- 1/2 cup cream, whipped

Combine all the ingredients and stir until blended. Chill, in a glass jar, until serving time. Place dressing in a bowl and surround with cooked shrimp, lobster or crabmeat. Yields about 2 1/2 cups dresssing.

Lemon Yogurt Dressing with Garlic & Onion

- 1 cup yogurt
- 2 tablespoons sugar
- 2 tablespoons lemon juice (or more to taste)
- 1 tablespoon chopped parsley
- 1 green onion, minced (Remove the whiskers and mince the whole onion.)
- 1/8 teaspoon garlic powder
- 2 tablespoons non-fat milk
  salt and pepper to taste

Well, you guessed it. This little dressing is designed for those of you who are counting. . . You may like to add some dill weed, celery seed or a pinch of tarragon. Merely combine all the ingredients and stir until blended. Refrigerate until serving time. Serve with salad greens, cucumbers or tomatoes. Yields 1 1/2 cups dressing.

Creamy Salad Dressing with Green Onions, Lemon & Cheese

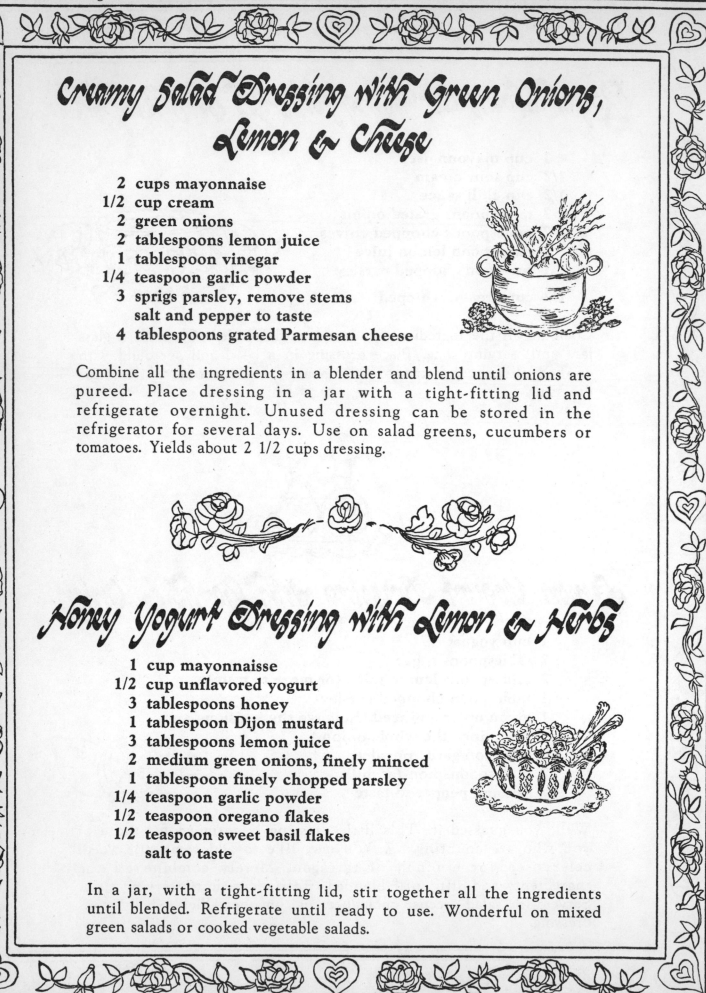

        2   cups mayonnaise
      1/2   cup cream
        2   green onions
        2   tablespoons lemon juice
        1   tablespoon vinegar
      1/4   teaspoon garlic powder
        3   sprigs parsley, remove stems
            salt and pepper to taste
        4   tablespoons grated Parmesan cheese

Combine all the ingredients in a blender and blend until onions are pureed. Place dressing in a jar with a tight-fitting lid and refrigerate overnight. Unused dressing can be stored in the refrigerator for several days. Use on salad greens, cucumbers or tomatoes. Yields about 2 1/2 cups dressing.

Honey Yogurt Dressing with Lemon & Herbs

        1   cup mayonnaisse
      1/2   cup unflavored yogurt
        3   tablespoons honey
        1   tablespoon Dijon mustard
        3   tablespoons lemon juice
        2   medium green onions, finely minced
        1   tablespoon finely chopped parsley
      1/4   teaspoon garlic powder
      1/2   teaspoon oregano flakes
      1/2   teaspoon sweet basil flakes
            salt to taste

In a jar, with a tight-fitting lid, stir together all the ingredients until blended. Refrigerate until ready to use. Wonderful on mixed green salads or cooked vegetable salads.

Good Old-Fashioned Thousand Island Dressing

- 1 cup mayonnaise
- 1/2 cup sour cream
- 1/4 cup ketchup
- 2 tablespoons chopped parsley
- 2 tablespoons lemon juice
- 1/4 small onion, (about 2 tablespoons chopped onion)

- 3 tablespoons sweet pickled relish
- 1 hard cooked egg, finely chopped
- 1 tablespoon slivered pimientos (optional)
- salt and pepper to taste

Place first 6 ingredients in blender container and blend for 1 minute. Stir in the remaining ingredients until blended. Store dressing in a glass jar with a tight-fitting lid. Yields about 2 cups dressing.

French Dressing with Lemon & Herbs

- 1/2 cup oil (can use part olive oil)
- 2 tablespoons lemon juice
- 2 tablespoons vinegar
- 1/2 teaspoon Dijon mustard
- 1 tablespoon minced parsley
- 1 tablespoon minced chives
- 1/2 teaspoon thyme leaves
- salt and pepper to taste

Combine all the ingredients in a jar with a tight-fitting lid and shake to blend. Yields about 3/4 cup dressing.

Mayonnaise

Once you've made homemade mayonnaise, you'll wonder how you ever did without it. Making mayonnaise is so easy and the results so divine, that I do hope you will have a chance to try some. The delicacy and freshness of homemade mayonnaise will elevate a hard-cooked egg to gastronomical heights. Tossing it with chicken, seafood, potato salad or just brushed on sandwiches is a delight. If you follow these few simple instructions, you will prepare perfect mayonnaise every time.

Easiest & Best Blender Mayonnaise

3 egg yolks
2 tablespoons lemon juice
1 tablespoon water
1/4 teaspoon salt (or to taste)
1/4 teaspoon Dijon mustard

1 cup oil, (use a good quality oil)
1 tablespoon water
1 tablespoon lemon juice

Place yolks in blender container and beat for 1 minute. Add the lemon juice, water, salt and mustard and beat for another minute. Now, slowly, drop by drop, drizzle in the salad oil, while the blender continues running at high speed. Do not stop until at least 1/2 cup of oil has been incorporated. Mixture will be very thick.

Now continue beating, adding a little water and lemon juice and oil until all the oil has been incorporated. When the mayonnaise is very thick, thin it out with a little water or lemon juice; then continue to drizzle in the oil. Now, that is **all** there is to it. You could add a little more oil than the 1 cup I specified, but the more oil you add, the greater the chance to curdle the emulsion. Yields about 1 1/2 cups mayonnaise.

IMPORTANT TIPS
1. Be certain to beat yolks until they begin to thicken.
2. Add oil very slowly, drop by drop, until you have a thick emulsion. If you add oil too rapidly, emulsion will break down.
3. As mayonnaise thickens, add a little water or lemon juice to thin it a little. Do this by the teaspoonful.

From the Beautiful Sea

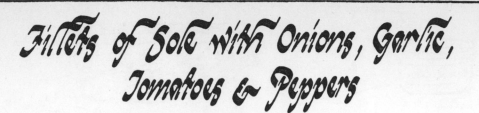

Fillets of Sole with Onions, Garlic, Tomatoes & Peppers

2 pounds fillets of sole, sprinkled with salt
  and pepper to taste

1 onion, finely chopped
2 cloves garlic, minced
1 small red pepper, cut into strips
1 green pepper, cut into strips
6 tablespoons butter
1 can (16 ounces) stewed tomatoes, finely chopped
2 tablespoons chopped parsley

Place fish in a 12x16-inch baking pan. Saute onions, garlic and peppers in butter until vegetables are tender. Add tomatoes and parsley and pour sauce over the fillets. Bake in a 350° oven for 20 minutes.

Cioppino Romano ~ Italian Fisherman's Stew

While this recipe seems lengthy, it is actually the essence of simplicity to prepare. All of the soup base ingredients are merely placed in the pan and simmered.

1/4 cup oil (you can use part olive oil)
2 onions, chopped
4 cloves garlic, finely minced
1 cup green onions, chopped
1 can (16 ounces) stewed tomatoes, chopped.
    Do not drain.
1 can (8 ounces) tomato sauce
1 cup dry red wine
1 can (7 ounces) minced clams. Do not drain.
2 cups clam juice
1/4 cup minced parsley
1 teaspoon oregano
1/4 teaspoon each, thyme and basil
1 teaspoon sugar
1/2 teaspoon red pepper flakes
1/4 teaspoon tumeric
    salt and pepper to taste

In a Dutch oven, combine all the ingredients and simmer mixture for 30 minutes, uncovered. Bring soup to a rolling boil and add:

2 pounds of assorted fish or shellfish, including cod, snapper, halibut, flounder, sole or haddock. Fish should be filleted and cut into 1 or 2-inch slices. Scallops, clams, crab and lobster add a wonderful dimension to this dish. There are no rules.

Keep soup at a rolling boil for about 10 minutes or until the fish become opaque. Do not overcook. Serve in deep soup bowls with some Crusty Italian bread. Serves 6.

Note: - If you use shrimp, make certain that the black veins are removed. Crab and lobster should be carefully scrubbed and cut into pieces. All clams that do not open should be discarded.

- Soup base can be prepared earlier in the day and refrigerated. At serving time, bring soup to a rolling boil and then add the fish before serving.

Fillets of Sole with Tomatoes & Onions

1 onion
6 shallots
4 cloves garlic
2 tablespoons butter

1 can (1 pound) stewed tomatoes, chopped. Do
    not drain.
1 tablespoon chopped parsley
1 teaspoon basil
2 tablespoons lemon juice

1 1/2 pounds fillets of sole
    salt and pepper to taste

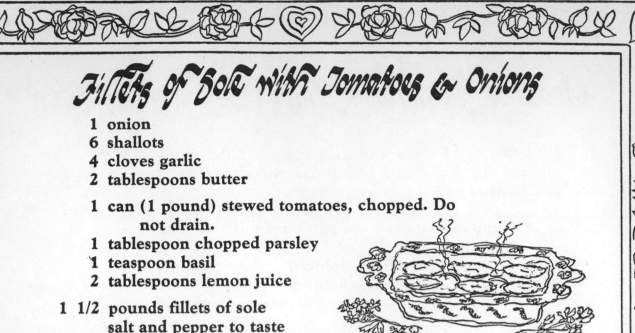

In a large skillet, saute onion, shallots and garlic in butter until
onions are soft. Add tomatoes, parsley, basil and lemon juice and
cook for 5 minutes, stirring occasionally.

Lay fillets, in one layer, in a 12x16-inch baking pan and sprinkle
with seasonings to taste. Spoon tomato mixture over the fish and
bake in a 350° oven for about 20 minutes or until fish flakes
easily with a fork. It is lovely served this way, but for a special
luncheon, a spoonful of Swiss Cream Sauce, spooned on top, adds
depth to the dish. Serves 6 for lunch.

Swiss Cheese Cream Sauce

1/2 cup cream
1/2 cup sour cream

1 cup grated Swiss cheese
1 tablespoon chopped parsley
2 tablespoons chopped chives
2 tablespoons lemon juice
1/8 teaspoon garlic powder
2 tablespoons grated Parmesan cheese
    salt and pepper to taste

In a saucepan, heat together cream and sour cream and stir until
blended. Add the remaining ingredients and continue, cooking and
stirring, over low heat, until cheese is melted.. Yields 1 1/2 cups
sauce.

*Note: - Sauce ingredients can be stirred together in the saucepan, earlier
in the day, and heated at serving time. Do not cook sauce until
serving time.*

Baked Mackerel in Tomato, Onion & Wine Sauce

When we were children, this was one of our favorites. I don't know how old I was when I stopped calling this fish "mirackel." And I must confess that when I serve this dish for dinner, all the kids join in unison (they are so tired of hearing this). "Please Be Careful with the Bones." As this fish is not fileted, I think that is very sage advice, don't you? In any case, please do be careful with the bones.

2 pounds mackerel, about. Ask the man at your
      fish market to remove the skin and to
      cut the fish into 1-inch slices,
      except for the tail section, which should be
      about 4-inches long. Place fish in a
      9x13-inch baking pan and drizzle it with 2
      tablespoons oil.

Tomato, Onion & Wine Sauce

1 onion, finely chopped
2 cloves garlic, finely minced
3 tomatoes, fresh or canned, peeled, seeded and chopped
1 tablespoon tomato paste
2 tablespoons lemon juice
1/4 cup dry white wine
1 tablespoon chopped parsley
1/2 teaspoon oregano
    pinch of thyme
    salt and pepper to taste

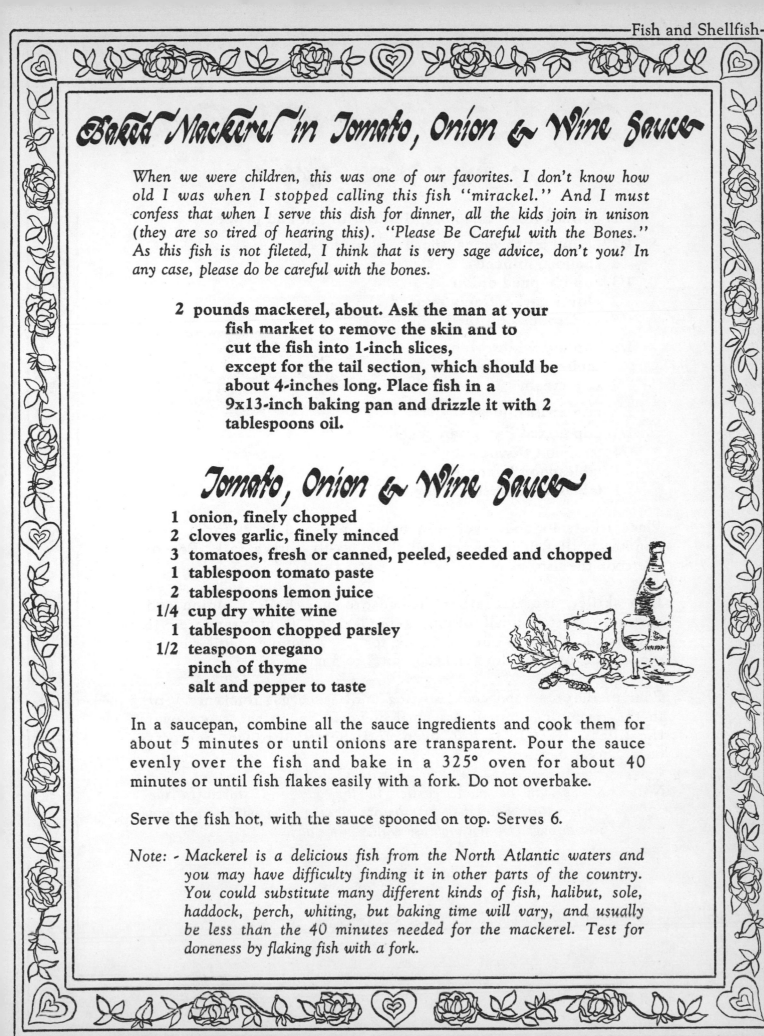

In a saucepan, combine all the sauce ingredients and cook them for about 5 minutes or until onions are transparent. Pour the sauce evenly over the fish and bake in a 325° oven for about 40 minutes or until fish flakes easily with a fork. Do not overbake.

Serve the fish hot, with the sauce spooned on top. Serves 6.

Note: - Mackerel is a delicious fish from the North Atlantic waters and you may have difficulty finding it in other parts of the country. You could substitute many different kinds of fish, halibut, sole, haddock, perch, whiting, but baking time will vary, and usually be less than the 40 minutes needed for the mackerel. Test for doneness by flaking fish with a fork.

Fillets of Sole with Creamed Mushrooms in Swiss Wine Sauce

2 pounds fillets of sole, sprinkle with salt and pepper

1/2 pound mushrooms, sliced
3 shallots, minced
1/3 cup chopped onion
2 cloves garlic, finely minced
3 tablespoons butter

1/3 cup dry white wine
3 tablespoons flour
1 cup cream

1/2 cup Swiss cheese
1/4 cup grated Parmesan cheese
1/4 teaspoon thyme
1 tablespoon lemon juice
1 tablespoon parsley, chopped

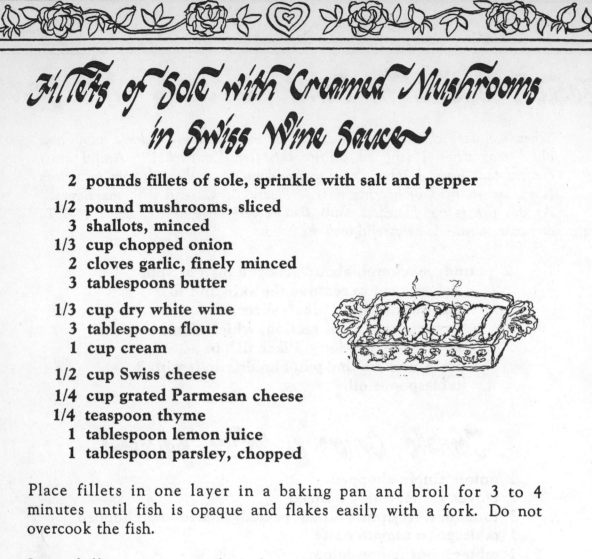

Place fillets in one layer in a baking pan and broil for 3 to 4 minutes until fish is opaque and flakes easily with a fork. Do not overcook the fish.

In a skillet, saute together the mushrooms, shallots, onion and garlic in butter until onion is tender and liquid rendered is evaporated. Add the wine and cook for a few minutes until wine is evaporated. Add the flour and cook for 2 to 3 minutes.

Pour in the cream and cook, stirring until sauce has thickened. Stir in the remaining ingredients until blended. Spoon the sauce over the fillets. Heat in a 350° oven until heated through. Serve at once. Serves 6.

Note: - Sauce can be made earlier in the day and stored in the refrigerator. Broil fish just before serving, top with sauce and heat through. Do not broil fish earlier in the day.

Baked Butterfish with Tomato Lemon Vinaigrette

2 pounds fillets of butterfish (or sole or red snapper),
sprinkled salt, pepper and lemon juice to taste.

2 tablespoons melted butter

1 can (1 pound) stewed tomatoes, finely chopped
3 green onions, finely chopped
2 tablespoons parsley, finely chopped
1/4 cup oil
2 tablespoons red wine vinegar
2 tablespoons lemon juice
salt and pepper to taste

Place fish in one layer in a 12x16-inch baking pan and drizzle tops with the melted butter. Bake fish in a 350° oven for about 10 minutes or until it flakes easily with a fork.

Meanwhile combine the remaining ingredients in a saucepan and heat it for about 5 minutes. Pour sauce evenly over the fish and serve hot. Serve with a simple pilaf and buttered green vegetable. Serves 6 to 8.

Note: - This is a sort of hot fish salad and a rather unusual way to serve fish. If you are counting calories, substitute 1/4 cup clam juice for the oil.
   - Sauce can be made earlier in the day and stored in the refrigerator. Heat before serving.

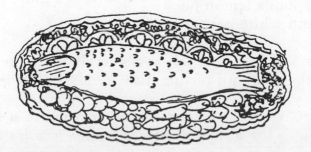

Broiled Salmon Steaks with Dilled Cream Mayonnaise

This is a lovely dish to consider on an evening when you are runnng late. The Dilled Cream Mayonnaise can be prepared 1 day earlier and the fish can be broiled just before serving.

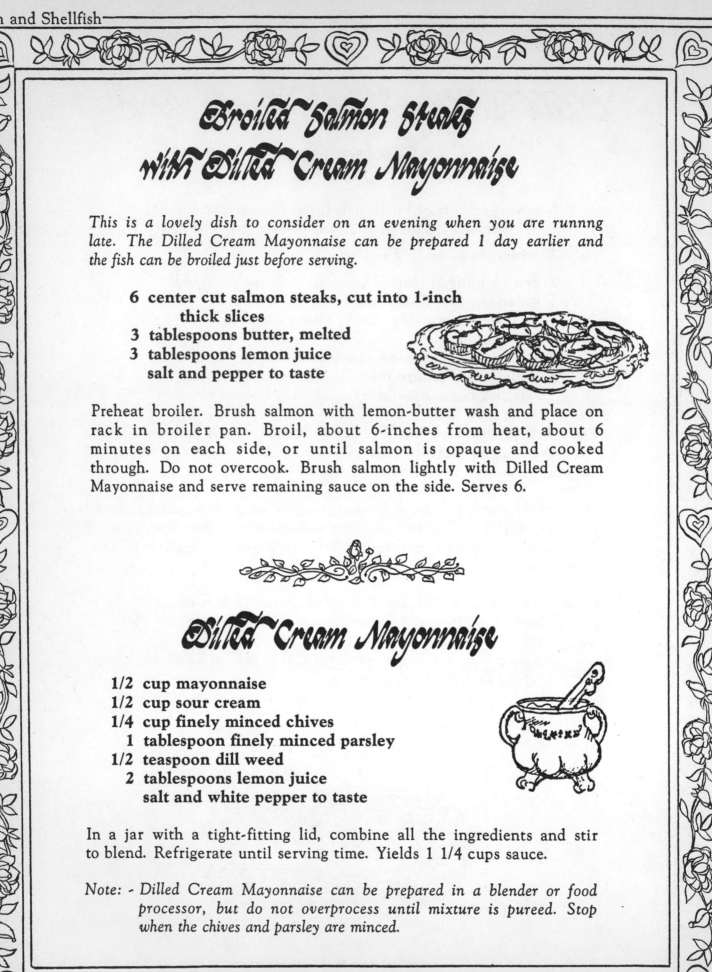

6 **center cut salmon steaks, cut into 1-inch thick slices**
3 **tablespoons butter, melted**
3 **tablespoons lemon juice**
    salt and pepper to taste

Preheat broiler. Brush salmon with lemon-butter wash and place on rack in broiler pan. Broil, about 6-inches from heat, about 6 minutes on each side, or until salmon is opaque and cooked through. Do not overcook. Brush salmon lightly with Dilled Cream Mayonnaise and serve remaining sauce on the side. Serves 6.

Dilled Cream Mayonnaise

1/2 **cup mayonnaise**
1/2 **cup sour cream**
1/4 **cup finely minced chives**
  1 **tablespoon finely minced parsley**
1/2 **teaspoon dill weed**
  2 **tablespoons lemon juice**
    salt and white pepper to taste

In a jar with a tight-fitting lid, combine all the ingredients and stir to blend. Refrigerate until serving time. Yields 1 1/4 cups sauce.

Note: - Dilled Cream Mayonnaise can be prepared in a blender or food processor, but do not overprocess until mixture is pureed. Stop when the chives and parsley are minced.

Scampi Alta Marinara with Garlic Marinara Sauce

2 pounds raw shrimp. Remove shells and black veins.
　　Sprinkle with salt and pepper and dust
　　lightly with flour.

1/2　cup (1 stick) butter
　4　cloves garlic, finely minced
　2　tablespoons minced parsley
1/2　teaspoon Italian Herb Seasoning
　2　teaspoons paprika

　2　tablespoons lemon juice

In a large skillet, heat butter until it is sizzling hot. Add the garlic and cook for a minute or two. Add the shrimp, and saute quickly, tossing and turning until shrimp are opaque. Do not overcook shrimp. Toss in the remainng ingredients and cook for a few seconds until blended.

Divide shrimp between 6 scallop shells. Drizzle shrimp with a little of the garlic butter. Can be served "natural" at this point.

However, for an irresistible touch, spoon a little Garlic Marinara Sauce over the shrimp and sprinkle with grated Parmesan cheese. Serves 6.

Garlic Marinara Sauce

　3　tablespoons oil (can use part olive oil)
　4　cloves garlic, finely minced
　1　can (1 pound) stewed tomatoes, very finely chopped
　1　can (8 ounces) tomato sauce
　1　tablespoon chopped parsley
1/4　cup dry red wine
　3　tablespoons grated onion
1/2　teaspoon Italian Herb Seasoning
1/2　bay leaf
　　salt and pepper to taste

In a saucepan, heat oil and saute garlic for 2 minutes. Add the remaining ingredients and simmer mixture for 25 minutes, uncovered.

Note: - Do not cook shrimp in sauce. Sauce can be prepared earlier in the day and reheated at time of serving. Spoon hot sauce over hot shrimp. If shrimp are overcooked, they get chewy and rubbery.

Giant Piroshkis with Shrimp in Herbed Mushroom Cream

Shrimp and Herbed Mushroom Cream Sauce Filling:
- 1 onion, finely chopped
- 4 shallots, minced
- 4 cloves garlic, minced
- 4 tablespoons butter

- 1/2 pound mushrooms, thinly sliced

- 2 tablespoons flour
- 1/2 teaspoon poultry seasoning
  salt and white pepper to taste

- 1/2 cup cream
- 1/2 cup sour cream
- 3 tablespoons lemon juice

- 1/4 pound cooked baby shrimp

In a large skillet, saute onions, shallots and garlic in butter until onions are soft. Add the mushrooms and continue sauteing until mushrooms are tender and liquid rendered is evaporated. Add the flour and seasonings and cook for 2 minutes, stirring. Stir in the cream, sour cream and lemon juice and cook for 2 minutes, stirring. Mixture should be very thick. Stir in the shrimp.

The Pastry:
- 2 packages frozen patty shells (12 shells), defrosted in refrigerator
- 2 eggs, beaten
- 1/2 cup grated Parmesan cheese

On a floured pastry cloth, roll out each patty shell to measure about 6-inches. Place 1/12 of the filling (about 2 tablespoons) on each shell, fold dough over and press edges down with the tines of a fork. Scallop the edges. Place piroshkis on a greased cookie sheet, brush tops with beaten egg and sprinkle with grated cheese. Pierce tops with the tines of a fork.

Bake at 400° for 25 minutes or until pastry is puffed and tops are golden brown. Yields 12 luncheon servings.

Note: - Filled piroshkis can be stored in the refrigerator earlier in the day and baked before serving.

Shrimp with Rice, Tomatoes, Peas & Artichokes
Shrimp Paella

This is an exciting casserole that does well for a main dish. Add a soup or salad and dinner is ready.

- 2 onions, chopped
- 1 can (4 ounces) diced green chiles
- 2 tomatoes, fresh or canned, chopped
- 4 tablespoons oil
- 1 clove garlic, minced

- 1 cup rice

- 1 package (10 ounces) frozen peas, defrosted
- 1 package (10 ounces) frozen artichoke hearts, defrosted
- 2 cups chicken broth, homemade or canned
- 1 tablespoon chopped parsley
  salt and pepper to taste
- 1/3 teaspoon tumeric

- 1 pound cooked baby shrimp

In a Dutch oven casserole, cook together first 5 ingredients until onions are transparent. Add the rice and cook for about 5 minutes, tossing and turning. Add the peas, artichoke hearts, broth, parsley and seasonings and stir to blend. Cover pan, and simmer mixture until rice is tender and liquid is absorbed, about 35 to 40 minutes. Add the shrimp and heat through. Serve with salad or fresh fruit. Serves 6.

Note: - Entire casserole can be prepared in advance up to the point where the shrimp are added. Shrimp toughen with overcooking, so add the shrimp just before you serve. Heat for a few minutes and then serve.

- An excellent addition would be 1 jar (2 ounces) pimiento strips, which you would add at the very end with the shrimp.

- Any leftover pieces of shredded chicken or pork can also be added with the shrimp.

Scallops with Mushrooms & Tomatoes in Wine Sauce

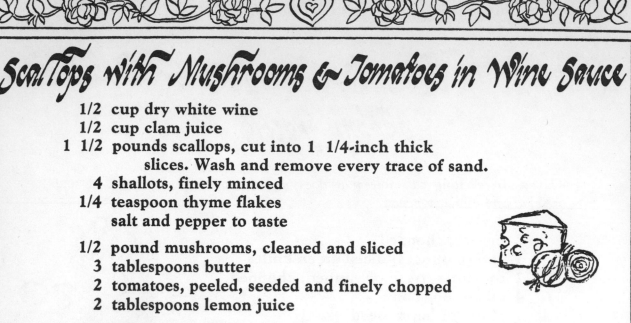

- 1/2 cup dry white wine
- 1/2 cup clam juice
- 1 1/2 pounds scallops, cut into 1 1/4-inch thick slices. Wash and remove every trace of sand.
- 4 shallots, finely minced
- 1/4 teaspoon thyme flakes
- salt and pepper to taste

- 1/2 pound mushrooms, cleaned and sliced
- 3 tablespoons butter
- 2 tomatoes, peeled, seeded and finely chopped
- 2 tablespoons lemon juice

- 3 tablespoons flour

- 1 cup cream
- Herbed Cheese Crumbs

In a saucepan, combine first 6 ingredients and bring to a boil. Reduce heat and simmer mixture for about 5 minutes or until scallops become opaque. Remove scallops with a slotted spoon and reduce liquid to 1/2.

Saute mushrooms in butter until tender. Add tomatoes and lemon juice and cook for 3 minutes, stirring, over high heat. Stir in the flour and cook for another 3 minutes, stirring. Stir in the cream and cook until sauce thickens. Add the scallops and the reduced wine sauce and stir until blended.

Spoon mixture into 8 individual buttered scallop shells. Sprinkle top with 2 tablespoons Herbed Cheese crumbs and heat in a 350° oven until heated through. Broil tops for a few seconds to lightly brown. Serves 8.

Herbed Cheese Crumbs:
- 1/4 cup melted butter
- 1/2 cup crushed Ritz cracker crumbs
- 1/4 cup grated Parmesan cheese
- 1/2 cup grated Swiss cheese
- 1 tablespoon chopped parsley
- 1 tablespoon chopped chives
- 1 tablespoon lemon juice

Combine all the ingredients in a glass jar with a screw-top lid and shake vigorously until mixture is blended. Store unused crumbs in the refrigerator and use over vegetables or casseroles.

Scallops & Tomatoes in Wine, Garlic & Herb Sauce

1 pound scallops, washed and cut into 1/4-inch
   thick slices. Sprinkle lightly with salt, pepper
   and paprika and dust lightly with flour.
4 tablespoons butter

Wine, Garlic & Herb Sauce

1 cup grated Swiss Cheese
4 tablespoons grated Parmesan cheese

Saute scallops in hot butter for just a minute or two until they become opaque. Place scallops in an oval porcelain baker. Pour Wine, Garlic & Herb Sauce over the scallops and sprinkle top with grated Swiss and Parmesan cheese.

Heat in a 350° oven until heated through and cheese on top is thoroughly melted. Serve at once with pink rice. Serves 4 to 5.

Wine, Garlic & Herb Sauce

1 onion, finely chopped
4 shallots, minced
2 cloves garlic, minced
2 tablespoons butter

1/2 cup dry white wine

3 tomatoes, fresh or canned, peeled, seeded and chopped
1 tablespoon tomato paste
1 tablespoon chopped parsley
1/2 teaspoon oregano
1/8 teaspoon thyme
1 tablespoon lemon juice
   salt and pepper to taste

In a large skillet, saute together onion, shallots and garlic in butter, until onions are tender. Add the wine and continue cooking until wine is reduced to half. Add the remaining ingredients and cook sauce at a simmer for 10 minutes.

Cucumber Sauce for Cold Salmon or Shellfish

1/2 cup mayonnaise
1/2 cup sour cream
2 tablespoons lemon juice
1/4 cup finely chopped green onions
1/2 teaspoon dried dill weed
2 tablespoons finely chopped parsley
salt and pepper to taste

1 cucumber, peeled, seeded and grated

Combine all the ingredients, except the cucumber, in a glass jar with a tight-fitting lid and stir until the mixture is thoroughly combined.

Salt the cucumber and let it drain in a strainer for 1 hour. Squeeze out the excess moisture. Add the cucumber to the dressing. Serve with cold poached salmon or shellfish. Yields 1 1/4 cups sauce.

Dilled Mustard Mayonnaise for Fish or Shellfish

1/2 cup mayonnaise
2 tablespoons sour cream
1 tablespoon Dijon-style mustard
2 tablespoons sugar
3 tablespoons wine vinegar
1/2 teaspoon dill weed

Combine all the ingredients in a glass jar with a tight-fitting lid and stir until the mixture is thoroughly combined. Serve with cold poached fish or shellfish. Yields about 1 cup sauce.

Note: - An excellent addition to the above would be 1 1/2 teaspoons of finely minced shallots.
- What a good time to try the above with homemade mayonnaise.

Meats

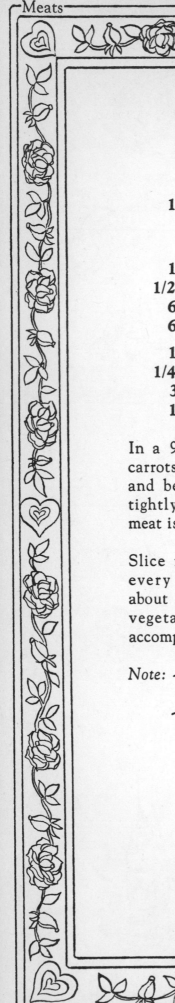

Country - Style Pot Roast with Prunes & Raisins

1 brisket of beef, about 4 pounds, lean and trimmed of fat. Sprinkle with salt, pepper, paprika and garlic powder.

1 package (6 ounces) pitted prunes
1/2 cup yellow raisins
6 medium carrots, peeled and cut in half, cross-wise
6 small whole onions

1 envelope onion soup mix
1/4 cup brown sugar
3 tablespoons ketchup
1 can (12 ounces) beer

In a 9x13-inch roasting pan, place meat. Arrange prunes, raisins, carrots and onions around meat. Combine soup mix, sugar, ketchup and beer and stir to blend. Pour this over the meat. Cover pan tightly with foil and bake at 350° for 2 1/2 to 3 hours or until meat is fork tender. Allow to cool.

Slice meat and return it to the pan with the gravy from which every trace of fat has been removed. Heat in a 350° oven for about 30 minutes or until heated through. Serve with the fruit and vegetables on the side. Potato pancakes are an excellent accompaniment. Serves 6.

Note: - As with all pot roasts, this is very good the next day, allowing flavors to blend.
- Gravy is delicious and does not need to be thickened.

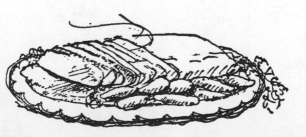

Old-Fashioned Hungarian Goulash with Spaetzel

This lovely goulash is an updated version of the traditional Hungarian stew. Usually made with a tougher cut of beef, cooking time was markedly longer. Using sirloin steak, not only decreases cooking time to minutes, but the beef is tender and succulent and I do believe, more delightful served this way.

- 2 pounds sirloin steak cut into 1x1x1/8-inch strips. Toss with 2 tablespoons Dijon mustard.
- 3 tablespoons butter

- 2 onions, chopped
- 2 cloves garlic, minced
- 1 carrot, grated (not traditional, but very good)
- 2 tablespoons brown sugar
- 2 tablespoons butter
- 1/4 cup dry white wine

- 1/4 cup tomato sauce
- 1 can (10 1/2 ounces) beef broth
- 1/2 teaspoon Bovril
- 2 tablespoons paprika
  salt and pepper to taste
- 1 1/2 cups sour cream
  salt and pepper to taste

Saute meat in very hot butter, turning and tossing, until meat loses its pinkness. Set aside.

In a Dutch oven casserole, saute onions, garlic, carrot in brown sugar and wine until onions are soft. Add the wine and cook for 1 or 2 minutes until wine is evaporated.

Add tomato sauce, broth, Bovril and seasonings and simmer sauce for about 10 minutes, uncovered, to reduce sauce a little. Stir in beef and sour cream and heat through. Do not boil at this point. Simply heat through. Serve with Spaetzel or Buttered Noodles with Poppy Seeds. Serves 6.

Buttered Noodles with Poppyseeds:
Cook 8 ounces of medium-wide noodles until tender but firm. Drain. Toss with 6 tablespoons melted butter, 1 tablespoon lemon juice, 1 tablespoon poppy seeds and salt to taste. Serves 6.

Note: - Goulash can be prepared earlier in the day and heated at time of serving. Add the sour cream to the heated goulash and then heat through as described above.

Easiest & Best Hungarian Spaetzel

Spaetzel are little Hungarian noodles that are a pleasant accompaniment to soups or stews. They can be served as a starch, very much like rice or potatoes. They can be served "natural," tossed in butter or with an infinite variety of sauces or gravies.

The recipe I am sharing today is made foolproof with the addition of a little baking powder. The Spaetzel are exceedingly light and the onion powder imparts a very delicate flavor.

Spaetzel are excellent served with stews or soups. As these are made in a minute in a mixer, you can depend on them when you are really pressed for time. Once you try these little "noodle-like dumplings" you will enjoy using them often. The shapes are very irregular, so don't think anything went wrong.

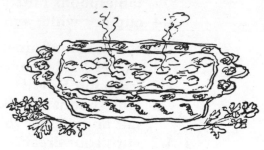

  3 eggs
2/3 cup milk

  2 cups flour
1/2 teaspoon baking powder
1/4 teaspoon onion powder
1/4 teaspoon salt

In the large bowl of an electric mixer, beat together eggs and milk until blended.

Combine the remaining ingredients and add them, all at once, to the egg mixture. Beat, for about 1 minute, or until batter is thoroughly blended.

Bring 4 quarts salted water to a boil. Place the batter inside a collander, and hold it over the boiling water. Let the batter drip into the boiling water. When the noodles float to the top, let them cook a minute more. Remove them with a slotted spoon. Noodles can be tossed in butter, with cheese (optional), in soups, alongside stews or with gravy. Serves 6.

Royal Prime Rib Roast with Old English Yorkshire Pudding & Creamy Horseradish Sauce

1 standing prime rib roast. Ask your butcher
to remove the chine bone, loosen the ribs and
tie them back in place. Use a 6-pound roast
(3 ribs) for 6 servings. Sprinkle with salt,
pepper and garlic powder.

Place roast, bone-side down, in a roasting pan and roast in a 300° oven until meat thermometer registers desired doneness.*

Remove roast from the oven. Remove the strings and place on a serving platter. Slice at the table and serve with Old English Yorkshire Pudding and Creamy Horseradish Sauce on the side.

Note: - *Meat thermometer should be inserted into the thickest part of the meat, making certain that it does not touch the bone. Meat thermometer should register for:

Very rare	-	130°
Rare	-	140°
Medium rare	-	150°
Medium	-	160° (not recommended)
Well done	-	170° (not recommended)

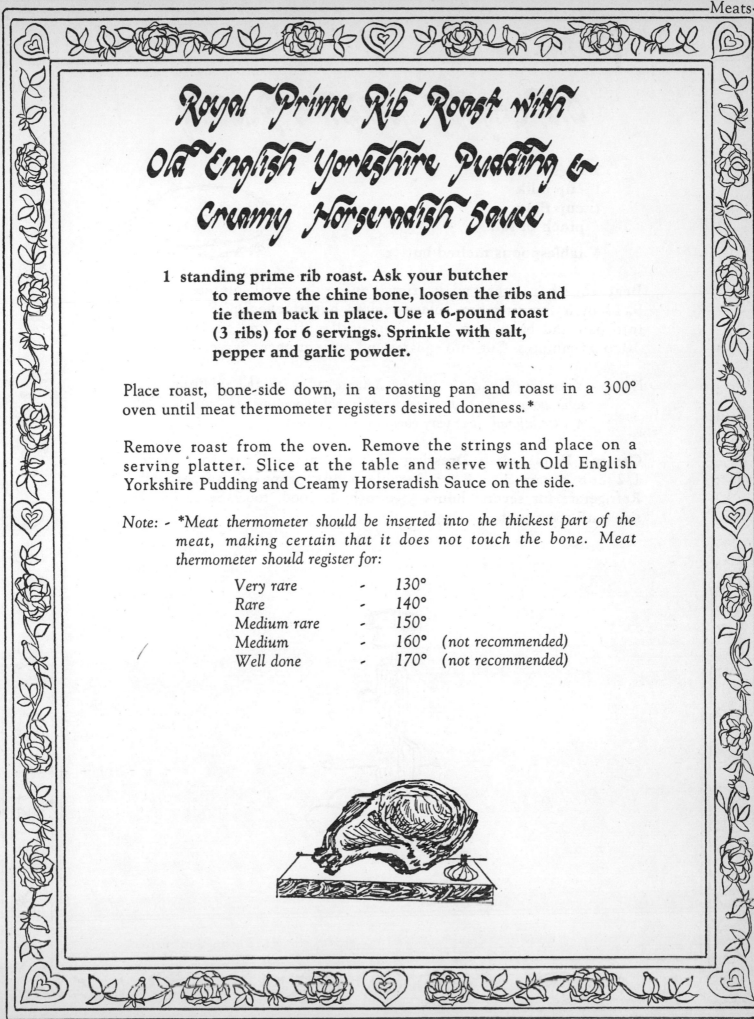

Old English Yorkshire Pudding

3 eggs
1 cup milk
1 cup flour
   pinch of salt

4 tablespoons melted butter

Beat together eggs, milk, flour and salt until blended. In a 9x13-inch roasting pan, place melted butter evenly. Pour batter into pan and bake in a 350° oven until puffed and golden, about 30 to 35 minutes. Cut into squares and serve at once. Serves 6.

Note: - Yorkshire pudding can be heightened with the addition of 2 tablespoons chopped chives and 1 tablespoon melted butter. While not traditional, it is very good.

Creamy Horseradish Dressing: Stir together 1/2 cup sour cream, 1/2 cup cream and 2 or 3 tablespoons prepared horseradish. Refrigerate for several hours (overnight is good, too.) Serve on the side with roast beef.

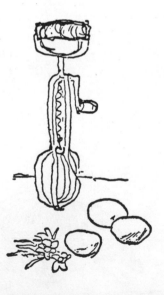

Bracciole ~ Roulades of Beef with Herb Stuffing, Bacon & Pine Nuts

These tender and very delicious beef roulades, filled with an herbed stuffing that is sparkled with bacon and pine nuts, is an incredible choice for the fanciest dinner party. Yet they are easy enough to make for a family dinner. They cook in minutes, and in spite of the fact that you start with an expensive cut of meat, they are really very economical.

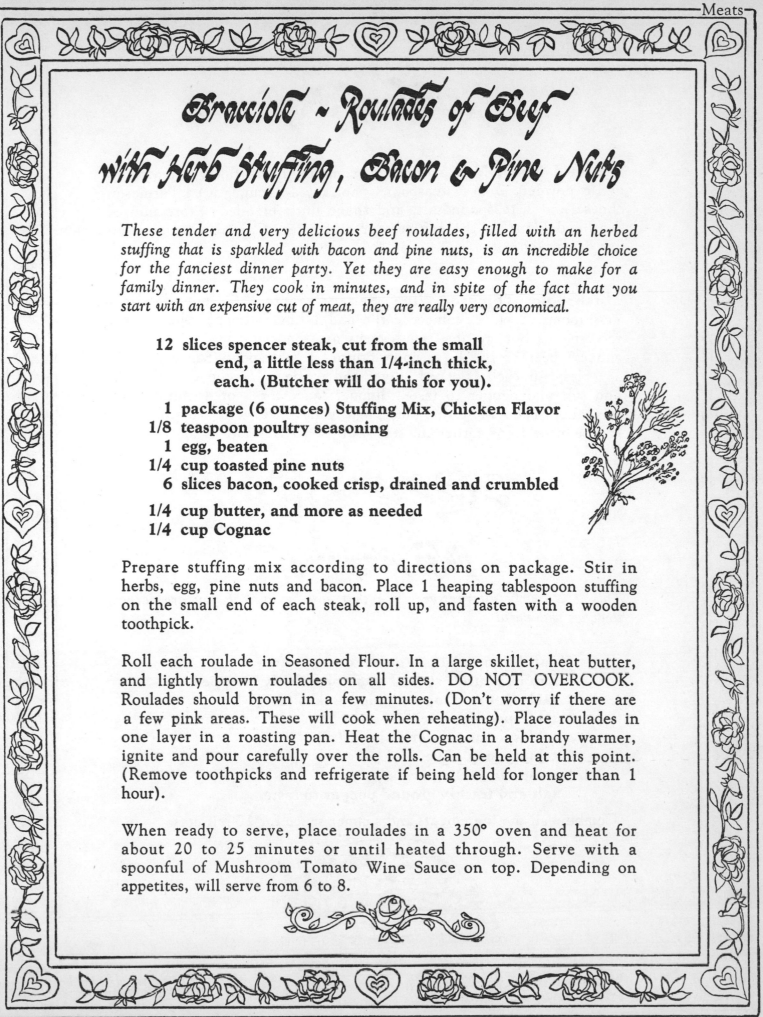

12 slices spencer steak, cut from the small
   end, a little less than 1/4-inch thick,
   each. (Butcher will do this for you).

 1 package (6 ounces) Stuffing Mix, Chicken Flavor
1/8 teaspoon poultry seasoning
 1 egg, beaten
1/4 cup toasted pine nuts
 6 slices bacon, cooked crisp, drained and crumbled

1/4 cup butter, and more as needed
1/4 cup Cognac

Prepare stuffing mix according to directions on package. Stir in herbs, egg, pine nuts and bacon. Place 1 heaping tablespoon stuffing on the small end of each steak, roll up, and fasten with a wooden toothpick.

Roll each roulade in Seasoned Flour. In a large skillet, heat butter, and lightly brown roulades on all sides. DO NOT OVERCOOK. Roulades should brown in a few minutes. (Don't worry if there are a few pink areas. These will cook when reheating). Place roulades in one layer in a roasting pan. Heat the Cognac in a brandy warmer, ignite and pour carefully over the rolls. Can be held at this point. (Remove toothpicks and refrigerate if being held for longer than 1 hour).

When ready to serve, place roulades in a 350° oven and heat for about 20 to 25 minutes or until heated through. Serve with a spoonful of Mushroom Tomato Wine Sauce on top. Depending on appetites, will serve from 6 to 8.

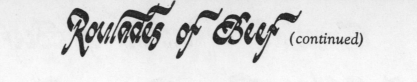

Roulades of Beef (continued)

Seasoned Flour: In a plastic bag, combine 1 cup flour, 2 teaspoons garlic powder, 2 to 3 teaspoons paprika, 1/4 cup grated Parmesan cheese and 1 teaspoon salt, and shake until blended. Store unused Seasoned Flour in the refrigerator or freezer. Can also be used on fish or chicken.

Mushroom Tomato Wine Sauce: Saute 1/2 pound sliced mushrooms, 2 cloves minced garlic and 1 finely chopped shallot in 3 tablespoons butter, until mushrooms are tender. Add 1 can (10 1/2 ounces) beef broth, 1 teaspoon Bovril, 1 tablespoon Sauce Robert, 1 tablespoon each chopped chives and parsley, 1/2 cup tomato sauce and salt and pepper to taste. Simmer sauce for 3 or 4 minutes and serve hot. (You want this sauce lightly flavored with tomato). Sauce can be made 1 day earlier and stored in the refrigerator.

Salsa Marinara

This is a lovely alternative sauce that can be used if you are serving roulades with pasta.

> 1 can (1 pound 12 ounces) tomato puree
> 1 can (1 pound) stewed tomatoes, finely chopped
> 2 tablespoons chopped onion flakes (dry)
> 2 tablespoons sugar
> 2 tablespoons parsley flakes (dry)
> 2 tablespoons olive oil
> 1/4 teaspoon garlic powder
> salt and freshly ground pepper to taste

Combine all the ingredients and simmer sauce for 10 minutes.

German Potted Beef Stew with Red Wine Gravy

This is a delicious sweet and sour stew that will surely satisfy on a bleak and raw winter night. It is wonderful for family dinners.

- 1 boneless chuck roast, about 3 pounds, cut into 1-inch cubes
- 2 onions, chopped
- 3 carrots, thinly sliced
- 4 cloves garlic, minced
- 1 cup dry red wine
- 1 can (10 1/2 ounces) beef broth
- 1/2 cup red wine vinegar
- 1/2 cup brown sugar
- salt and pepper to taste

Combine all the ingredients in a bowl and toss until they are nicely mixed. Cover and refrigerate overnight.

Place all the ingredients in a Dutch oven casserole and bring mixture to a boil. Lower heat and simmer casserole for about 2 hours or until meat is tender.

Skim off any trace of fat. If you would like to thicken the gravy, add:

1/2 cup ginger snap cookie crumbs

Serve with dumplings or spaetzel or potato pancakes. Sweet and Sour Red Cabbage is very traditional. Serves 6.

Note: - If you wish, you can omit marinating the beef overnight. Flavor will be very good, but not as intense.

Sweet & Sour Red Cabbage

- 1 small head red cabbage, grated or very thinly sliced
- 2 apples, peeled, cored and grated
- 1/3 cup yellow raisins
- 1 can (10 1/2 ounces) beef broth
- 2 tablespoons bacon fat or oil
- 3 tablespoons vinegar
- 3 tablespoons brown sugar
- salt and pepper to taste

Combine all the ingredients in a Dutch oven casserole and bring to a boil. Cover casserole, lower heat and simmer mixture until cabbage is tender, about 30 minutes. Serves 6.

Farmhouse Pot Roast with Peaches & Prunes

When the weather starts to turn chilly, this hearty dish is a grand one to consider. It is bursting with goodness and flavor, and is a fine choice for a family dinner.

4   **pounds brisket of beef, trimmed of all fat**
3   **cloves garlic, minced**
2   **onions, chopped**
4   **carrots, cut into 1-inch pieces**
1   **package (6 ounces) dried peaches**
12   **pitted prunes**

1/2   **cup peach jam**
4   **tablespoons brown sugar**
1/4   **cup ketchup**
1   **can (10 1/2 ounces) beef broth**
1/2   **cup dry white wine**
    salt and pepper to taste

In a 9x13-inch pan, place first 6 ingredients. Stir together the remaining ingredients and pour over the meat. Cover the pan tightly with foil and bake in a 350° oven until meat is tender, about 2 to 2 1/2 hours.

Remove from the oven, allow to cool and remove every trace of fat. Slice the meat and return it to the pan with the gravy. When ready to serve, heat in a 350° oven, covered, for about 30 minutes or until heated through. Serve with brown rice or toasted egg barley. Serves 6 to 8.

Note: - Gravy is delicious and does not need to be thickened.
    - Entire dish can be prepared 1 day earlier with excellent results. Reheat at time of serving.

Fluffy Meatballs in a Quick, Light Tomato Sauce

1 pound lean ground beef
1 pound lean ground pork
1 small onion, peeled and grated
4 slices fresh bread, crusts removed, soaked in
    water and squeezed dry
2 eggs
1 clove garlic, minced
4 tablespoons tomato sauce
    salt and pepper to taste

In a bowl, combine all the ingredients and stir until mixture is blended. Shape meat into 1-inch balls and saute them in a large skillet, in one layer, shaking pan frequently so that the meatballs brown on all sides. Continue with remaining meatballs.

Place browned meatballs in the Dutch oven with the Quick, Light Tomato Sauce, and simmer meatballs in sauce for about 20 to 30 minutes. Serve over cooked pasta or noodles. Serves 8.

Quick, Light Tomato Sauce

2 cans (1 pound 12 ounces, each) crushed tomatoes
    in tomato puree. (A good brand to use is
    PROGRESSO)
4 tablespoons dried minced onions
1/2 teaspoon coarse grind garlic powder. (A good
    brand to use is LAWRY'S)
6 tablespoons chopped parsley (or 2 tablespoons
    dried parsley)
1 tablespoon Italian Herb Seasoning
2 tablespoons sugar
3 tablespoons oil
    salt and pepper to taste

Combine all the ingredients in a Dutch oven casserole and simmer sauce for 5 minutes.

Country Potted Beef with Apples & Prunes

This is a dish we often enjoyed on Sundays as a pleasant change from chicken. The gravy is delicious so have some crusty French bread for dipping. The Brown Rice is a perfect accompaniment.

1 brisket of beef (about 4 pounds). Sprinkle with
salt, pepper, garlic powder. Spread meat with 3
tablespoons Dijon mustard and sprinkle with
1/2 cup brown sugar

12 prunes
3 apples, peeled, cored and sliced into quarters
4 carrots, peeled and cut into thick slices
1 cup whole berry cranberry sauce (canned)
1 large onion, chopped
1 can (10 1/2 ounces) beef broth
1 cup dry white wine

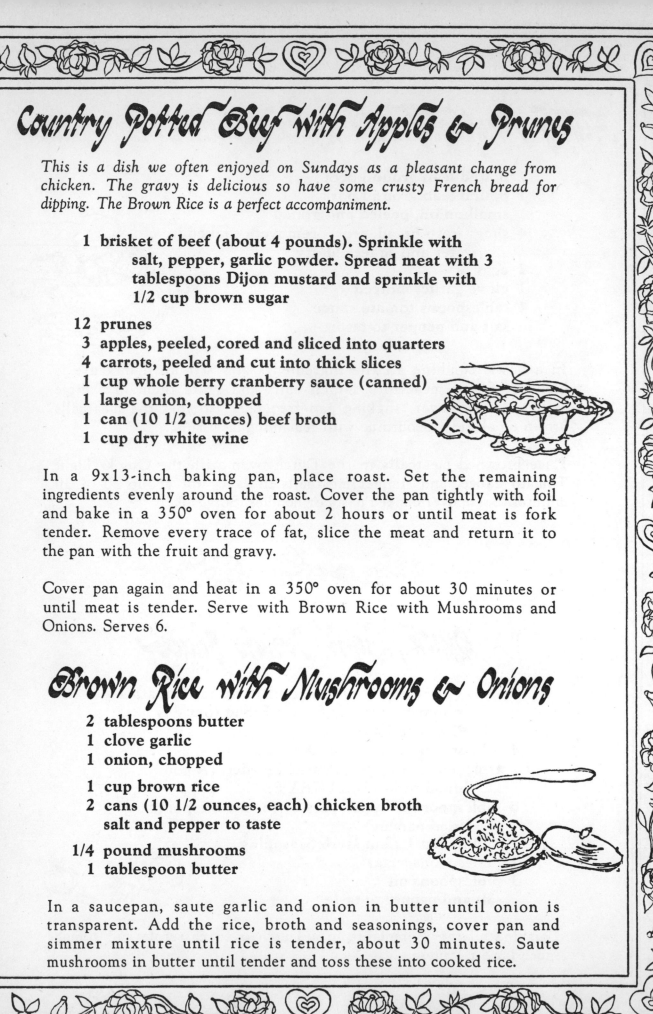

In a 9x13-inch baking pan, place roast. Set the remaining ingredients evenly around the roast. Cover the pan tightly with foil and bake in a 350° oven for about 2 hours or until meat is fork tender. Remove every trace of fat, slice the meat and return it to the pan with the fruit and gravy.

Cover pan again and heat in a 350° oven for about 30 minutes or until meat is tender. Serve with Brown Rice with Mushrooms and Onions. Serves 6.

Brown Rice with Mushrooms & Onions

2 tablespoons butter
1 clove garlic
1 onion, chopped

1 cup brown rice
2 cans (10 1/2 ounces, each) chicken broth
salt and pepper to taste

1/4 pound mushrooms
1 tablespoon butter

In a saucepan, saute garlic and onion in butter until onion is transparent. Add the rice, broth and seasonings, cover pan and simmer mixture until rice is tender, about 30 minutes. Saute mushrooms in butter until tender and toss these into cooked rice.

Farmhouse Sweet & Sour Pot Roast with Apples & Raisins

This sweet and sour pot roast is the essence of simplicity and a triumph of taste. It assembles in minutes and produces the finest tasting pot roast.

1 brisket of beef, about 4 pounds, trimmed of all fat and sprinkled with salt, pepper and garlic powder

1 jar (1 pound) sweet-sour red cabbage
1/2 cup brown sugar
1/4 cup vinegar
1/2 cup dry white wine
1 onion, chopped
1/2 cup yellow raisins
1 apple, peeled, cored and grated
salt and pepper to taste

In a 9x13-inch roasting pan, place brisket. Combine all the remaining ingredients and pour over the meat. Cover pan tightly with foil and bake in a 350° oven until meat is fork tender, about 2 hours. Remove from the oven and allow to cool.

Slice meat and return it to the pan with the gravy, from which every trace of fat has been removed. When ready to serve, heat in a 350° oven, covered, for another 30 minutes. Serve with dumplings or potato pancakes. Serves 6.

Note: - Gravy is delicious and does not need to be thickened.
- Entire dish can be prepared earlier in the day and stored in the refrigerator.
- Entire dish can be made 1 day earlier and stored in the refrigerator.

Spinach & Beef Dumplings with Yogurt Dill Sauce

This is an economical main course, that can also be served as a small entree or hors d'oeuvre. Whichever way it is served it is delicious as well as unusual.

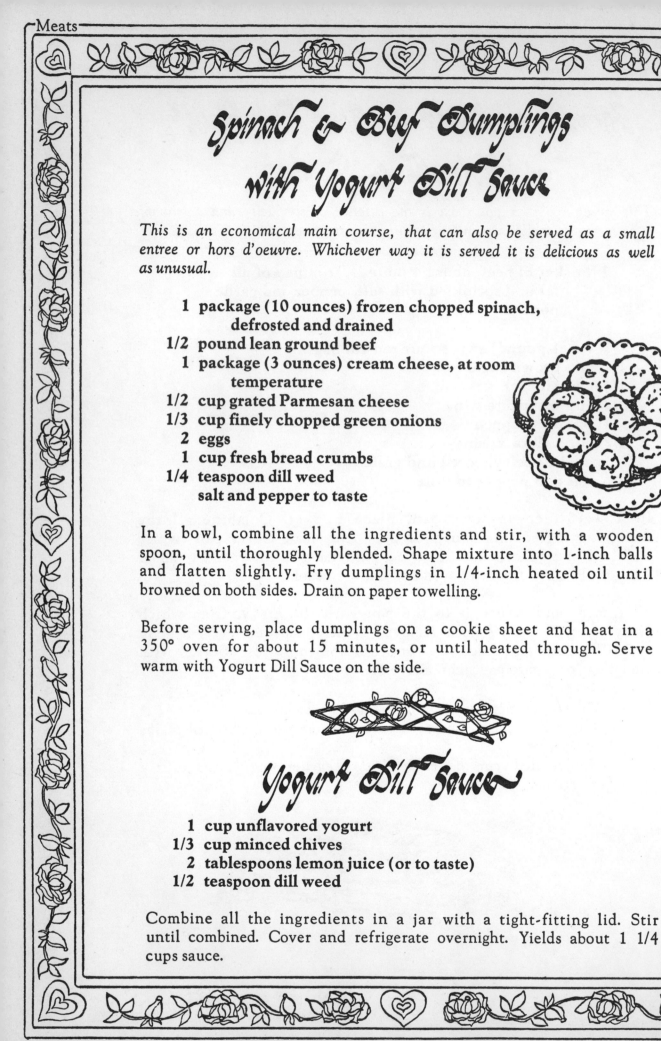

- 1 **package (10 ounces) frozen chopped spinach, defrosted and drained**
- 1/2 **pound lean ground beef**
- 1 **package (3 ounces) cream cheese, at room temperature**
- 1/2 **cup grated Parmesan cheese**
- 1/3 **cup finely chopped green onions**
- 2 **eggs**
- 1 **cup fresh bread crumbs**
- 1/4 **teaspoon dill weed**
  salt and pepper to taste

In a bowl, combine all the ingredients and stir, with a wooden spoon, until thoroughly blended. Shape mixture into 1-inch balls and flatten slightly. Fry dumplings in 1/4-inch heated oil until browned on both sides. Drain on paper towelling.

Before serving, place dumplings on a cookie sheet and heat in a 350° oven for about 15 minutes, or until heated through. Serve warm with Yogurt Dill Sauce on the side.

Yogurt Dill Sauce

- 1 **cup unflavored yogurt**
- 1/3 **cup minced chives**
- 2 **tablespoons lemon juice (or to taste)**
- 1/2 **teaspoon dill weed**

Combine all the ingredients in a jar with a tight-fitting lid. Stir until combined. Cover and refrigerate overnight. Yields about 1 1/4 cups sauce.

Beef & Peppers Romano in Tomato & Cheese Sauce

What a wonderful dish to serve family and friends. Succulent strips of beef in a rich and flavorful tomato sauce with peppers and garlic is just bursting with flavor.

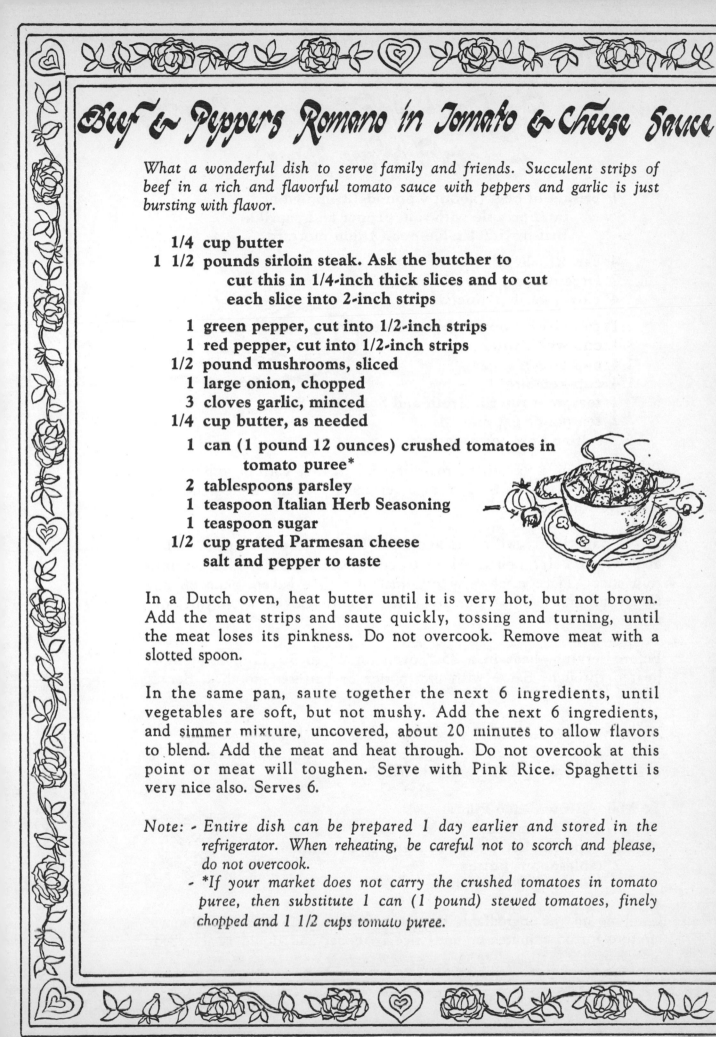

> 1/4 cup butter
> 1 1/2 pounds sirloin steak. Ask the butcher to cut this in 1/4-inch thick slices and to cut each slice into 2-inch strips
>
> 1 green pepper, cut into 1/2-inch strips
> 1 red pepper, cut into 1/2-inch strips
> 1/2 pound mushrooms, sliced
> 1 large onion, chopped
> 3 cloves garlic, minced
> 1/4 cup butter, as needed
>
> 1 can (1 pound 12 ounces) crushed tomatoes in tomato puree*
> 2 tablespoons parsley
> 1 teaspoon Italian Herb Seasoning
> 1 teaspoon sugar
> 1/2 cup grated Parmesan cheese
> salt and pepper to taste

In a Dutch oven, heat butter until it is very hot, but not brown. Add the meat strips and saute quickly, tossing and turning, until the meat loses its pinkness. Do not overcook. Remove meat with a slotted spoon.

In the same pan, saute together the next 6 ingredients, until vegetables are soft, but not mushy. Add the next 6 ingredients, and simmer mixture, uncovered, about 20 minutes to allow flavors to blend. Add the meat and heat through. Do not overcook at this point or meat will toughen. Serve with Pink Rice. Spaghetti is very nice also. Serves 6.

Note: - *Entire dish can be prepared 1 day earlier and stored in the refrigerator. When reheating, be careful not to scorch and please, do not overcook.*
- **If your market does not carry the crushed tomatoes in tomato puree, then substitute 1 can (1 pound) stewed tomatoes, finely chopped and 1 1/2 cups tomato puree.*

Farmhouse Pot Roast with Onions & Carrots & Garlic Wine Sauce

1 brisket of beef (about 4 pounds) trimmed of
  fat. Sprinkle with salt, pepper and paprika.
  Brush with 1 tablespoon Dijon mustard.

4 carrots, sliced
2 large onions, coarsely chopped
4 cloves garlic, minced

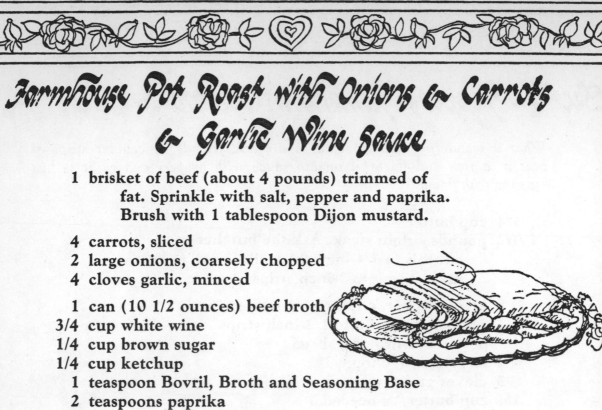

1 can (10 1/2 ounces) beef broth
3/4 cup white wine
1/4 cup brown sugar
1/4 cup ketchup
1 teaspoon Bovril, Broth and Seasoning Base
2 teaspoons paprika
  salt and pepper to taste

Place meat in a 9x13-inch roasting pan. Scatter carrots, onions and garlic around the meat. Stir together the remaining ingredients and pour over the meat.

Cover pan tightly with foil and bake in a 350° oven until tender, about 2 to 2 1/2 hours. Allow to cool. Remove meat and cut into thin slices. Place meat in a 9x13-inch porcelain baker. Skim off any fat from gravy and pour over the meat. Cover with foil and refrigerate.

Before serving, heat in a 350° oven for 25 to 30 minutes or until heated through. Serve with brown rice or buttered noodles. Serves 6.

Note: - Gravy is delicious and does not need to be thickened.
  - Entire dish can be prepared 1 day earlier and stored in the refrigerator, with excellent results.

To Make Brown Rice Pilaf:

1 cup brown rice
2 1/2 cups chicken broth, homemade or canned
2 tablespoons butter
  salt and pepper to taste

Combine all the ingredients in a saucepan and stir to blend. Simmer mixture for 35 minutes or until rice is tender and liquid is absorbed. Serves 6.

Great Sesame Ginger Beef with Garlic & Chili

    1 pound sirloin steak (or flank steak), cut
        into strips, about 2x1x1/8-inches. (Place
        meat in freezer for about 1 hour to
        facilitate cutting . . . or ask your butcher
        to do this for you.)
    1 egg white (save the yolk for your fried rice)
    1 tablespoon cornstarch
    2 teaspoons sesame seeds

Sauce:
    2 tablespoons sherry (or white wine)
    2 tablespoons dark soy sauce
    1 teaspoon ground ginger (or more to taste)
    1/2 teaspoon coarse grind garlic powder
    1 tablespoon Beef Stock Base
    2 teaspoons cornstarch
    2 teaspoons sugar
    1/2 teaspoon Kimchee Base (This is a base made
        of garlic, chili and ginger.)
    2 teaspoons sesame oil

Preheat wok with 2 tablespoons oil. In a bowl, stir and toss beef, the egg white, cornstarch and sesame seeds. Add to hot oil and stir-fry for 1 or 2 minutes or until meat loses its pinkness.

Combine the sauce ingredients and stir until blended. Pour sauce ingredients over the beef and continue cooking and stir-frying until sauce has thickened, about 1 or 2 minutes. Serve with fried rice. Serves 4.

Note: - This dish can be extended with the addition of 1 pound fresh broccoli or asparagus. Trim the tough end of the spears and cut vegetables into 1-inch pieces. In this instance, you will have to stir-fry in 2 steps. First, stir-fry the vegetables and remove them from the wok. Then stir-fry the meat. Now, add the vegetables and the sauce, and continue as above.

Irish Beef Stew with Carrots & Onions

2 pounds boneless chuck, cut into 1-inch cubes.
　　Sprinkle with salt and pepper and dust with flour.
3 onions, coarsely chopped
2 carrots, cut into 1/2-inch slices
3 tablespoons butter

1 cup beer
3/4 cup beef broth
1 teaspoon Bovril, meat extract
3 tablespoons brown sugar
1/4 teaspoon thyme
1/2 teaspoon prepared mustard
　　salt and pepper to taste

In a Dutch oven, combine first 4 ingredients together and cook over moderately high heat, tossing and stirring until onions are transparent.

Add the remaining ingredients and bring mixture to a boil. Lower heat and simmer stew, covered, for about 2 hours or until meat is tender. Serve stew with creamy mashed potatoes. Serves 4 or 5.

Note: - If gravy needs a little more flavor, add 1/2 teaspoon Bovril.

Creamy Mashed Potatoes

3 cups mashed potatoes (can use instant
　　mashed potatoes)
3 eggs
1/2 teaspoon onion powder
3 tablespoons flour
1 cup cream
2 tablespoons butter
　　salt and pepper to taste

Beat together all the ingredients until blended. Place mixture into a 1 1/2-quart buttered souffle dish and bake in a 350° oven for about 45 minutes or until top is lightly browned. Serves 4 or 5.

Moroccan Lamb Dumplings with Apples & Raisins

This lovely and economical dish is just right for a cold night. Serve it with Cous Cous with Raisins & Pine Nuts for a really exciting meal with family and friends. If you are planning a dinner party then substitute the lamb dumplings with cubes of leg of lamb.

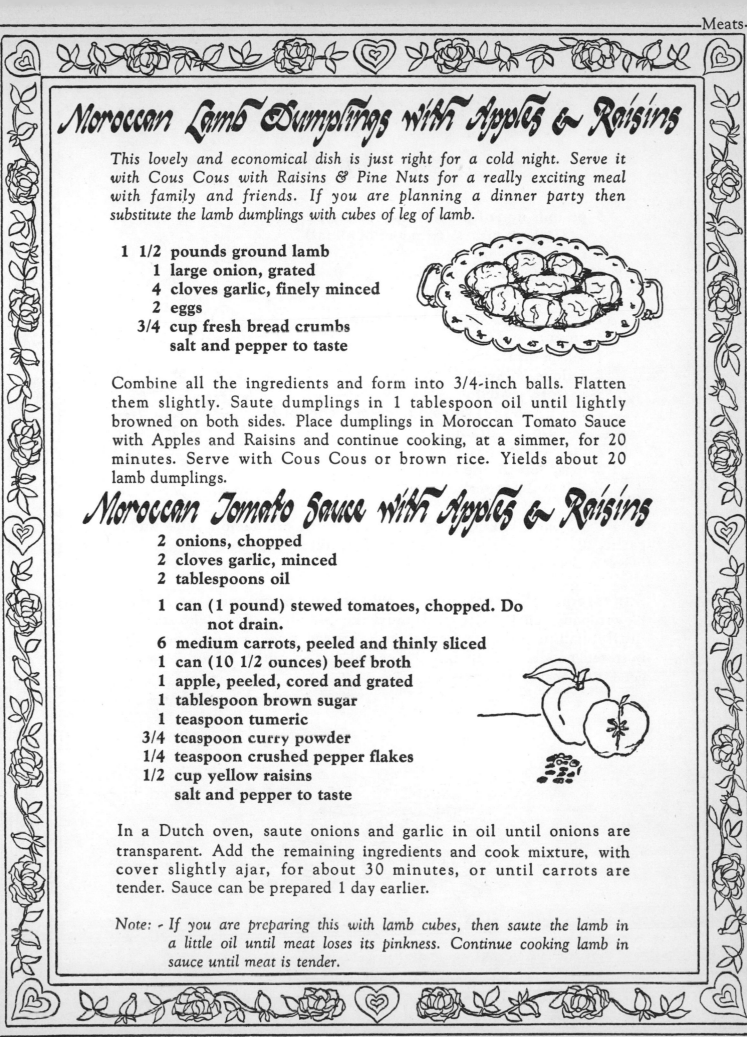

- 1 1/2 pounds ground lamb
- 1 large onion, grated
- 4 cloves garlic, finely minced
- 2 eggs
- 3/4 cup fresh bread crumbs
- salt and pepper to taste

Combine all the ingredients and form into 3/4-inch balls. Flatten them slightly. Saute dumplings in 1 tablespoon oil until lightly browned on both sides. Place dumplings in Moroccan Tomato Sauce with Apples and Raisins and continue cooking, at a simmer, for 20 minutes. Serve with Cous Cous or brown rice. Yields about 20 lamb dumplings.

Moroccan Tomato Sauce with Apples & Raisins

- 2 onions, chopped
- 2 cloves garlic, minced
- 2 tablespoons oil

- 1 can (1 pound) stewed tomatoes, chopped. Do not drain.
- 6 medium carrots, peeled and thinly sliced
- 1 can (10 1/2 ounces) beef broth
- 1 apple, peeled, cored and grated
- 1 tablespoon brown sugar
- 1 teaspoon tumeric
- 3/4 teaspoon curry powder
- 1/4 teaspoon crushed pepper flakes
- 1/2 cup yellow raisins
- salt and pepper to taste

In a Dutch oven, saute onions and garlic in oil until onions are transparent. Add the remaining ingredients and cook mixture, with cover slightly ajar, for about 30 minutes, or until carrots are tender. Sauce can be prepared 1 day earlier.

Note: - If you are preparing this with lamb cubes, then saute the lamb in a little oil until meat loses its pinkness. Continue cooking lamb in sauce until meat is tender.

Oven~Braised Lamb with Onions & Carrots in Tomato Wine Sauce

3 pounds boned lamb (from the leg), cut into
    1-inch cubes (trimmed of all fat)
2 tablespoons oil
4 tablespoons lemon juice
4 cloves garlic, minced

1 can (10 1/2 ounces) beef broth
1/2 cup dry red wine
1 teaspoon Bovril, beef extract
2 onions, minced
3 carrots, grated
1 can (1 pound) stewed tomatoes, chopped.
    Do not drain.
1/2 cup tomato paste
1/2 teaspoon thyme flakes
    salt and pepper to taste

In a 9x13-inch baking pan, toss lamb with oil, lemon juice and garlic. Bake in a 400° oven for 20 minutes. Remove lamb from oven. Reduce temperature to 350°.

Stir together the remaining ingredients and place over the lamb. Cover pan tightly with foil and bake for about 1 1/2 hours or until lamb is tender. Serve with brown rice or on a bed of buttered noodles. Oven-Baked Toasted Barley with Onions is very good, too. Serves 6.

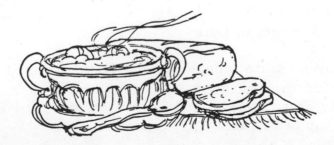

Butterflied Leg of Lamb with Lemon, Garlic & Dill Sauce

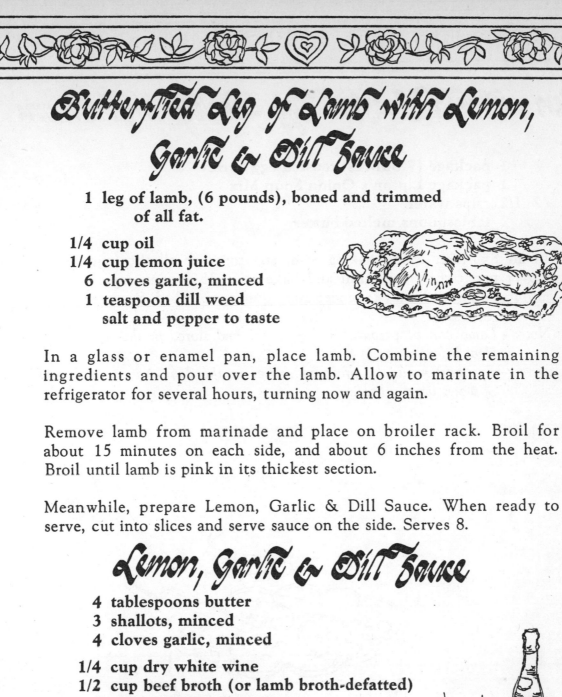

1 leg of lamb, (6 pounds), boned and trimmed of all fat.

1/4 cup oil
1/4 cup lemon juice
6 cloves garlic, minced
1 teaspoon dill weed
salt and pepper to taste

In a glass or enamel pan, place lamb. Combine the remaining ingredients and pour over the lamb. Allow to marinate in the refrigerator for several hours, turning now and again.

Remove lamb from marinade and place on broiler rack. Broil for about 15 minutes on each side, and about 6 inches from the heat. Broil until lamb is pink in its thickest section.

Meanwhile, prepare Lemon, Garlic & Dill Sauce. When ready to serve, cut into slices and serve sauce on the side. Serves 8.

Lemon, Garlic & Dill Sauce

4 tablespoons butter
3 shallots, minced
4 cloves garlic, minced

1/4 cup dry white wine
1/2 cup beef broth (or lamb broth-defatted)
1 teaspoon Bovril
1 tablespoon lemon juice
1/2 teaspoon dill weed
1 teaspoon chopped parsley
1 teaspoon chopped chives

Saute shallots and garlic in butter until shallots are tender. Add wine and simmer mixture until wine has evaporated. Add the remaining ingredients and simmer sauce for 2 or 3 minutes. Serve hot. Yields about 3/4 cup sauce.

Note: - Sauce can be made 1 day earlier and stored in the refrigerator. Heat before serving.
- Lamb can be marinated overnight.

Oven~Baked Toasted Egg Barley with Onions

1 package (7 ounces) toasted egg barley
1 package Lipton's Onion Soup Mix
2 1/2 cups water
2 tablespoons melted butter

In an 8x3-inch round baking dish, stir together all the ingredients. Cover pan tightly with foil and bake in a 350° oven for about 45 minutes or until barley is tender and liquid is absorbed. Serves 6.

Note: - Lamb can be prepared 1 day earlier and stored in the refrigerator. Heat before serving.
 - Egg barley can be prepared earlier in the day. Add a few drops of water when reheating.

Roast Leg of Lamb with Lemon, Garlic & Yogurt

1 leg of lamb, about 5 pounds, boned, sprinkled
    with salt and pepper
1 cup yogurt
1 onion, finely chopped
1/4 cup oil
3 tablespoons lemon juice
3 cloves garlic, minced
1/2 teaspoon dill weed

In a ceramic or plastic bowl, place the leg of lamb. Combine the remaining ingredients and spread it on all sides of the lamb. Cover the bowl with plastic wrap and refrigerate it overnight. The next day, turn it once or twice, so that it marinates evenly.

Lay the boned lamb in a 9x13-inch roasting pan, and spread the yogurt mixture on the cut side of the lamb. Roast the lamb, skin side down, in a 350° oven for about 1 1/2 hours or until a meat thermometer, inserted in the fleshiest part of the lamb, registers 165° for medium and 150° for medium rare.

Remove any trace of fat from the juices, slice the lamb and drizzle the natural juices over the lamb. Serve with rice seasoned with lemon and dill, or brown rice with lentils. Cucumber salad is a nice accompaniment. Serves 6 to 8.

Note: - When I last made the lamb, I roasted it in the following manner. It was a bit unconventional, but the results were so excellent, that I will share them with you. To avoid last minute reheating, I started the lamb about 3 hours before serving. I roasted it at 350° for 1 hour, reduced the oven temperature to 150° and continued roasting for 2 hours. Somewhere, in between, I defatted the natural juices, and at serving time, the lamb was pink and juicy and perfect for serving. Carve it at the table and serve with pride.

    - Whichever method you choose, be certain to check your meat thermometer for the degree of doneness.

Casserole of Pork & Onions with Sauerkraut & Apples

1 1/2 pounds boneless pork roast, cut into 3/4-inch
         cubes. Sprinkle meat with salt and
         garlic powder
2 onions, chopped
1 jar (1 pound) sauerkraut
1 jar (1 pound) sweet and sour red cabbage
2 apples, peeled and grated
1/2 cup yellow raisins
3 tablespoons brown sugar

Combine all the ingredients in a Dutch oven casserole and simmer mixture until meat is tender. (Time will depend on cut of pork you are using.) Serve with crusty black bread to soak up the delicious gravy. Serves 4 to 5.

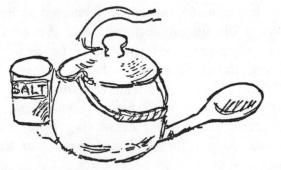

Honey & Currant Glazed Pork Roast with Baked Apples

1   loin of pork roast (about 4 to 5 pounds.) Ask butcher to remove chine bone. Sprinkle with salt and garlic powder.

6   apples, cored and cut into halves

1/2   cup currant jelly
1/2   cup honey
1   teaspoon Dijon-style mustard
2   tablespoons lemon juice

Place roast in a roasting pan, bone side down. Roast it in a 350° oven for about 2 hours. Now, place apples, cut side up around the roast, and continue baking for about 30 minutes.

Combine currant jelly, honey, mustard and lemon juice in a saucepan and heat until mixture is blended. Brush roast and apples with this glaze during the last 30 minutes of baking. Use a thermometer inserted in the thickest part of the meat (do not touch the bone) and internal temperature of pork should be about 175°. Pork and apples should be highly glazed.

Serve with brown rice and sweet and sour red cabbage. Serves about 4 to 5.

Note: - Please make certain that pork is well done.

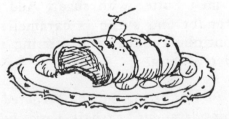

Apple Glazed Pork with Brandied Cream Apples

This is an excellent choice for a special dinner party, yet easy enough to make at any time. Succulent pork, accompanied with brandied apples will turn an ordinary evening into a banquet.

2 pork tenderloins, about 1 1/2 to 2 pounds each. Sprinkle with salt, pepper, garlic powder and paprika.

1 cup apple jelly
1/4 cup orange juice
2 teaspoons Dijon mustard

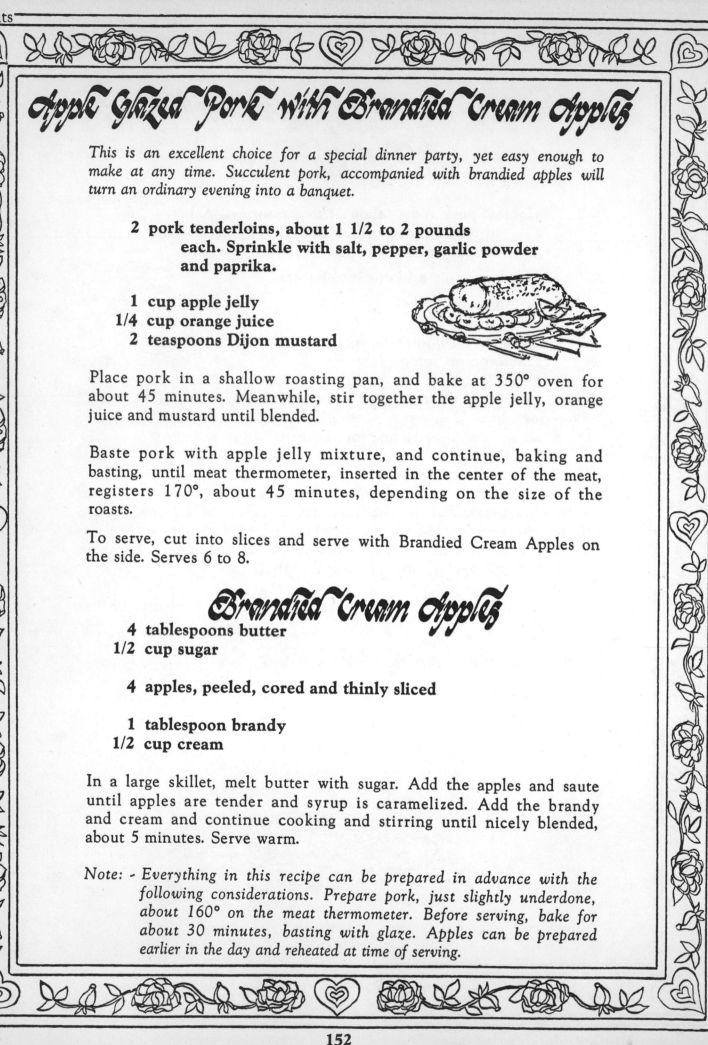

Place pork in a shallow roasting pan, and bake at 350° oven for about 45 minutes. Meanwhile, stir together the apple jelly, orange juice and mustard until blended.

Baste pork with apple jelly mixture, and continue, baking and basting, until meat thermometer, inserted in the center of the meat, registers 170°, about 45 minutes, depending on the size of the roasts.

To serve, cut into slices and serve with Brandied Cream Apples on the side. Serves 6 to 8.

Brandied Cream Apples

4 tablespoons butter
1/2 cup sugar

4 apples, peeled, cored and thinly sliced

1 tablespoon brandy
1/2 cup cream

In a large skillet, melt butter with sugar. Add the apples and saute until apples are tender and syrup is caramelized. Add the brandy and cream and continue cooking and stirring until nicely blended, about 5 minutes. Serve warm.

Note: - Everything in this recipe can be prepared in advance with the following considerations. Prepare pork, just slightly underdone, about 160° on the meat thermometer. Before serving, bake for about 30 minutes, basting with glaze. Apples can be prepared earlier in the day and reheated at time of serving.

Sweet & Sour Pork Loin Chops with Raisins

This is an especially good dish to serve with dumplings, a grand accompaniment to the delicious gravy. It is a good choice for an informal dinner. Sweet and sour red cabbage is traditional with this dish.

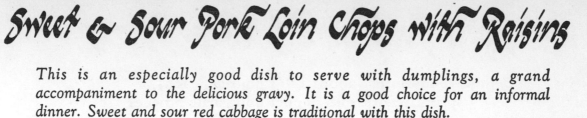

- 1/4 cup brown sugar
- 1/4 cup vinegar
- 1 large onion, chopped
- 2 cloves garlic, minced
- 1/2 cup yellow raisins
- 1 bay leaf
- 6 peppercorns
- 1/8 teaspoon ground cloves
- 1 can (10 1/2 ounces) chicken broth
  salt and pepper to taste

- 2 pounds pork loin chops (about 4 chops)
  trimmed of all fat

- 1/4 cup ginger snap cookie crumbs

In a Dutch oven, combine first 10 ingredients and bring mixture to a boil. Place chops in pan, cover and simmer mixture for about 2 hours or until meat is tender. Remove every trace of fat from the gravy.

Add the ginger snap crumbs, 1 tablespoon at a time, until gravy is slightly thickened. Cook for 1 minute. Serve with dumplings or potato pancakes with applesauce. Serves 4.

Note: - This dish improves with age, and is very delicious when made 1 day earlier and stored in the refrigerator.

Roast Pork with Apples & Prunes

2 pork tenderloins (about 1 1/2 pounds, each),
    sprinkle with salt, pepper and garlic powder

3 apples, peeled, cored and sliced
1 package (6 ounces) pitted prunes
1 carrot, grated
1 onion, finely chopped
    salt and pepper to taste

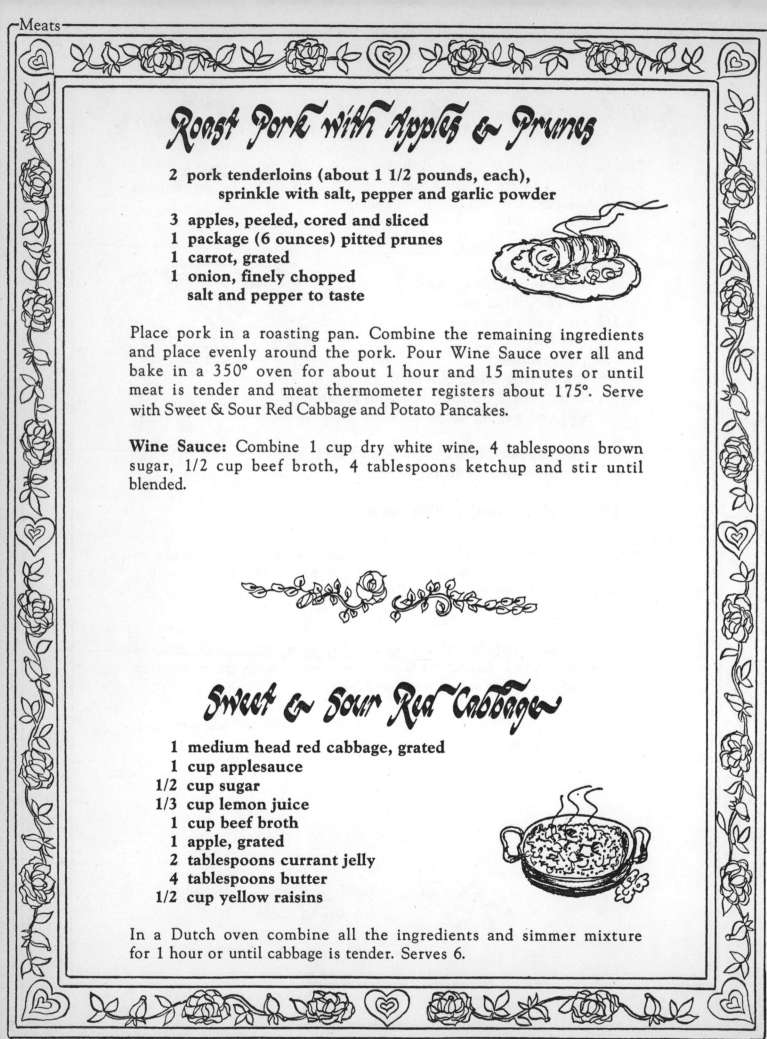

Place pork in a roasting pan. Combine the remaining ingredients and place evenly around the pork. Pour Wine Sauce over all and bake in a 350° oven for about 1 hour and 15 minutes or until meat is tender and meat thermometer registers about 175°. Serve with Sweet & Sour Red Cabbage and Potato Pancakes.

Wine Sauce: Combine 1 cup dry white wine, 4 tablespoons brown sugar, 1/2 cup beef broth, 4 tablespoons ketchup and stir until blended.

Sweet & Sour Red Cabbage

1 medium head red cabbage, grated
1 cup applesauce
1/2 cup sugar
1/3 cup lemon juice
1 cup beef broth
1 apple, grated
2 tablespoons currant jelly
4 tablespoons butter
1/2 cup yellow raisins

In a Dutch oven combine all the ingredients and simmer mixture for 1 hour or until cabbage is tender. Serves 6.

Honey Plum Barbecued Spareribs

**4 pounds pork spareribs, cut into 2-rib pieces
and sprinkled generously with salt**

Honey Plum Barbecue Sauce

In a large Dutch oven, cook pork in simmering water for 30 minutes. Remove meat from pan and discard water.

Place the partially cooked pork in a roasting pan and baste on all sides with Honey Plum Barbecue Sauce. Bake in a 350° oven, basting often with the barbecue sauce, for about 30 minutes or until the ribs are cooked through. Serves 4.

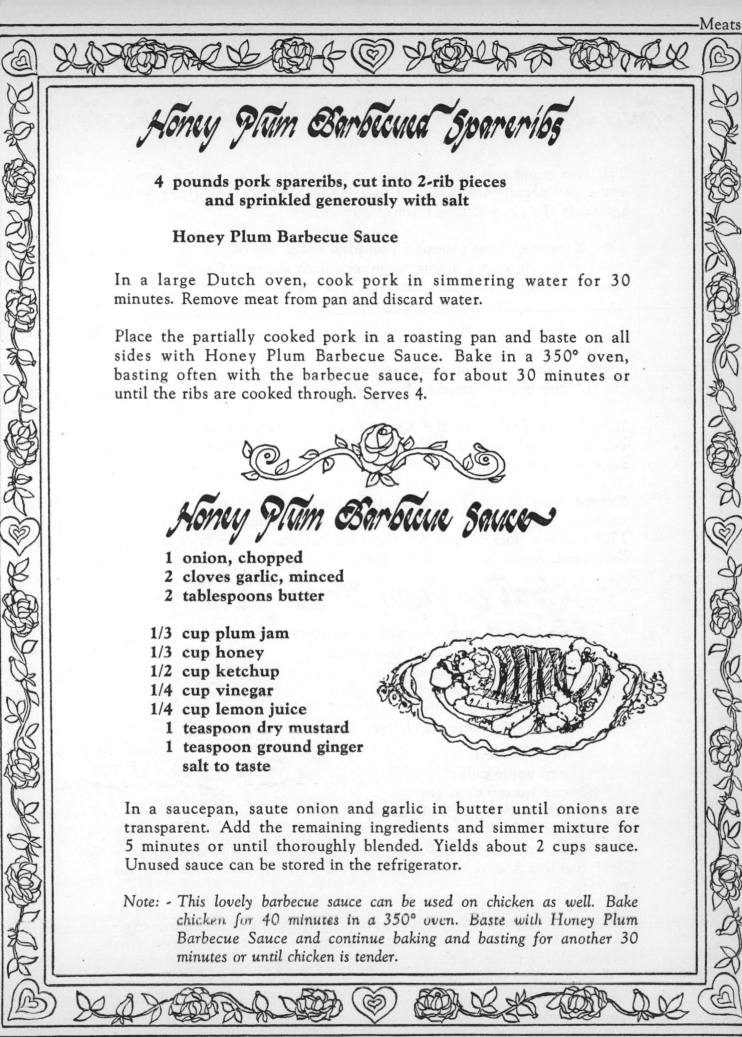

Honey Plum Barbecue Sauce

1 onion, chopped
2 cloves garlic, minced
2 tablespoons butter

1/3 cup plum jam
1/3 cup honey
1/2 cup ketchup
1/4 cup vinegar
1/4 cup lemon juice
1 teaspoon dry mustard
1 teaspoon ground ginger
salt to taste

In a saucepan, saute onion and garlic in butter until onions are transparent. Add the remaining ingredients and simmer mixture for 5 minutes or until thoroughly blended. Yields about 2 cups sauce. Unused sauce can be stored in the refrigerator.

Note: - This lovely barbecue sauce can be used on chicken as well. Bake chicken for 40 minutes in a 350° oven. Baste with Honey Plum Barbecue Sauce and continue baking and basting for another 30 minutes or until chicken is tender.

Honey ~ Baked Ham with Apple & Pecan Pudding

This is a grand way to serve ham, accompanied with a deeply fragrant apple and pecan pudding. The pudding is basically a stuffing baked separately. This is good served with chicken or turkey.

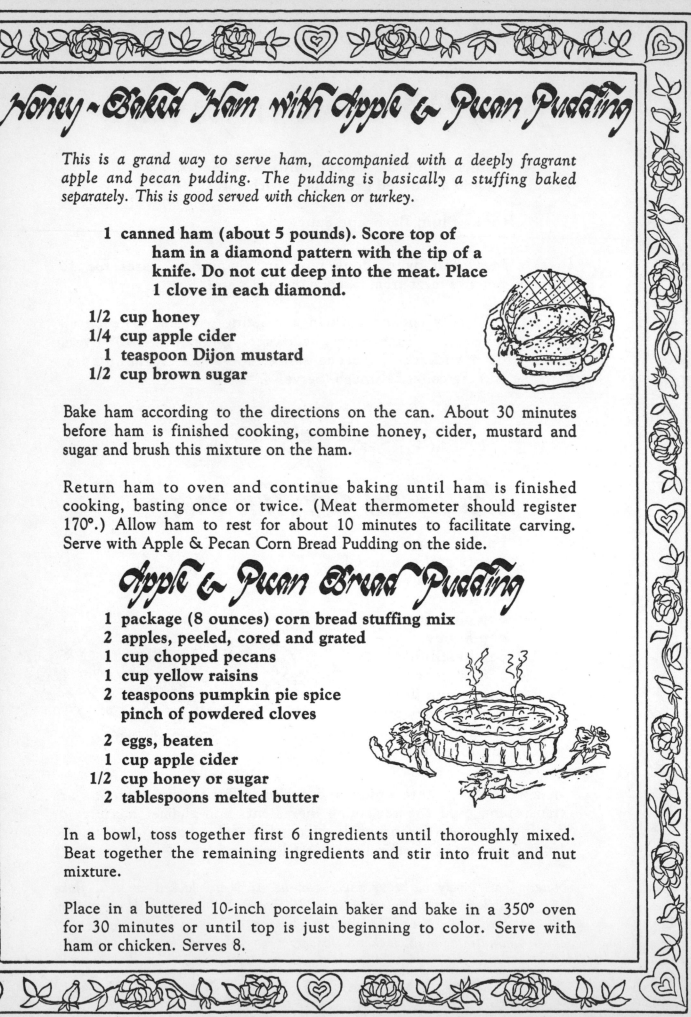

1 canned ham (about 5 pounds). Score top of
ham in a diamond pattern with the tip of a
knife. Do not cut deep into the meat. Place
1 clove in each diamond.

1/2 cup honey
1/4 cup apple cider
1 teaspoon Dijon mustard
1/2 cup brown sugar

Bake ham according to the directions on the can. About 30 minutes before ham is finished cooking, combine honey, cider, mustard and sugar and brush this mixture on the ham.

Return ham to oven and continue baking until ham is finished cooking, basting once or twice. (Meat thermometer should register 170°.) Allow ham to rest for about 10 minutes to facilitate carving. Serve with Apple & Pecan Corn Bread Pudding on the side.

Apple & Pecan Bread Pudding

1 package (8 ounces) corn bread stuffing mix
2 apples, peeled, cored and grated
1 cup chopped pecans
1 cup yellow raisins
2 teaspoons pumpkin pie spice
   pinch of powdered cloves

2 eggs, beaten
1 cup apple cider
1/2 cup honey or sugar
2 tablespoons melted butter

In a bowl, toss together first 6 ingredients until thoroughly mixed. Beat together the remaining ingredients and stir into fruit and nut mixture.

Place in a buttered 10-inch porcelain baker and bake in a 350° oven for 30 minutes or until top is just beginning to color. Serve with ham or chicken. Serves 8.

Teriyaki Pork Roast with Honey Apple Glaze

2 pork tenderloins (about 1 1/2 pounds, each),
    sprinkle with salt and pepper
6 apples, peeled, cored and cut into halves
1/2 cup apple jelly
1/2 cup honey
1/2 cup apple juice
1/4 cup teriyaki marinade
1 teaspoon ground ginger
1 teaspoon dry mustard
1 tablespoon lemon juice
    salt and pepper to taste

Place pork and apples in a roasting pan and bake in a 350° oven for 30 minutes. Meanwhile combine the remaining ingredients in a saucepan and heat until blended.

Baste pork and apples with honey mixture, every 15 minutes until meat is tender and meat thermometer registers about 175°, about another 40 minutes. Serve with Fried Rice with Green Onions. Serves 6.

Fried Rice with Green Onions

1 cup long grain rice
1 can (10 1/2 ounces) beef broth
1 tablespoon teriyaki marinade (or soy sauce)
1 cup water
    salt and pepper to taste
2 tablespoons butter

Combine all the ingredients in a saucepan. Cover and simmer mixture until rice is tender and liquid is absorbed. When rice is cooked, add:

1/2 cup finely chopped green onions
1 egg (which has been scrambled and cooked in
    1 tablespoon butter)
1/4 cup toasted slivered almonds
6 strips bacon, cooked crisp, drained and crumbled

Toss everything together until nicely blended. Place rice in a porcelain baker and serve with the pork and apples. Serves 6.

Fluffy Pork Dumplings in Brandy Apple Cream

This is a fairly economical dish that imparts elegance to ground pork. If you are splurging one evening, the sauce can be used with medallions of pork tenderloin for a truly exquisite dish.

Pork Dumplings:

1 1/2 pounds ground pork, very lean
1 small onion, grated
1/4 teaspoon garlic powder
4 slices egg bread, crusts removed. Soak bread in water and squeeze dry.
2 eggs
salt and pepper to taste

Combine all the ingredients in a large bowl and blend, with a wooden spoon (if you do not like to use your hands.) Shape mixture, with moistened hands, into 1-inch balls. Saute pork dumplings in a skillet, until browned on all sides.

Place meatballs in a Dutch oven casserole and spoon Brandy Apple Cream Sauce on the top. Cook for 15 minutes or until heated through. Serves 6.

Brandy Apple Cream Sauce

2 apples, peeled, cored and sliced
1 onion, finely chopped
1 tablespoon sugar
2 tablespoons butter

1 cup apple juice
1/2 cup cream
1 tablespoon Cognac or brandy

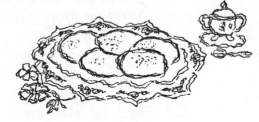

In a skillet, saute apples and onion in sugar and butter until apples are soft. Add the apple juice, cream and brandy and simmer mixture for 10 minutes or until sauce has thickened. Yields about 2 cups sauce.

Note: - If you are using medallions or scallops of pork tenderloin, then dust them with seasoned flour and saute them for a few minutes on each side. Place in a shallow porcelain baker and spoon sauce on top. Heat in a 350° oven until heated through. This can be prepared earlier in the day and heated at serving time.

Osso Bucco alla Milanese

Try this marvelous recipe one night soon. It is such fun to pick the meat off the bones and scoop out every little morsel of marrow. The Gremolada is optional. The results are rich and glorious without it, but I am adding the information on the Gremolada at the very end, in the event you may like to try it.

3 **veal shanks (also called shinbones) about 6 pounds. Ask the butcher to saw them into 3-inch pieces. Sprinkle them with salt and pepper and lightly dust with flour.**

6 **medium onions, cut into fourths and separated into single pieces.**

2 **cans (1 pound, each) stewed tomatoes, chopped. Discard seeds.**

1 **can (8 ounces) tomato paste**

1 **cup dry white wine**

2 **teaspoons beef stock base**

1 **carrot, finely grated**

1 **tablespoon sugar**

3 **tablespoons olive oil**

4 **cloves garlic, minced**

1/2 **teaspoon each, oregano, basil and thyme (or 1 1/2 teaspoons Italian Herb Seasoning) salt and pepper to taste**

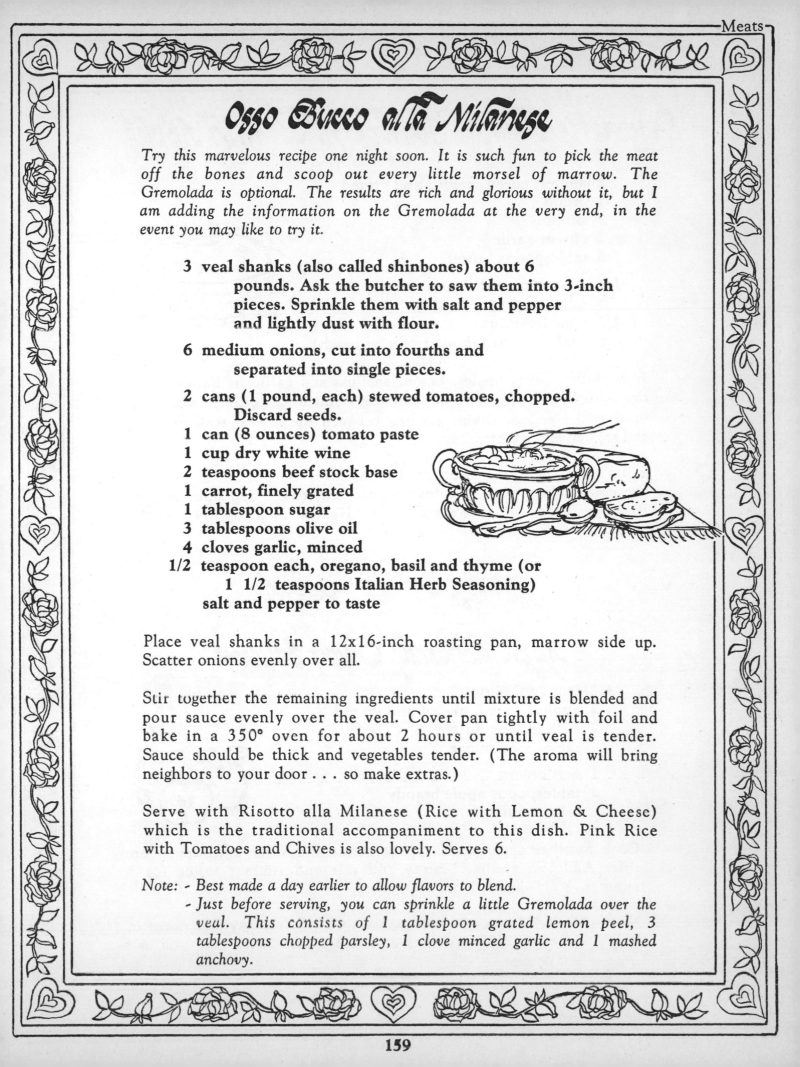

Place veal shanks in a 12x16-inch roasting pan, marrow side up. Scatter onions evenly over all.

Stir together the remaining ingredients until mixture is blended and pour sauce evenly over the veal. Cover pan tightly with foil and bake in a 350° oven for about 2 hours or until veal is tender. Sauce should be thick and vegetables tender. (The aroma will bring neighbors to your door . . . so make extras.)

Serve with Risotto alla Milanese (Rice with Lemon & Cheese) which is the traditional accompaniment to this dish. Pink Rice with Tomatoes and Chives is also lovely. Serves 6.

Note: - Best made a day earlier to allow flavors to blend.
- Just before serving, you can sprinkle a little Gremolada over the veal. This consists of 1 tablespoon grated lemon peel, 3 tablespoons chopped parsley, 1 clove minced garlic and 1 mashed anchovy.

Paupiettes of Veal Scallops filled with Apples

2 apples, cored, peeled and grated
1 onion
3 shallots
2 cloves garlic
6 tablespoons butter

1/2 teaspoon poultry seasoning
   salt and pepper to taste
1 1/2 cups fresh bread crumbs
8 veal scallops (about 3 ounces, each)

In a skillet, saute apples, onion, shallots and garlic in butter until the onions are soft. Stir in seasonings and bread crumbs and toss until well blended. Divide stuffing between the 8 veal scallops, roll and skewer with a toothpick.

Saute veal rolls in butter until meat loses its pinkness. Do not overcook. Place veal in a lovely porcelain baker and pour Apple Brandy Cream Sauce over the top. Heat in a 350° oven until heated through. Serves 4.

Apple Brandy Cream Sauce

1/2 cup apple juice
2 apples, cored, peeled and grated
2 tablespoons butter
1 tablespoon sugar

1 cup cream
2 tablespoons apple brandy
   salt to taste

Cook together apple juice, apples, butter and sugar until apples are soft. Add the cream, brandy and salt and simmer sauce for 5 minutes. Yields about 1 1/2 cups sauce.

Note: - Veal and sauce can be cooked earlier in the day and stored in the refrigerator. At time of serving, pour sauce over veal and heat through.

Royal Veal Ring with Mushrooms & Cinnamon Rice

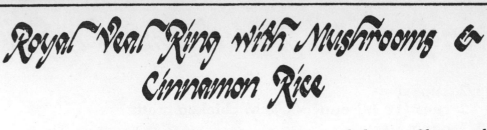

What a nice, homey dish to serve for a casual dinner. Shaping the veal into a ring adds a touch of glamor. Fill the center with Cinnamon Rice or buttered vegetables.

1 1/2 pounds ground veal
  1/2 pound ground pork
    1 medium onion, grated or very finely
         chopped in food processor
  1/4 pound mushrooms, thinly sliced. Place
         in a kitchen towel and squeeze out
         some of the liquid.
    3 slices fresh egg bread, moistened in
         water and squeezed dry
    1 carrot, peeled and finely grated
    1 cup sour cream
    1 egg
       salt and pepper to taste

Combine all the ingredients in a large bowl and mix until blended. Butter and flour a ring mold and place meat evenly in mold. Place on a cookie sheet and bake in a 350° oven for about 1 hour or until meat is cooked through. Ease the sides of the mold with a knife and invert onto serving platter. Fill center with rice or vegetables. Serves 8.

Note: - Veal ring can be prepared earlier in the day and reheated at time of serving.

Cinnamon Rice with Toasted Almonds & Raisins

1 1/2   cups rice
    2   cans (10 1/2 ounces, each) chicken broth
1/2   cup water
1/4   cup butter (1/2 stick)
1/8   teaspoon cinnamon
      salt to taste

1/2   cup chopped toasted almonds
1/2   cup yellow raisins, plumped in boiling
      water and drained

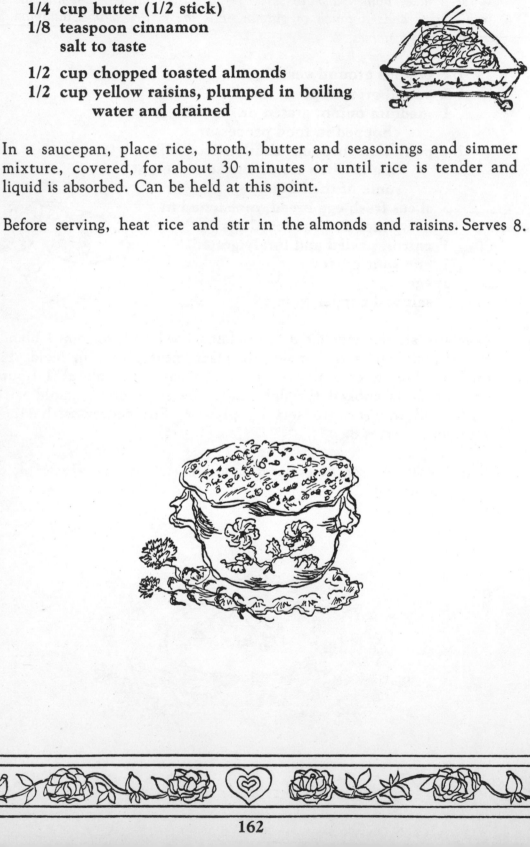

In a saucepan, place rice, broth, butter and seasonings and simmer mixture, covered, for about 30 minutes or until rice is tender and liquid is absorbed. Can be held at this point.

Before serving, heat rice and stir in the almonds and raisins. Serves 8.

Veal Roast Persillade with Garlic, Tomato & Wine Sauce

1   boneless veal roast (about 3 1/2 pounds), from the
      leg, rolled and tied. (Butcher can do this
      for you.) Sprinkle with salt and pepper.
3/4 cup herb seasoned stuffing mix
1/4 cup chopped parsley
6   cloves garlic
1/3 cup grated Parmesan cheese
3   tablespoons lemon juice
3   tablespoons olive oil
1   teaspoon sweet basil flakes

Place roast in a 9x13-inch roasting pan. Combine the remaining ingredients in a food processor and blend until mixture is finely minced. Pat mixture over the roast. Pour Garlic Tomato Wine Sauce around the meat and bake in a 325° oven for about 1 hour 15 minutes or until meat is tender. Remove strings, carve into 1/4-inch slices and serve with a spoonful of sauce over all. Have some crusty Italian bread close by to soak up the delicious gravy. Serves 6 to 8.

Garlic, Tomato & Wine Sauce

2   onions, finely chopped
2   carrots, grated
2   cloves garlic, minced
2   tablespoons oil
1   can (1 pound) stewed tomatoes, chopped
3   tablespoons tomato paste
1/2 cup dry white wine
1/2 teaspoon sweet basil flakes
2   teaspoons sugar
2   teaspoons lemon juice

In a bowl, stir together all the ingredients until blended.

Note: - A veal roast, cut from the leg, is very tender and cooks rapidly. It is however, very expensive. If you use the shoulder cut, it is equally delicious and about 1/2 the price. In this case, you would follow the above instructions, except the pan must be tightly covered with foil. Increase baking time to about 2 hours.

Dilled Veal with Onions & Mushrooms & Creme Fraiche

This is a grand dish to serve family and friends. I enjoy preparing it with veal scallops. They are tender and succulent, but expensive. You can use a less expensive cut of veal. In this case, saute the veal and then cook it with the vegetables for 1 1/2 hours.

1 1/2 pounds veal scallops, cut into 1-inch pieces. Season with salt and white pepper.

2 tablespoons butter
1 large onion, chopped
2 cloves garlic, minced
1/2 pound mushrooms, sliced
3 medium carrots, grated
2 shallots, finely chopped
2 tablespoons butter

1/4 cup dry white wine
3 tablespoons flour

1/2 teaspoon dried dill weed
1 can (10 1/2 ounces) chicken broth

1 cup Creme Fraiche

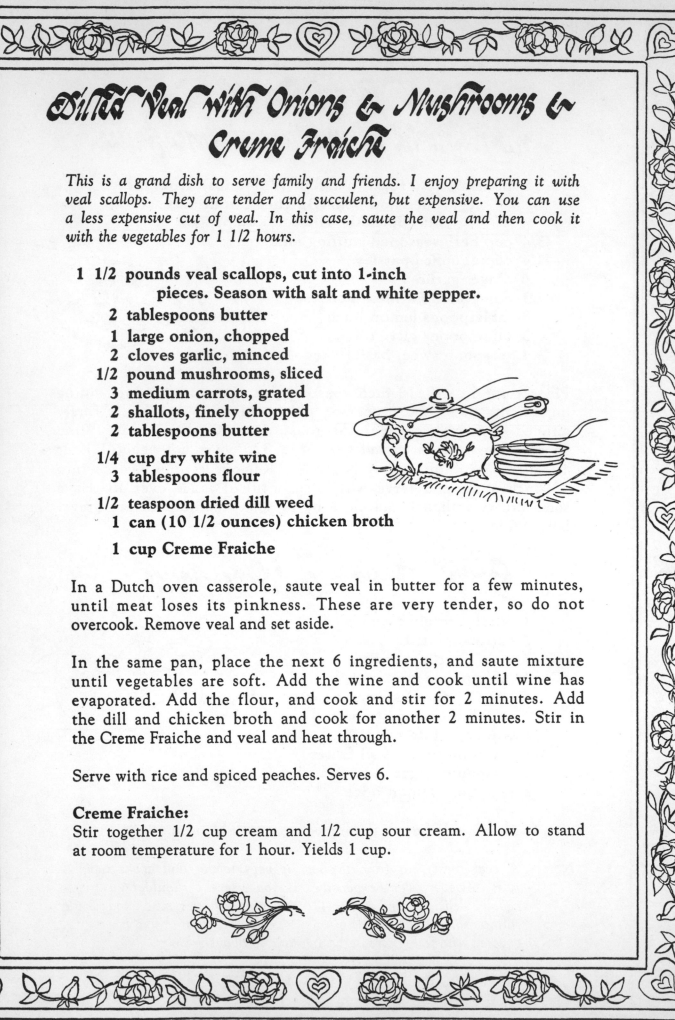

In a Dutch oven casserole, saute veal in butter for a few minutes, until meat loses its pinkness. These are very tender, so do not overcook. Remove veal and set aside.

In the same pan, place the next 6 ingredients, and saute mixture until vegetables are soft. Add the wine and cook until wine has evaporated. Add the flour, and cook and stir for 2 minutes. Add the dill and chicken broth and cook for another 2 minutes. Stir in the Creme Fraiche and veal and heat through.

Serve with rice and spiced peaches. Serves 6.

Creme Fraiche:
Stir together 1/2 cup cream and 1/2 cup sour cream. Allow to stand at room temperature for 1 hour. Yields 1 cup.

Chicken Delights

Chicken Casserole with Small White Onions & Carrots

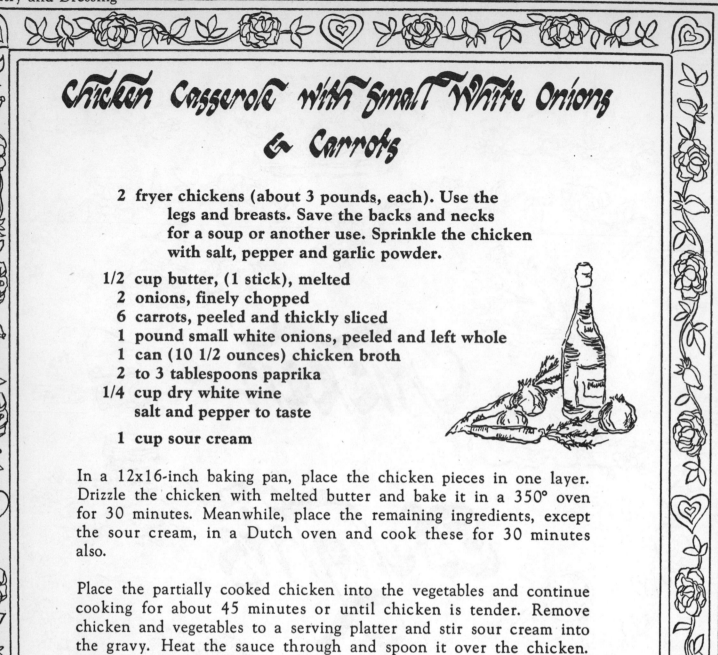

2 fryer chickens (about 3 pounds, each). Use the
   legs and breasts. Save the backs and necks
   for a soup or another use. Sprinkle the chicken
   with salt, pepper and garlic powder.

1/2 cup butter, (1 stick), melted
2 onions, finely chopped
6 carrots, peeled and thickly sliced
1 pound small white onions, peeled and left whole
1 can (10 1/2 ounces) chicken broth
2 to 3 tablespoons paprika
1/4 cup dry white wine
   salt and pepper to taste

1 cup sour cream

In a 12x16-inch baking pan, place the chicken pieces in one layer.
Drizzle the chicken with melted butter and bake it in a 350° oven
for 30 minutes. Meanwhile, place the remaining ingredients, except
the sour cream, in a Dutch oven and cook these for 30 minutes
also.

Place the partially cooked chicken into the vegetables and continue
cooking for about 45 minutes or until chicken is tender. Remove
chicken and vegetables to a serving platter and stir sour cream into
the gravy. Heat the sauce through and spoon it over the chicken.
Do not boil the sauce.

Serve over noodles. Rice is good, too. Serves 6.

Note: - You can add 1 chopped tomato and 1 small green pepper chopped
     to the vegetable mixture. It adds a totally different character to
     this dish and is very good.
    - Entire dish can be prepared earlier in the day and even 1 day
     earlier. Add the sour cram just before serving.

Moroccan Chicken with Carrots & Apples & Cous Cous with Cici Peas

This is a variation of my Moroccan Lamb, but it is so good, it is worth repeating. While the recipe seems lengthy, it is quite simple to prepare and the results will make it all worthwhile. The entire dish can be prepared 1 day earlier and carefully reheated at time of serving. This is an excellent choice for dinner with family and friends. Green Onion Flat Bread goes well with this.

3 pounds chicken wings, tips removed and split at the joints. Sprinkle with salt and garlic powder. Baste with a little butter and bake in a 350° oven for 40 minutes.

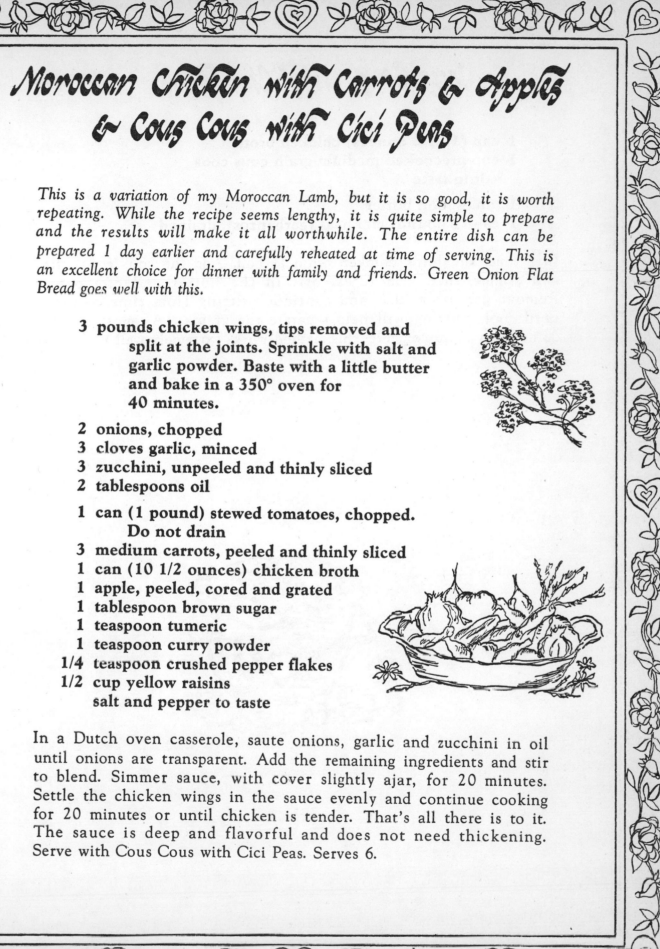

2 onions, chopped
3 cloves garlic, minced
3 zucchini, unpeeled and thinly sliced
2 tablespoons oil

1 can (1 pound) stewed tomatoes, chopped. Do not drain
3 medium carrots, peeled and thinly sliced
1 can (10 1/2 ounces) chicken broth
1 apple, peeled, cored and grated
1 tablespoon brown sugar
1 teaspoon tumeric
1 teaspoon curry powder
1/4 teaspoon crushed pepper flakes
1/2 cup yellow raisins
salt and pepper to taste

In a Dutch oven casserole, saute onions, garlic and zucchini in oil until onions are transparent. Add the remaining ingredients and stir to blend. Simmer sauce, with cover slightly ajar, for 20 minutes. Settle the chicken wings in the sauce evenly and continue cooking for 20 minutes or until chicken is tender. That's all there is to it. The sauce is deep and flavorful and does not need thickening. Serve with Cous Cous with Cici Peas. Serves 6.

Cous Cous with Cici Peas

1 can (10 1/2 ounces) chicken broth
1 cup precooked medium-grain cous cous
salt to taste

1 tablespoon butter
1 can (1 pound) cici peas (garbanzos), drained

In a saucepan, bring chicken broth to boil. Add the cous cous, stir and simmer for 3 minutes. Stir in the butter and cici peas. Remove pan from heat and continue stirring from time to time until cool. Stirring will help separate the grains. (As most people do not own a couscousiere, this method works extremely well.)

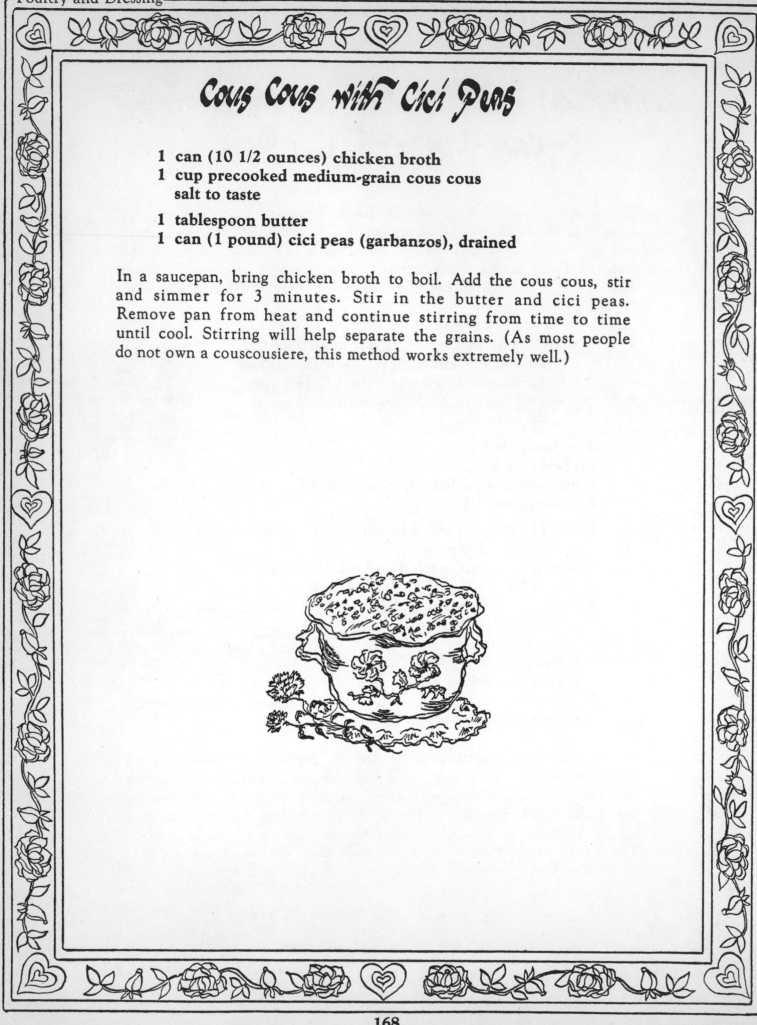

Chicken Breasts alla Parmigiana in a Light Tomato Sauce

This is a grand dish to serve family or friends. It is just bursting with flavor and goodness. Entire dish can be prepared earlier in the day and baked before serving.

12 half chicken breasts, boned, skinned and
    pounded gently to flatten.

2 cups bread crumbs
1 cup grated Parmesan cheese
1/2 teaspoon garlic powder
1 teaspoon paprika
    salt and pepper to taste
2 eggs, beaten

In a plastic bag, place crumbs, cheese, garlic powder, paprika and seasonings, and shake to blend. Dip chicken breasts into beaten egg and then into crumb mixture, coating evenly. Place on waxed paper, in one layer. Saute breasts in butter, until browned on both sides.

Light Tomato Sauce:
1 onion, finely chopped
2 cloves garlic, minced
2 tablespoons oil

1 can (1 pound 12 ounces) crushed tomatoes in
    tomato puree
1 tablespoon sugar
1 teaspoon Italian Herb Seasoning
1/2 teaspoon sweet basil flakes
    salt and pepper to taste

Saute onion and garlic in oil until onions are soft. Add the remaining ingredients and simmer sauce for 10 minutes, with cover slightly ajar.

To Assemble:
Spoon a little sauce in a 12x16-inch roasting pan. Place chicken breasts in pan in one layer. Sprinkle top with 8 ounces of grated Mozzarella cheese and 1/2 cup grated Parmesan cheese. Spoon remaining sauce on top. Bake at 350° for 20 minutes or until heated through and cheese is melted. Serves 12.

Easiest & Best Hungarian Chicken with Onions & Sour Cream

        2 onions, finely chopped
        3 tablespoons butter
        2 tablespoons brown sugar

   1/4 cup dry white wine

        1 can (10 1/2 ounces) chicken broth
        1 teaspoon Escoffier's Sauce Robert
        2 tablespoons paprika
          salt and pepper to taste

        2 fryer chickens (about 2 1/2 pounds, each) cut
             up and brushed with 1 tablespoon Dijon mustard
        1 cup sour cream

In a Dutch oven, saute onions in butter with sugar until onions are soft. Add wine and cook for 2 minutes or until wine has evaporated. Add the next 4 ingredients and stir until blended. Arrange chicken pieces over the sauce, cover pan and simmer for 1 hour 15 minutes or until chicken is tender. Just before serving, add sour cream and heat through. Do not boil or sauce will curdle. Serves 8.

Easiest & Best New Orleans Spicy~Hot Fried Chicken

Our friends returned from New Orleans with a huge bagful of spicy, peppery fried chicken, that I must admit was awfully good. As you probably know, I do not have a special fondness for peppery dishes that make your eyes tear and your breath come short. But this chicken, in spite of this, was astonishingly good. I have tried to duplicate it for you, but have cut down on the amount of pepper. If you are "bravo" and stout of heart, double the amount of cayenne pepper.

> 2 **fryer chickens, (about 2 1/2 pounds, each). Ask the butcher to cut each chicken into 10 pieces, (2 legs, 2 thighs, 2 wings and 4 breast pieces.) Save the backs and necks for another use.**
>
> **Pepper Seasoned Coating**
>
> 2 **eggs**
> 2 **tablespoons water**

Roll the chicken pieces in the Pepper Seasoned Coating until they are nicely coated. In a large skillet, heat about 1/2-inch of oil. Beat together the eggs with the water until blended.

Dip the coated chicken pieces in the egg mixture and fry them until they are golden brown on all sides. Drain chicken pieces on absorbent paper and place them in a 12x16-inch roasting pan.

Heat in a 350° oven for about 20 minutes before serving. Serves 8.

Pepper Seasoned Coating

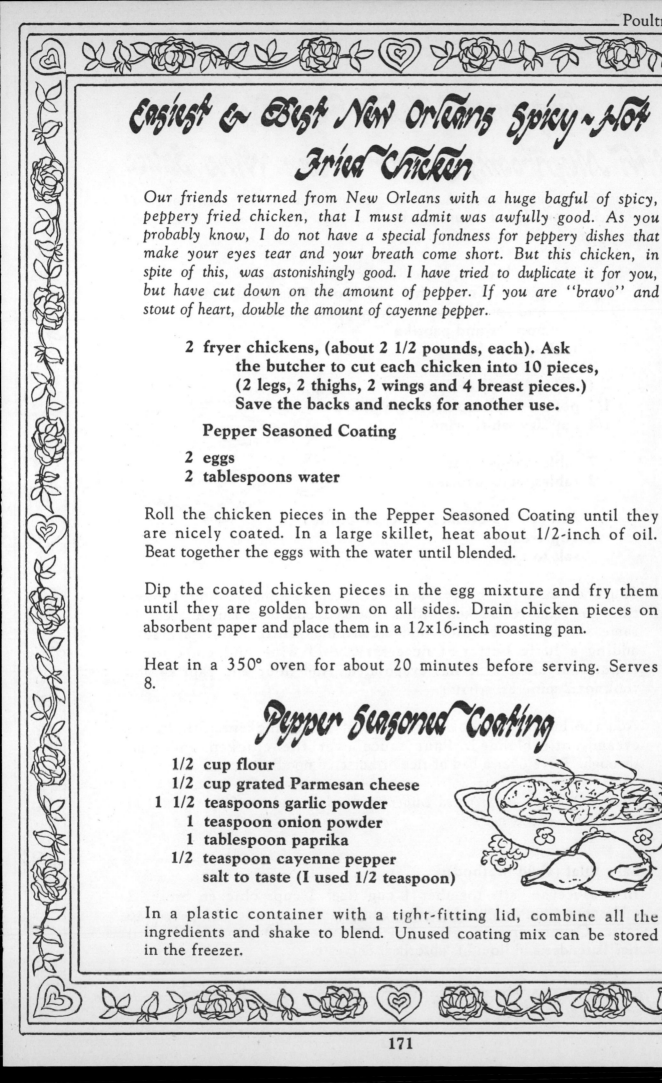

> 1/2 **cup flour**
> 1/2 **cup grated Parmesan cheese**
> 1 1/2 **teaspoons garlic powder**
> 1 **teaspoon onion powder**
> 1 **tablespoon paprika**
> 1/2 **teaspoon cayenne pepper**
> **salt to taste (I used 1/2 teaspoon)**

In a plastic container with a tight-fitting lid, combine all the ingredients and shake to blend. Unused coating mix can be stored in the freezer.

Hungarian Chicken Paprikash with Mushrooms & Sour Cream Wine Sauce

This is a family favorite that is delicate and delicious. Tender morsels of chicken in an elegant cream sauce is just lovely for informal dinners with family or friends.

3 chicken breasts, boned and cut into 1-inch
        pieces. Toss with 1 tablespoon Dijon mustard
        and sprinkle with salt, pepper, garlic
        powder and paprika
4 tablespoons butter

1 onion, finely chopped
1/2 pound mushrooms, thinly sliced
1/4 cup dry white wine

2 tablespoons flour
2 tablespoons paprika

1 can (10 1/2 ounces) chicken broth
1 cup cream
    salt to taste

Saute chicken in butter until chicken is opaque and cooked through. Remove chicken with a slotted spoon to a Dutch oven. In same skillet, saute onion and mushrooms until onions are soft, adding a little butter if necessary. Add wine and cook for 2 minutes or until wine has evaporated. Add flour and paprika and cook for 2 minutes, stirring.

Add the broth and cook stirring until sauce thickens. Stir in the cream until blended. Pour sauce over the chicken and heat through. Serve over a bed of rice or buttered noodles. Serves 6.

Note: - Dish can be prepared earlier in the day, and carefully reheated at time of serving.

Easy Pilaf (Cold Method):

In a saucepan, stir together 1 cup rice, 2 cups chicken broth, 2 tablespoons butter, 1 tablespoon chopped chives, salt and pepper to taste. Cover pan and simmer rice for about 30 minutes or until rice is tender and liquid is absorbed. Serves 6.

Butter Honey Glazed Chicken with Fruit & Rice Stuffing

This is a great dish for a Sunday dinner with family and friends. You could prepare the stuffing separately. In this instance, you can use cut-up chicken parts, eliminating last minute carving at the table.

2 fryer chickens (about 3 pounds, each), sprinkle with salt, pepper and dust lightly with flour. Fill opening with Fruit and Rice Stuffing, skewer the opening and tie legs together.

1/2 cup honey
1/2 cup butter, melted

Place chicken in a roasting pan and bake in a 350° oven for 40 minutes. Combine honey and butter and baste chicken with this mixture. Continue baking and basting until chickens are tender and deeply glazed, about 40 minutes longer. Carve at the table and serve with buttered carrots. Serves 6 to 8.

Fruit & Rice Stuffing

1/2 cup butter (1 stick)
1 large onion, finely chopped
1/2 pound mushrooms, thinly sliced
2 apples, peeled, cored and grated
1/4 cup yellow raisins, chopped
1/2 teaspoon poultry seasoning
    salt to taste

3 cups cooked rice*

In a saucepan, saute together first 7 ingredients until vegetables and apples are tender and most of the liquid rendered is absorbed. Stir in the cooked rice. Enough to fill 2 chickens.

***To prepare Rice:** In a saucepan, simmer together 1 cup long grain rice, 2 tablespoons butter, 1 can (10 1/2 ounces) chicken broth, 1 cup water and salt and pepper to taste, until rice is tender and liquid is abosrbed. Yields 3 cups cooked rice.

Note: - If you are preparing stuffing separately, then place it in a casserole or souffle dish, cover it tightly with foil, and heat it in a 300° oven until heated through.

Apricot Glazed Chicken with Peaches & Raisins

Chicken with fruit is one of the ways to prepare chicken that I admire the most. Somehow, the flavors marry so well. In this case, serve the hot fruit on the side as a lovely accompaniment.

2 fryer chickens, cut into serving pieces (about
    3 pounds, each). Sprinkle lightly with salt and
    garlic powder. Baste with 1/4 cup melted butter.
1 package (12 ounces) dried peaches
3/4 cup yellow raisins
3/4 cup white wine

3/4 cup sieved apricot jam
1/4 cup white wine

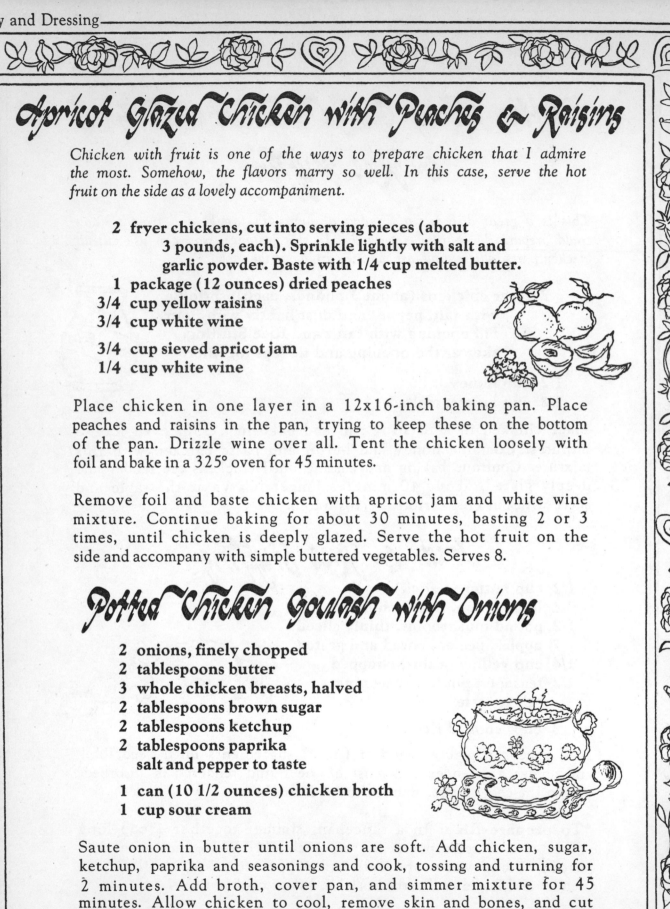

Place chicken in one layer in a 12x16-inch baking pan. Place peaches and raisins in the pan, trying to keep these on the bottom of the pan. Drizzle wine over all. Tent the chicken loosely with foil and bake in a 325° oven for 45 minutes.

Remove foil and baste chicken with apricot jam and white wine mixture. Continue baking for about 30 minutes, basting 2 or 3 times, until chicken is deeply glazed. Serve the hot fruit on the side and accompany with simple buttered vegetables. Serves 8.

Potted Chicken Goulash with Onions

2 onions, finely chopped
2 tablespoons butter
3 whole chicken breasts, halved
2 tablespoons brown sugar
2 tablespoons ketchup
2 tablespoons paprika
    salt and pepper to taste

1 can (10 1/2 ounces) chicken broth
1 cup sour cream

Saute onion in butter until onions are soft. Add chicken, sugar, ketchup, paprika and seasonings and cook, tossing and turning for 2 minutes. Add broth, cover pan, and simmer mixture for 45 minutes. Allow chicken to cool, remove skin and bones, and cut into 1-inch chunks. Return to pan and stir in sour cream, stirring until blended. Heat chicken through, but do not let it boil. Serve on a bed of rice. Serves 4.

Cinnamon Chicken Espagnole with Tomatoes, Raisins & Wine

This is a lovely chicken dish with a Spanish "feel" but very American in style. The sauce is incredibly delicious and the cinnamon adds the nicest accent.

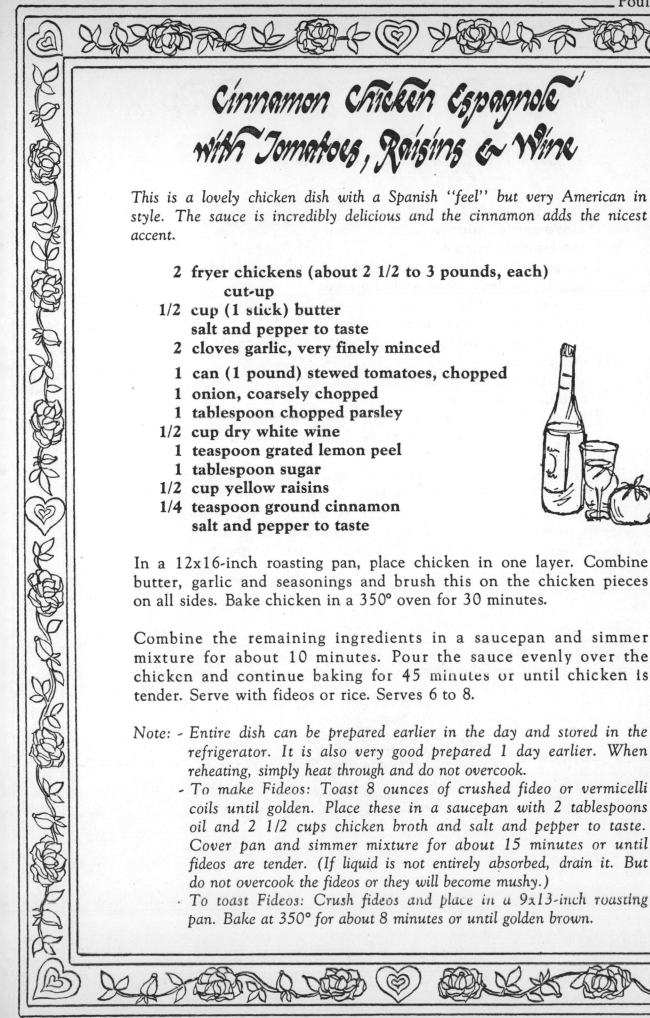

2 **fryer chickens (about 2 1/2 to 3 pounds, each)**
    cut-up
1/2 **cup (1 stick) butter**
    salt and pepper to taste
2 **cloves garlic, very finely minced**

1 **can (1 pound) stewed tomatoes, chopped**
1 **onion, coarsely chopped**
1 **tablespoon chopped parsley**
1/2 **cup dry white wine**
1 **teaspoon grated lemon peel**
1 **tablespoon sugar**
1/2 **cup yellow raisins**
1/4 **teaspoon ground cinnamon**
    salt and pepper to taste

In a 12x16-inch roasting pan, place chicken in one layer. Combine butter, garlic and seasonings and brush this on the chicken pieces on all sides. Bake chicken in a 350° oven for 30 minutes.

Combine the remaining ingredients in a saucepan and simmer mixture for about 10 minutes. Pour the sauce evenly over the chicken and continue baking for 45 minutes or until chicken is tender. Serve with fideos or rice. Serves 6 to 8.

Note: - Entire dish can be prepared earlier in the day and stored in the refrigerator. It is also very good prepared 1 day earlier. When reheating, simply heat through and do not overcook.
- To make Fideos: Toast 8 ounces of crushed fideo or vermicelli coils until golden. Place these in a saucepan with 2 tablespoons oil and 2 1/2 cups chicken broth and salt and pepper to taste. Cover pan and simmer mixture for about 15 minutes or until fideos are tender. (If liquid is not entirely absorbed, drain it. But do not overcook the fideos or they will become mushy.)
- To toast Fideos: Crush fideos and place in a 9x13-inch roasting pan. Bake at 350° for about 8 minutes or until golden brown.

German Style Sweet & Sour Chicken with Apples & Bacon

- 2 onions, chopped
- 1 clove garlic, minced
- 4 tablespoons butter
- 4 strips bacon, cooked crisp, drained and crumbled
- 2 apples, peeled, cored and chopped
- 4 tablespoons cider vinegar
- 4 tablespoons brown sugar
- 4 cups finely grated cabbage (about 1 small head)
- 1/2 cup raisins
  salt and pepper to taste
- 1/2 cup dry white wine
- 2 fryer chickens, (about 3 pounds) cut into
      serving pieces. Do not use backs or necks.

In a Dutch oven casserole place all the ingredients, except the chicken, and bring mixture to a boil. Lower heat and simmer for about 10 minutes, or until cabbage is wilted. Place chicken in casserole, cover pan, and simmer for about 1 hour or until chicken is tender. Serve with potato pancakes or dumplings. Serves 6.

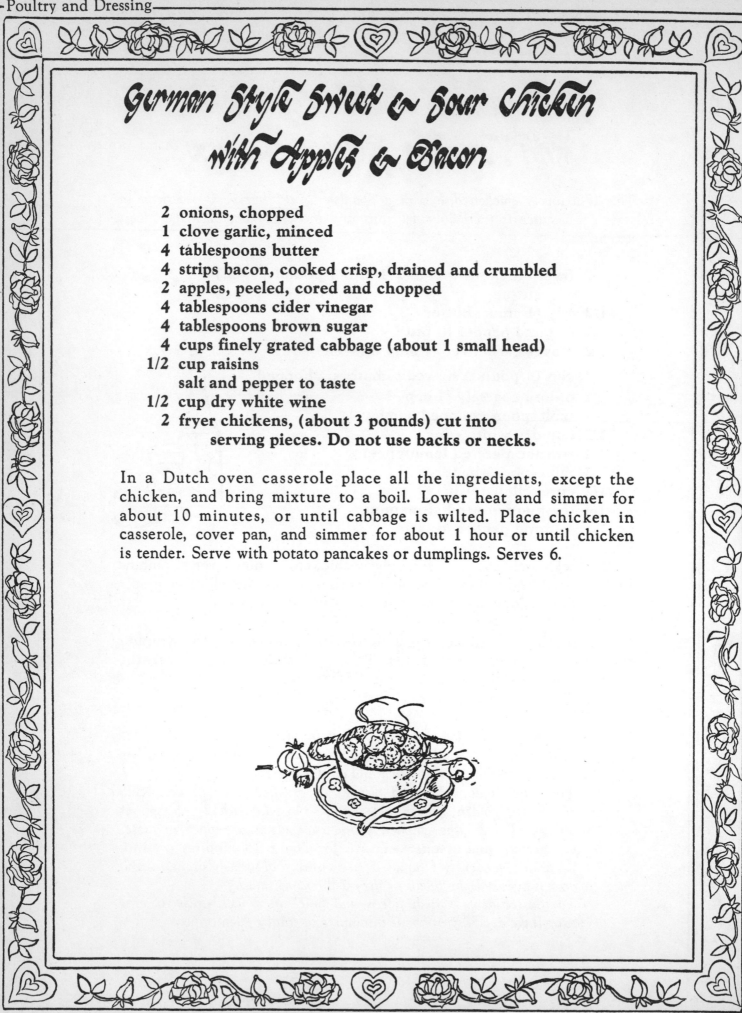

Oven - Fried Chicken with Cinnamon Apple Bread Pudding

This delicious chicken dish is excellent for a Sunday dinner with family or friends. Everyone will be cooing like pidgeons when they bite into the delightful Apple Pudding, which is much like an apple stuffing.

2 fryer chickens (about 2 1/2 to 3 pounds, each)
    cut up into serving pieces

1/2 cup (1 stick) melted butter

2 cups fresh bread crumbs (about 6 slices)
1/2 cup grated Parmesan cheese
1/2 teaspoon garlic powder
1/2 teaspoon paprika
    salt and pepper to taste

In a 12x16-inch pan, place chicken pieces in one layer. Brush chicken with melted butter. Combine the remaining ingredients and dip chicken pieces in crumb mixture and return to pan. Bake in a 350° oven for about 1 hour and 15 minutes or until chicken is tender. Serve with Cinnamon Apple Bread Pudding as a lovely accompaniment. Serves 8.

Cinnamon Apple Bread Pudding

4 large apples, peeled, cored and coarsely chopped
1 1/2 teaspoons cinnamon
4 tablespoons sugar
1/4 cup butter

6 slices egg bread, cut into cubes
3 eggs, beaten
1/3 cup apple juice, or enough to moisten pudding

In a skillet, saute apples in cinnamon, sugar and butter until apples are tender. In a large bowl, place apples, bread, eggs and apple juice and mix and toss until mixture is blended. Place in a buttered 2-quart souffle dish and bake in a 350° oven until pudding is set and top is browned, about 40 minutes. Serves 8.

Note: - Chicken and pudding can be prepared earlier in the day and reheated at time of serving.

Country Chicken
with Sweet & Sour Cabbage & Tomatoes

2 onions, chopped
4 tablespoons butter
4 cups finely grated cabbage (about 1 small head)
4 tablespoons brown sugar
1/4 cup lemon juice
1 can (8 ounces) tomato sauce
2 tomatoes, chopped
1 can chicken broth (10 1/2 ounces)
1/2 cup yellow raisins
salt and pepper to taste

2 fryer chickens, about 2 1/2 to 3 pounds) cut
into serving pieces. Do not use backs or necks.

In a Dutch oven casserole, place first 9 ingredients and bring mixture to a boil. Lower heat and simmer for about 10 minutes, or until cabbage is wilted.

Place chicken evenly in casserole. Cover pan and simmer chicken for about 1 hour, or until chicken is tender. Serve with brown rice or toasted barley. Serves 6.

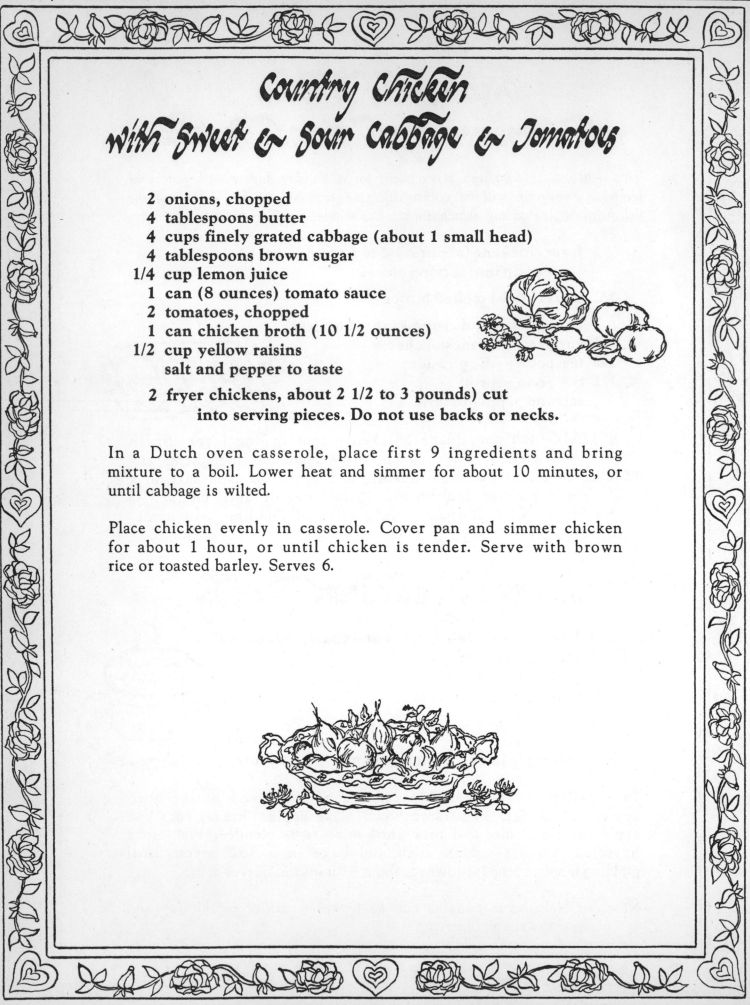

Curried Chicken with Honey Ginger Sauce

This extremely palatable chicken is gently spiced and highly glazed with honey, curry and ginger. It is marvellously delicious served with brown rice or fried rice.

2 fryer chickens, (about 2 1/2 to 3 pounds), cut up into serving pieces. Baste chicken with teriyaki marinade or soy sauce. Sprinkle with salt, pepper and garlic powder.

Honey Ginger Sauce:
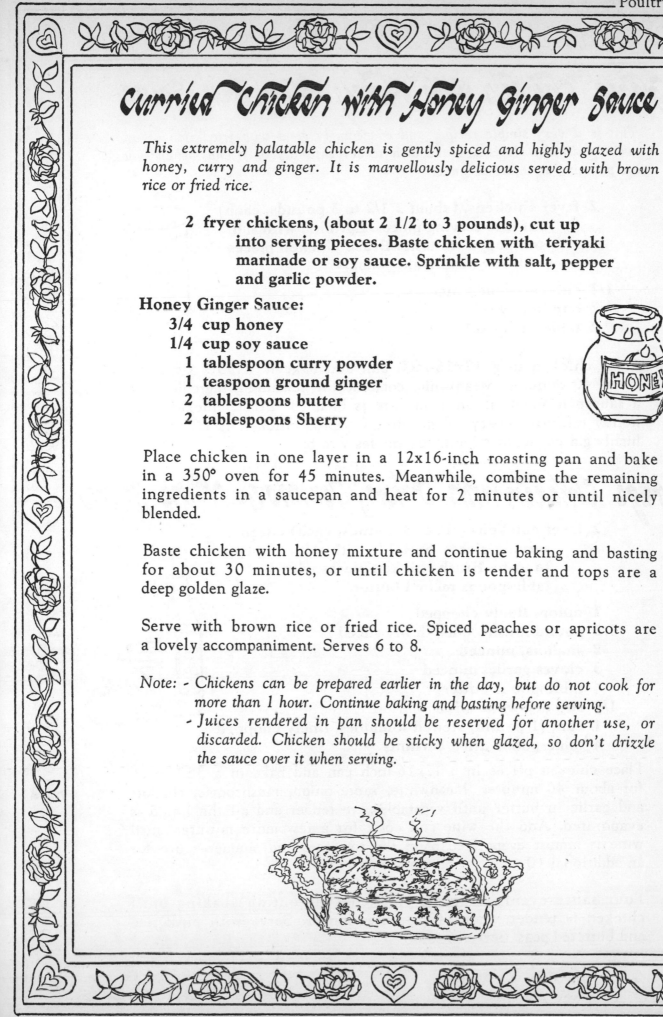
3/4 cup honey
1/4 cup soy sauce
1 tablespoon curry powder
1 teaspoon ground ginger
2 tablespoons butter
2 tablespoons Sherry

Place chicken in one layer in a 12x16-inch roasting pan and bake in a 350° oven for 45 minutes. Meanwhile, combine the remaining ingredients in a saucepan and heat for 2 minutes or until nicely blended.

Baste chicken with honey mixture and continue baking and basting for about 30 minutes, or until chicken is tender and tops are a deep golden glaze.

Serve with brown rice or fried rice. Spiced peaches or apricots are a lovely accompaniment. Serves 6 to 8.

Note: - Chickens can be prepared earlier in the day, but do not cook for more than 1 hour. Continue baking and basting before serving.
- Juices rendered in pan should be reserved for another use, or discarded. Chicken should be sticky when glazed, so don't drizzle the sauce over it when serving.

Glazed Chicken with Honey Barbecue Sauce

This is a very simple recipe, and exceedingly good with fried rice as an accompaniment. It is a grand dish to serve family or friends when you are planning an informal dinner.

2 **fryer chickens, (about 2 1/2 to 3 pounds, each) cut into serving pieces. Sprinkle with salt and pepper to taste. Brush chicken pieces with soy or teriyaki sauce.**

1/2 **cup barbecue sauce**
1/2 **cup honey**
2 **tablespoons oil**

Place chicken in a 12x16-inch pan and bake in a 350° oven for about 40 minutes. Meanwhile, combine the remaining ingredients in a saucepan and heat until mixture is blended. Brush chicken with honey mixture, every 10 minutes or until chicken is tender and highly glazed, about 40 minutes. Serves 6 to 8.

Cottage Chicken with Onion, Tomato & Wine Sauce

2 **fryer chickens (about 3 pounds, each) cut into serving pieces. Sprinkle with salt and pepper to taste. Brush chicken pieces with 4 tablespoons melted butter.**

1 **onion, finely chopped**
1/2 **pound mushrooms, thinly sliced**
2 **shallots, minced**
3 **cloves garlic, minced**
4 **tablespoons butter**
1/3 **cup dry white wine**
1 **can, (1 pound) stewed tomatoes, finely chopped**
4 **tablespoons dried currants**

Place chicken pieces in a 12x16-inch pan and bake in a 350° oven for about 40 minutes. Meanwhile, saute onion, mushrooms, shallots and garlic in butter until vegetables are tender and all the liquid is evaporated. Add the wine and cook for a few more minutes until wine is almost evaporated. Add the tomatoes and simmer sauce for an additional 10 minutes. Stir in the currants.

Pour sauce evenly over the chicken and continue baking until chicken is tender, about 40 minutes longer. Serve with pink rice and buttered peas. Serves 6 to 8.

Poulet Dijonnaise with Sour Cream Sauce

This simple little chicken dish is by no means "plain." It is a grand choice when you are running late one evening. The results will simply amaze you. Serve it on a bed of rice and with a buttered vegetable, and no one will ever guess the simplicity of preparation.

2 onions, chopped (frozen onions can be used)
2 cloves garlic, minced
1/4 cup (1/2 stick) butter

3 boned chicken breasts, cut into 1-inch pieces
2 tablespoons Dijon mustard

1 cup sour cream
salt and white pepper to taste

In a skillet, saute onions and garlic in butter until onion is soft. Add chicken and cook and stir until chicken is opaque and cooked through, about 5 minutes. Do not overcook. Add the mustard and cook and stir for 1 minute. Add sour cream and seasonings and cook and toss for 1 or 2 minutes or until heated through. Do not boil.

Serve on a bed of rice or buttered noodles. Serves 6.

Buttered Noodles with Lemon & Poppy Seeds

3/4 pound medium-width noodles, cooked "al dente"
and drained
4 tablespoons butter, melted
3 tablespoons lemon juice
2 tablespoons poppy seeds
salt to taste

1/3 cup toasted slivered almonds

In a large pan, stir together noodles, butter, lemon juice, salt and poppy seeds. Toss in the almonds just before serving. Serves 6.

Peasant Chicken with Tomatoes, Cabbage & Bacon

2 onions, chopped
1 can (1 pound) stewed tomatoes, chopped
2 cans (8 ounces, each) tomato sauce
1 can (10 1/2 ounces) chicken broth
6 tablespoons lemon juice
2 tablespoons brown sugar
3 tablespoons sugar
   salt and pepper to taste

1 small head cabbage (about 1 pound)

1 fryer chicken (about 3 pounds), cut into 8
   serving pieces

6 slices bacon, cooked crisp, drained and crumbled

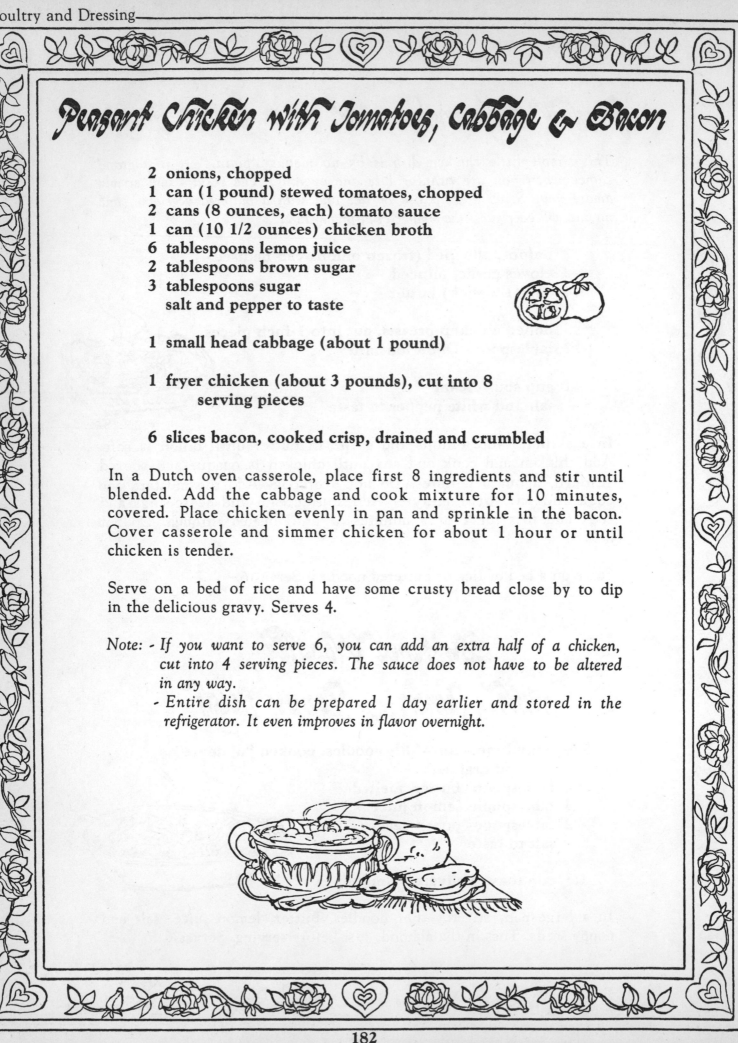

In a Dutch oven casserole, place first 8 ingredients and stir until blended. Add the cabbage and cook mixture for 10 minutes, covered. Place chicken evenly in pan and sprinkle in the bacon. Cover casserole and simmer chicken for about 1 hour or until chicken is tender.

Serve on a bed of rice and have some crusty bread close by to dip in the delicious gravy. Serves 4.

Note: - If you want to serve 6, you can add an extra half of a chicken, cut into 4 serving pieces. The sauce does not have to be altered in any way.
 - Entire dish can be prepared 1 day earlier and stored in the refrigerator. It even improves in flavor overnight.

Red Currant Glazed Chicken with Fruit Compote

2 fryer chickens (about 3 pounds, each) cut into
    serving pieces. Brush lightly with butter and
    sprinkle with salt, pepper and garlic powder.

Red Currant Glaze:
- 1 cup red currant jelly
- 1/4 cup orange juice
- 2 tablespoons lemon juice
- 1 tablespoon Dijon mustard
- 1 tablespoon grated orange peel

Place chicken in a 12x16-inch pan, in one layer, and bake in a
350° oven for 40 minutes. Meanwhile, heat together glaze
ingredients until blended. Baste chicken with glaze and continue
baking and basting, until chicken is tender about 35 minutes.
Chicken will be a rich, golden color.

Serve with Hot Sherried Fruit on the side. Serves 8.

Hot Sherried Fruit Compote

- 4 tablespoons butter
- 2 apples, peeled, cored and sliced
- 1/4 cup sugar or more to taste
- 1/2 teaspoon cinnamon

- 3 bananas, cut on the diagonal
- 1 orange, peeled and cut into sections
- 1/2 cup yellow raisins
- 1/3 cup sherry

- 1/4 cup toasted slivered almonds

In a large skillet, place butter, apples, sugar and cinnamon and
saute apples until they are tender. Add bananas and saute for 3 or
4 minutes. Add orange, raisins and sherry and continue cooking
and stirring for 3 minutes, or until sherry is evaporated. Stir in
the toasted almonds, and serve warm. Serves 8.

Note: - Fruit can be prepared earlier in the day and stored in the
    refrigerator. Add the almonds just before serving.
    - Chicken can be prepared earlier in the day. Bake for 1 hour.
    Continue baking time before serving.

Old World Peasant Chicken with Sauerkraut & Raisins

On a cold, wintry night when you are looking for a hearty and robust dish, try this delicious sweet and sour chicken. Serve it with noodles or brown rice and a crusty bread to dip into the delicious gravy.

> **2 fryer chickens (about 2 1/2 pounds, each) cut up. Sprinkle with salt, pepper and garlic powder. Reserve backs for another use.**

> **1 tablespoon oil**
> **1 can (16 ounces) tomato sauce**
> **1 cup sauerkraut, undrained**
> **1 onion, finely chopped**
> **1 small carrot, grated**
> **1/2 cup brown sugar**
> **1 cup yellow raisins**
> **salt and pepper to taste**

In a Dutch oven combine all the ingredients, except the chicken and bring mixture to a boil. Set chicken pieces evenly in pan. Cover pan and simmer mixture for about 1 1/2 hours or until chicken is tender. Allow chicken to cool for several hours and then carefully reheat at serving time. Serves 8.

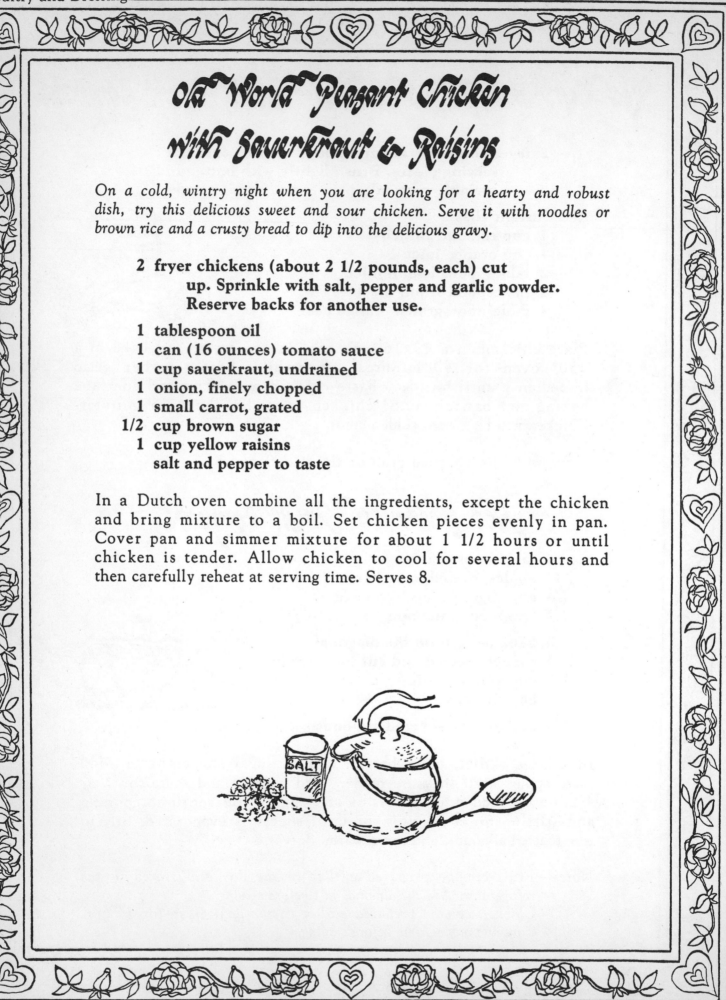

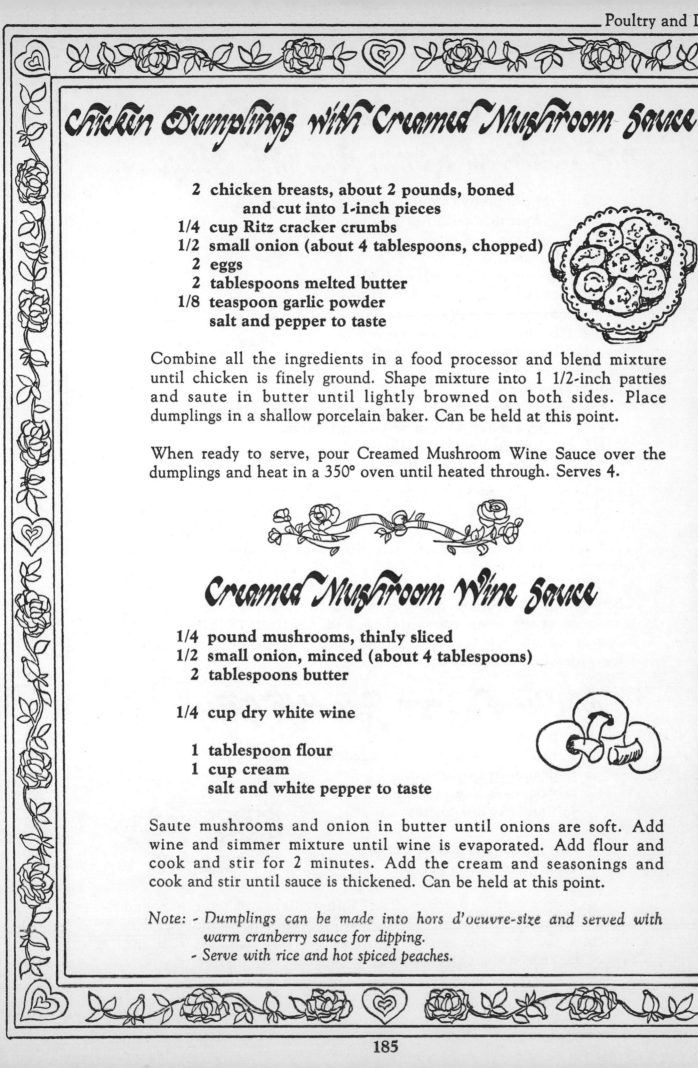

Chicken Dumplings with Creamed Mushroom Sauce

    2   chicken breasts, about 2 pounds, boned
            and cut into 1-inch pieces
    1/4 cup Ritz cracker crumbs
    1/2 small onion (about 4 tablespoons, chopped)
    2   eggs
    2   tablespoons melted butter
    1/8 teaspoon garlic powder
        salt and pepper to taste

Combine all the ingredients in a food processor and blend mixture until chicken is finely ground. Shape mixture into 1 1/2-inch patties and saute in butter until lightly browned on both sides. Place dumplings in a shallow porcelain baker. Can be held at this point.

When ready to serve, pour Creamed Mushroom Wine Sauce over the dumplings and heat in a 350° oven until heated through. Serves 4.

Creamed Mushroom Wine Sauce

    1/4 pound mushrooms, thinly sliced
    1/2 small onion, minced (about 4 tablespoons)
    2   tablespoons butter

    1/4 cup dry white wine

    1   tablespoon flour
    1   cup cream
        salt and white pepper to taste

Saute mushrooms and onion in butter until onions are soft. Add wine and simmer mixture until wine is evaporated. Add flour and cook and stir for 2 minutes. Add the cream and seasonings and cook and stir until sauce is thickened. Can be held at this point.

Note: - Dumplings can be made into hors d'oeuvre-size and served with
        warm cranberry sauce for dipping.
      - Serve with rice and hot spiced peaches.

Crusty Garlic Lemon Chicken with Buttered Lemon Rice with Cheese

2 fryer chickens (about 3 pounds, each) cut up. Sprinkle with salt and pepper.

Basting Mixture:
- 1/2 cup butter (1 stick), melted
- 2 cloves garlic, minced
- 1 teaspoon paprika
- 4 tablespoons lemon juice
- 1 tablespoon Dijon mustard

Crumb Topping:
- 1/2 cup cracker crumbs. Use a tasty cracker such as French Onion or Green Onion.
- 1/2 cup grated Parmesan cheese
- 1/4 teaspoon garlic powder

Lay chicken pieces in one layer in a 12x16-inch roasting pan. Combine all the ingredients of basting mixture and stir until blended. Brush chicken on all sides with basting mixture. Bake at 350° for about 40 minutes, brushing 2 or 3 times with basting mixture.

Combine crumb topping ingredients and stir until blended. Sprinkle crumb mixture over the chicken and continue baking for 40 minutes or until chicken is tender. Serve with Buttered Lemon Rice with Cheese. Serves 6.

Buttered Lemon Rice with Cheese

- 1 cup rice
- 2 cups chicken broth, homemade or canned
- 2 tablespoons butter
- 2 tablespoons lemon juice
- salt and pepper to taste

- 1/3 cup grated Parmesan cheese
- 2 tablespoons chopped chives

In a saucepan, stir together first 5 ingredients. Cover pan and simmer mixture for 30 minutes or until rice is tender and liquid is absorbed. Can be held at this point. Before serving, heat rice and toss in the cheese and chives. Serves 6.

Roast Turkey with Old-Fashioned Herbed Vegetable Stuffing

1 turkey, about 15 pounds, thoroughly cleaned and patted dry

Basting Mixture:
- **1 cup melted butter**
- **1 teaspoon salt**
- **1/4 teaspoon pepper**
- **1 tablespoon paprika**
- **6 cloves garlic,**

Place all the ingredients in a blender container and blend until garlic is ground. Baste turkey generously, inside and out, with basting mixture. Stuff turkey with Herbed Vegetable Stuffing and skewer opening with poultry pins.

Place turkey on a rack in roasting pan, breast side down. Bake at 300°, approximately 25 minutes per pound, for under 15 pounds; for over 15 pounds, approximately 20 minutes per pound. Tent the turkey loosely with foil and baste often with the juices. About 1 1/2 hours before turkey is finished cooking, turn it breast side up, and continue baking, uncovered, until meat thermometer (inserted in the thickest part of the thigh—not touching the bone) registers 185° to 190°.

You can also test for doneness by moving the drumstick up and down. If it gives easily, turkey is done. Remove any fat from the gravy. Gravy is very flavorful and does not need to be thickened.

Old-Fashioned Herbed Vegetable Stuffing

1 cup butter (2 sticks)
2 large onions, finely chopped
3 carrots, grated
1 cup celery, finely chopped
1/2 pound mushrooms, thinly sliced

2 eggs
1/4 cup finely minced parsley
2 teaspoons poultry seasoning
2 cans (10 1/2 ounces, each) chicken broth
salt and pepper to taste

2 packages (8 ounces, each) herbed seasoned
stuffing mix

In a skillet, saute together first 5 ingredients until onions are soft. Add remaining ingredients, using only enough chicken broth to hold stuffing together. Will stuff a 15 to 18 pound turkey.

Important:

Note: - Do not stuff turkey in advance. Remove stuffing before storing leftover turkey. Improper handling of stuffing can lead to growth of harmful bacteria. So, please take care to stuff turkey shortly before roasting and remove stuffing from turkey right after serving.

- Stuffing can be baked separately in a casserole, at 350° for about 30 minutes, which I prefer and recommend.

Duckling with Apple Raisin Stuffing & Brandy Orange Glaze

This is a nice homey dish for a good change-of-pace dinner. The stuffing is fruity and delicious. The rich and flavorful glaze makes gravy unnecessary.

2 **ducklings (about 5 pounds, each). Sprinkle lightly with salt, garlic powder and paprika.**

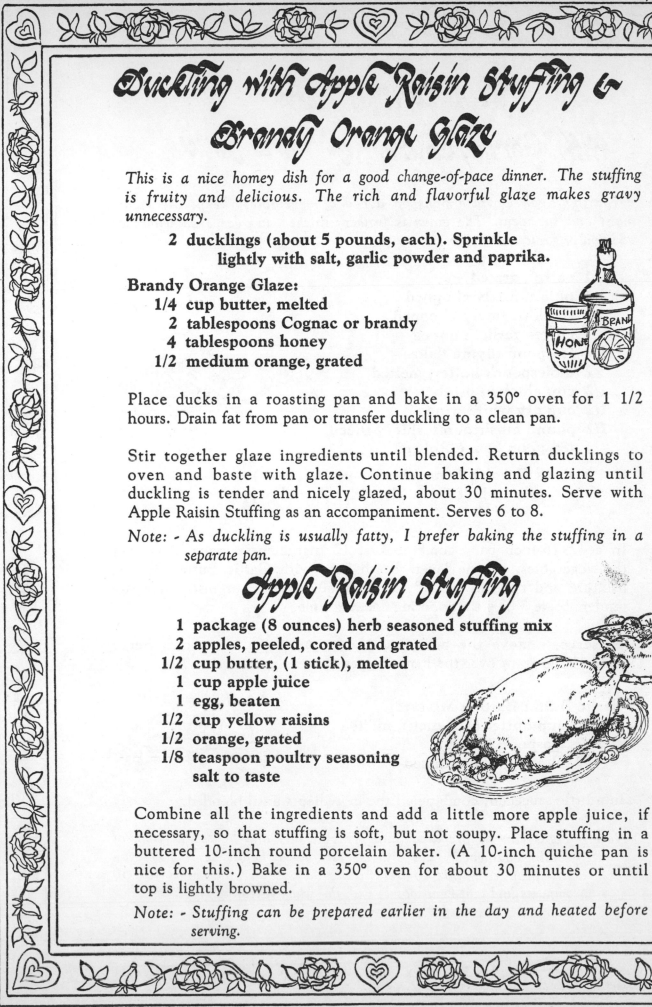

Brandy Orange Glaze:
- 1/4 **cup butter, melted**
- 2 **tablespoons Cognac or brandy**
- 4 **tablespoons honey**
- 1/2 **medium orange, grated**

Place ducks in a roasting pan and bake in a 350° oven for 1 1/2 hours. Drain fat from pan or transfer duckling to a clean pan.

Stir together glaze ingredients until blended. Return ducklings to oven and baste with glaze. Continue baking and glazing until duckling is tender and nicely glazed, about 30 minutes. Serve with Apple Raisin Stuffing as an accompaniment. Serves 6 to 8.

Note: - *As duckling is usually fatty, I prefer baking the stuffing in a separate pan.*

Apple Raisin Stuffing

- 1 **package (8 ounces) herb seasoned stuffing mix**
- 2 **apples, peeled, cored and grated**
- 1/2 **cup butter, (1 stick), melted**
- 1 **cup apple juice**
- 1 **egg, beaten**
- 1/2 **cup yellow raisins**
- 1/2 **orange, grated**
- 1/8 **teaspoon poultry seasoning**
  salt to taste

Combine all the ingredients and add a little more apple juice, if necessary, so that stuffing is soft, but not soupy. Place stuffing in a buttered 10-inch round porcelain baker. (A 10-inch quiche pan is nice for this.) Bake in a 350° oven for about 30 minutes or until top is lightly browned.

Note: - *Stuffing can be prepared earlier in the day and heated before serving.*

Rock Cornish Hens with Garlic, Butter & Wine Sauce

Preparing Rock Cornish hens on a bed of vegetables, keeps the meat moist and succulent. The gravy is further enriched and deepened with the addition of garlic and thyme.

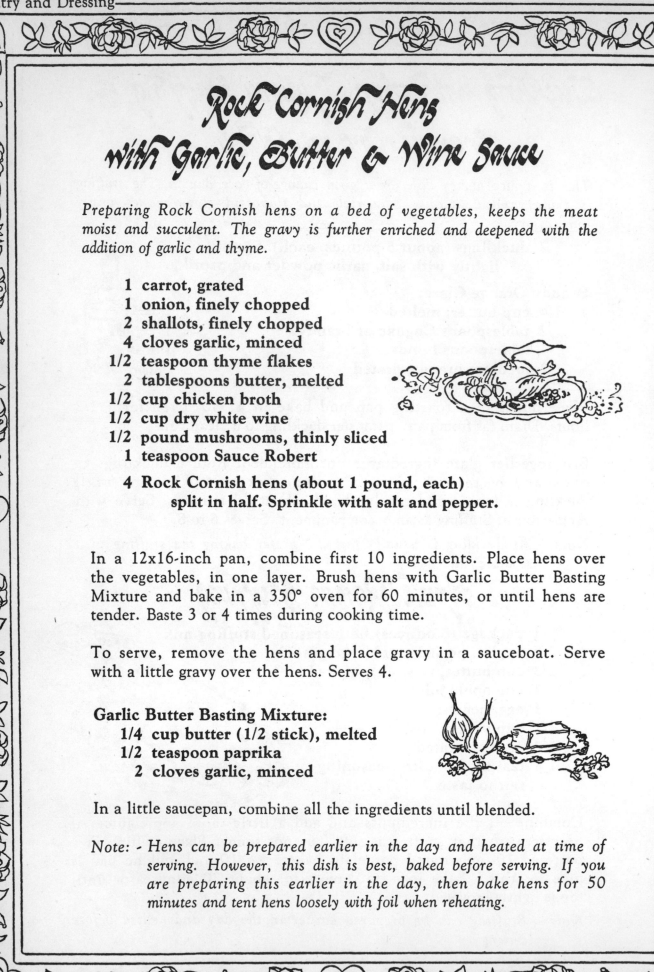

- 1 **carrot, grated**
- 1 **onion, finely chopped**
- 2 **shallots, finely chopped**
- 4 **cloves garlic, minced**
- 1/2 **teaspoon thyme flakes**
- 2 **tablespoons butter, melted**
- 1/2 **cup chicken broth**
- 1/2 **cup dry white wine**
- 1/2 **pound mushrooms, thinly sliced**
- 1 **teaspoon Sauce Robert**

4 **Rock Cornish hens (about 1 pound, each)**
     split in half. Sprinkle with salt and pepper.

In a 12x16-inch pan, combine first 10 ingredients. Place hens over the vegetables, in one layer. Brush hens with Garlic Butter Basting Mixture and bake in a 350° oven for 60 minutes, or until hens are tender. Baste 3 or 4 times during cooking time.

To serve, remove the hens and place gravy in a sauceboat. Serve with a little gravy over the hens. Serves 4.

Garlic Butter Basting Mixture:
- 1/4 **cup butter (1/2 stick), melted**
- 1/2 **teaspoon paprika**
- 2 **cloves garlic, minced**

In a little saucepan, combine all the ingredients until blended.

Note: - Hens can be prepared earlier in the day and heated at time of serving. However, this dish is best, baked before serving. If you are preparing this earlier in the day, then bake hens for 50 minutes and tent hens loosely with foil when reheating.

Peach & Wine Glazed Rock Cornish Hens with Peach & Raisin Stuffing

6 Rock Cornish Hens, cleaned and seasoned
lightly with salt, garlic powder and ginger.
Dust lightly with flour.

Peach & Raisin Stuffing:

    2 apples, peeled, cored and coarsely chopped
    1 cup frozen peaches, coarsely chopped. (You can
        use fresh peaches, but you must peel them and
        remove the stones.)
1/2 cup yellow raisins
    1 tablespoon grated orange peel
    1 cup orange juice or more, as needed
    2 tablespoons sugar
1/2 cup butter (1 stick)

    1 package (8 ounces) herb seasoned stuffing mix

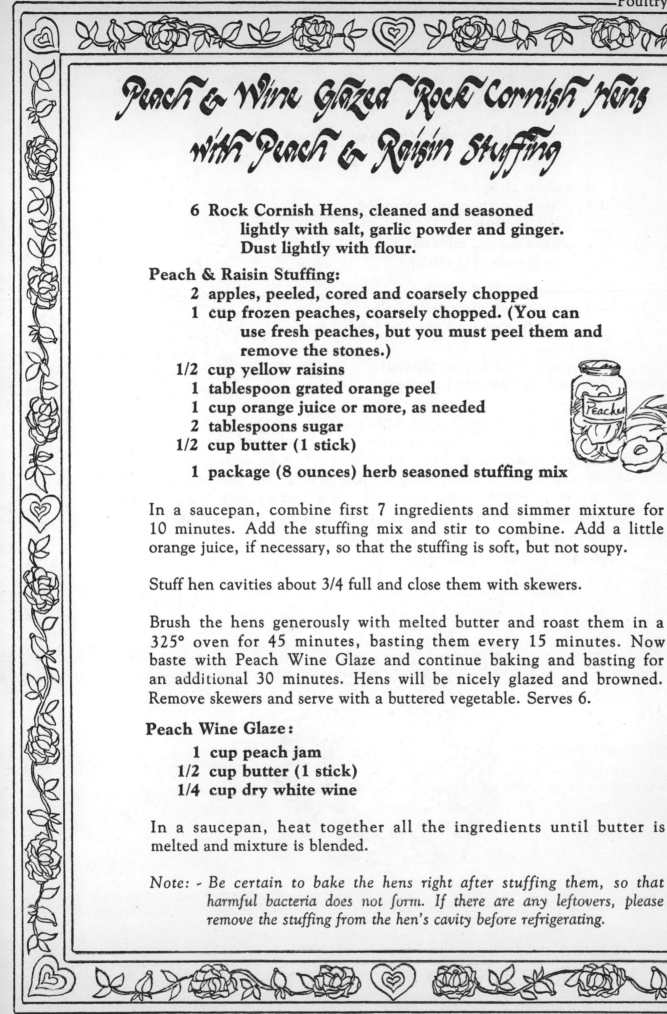

In a saucepan, combine first 7 ingredients and simmer mixture for 10 minutes. Add the stuffing mix and stir to combine. Add a little orange juice, if necessary, so that the stuffing is soft, but not soupy.

Stuff hen cavities about 3/4 full and close them with skewers.

Brush the hens generously with melted butter and roast them in a 325° oven for 45 minutes, basting them every 15 minutes. Now baste with Peach Wine Glaze and continue baking and basting for an additional 30 minutes. Hens will be nicely glazed and browned. Remove skewers and serve with a buttered vegetable. Serves 6.

Peach Wine Glaze:

    1 cup peach jam
1/2 cup butter (1 stick)
1/4 cup dry white wine

In a saucepan, heat together all the ingredients until butter is melted and mixture is blended.

Note: - Be certain to bake the hens right after stuffing them, so that harmful bacteria does not form. If there are any leftovers, please remove the stuffing from the hen's cavity before refrigerating.

Easiest & Best Onion, Shallot & Mushroom Stuffing

1 onion, chopped
1/4 pound mushrooms, chopped
2 shallots, minced
2 cloves garlic, minced
1/4 cup butter (1/2 stick)

1 teaspoon lemon juice
1 tablespoon chopped parsley
3 cups fresh bread crumbs (about 6 slices)
1 egg
1/3 cup cream (or as needed)
    salt and pepper to taste

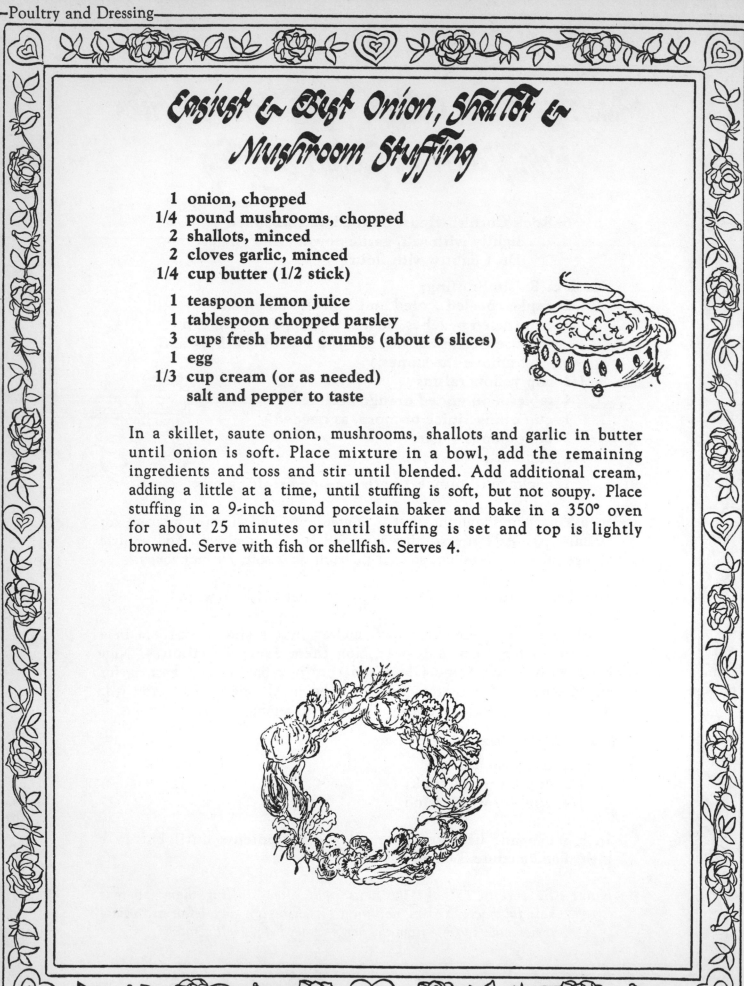

In a skillet, saute onion, mushrooms, shallots and garlic in butter until onion is soft. Place mixture in a bowl, add the remaining ingredients and toss and stir until blended. Add additional cream, adding a little at a time, until stuffing is soft, but not soupy. Place stuffing in a 9-inch round porcelain baker and bake in a 350° oven for about 25 minutes or until stuffing is set and top is lightly browned. Serve with fish or shellfish. Serves 4.

Old Fashioned Cracker Stuffing with Garlic & Herbs

This is a very old recipe for cracker stuffing which is very good indeed. Its goodness comes from onions and shallots and mushrooms and garlic and herbs.

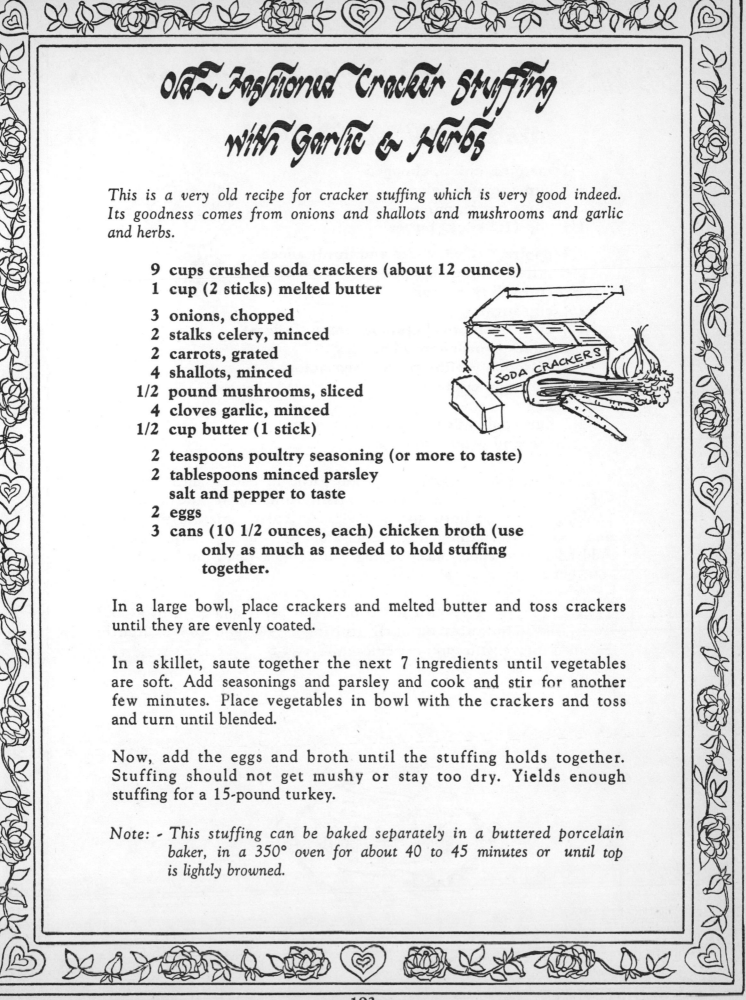

9 cups crushed soda crackers (about 12 ounces)
1 cup (2 sticks) melted butter

3 onions, chopped
2 stalks celery, minced
2 carrots, grated
4 shallots, minced
1/2 pound mushrooms, sliced
4 cloves garlic, minced
1/2 cup butter (1 stick)

2 teaspoons poultry seasoning (or more to taste)
2 tablespoons minced parsley
  salt and pepper to taste
2 eggs
3 cans (10 1/2 ounces, each) chicken broth (use
    only as much as needed to hold stuffing
    together.

In a large bowl, place crackers and melted butter and toss crackers until they are evenly coated.

In a skillet, saute together the next 7 ingredients until vegetables are soft. Add seasonings and parsley and cook and stir for another few minutes. Place vegetables in bowl with the crackers and toss and turn until blended.

Now, add the eggs and broth until the stuffing holds together. Stuffing should not get mushy or stay too dry. Yields enough stuffing for a 15-pound turkey.

Note: - This stuffing can be baked separately in a buttered porcelain baker, in a 350° oven for about 40 to 45 minutes or until top is lightly browned.

Easiest & Best Apple, Prune & Raisin Stuffing with Cinnamon & Spice

    1 medium onion, chopped
  1/3 cup chopped celery
    1 clove garlic, minced
  1/4 cup (1/2 stick) butter

    3 apples, peeled, cored and thinly sliced
    6 pitted prunes, snipped
  1/2 cup yellow raisins
  1/4 cup sugar
    4 cups fresh bread crumbs (about 8 slices)
    2 tablespoons chopped parsley
  1/4 teaspoon ground poultry seasoning
  1/8 teaspoon cinnamon
    1 egg
  1/2 cup apple juice (or more as needed)
      salt and pepper to taste

In a skillet, saute onion, celery and garlic in butter, until onion is soft. Add the apples, prunes, raisins and sugar and continue cooking, covered, until apples are tender. Place mixture in a bowl and add the remaining ingredients and toss and stir until blended. Add additional apple juice, adding a little at a time, until stuffing is soft, but not soupy.

Place stuffing in a 10-inch round porcelain baker and bake in a 350° oven for 30 minutes or until stuffing is set and top is lightly browned. Serve with turkey or chicken. Serves 6.

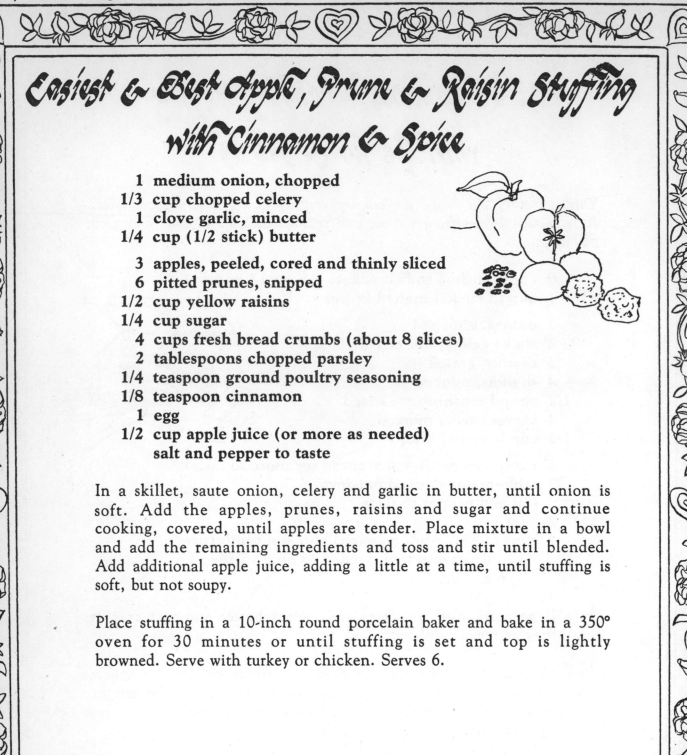

Molds

Cranberry Bavarian with Orange, Lemons & Raisins

1 **can (1 pound) whole cranberry sauce**
1/2 **cup orange juice**
2 **tablespoons lemon juice**
2 **tablespoons grated orange peel**
2 **tablespoons unflavored gelatin**
1/2 **cup water**

1/2 **cup chopped toasted walnuts**
1/2 **cup chopped yellow raisins**

2 **cups cream**

In a saucepan, heat together cranberries, orange juice, lemon juice and orange peel until cranberries are loosened and sauce is dissolved. Soften gelatin in water and place it in a larger pan with hot water until it is dissolved. Add gelatin to cranberry mixture. Allow gelatin to come to room temperature.

Stir walnuts and raisins into cranberry mixture. Whip cream until it is stiff and fold it into the cranberry mixture. Pour into a 2-quart mold and refrigerate until firm. Unmold onto a lovely platter and decorate with frosted cranberries. (Cranberries brushed with egg white, rolled in sugar and allowed to dry.)

Apricot Mold With Oranges & Cream

- 1 package (6 ounces) apricot gelatin
- 2 cups boiling water
- 1 can (1 pound 12 ounces) apricots. Remove seeds and whirl in a blender or food processor to coarsely chop.
- 1/2 orange grated. Use juice, peel and fruit. Remove any large pieces of membranes.

- 1 cup sour cream
- 1 cup cream

Dissolve gelatin in boiling water and place mixture into the large bowl of an electric mixer. Now beat in the remaining ingredients until the mixture is blended.

Pour gelatin mixture into a 2-quart mold and refrigerate until firm. Unmold on a lovely platter and decorate with orange slices and green leaves. Serves 10 or 12.

Orange Mold With Fresh Fruit, Raisins & Walnuts

- 1 package (6 ounces) orange gelatin
- 2 cups boiling water

- 2 oranges, peeled and cut into sections
- 2 bananas, sliced
- 2 peaches, peeled and thinly sliced
- 2 pears, peeled and thinly sliced
- 1/2 cup yellow raisins
- 1/2 cup coarsely chopped walnuts
- 2 cups orange juice

Dissolve gelatin in boiling water and place mixture into a large bowl. In another bowl, stir together the remaining ingredients. Combine the two mixtures and spoon mixture into a 2-quart mold. Refrigerate until firm.

Unmold on a lovely platter and decorate with green leaves. Serves 10 or 12.

Molded Cranberry Relish with Yogurt, Orange & Walnuts

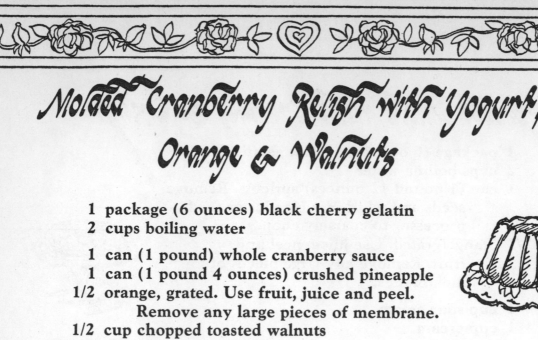

1 package (6 ounces) black cherry gelatin
2 cups boiling water

1 can (1 pound) whole cranberry sauce
1 can (1 pound 4 ounces) crushed pineapple
1/2 orange, grated. Use fruit, juice and peel.
　　Remove any large pieces of membrane.
1/2 cup chopped toasted walnuts
1 cup unflavored yogurt

Stir gelatin in boiling water until it is thoroughly dissolved. Add the cranberries and stir until cranberries are loosened and the sauce is dissolved. Add the remaining ingredients and stir until it is nicely blended.

Place mixture in a 2-quart mold and refrigerate until firm. Unmold on a lovely platter and decorate with green leaves and orange slices. Serves 12.

Coeur a la Creme with Raspberry Sauce

    1   tablespoon unflavored gelatin
    1/4 cup water

  1 1/2 cups cream
    3/4 cup sifted powdered sugar

    1   package (8 ounces) cream cheese, at room
             temperature
    1   teaspoon vanilla
    1   tablespoon grated lemon peel
    2   tablespoons lemon juice

In a metal measuring cup, soften gelatin in water. Place cup in a pan with 1-inch simmering water until gelatin is dissolved.

Beat cream with sugar until thickened. Beat cream cheese with vanilla, lemon peel and juice until nice and fluffy. Beat in the whipped cream and dissolved gelatin until blended.

Pour mixture into a 6-cup heart-shaped mold and refrigerate it until mold is set.

To unmold, run a knife along the edge, dip the mold quickly in hot water and invert on a serving platter. Serve with a spoonful of Raspberry Sauce on the top. Serves 6.

Raspberry Sauce

    1   package (10 ounces) frozen raspberries in syrup
    1   tablespoon lemon juice
    1   teaspoon grated lemon peel

Sieve the raspberries to remove the seeds. Add the lemon juice and peel. Yields about 1 cup sauce.

Note: - Mold can be prepared 1 day earlier and stored in the refrigerator.
*   - To facilitate unmolding, you can line the mold with plastic wrap and extend it about 4-inches on each side.*

Apricot & Sour Cream Mold with Dates & Walnuts

1 package (6 ounces) apricot flavored gelatin
2 cups boiling water

1 can (1 pound 14 ounces) peeled apricot
   halves (pit these if whole)
1 cup sour cream
1 package (3 ounces) cream cheese, cut
   into 1/4-inch squares
1/2 cup finely chopped dates
1/2 cup finely chopped walnuts

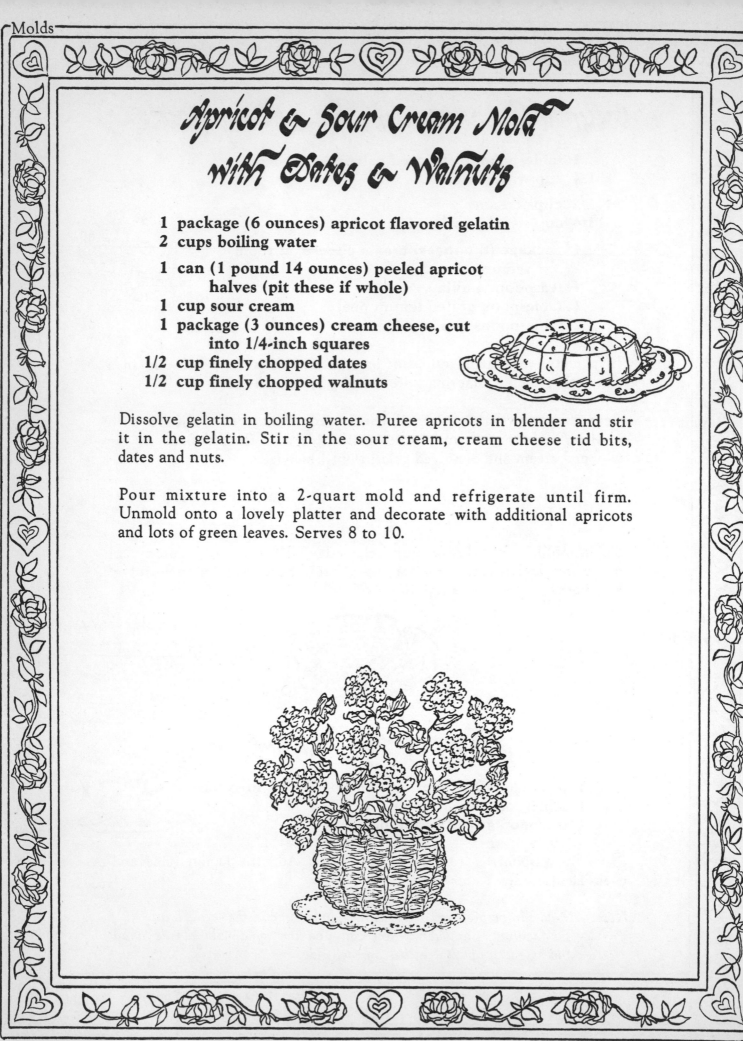

Dissolve gelatin in boiling water. Puree apricots in blender and stir it in the gelatin. Stir in the sour cream, cream cheese tid bits, dates and nuts.

Pour mixture into a 2-quart mold and refrigerate until firm. Unmold onto a lovely platter and decorate with additional apricots and lots of green leaves. Serves 8 to 10.

Strawberry Mold with Yogurt & Bananas

1 package (6 ounces) wild strawberry flavored
   gelatin
2 cups boiling water

1 package (10 ounces) frozen strawberries in
   syrup. Drain.
1 pint (2 cups) unflavored yogurt
2 bananas sliced

Dissolve gelatin in boiling water. Drain strawberries and add the juice to the gelatin. Stir in the yogurt until mixture is blended. Stir in the reserved strawberries and sliced bananas.

Pour mixture into a 2-quart mold and refrigerate until firm. Unmold onto a lovely platter and decorate with whole strawberries. In absence of these, decorate with green leaves. Serves 8 to 10.

Melba Mold with Peaches & Cream & Raspberry Sauce

1 package (6 ounces) peach flavored gelatin
1 1/2 cups boiling water

1/2 cup orange juice
1 pint vanilla ice cream, softened
1 package (10 ounces) frozen peaches in syrup
   undrained
2 bananas, sliced

Dissolve gelatin in boiling water. Stir in the orange juice and vanilla ice cream until blended. Stir in the peaches and bananas. Pour mixture into a 2-quart mold and refrigerate until firm. Unmold onto a lovely platter. Serve with a spoonful of Raspberry Sauce. Serves 8 to 10.

Raspberry Sauce: Stir together 1 package (10 ounces) raspberries in syrup with 1/4 can (1 1/2 ounces) undiluted concentrated frozen orange juice.

Orange Ambrosia Mold with Pineapple, Oranges & Walnuts

This is a spectacular mold and just right to serve with a backyard luau. I have used the more readily available fruit, but if you can substitute mangoes or papayas, it would be just lovely.

- 1 **package (6 ounces) orange gelatin**
- 2 **cups pineapple juice**
- 1 **cup sour cream**
- 1 **can (14 ounces) crushed pineapple**
- 2 **oranges, peeled, remove membranes and chop coarsely**
- 1 **cup miniature marshmallows**
- 1/2 **cup coarsely chopped walnuts**
- 1/4 **cup coconut flakes (sweetened)**
- 1/4 **cup finely chopped maraschino cherries**

In a saucepan, heat together gelatin and pineapple juice until gelatin is dissolved. Stir in the sour cream until mixture is thoroughly blended. Stir in the remaining ingredients.

Pour mixture into a 1 1/2-quart mold and refrigerate until firm. To serve, unmold on a lovely footed platter and decorate with orange slices, cherries and a profusion of green leaves. Serves 10 to 12.

Note: - *To peel oranges, remove the skin and the pith (the white part) with a very sharp knife. This will expose all the segments. Now run the knife down along the membranes, and the orange segments will come free.*
    - *This recipe can be considered a very general one. If coconut is not to your liking, omit it. If you wish, you can substitute tropical fruit for the pineapple and oranges. Feel free to add more oranges or walnuts if your prefer. However the mold is excellent "as is."*

Honey & Yogurt Spiced Peach Mold with Raisins & Walnuts

- 1 package (6 ounces) peach gelatin
- 2 cups boiling water
- 2 tablespoons honey
- 1 cup yellow raisins

- 1 cup yogurt
- 1 can (1 pound 13 ounces) spiced peaches in syrup.
  Drain the fruit and reserve the syrup. Remove
  the stones and chop the fruit coarsely.
- 3/4 cup chopped walnuts, toasted
- 1 cup reserved syrup

Stir together the gelatin and boiling water until gelatin is dissolved. Stir in the honey and raisins. Stir in the remaining ingredients until blended. Pour mixture into a 6-cup mold and refrigerate until firm. Unmold onto a lovely serving platter and decorate with lots of green leaves. Sift some powdered sugar on the leaves to resemble snow. Just lovely! Serves 8 to 10.

Egg Nog Mold with Raspberries & Cream

- 1 package (6 ounces) raspberry gelatin
- 1 package (3 ounces) raspberry gelatin
- 2 cups boiling water

- 3 cups prepared egg nog
- 1 package (10 ounces) frozen raspberries in syrup.
  slightly thawed. Do not drain
- 1 cup cream

Dissolve gelatin in boiling water. Stir in the egg nog and raspberries until blended. Allow mixture to come to room temperature. Beat the cream until stiff and fold it into the gelatin. This can be done on the lowest speed in your electric mixer.

Pour gelatin into a 2-quart mold and refrigerate until firm. Unmold onto a decorative serving platter and decorate with lots of green leaves. Sift some powdered sugar on the leaves to resemble snow. Serves 12.

Banana & Apricot Mold with Coconut & Lemon

1 package (6 ounces) apricot gelatin
2 cups boiling water

1 can (1 pound) apricots in syrup. Coarsely
    chop apricots and do not drain.
1 cup sour cream
2 bananas, sliced
1 tablespoon grated lemon peel

Dissolve gelatin in boiling water. Stir in the remaining ingredients until blended. Pour mixture into a 6-cup mold and refrigerate until firm.

Unmold on a lovely platter and serve with a dollup of Coconut Lemon Cream. Serves 8.

Coconut Lemon Cream

1 cup sour cream
1/4 cup sweetened coconut flakes
1 tablespoon sugar (or to taste)
2 tablespoons lemon juice
2 teaspoons grated lemon peel

Combine all the ingredients and stir until blended. Yields 1 1/4 cups sauce.

California Sunshine Citrus Mold with Pineapple & Bananas

1 package (6 ounces) orange gelatin
2 cups boiling water

1 can grapefruit sections (1 pound), drained.
    Reserve syrup.
1 can mandarin orange sections (12 ounces),
    drained. Reserve syrup.
1 can crushed pineapple (8 ounces)
2 bananas, sliced
1 tablespoon grated orange peel
1 cup reserved syrup from above

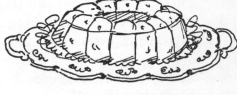

Dissolve gelatin in boiling water. Stir in the remaining ingredients. Pour mixture into a 6-cup mold and refrigerate until firm. Unmold on a lovely platter and decorate with green leaves and scored orange slices. Serves 8.

Rhubarb & Strawberry Mold with Raisins & Walnuts

1 package (6 ounces) strawberry gelatin
2 1/2 cups boiling water

1 package (10 ounces) frozen rhubarb, cooked
    according to directions on package.
1 package (10 ounces) frozen strawberries in
    syrup, defrosted.
2 tablespoons lemon juice

1/2 cup yellow raisins
1/2 cup chopped walnuts

Dissolve gelatin in boiling water. Stir in the remaining ingredients until blended. Pour mixture into a 2-quart mold and chill until firm. Unmold on a lovely footed platter and decorate with green leaves and fresh strawberries. Serve as a relish with roast chicken or veal. Serves 8 to 10.

Strawberry Mold with Raspberries & Sour Cream

    1 package (6 ounces) strawberry gelatin
1 1/2 cups boiling water

    1 cup sour cream
    1 package (3 ounces) cream cheese, at room temperature

    1 package (10 ounces) frozen raspberries in heavy syrup
    1 tablespoon lemon juice

Dissolve gelatin in boiling water. Beat together the sour cream and cream cheese until blended. Beat gelatin into the cream mixture. Stir in the raspberries and lemon juice.

Pour mixture into a 2-quart mold and refrigerate it until firm. Unmold on a lovely platter and decorate with pretty leaves and fresh strawberries. Serves 10 or 12.

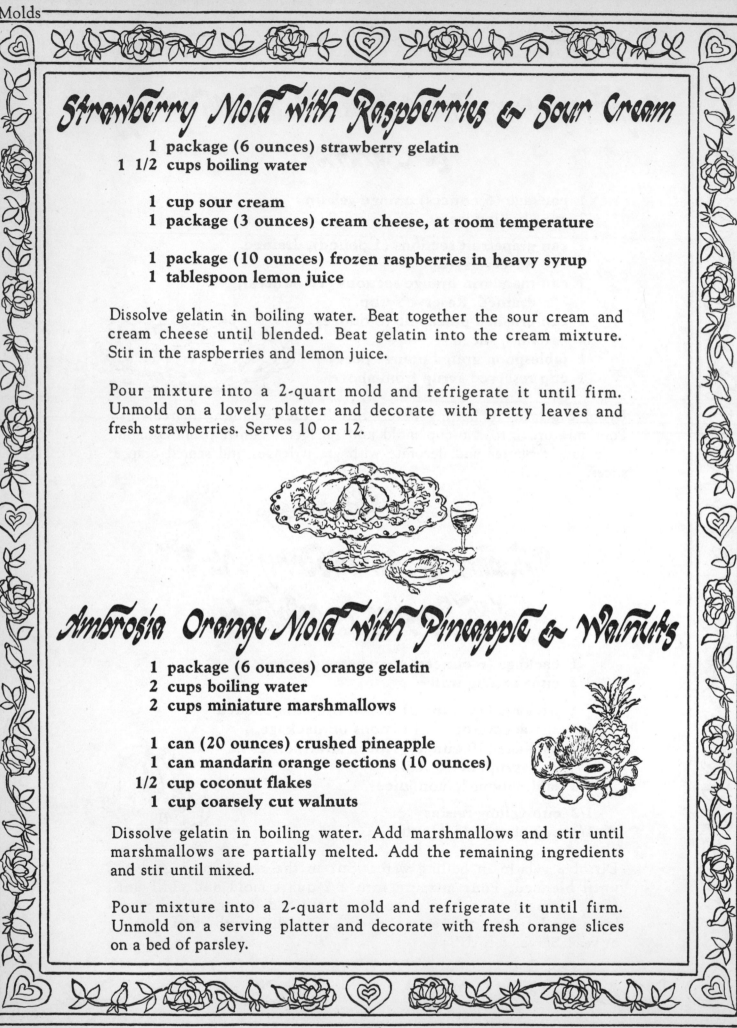

Ambrosia Orange Mold with Pineapple & Walnuts

    1 package (6 ounces) orange gelatin
    2 cups boiling water
    2 cups miniature marshmallows

    1 can (20 ounces) crushed pineapple
    1 can mandarin orange sections (10 ounces)
1/2 cup coconut flakes
    1 cup coarsely cut walnuts

Dissolve gelatin in boiling water. Add marshmallows and stir until marshmallows are partially melted. Add the remaining ingredients and stir until mixed.

Pour mixture into a 2-quart mold and refrigerate it until firm. Unmold on a serving platter and decorate with fresh orange slices on a bed of parsley.

Spiced Apricot Sour Cream Mold

- 1 package apricot gelatin (6 ounces)
- 2 cups boiling water
- 1 can (1 pound 12 ounces) spiced apricots, pitted
- 1 1/2 cups sour cream

In a bowl, dissolve gelatin in boiling water, stirring. Drain the apricots and place the juice into the bowl with the gelatin. Puree the apricots in a blender or food processor.

Beat the sour cream into the gelatin mixture until blended. Stir in the pureed apricots until blended. Pour mixture into a 2-quart mold and refrigerate until firm. Unmold onto a lovely platter and decorate with green leaves and spiced apricot halves. Serves 10.

Note: - Please don't be misled by the simplicity of this recipe. It produces a delicious mold, fruity and tart. If you are planning to serve this as a light dessert, then spoon a teaspoon of raspberries in syrup on the top.

Ambrosia Mold with Pineapple & Coconut

- 1 package (6 ounces) orange gelatin
- 2 cups boiling water
- 1 can (1 pound 4 ounces) crushed pineapple, undrained
- 1 can (11 ounces) mandarin orange segments, undrained
- 1 cup sour cream
- 1/4 cup chopped maraschino cherries
- 1 cup miniature marshmallows
- 1/2 cup chopped walnuts
- 1/2 cup sweetened coconut flakes

Dissolve gelatin in boiling water. Add the remaining ingredients and stir until blended. Pour mixture into a 2-quart mold and refrigerate until firm. Unmold onto a lovely platter and decorate with green leaves and orange slices. Serves 10 to 12.

Raspberry & Strawberry Lemon Cream Mold

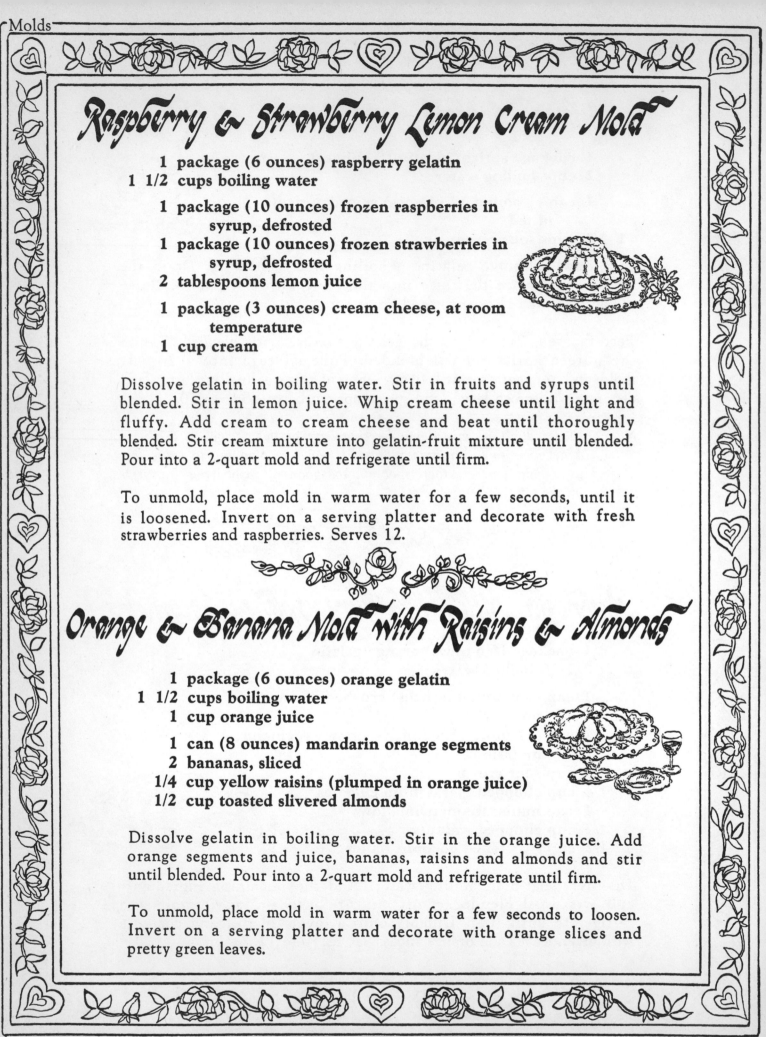

        1 package (6 ounces) raspberry gelatin
    1 1/2 cups boiling water

        1 package (10 ounces) frozen raspberries in
           syrup, defrosted
        1 package (10 ounces) frozen strawberries in
           syrup, defrosted
        2 tablespoons lemon juice

        1 package (3 ounces) cream cheese, at room
           temperature
        1 cup cream

Dissolve gelatin in boiling water. Stir in fruits and syrups until blended. Stir in lemon juice. Whip cream cheese until light and fluffy. Add cream to cream cheese and beat until thoroughly blended. Stir cream mixture into gelatin-fruit mixture until blended. Pour into a 2-quart mold and refrigerate until firm.

To unmold, place mold in warm water for a few seconds, until it is loosened. Invert on a serving platter and decorate with fresh strawberries and raspberries. Serves 12.

Orange & Banana Mold with Raisins & Almonds

        1 package (6 ounces) orange gelatin
    1 1/2 cups boiling water
        1 cup orange juice

        1 can (8 ounces) mandarin orange segments
        2 bananas, sliced
      1/4 cup yellow raisins (plumped in orange juice)
      1/2 cup toasted slivered almonds

Dissolve gelatin in boiling water. Stir in the orange juice. Add orange segments and juice, bananas, raisins and almonds and stir until blended. Pour into a 2-quart mold and refrigerate until firm.

To unmold, place mold in warm water for a few seconds to loosen. Invert on a serving platter and decorate with orange slices and pretty green leaves.

Noodles, Rice & Pastas

Oven - Baked Rice & Vermicelli with Onions & Mushrooms

1 cup rice
1 cup vermicelli(fideos) crushed into 1-inch pieces
4 tablespoons butter

3 cans (10 1/2 ounces, each) chicken broth
salt and pepper to taste

1 onion, chopped
1/2 pound mushrooms, sliced
3 tablespoons butter

In a skillet, saute rice and vermicelli in butter until vermicelli is just beginning to color. Spoon mixture into a round baking pan, 8x3-inches. Add chicken broth and seasonings, cover pan tightly and bake in a 350° oven for about 40 minutes or until rice is tender and liquid is absorbed.

Meanwhile, in a skillet, saute mushrooms and onion in butter until onions are soft. Stir mushroom mixture into rice and continue baking, covered, until heated through. To serve, garnish top with finely chopped green onions. Serves 6.

Brown Rice & Lentil Casserole with Carrots & Onions

What a nice family dish to serve on a frosty night when the weather is storming outside. It is a hearty, satisfying dish that is especially good with pot roast or potted chicken.

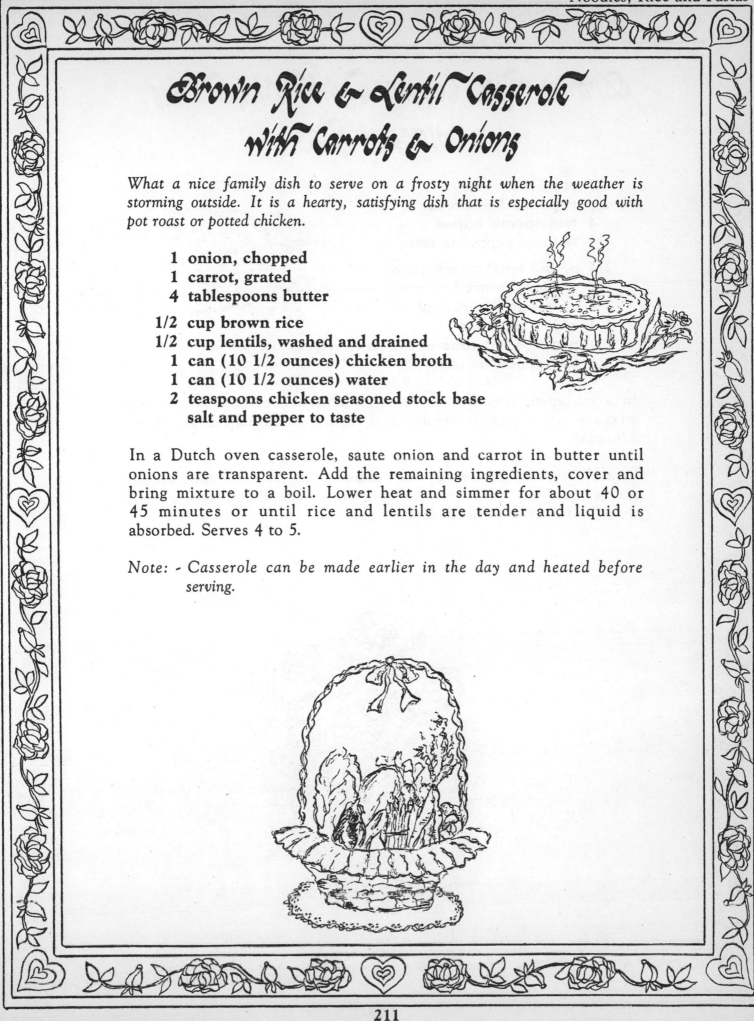

1 onion, chopped
1 carrot, grated
4 tablespoons butter

1/2 cup brown rice
1/2 cup lentils, washed and drained
1 can (10 1/2 ounces) chicken broth
1 can (10 1/2 ounces) water
2 teaspoons chicken seasoned stock base
salt and pepper to taste

In a Dutch oven casserole, saute onion and carrot in butter until onions are transparent. Add the remaining ingredients, cover and bring mixture to a boil. Lower heat and simmer for about 40 or 45 minutes or until rice and lentils are tender and liquid is absorbed. Serves 4 to 5.

Note: - *Casserole can be made earlier in the day and heated before serving.*

Brown Rice Casserole with Mushrooms, Onions & Peas

- 1 cup brown rice
- 2 1/2 cups chicken broth
- 4 tablespoons butter
  salt and pepper to taste

- 1/4 pound mushrooms, sliced
- 2 shallots, minced
- 2 cloves garlic, minced
- 1 onion, chopped
- 1 package (10 ounces) frozen baby peas
- 4 tablespoons butter

In a saucepan, combine first 4 ingredients, cover pan and simmer mixture until rice is tender and liquid is absorbed, about 40 minutes.

In a skillet, saute together the remaining ingredients until onions are tender and liquid rendered is abosrbed. Combine rice and vegetables and toss to blend. Serves 5 to 6.

Brown Rice with Apples & Almonds

Fruited rice is a grand accompaniment to pork or chicken. It adds a festive touch to a meal and is especially attractive served molded.

3 tablespoons butter
1 clove garlic
1 onion, chopped

1 cup brown rice
2 cans (10 1/2 ounces, each) chicken broth
salt and pepper to taste

1 apple, peeled, cored and grated
1 tablespoon butter
3 tablespoons brown sugar
1/2 cup chopped and toasted almonds

In a saucepan, saute together garlic and onion in butter until onion is transparent. Add rice, broth and seasonings, cover pan and simmer mixture until liquid is absorbed and rice is tender.

Meanwhile saute apple with butter and brown sugar until apple is soft. Add the chopped almonds. Stir apple mixture into rice until all is nicely blended. To serve, place hot rice into a ring mold, press it down and invert it onto a serving platter. Serve with roast chicken or pork. Serves 6.

Rice with Dates, Raisins & Almonds

1 cup rice
3 tablespoons butter
1 can (10 1/2 ounces) chicken broth
1 cup water
salt and pepper to taste

1/2 cup chopped dates
1/2 cup raisins
1/2 cup chopped apricots
1/2 cup brown sugar
2 tablespoons butter

1/2 cup chopped toasted almonds

In a saucepan, place first 5 ingredients, cover pan and simmer mixture until rice is tender and liquid is absorbed. Meanwhile, saute together dates, raisins, apricots, sugar and butter until fruits are tender. Stir in chopped almonds and combine rice and fruit mixture. Serve with roast pork or curries. Serves 6.

Green Rice with Onions & Herbs

1 small onion, finely chopped
2 tablespoons butter

1 cup rice
1 can (10 1/2 ounces) chicken broth
3/4 cup water
1/8 teaspoon thyme
2 tablespoons finely chopped parsley
   salt and pepper to taste

In a saucepan, saute onion in butter until onion is transparent. Add rice and cook and stir for 2 minutes. Add the remaining ingredients, stir and cover pan. Simmer rice until liquid is absorbed and rice is tender. Serves 4 to 6.

Pink Rice with Tomatoes & Onions

2 tablespoons butter
1 small onion chopped

1 cup rice
1 can (10 1/2 ounces) chicken broth
3/4 cup water
3 tablespoons tomato sauce
   salt and pepper to taste

Saute onion in butter until onion is transparent. Add the remaining ingredients, stir and cover pan. Simmer rice until liquid is absorbed and rice is tender. Serves 4 to 6.

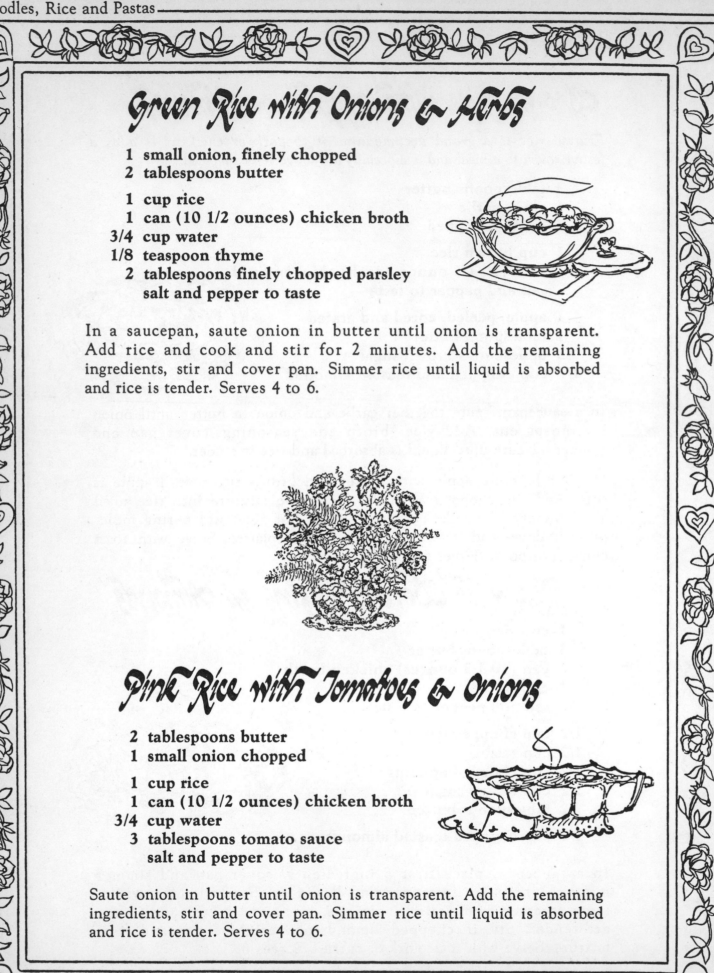

Spanish Rice with Onions, Peppers & Mushrooms

1 cup rice
1 can (10 1/2 ounces) chicken broth
4 tablespoons butter
  salt and pepper to taste

2 onions, chopped
2 cloves garlic, minced
1 green pepper, seeded and chopped
1 red pepper, seeded and chopped
1/4 pound mushrooms, sliced
1 teaspoon oregano
1/4 teaspoon sweet basil
1 can (1 pound) stewed tomatoes (do not drain)

In a saucepan, simmer first 4 ingredients until rice is tender and liquid is absorbed. In a skillet, place remaining ingredients and simmer mixture uncovered for 20 to 25 minutes or until liquid is almost evaporated. Stir together rice and vegetables in saucepan and heat through. Serves 6.

Note: - *Leftover cooked meat or chicken can be added to above for a hearty, satisfying meal.*

Yellow Rice with Onions & Cheese

4 tablespoons butter
1 small onion, finely chopped
1 cup rice

2 cups chicken broth, homemade or canned
1/4 teaspoon tumeric
  salt and pepper to taste

4 tablespoons grated Parmesan cheese
1 teaspoon grated lemon peel
1 tablespoon melted butter

Saute onion in butter until onion is soft. Add rice and saute for 2 minutes, stirring. Carefully add broth (it will splatter for a few seconds) and seasonings. Stir and cover pan and simmer rice for about 30 minutes or until rice is tender and liquid is absorbed. Stir in cheese, lemon peel and butter and toss to blend. Serves 6.

Confetti Rice with Chicken & Onions

      2 tablespoons butter
      1 cup long grain rice
      2 cans chicken broth (homemade or canned)
    1/3 cup chopped green onions
      2 tablespoons chopped parsley
      1 jar (2 ounces) pimiento strips drained
      1 cup finely chopped cooked chicken
      1 package (10 ounces) frozen green peas
         salt and pepper to taste

In a 1 1/2-quart souffle dish, combine all the ingredients and stir until mixture is well combined. Cover top tightly with foil and place in a 350° oven. Bake for about 45 minutes or until rice is tender and liquid is absorbed.

Serve with a green salad and fresh fruit mold. Serves 4 or 5.

Yellow Mexican Rice with Chiles & Cheese

      4 cups cooked rice*
    3/4 cup chopped canned tomatoes with
            about 2 tablespoons of juice
      1 cup grated Monterey Jack cheese
      1 can (4 ounces) diced green chile peppers
      1 cup sour cream
    1/2 teaspoon tumeric
         salt and pepper to taste

Stir together all the ingredients until blended. Place mixture into a buttered 2-quart casserole. Cover with foil and bake in a 350° oven until piping hot, about 30 minutes. Serves 6.

Note: - *To cook rice: Place 1 1/2 cups rice in a saucepan with 2 tablespoons oil and 3 cups chicken broth. Add salt and pepper to taste. Cover pan and simmer mixture for about 30 minutes or until rice is tender and liquid is absorbed.
   - Entire casserole can be assembled earlier in the day and stored in the refrigerator. Heat according to the directions above before serving.
   - This rice is "bravo" but not exceedingly hot. If you like, you can cut down on the amount of chile peppers.

Country-Style Noodle Pudding with Orange, Raisins & Pineapple

What a delectable pudding to serve with roast chicken on Sunday night when the whole family gets together. Invite a few friends for this recipe serves 12.

> 1 package (8 ounces) medium noodles, cooked according to the directions on the package.
> 1/2 cup (1 stick) melted butter
>
> 4 eggs
> 1 cup sugar
> 2 cups sour cream
> 1 teaspoon vanilla
> 1/4 teaspoon salt
>
> 1 can (8 ounces) crushed pineapple. Do not drain.
> 1/2 orange, grated. Use fruit, juice and peel.
> 1 cup yellow raisins
>
> cinnamon sugar

In a 9x13-inch pan, toss together cooked noodles with melted butter until blended.

Beat together eggs, sugar, sour cream, vanilla and salt until blended. Stir in pineapple, orange and yellow raisins. Pour mixture evenly over the noodles and ease noodles so that the filling flows to the bottom. Sprinkle top with cinnamon sugar.

Bake in a 350° oven for 1 hour or until top is golden brown. Cut into squares and serve warm. Serves 10 to 12.

Crown Mold of Noodles, Spiced Peaches & Raisins

1 package (8 ounces) medium noodles, cooked
    and drained
1/2 cup (1 stick) butter, melted
4 tablespoons cinnamon sugar
1 can (1 pound) spiced peaches, drained, pitted
    and chopped. Reserve juice for another use.
1/2 cup yellow raisins

3 eggs
1 1/2 cups sour cream
3/4 cup sugar
1 teaspoon vanilla
1/4 teaspoon salt

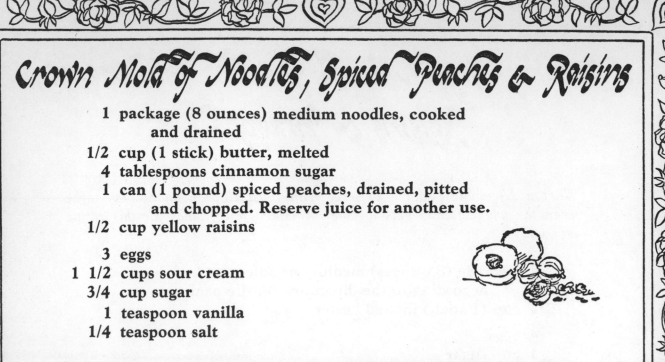

In a bowl, toss together first 5 ingredients until blended. Place mixture into a 2-quart ring mold that is sprayed with a non-stick spray and heavily buttered.

Beat together the remaining ingredients and pour mixture into the mold. Place mold on a cookie sheet and bake in a 350° oven for about 1 hour or until top is golden and custard is set. Unmold onto a lovely platter and serve warm. Serves 10.

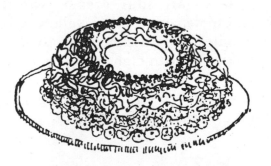

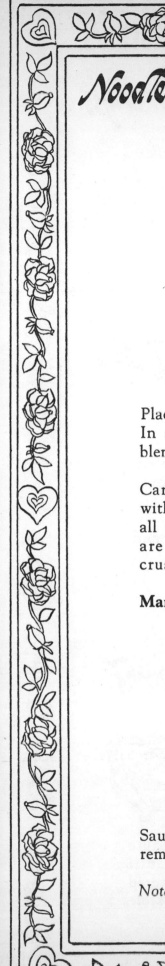

Noodle & Spinach Casserole with Marinara Sauce

1 pound wide egg noodles, cooked until
tender but firm. Drain and toss noodles
in 1/2 cup (1 stick) butter.
1 package (8 ounces) cream cheese
2 cups Ricotta cheese
1 package (8 ounces) Mozzarella chesse,
grated
2 green onions, finely chopped
1 package (10 ounces) frozen spinach,
defrosted and drained
2 eggs
1/2 teaspoon Italian Herb Seasoning
salt and pepper to taste
1/2 cup grated Parmesan cheese

Place half the cooked noodles in a buttered 9x13-inch baking pan. In a bowl, stir together the remaining ingredients until mixture is blended.

Carefully, spread spinach mixture over the noodles, and top this with the remaining noodles. Pour Marinara and Cheese Sauce over all and bake in a 350° oven for about 35 minutes or until noodles are beginning to brown. Serve hot with a spicy salad and some crusty Italian bread. Serves 8 to 10.

Marinara & Cheese Sauce:
1 carrot, finely grated
1 onion, chopped
2 cloves garlic, minced
2 tablespoons oil

1 can (1 pound 12 ounces) crushed tomatoes in
tomato puree
1 teaspoon Italian Herb Seasoning
1 teaspoon sugar
salt and pepper to taste
1/4 cup grated Parmesan cheese

Saute carrot, onion and garlic in oil until onion is tender. Add the remaining ingredients and simmer sauce for 10 minutes.

Note: - Entire casserole can be assembled earlier in the day and stored in the refrigerator. Cook as described above, but add a few minutes to cooking time.

Cinnamon Noodle Pudding with Apples & Oranges

2 apples, cored, peeled and very thinly sliced
1/2 cup yellow raisins
1 tablespoon grated orange peel
4 tablespoons butter

1 package (8 ounces) medium noodles, cooked
   and drained
1/4 cup (1/2 stick) butter, melted
4 tablespoons cinnamon sugar

4 eggs
2 cups sour cream
1 cup sugar
3/4 teaspoon vanilla
1/4 teaspoon salt

Saute apples, raisins and orange peel in butter until apples are tender. Stir together noodles, butter and cinnamon sugar. Stir in cooked apples. Place mixture into a 9x13-inch buttered porcelain casserole. Beat together the remaining ingredients and pour over the noodles.

Bake in a 350° oven for about 1 hour or until top is golden and custard is set. Cut into squares and serve. Serves 10.

Noodles tossed with Butter & Bread Crumbs

1 package (8 ounces) medium noodles, cooked
   and drained
6 tablespoons butter, divided
1 clove garlic, put through a press
1/2 cup bread crumbs
   salt and pepper to taste

Prepare noodles and toss with 4 tablespoons melted butter. Saute garlic and breadcrumbs in remaining 2 tablespoons butter until crumbs are toasted. Add seasonings and toss crumbs with buttered noodles until well combined. Place noodles in a buttered casserole and heat through. Serves 6.

Green Pasta with Ham & Cheese & Fresh Light Tomato Sauce

This is a lovely dish to serve on a night when you are expecting a few extra friends for dinner. it is incredibly easy to prepare and is glorious to serve.

- 1 package (8 ounces) green medium noodles, cooked tender but firm and drained
- 3 ounces (3/4 stick) butter, melted

- 1/4 pound sliced ham, cut into strips
- 1 container (16 ounces) Ricotta cheese
- 1/2 cup grated Parmesan cheese
- 1 package (8 ounces) Mozzarella cheese, grated
- 3 eggs
- 1 tablespoon chopped parsley
- 3 tablespoons chopped chives
- 1 teaspoon Italian Herb Seasoning
  salt and pepper to taste

In a large bowl, toss noodles with melted butter until noodles are nicely coated.

In another bowl, stir together the remaining ingredients until blended. Stir in the noodles and mix until everything is nicely combined. Place mixture in a buttered 9x13-inch baking pan and spread to even. Bake in a 350° oven for about 50 minutes or until top is lightly browned. Serve with Fresh Light Tomato Sauce on top. Enjoy!

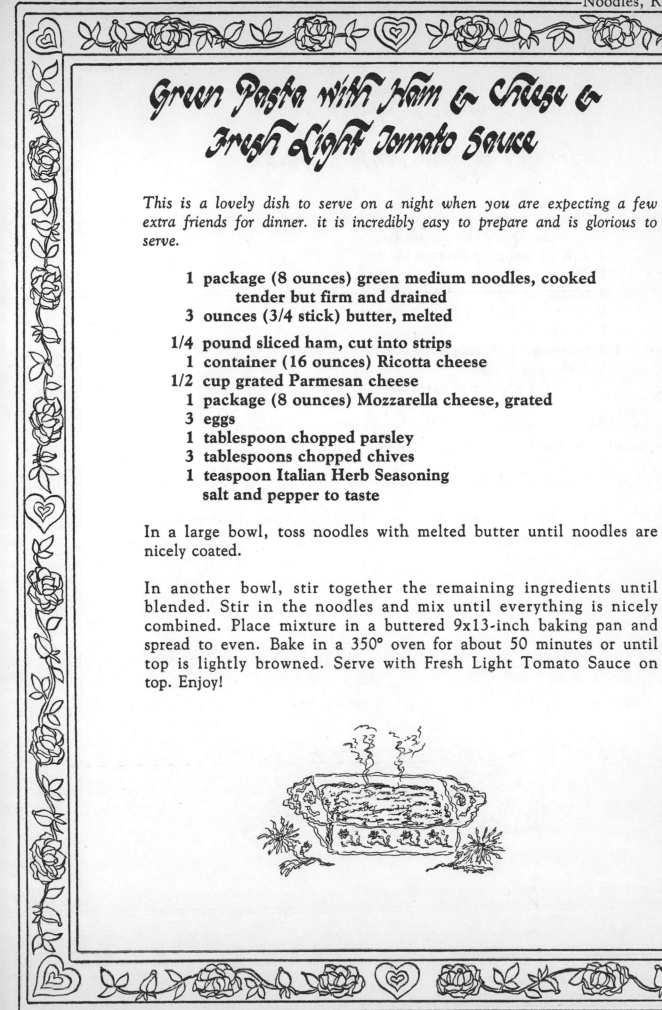

Green Pasta (continued)
Fresh Light Tomato Sauce

2 cans (1 pound, each) stewed tomatoes, finely
   chopped. Do not drain.
1 can (8 ounces) tomato sauce
1 teaspoon sugar
1/4 teaspoon coarse grind garlic powder
1 teaspoon Italian Herb Seasoning
1 bay leaf
1/8 teaspoon red pepper flakes
1 tablespoon oil
   salt and pepper to taste

In a saucepan, combine all the ingredients and simmer sauce for 10 minutes. Remove bay leaf. Serve warm.

Note: - Casserole can be assembled earlier in the day and baked before serving.
- Tomato sauce can be prepared earlier in the day and heated before serving.

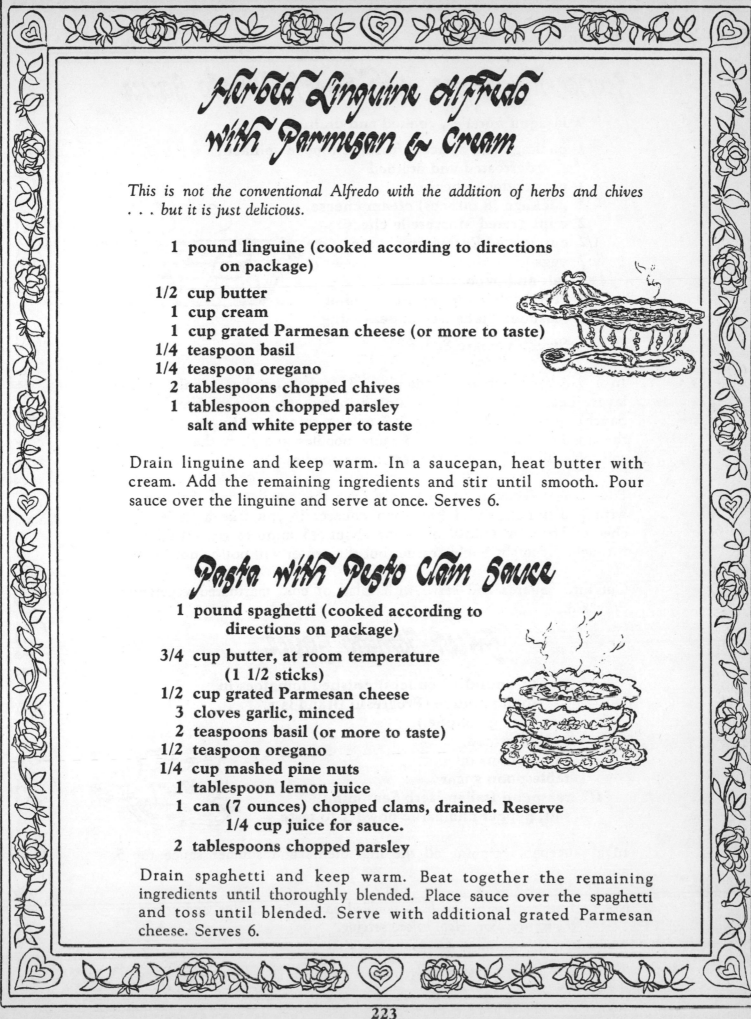

Herbed Linguine Alfredo with Parmesan & Cream

This is not the conventional Alfredo with the addition of herbs and chives . . . but it is just delicious.

- 1 **pound linguine (cooked according to directions on package)**

- 1/2 **cup butter**
- 1 **cup cream**
- 1 **cup grated Parmesan cheese (or more to taste)**
- 1/4 **teaspoon basil**
- 1/4 **teaspoon oregano**
- 2 **tablespoons chopped chives**
- 1 **tablespoon chopped parsley**
  salt and white pepper to taste

Drain linguine and keep warm. In a saucepan, heat butter with cream. Add the remaining ingredients and stir until smooth. Pour sauce over the linguine and serve at once. Serves 6.

Pasta with Pesto Clam Sauce

- 1 **pound spaghetti (cooked according to directions on package)**

- 3/4 **cup butter, at room temperature (1 1/2 sticks)**
- 1/2 **cup grated Parmesan cheese**
- 3 **cloves garlic, minced**
- 2 **teaspoons basil (or more to taste)**
- 1/2 **teaspoon oregano**
- 1/4 **cup mashed pine nuts**
- 1 **tablespoon lemon juice**
- 1 **can (7 ounces) chopped clams, drained. Reserve 1/4 cup juice for sauce.**
- 2 **tablespoons chopped parsley**

Drain spaghetti and keep warm. Beat together the remaining ingredients until thoroughly blended. Place sauce over the spaghetti and toss until blended. Serve with additional grated Parmesan cheese. Serves 6.

Spinach Lasagna with Sweet Tomato Sauce

9 lasagna noodles, cooked and drained

1 package (10 ounces) frozen chopped spinach,
    defrosted and drained

1 pint cottage cheese

1 package (8 ounces) cream cheese

2 cups grated Mozzarella cheese

1/2 cup grated Parmesan cheese

2 eggs
    salt and pepper to taste

1/2 cup finely chopped green onion

1/2 teaspoon Italian Herb Seasoning

Sweet Tomato Sauce

In a 9x13-inch greased pan, place 3 cooked noodles evenly in one layer. Beat together the remaining ingredients (except the Tomato Sauce) until blended. Place 1/2 of the spinach filling evenly over the noodles. Continue with 3 more noodles and then the remaining spinach filling. Top with the remaining noodles.

Pour Sweet Tomato Sauce evenly over the noodles and sprinkle top with additional grated Parmesan cheese, if you like a little more cheese. Heat in a 350° oven for about 45 minutes or until heated through. (It might bubble earlier but the center will not be hot.)

Cut into squares and serve with salad or cold marinated vegetables. Serves 8.

Sweet Tomato Sauce

1 can (1 pound 12 ounces) crushed tomatoes in
    tomato puree (Progresso Brand is a
    very good one.)

1 onion, grated

2 tablespoons oil

1 tablespoon sugar

1/2 teaspoon Italian Herb Seasoning
    salt, pepper and garlic powder to taste

In a saucepan, combine all the ingredients and simmer sauce for 5 minutes.

Note: - Entire casserole cn be assembled earlier in the day and stored in the refrigerator. Heat before serving.

Fettuccini Alla Romano with Onions, Peppers & Cheese

I still remember with fondness a dish, like this one, that we enjoyed in Italy. It is a total delight and indescribably delicious.

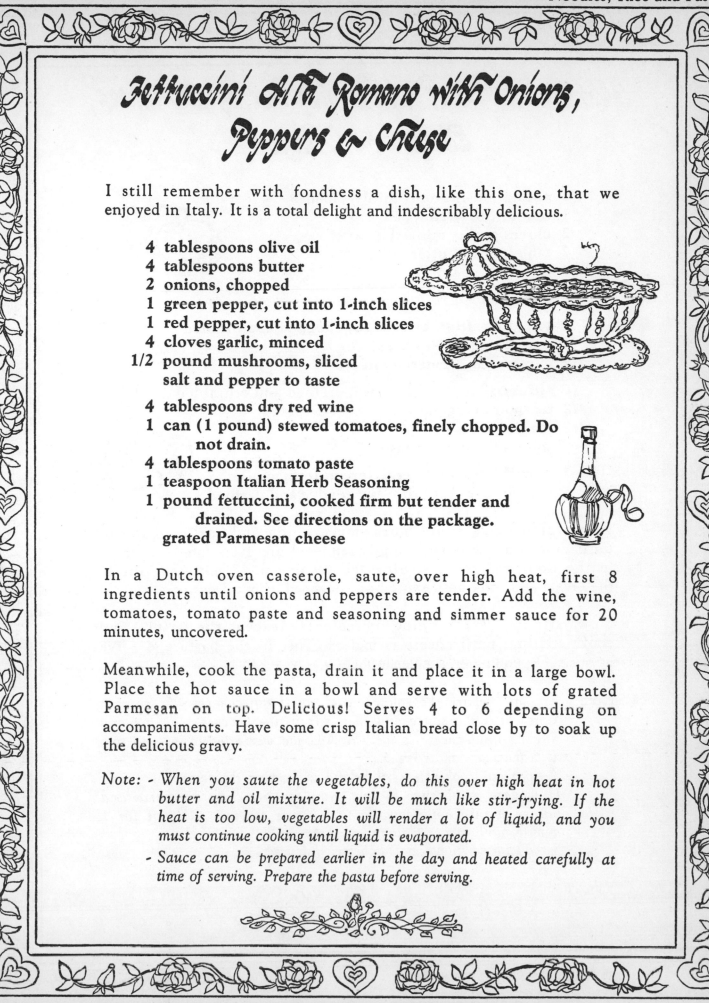

        4   tablespoons olive oil
        4   tablespoons butter
        2   onions, chopped
        1   green pepper, cut into 1-inch slices
        1   red pepper, cut into 1-inch slices
        4   cloves garlic, minced
      1/2   pound mushrooms, sliced
            salt and pepper to taste

        4   tablespoons dry red wine
        1   can (1 pound) stewed tomatoes, finely chopped. Do
                not drain.
        4   tablespoons tomato paste
        1   teaspoon Italian Herb Seasoning
        1   pound fettuccini, cooked firm but tender and
                drained. See directions on the package.
            grated Parmesan cheese

In a Dutch oven casserole, saute, over high heat, first 8 ingredients until onions and peppers are tender. Add the wine, tomatoes, tomato paste and seasoning and simmer sauce for 20 minutes, uncovered.

Meanwhile, cook the pasta, drain it and place it in a large bowl. Place the hot sauce in a bowl and serve with lots of grated Parmesan on top. Delicious! Serves 4 to 6 depending on accompaniments. Have some crisp Italian bread close by to soak up the delicious gravy.

Note: - *When you saute the vegetables, do this over high heat in hot butter and oil mixture. It will be much like stir-frying. If the heat is too low, vegetables will render a lot of liquid, and you must continue cooking until liquid is evaporated.*

   - *Sauce can be prepared earlier in the day and heated carefully at time of serving. Prepare the pasta before serving.*

Fettuccini Verdi with Mushrooms, Tomatoes, Bacon & Cheese

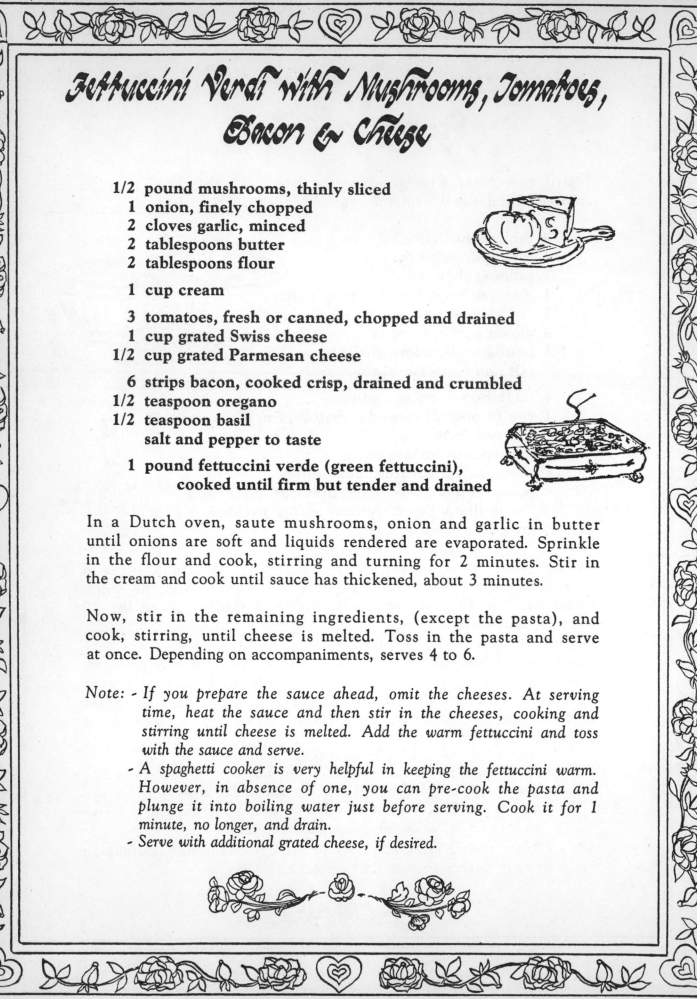

1/2 pound mushrooms, thinly sliced
1 onion, finely chopped
2 cloves garlic, minced
2 tablespoons butter
2 tablespoons flour

1 cup cream

3 tomatoes, fresh or canned, chopped and drained
1 cup grated Swiss cheese
1/2 cup grated Parmesan cheese

6 strips bacon, cooked crisp, drained and crumbled
1/2 teaspoon oregano
1/2 teaspoon basil
   salt and pepper to taste

1 pound fettuccini verde (green fettuccini),
   cooked until firm but tender and drained

In a Dutch oven, saute mushrooms, onion and garlic in butter until onions are soft and liquids rendered are evaporated. Sprinkle in the flour and cook, stirring and turning for 2 minutes. Stir in the cream and cook until sauce has thickened, about 3 minutes.

Now, stir in the remaining ingredients, (except the pasta), and cook, stirring, until cheese is melted. Toss in the pasta and serve at once. Depending on accompaniments, serves 4 to 6.

Note: - If you prepare the sauce ahead, omit the cheeses. At serving time, heat the sauce and then stir in the cheeses, cooking and stirring until cheese is melted. Add the warm fettuccini and toss with the sauce and serve.
- A spaghetti cooker is very helpful in keeping the fettuccini warm. However, in absence of one, you can pre-cook the pasta and plunge it into boiling water just before serving. Cook it for 1 minute, no longer, and drain.
- Serve with additional grated cheese, if desired.

Spaghetti alla Bolognese with Tomato Meat Sauce

This rich and flavorful meat and tomato sauce is probably one of the best loved sauces in all Italy. It can be used over veal, eggplant and many other pastas.

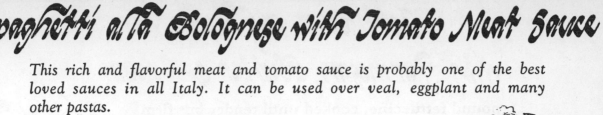

1 onion, finely chopped
1/2 cup finely grated carrots
3 cloves garlic, minced
2 tablespoons butter
2 tablespoons olive oil

1 pound lean ground beef

2 cans (1 pound, each) stewed tomatoes, finely chopped
1 can (8 ounces) tomato paste
1/2 cup dry white wine
4 tablespoons minced parsley (or 2 teaspoons dried parsley flakes)
2 teaspoons Italian Herb Seasoning (or 1 teaspoon oregano and 1 teaspoon basil)
1 bay leaf
2 teaspoons sugar
salt and freshly ground pepper to taste

In a Dutch oven or large saucepan, saute onion, carrots and garlic in butter and olive oil until the vegetables are soft. Add the ground beef and continue sauteing until the meat loses its pinkness.

Add the remaining ingredients and stir until the mixture is well blended. Simmer the sauce, uncovered, for about 40 minutes. Remove bay leaf and adjust seasonings. Serve with pastas, chicken, eggplant or veal. Yields about 1 quart sauce, enough for about 1 pound of spaghetti.

Spaghetti

I like using a spaghetti cooker for pastas. It facilitates draining and can be used to keep the pasta warm for a short while. In absence of this, use a large pot, allowing about 3 quarts of water for each pound of pasta. Add 2 tablespoons oil to the water to help prevent pasta from sticking. Bring water to a boil, add 3 teaspoons salt, and gradually add pasta so that the water keeps boiling briskly. Do not break the spaghetti, but place it in the water and as it softens, it will sink into the pot. Stir occasionally with a wooden spoon. Cook about 12 minutes or until pasta is cooked but firm. Drain in collander.

Fettuccine Alfredo with Parmesan, Butter & Cream

1 pound fettuccine, cooked until tender but firm

1/2 cup butter, melted
1 cup grated Parmesan cheese
1 cup heavy cream
salt and white pepper to taste

In a large bowl, toss together the hot pasta with the remaining ingredients, until blended. Serve at once. Delicious. Serves 6.

Note: - If you own a spaghetti cooker, then you can prepare the pasta earlier and keep it in the upper strainer, drained. To serve, bring water to a boil, lower pasta into boiling water and cook for 2 minutes.
- I like to add 2 tablespoons oil to the boiling water, when cooking pasta. It helps keep the pasta from sticking.

Pasta alla Marinara with Bacon & Cheese

12 ounces fettuccine rigatoni or other shaped pasta, cooked until tender but firm ("al dente")

1 small onion, minced
2 cloves garlic, minced
2 tablespoons oil
1 can (1 pound 12 ounces) crushed tomatoes in tomato puree
1 teaspoon sugar
1 teaspoon Italian Herb Seasoning
1/2 pound bacon, cooked crisp, drained and finely crumbled
1/2 cup grated Parmesan cheese
salt and pepper to taste

Saute onion and garlic in oil until onion is transparent. Now add the remaining ingredients and simmer sauce for 15 minutes, uncovered. Toss pasta with sauce and serve at once.

Giant Shells Filled with Spinach & Cheese

This is a grand family dish, exceedingly attractive and simple to prepare. It can be prepared ahead and heated at serving time.

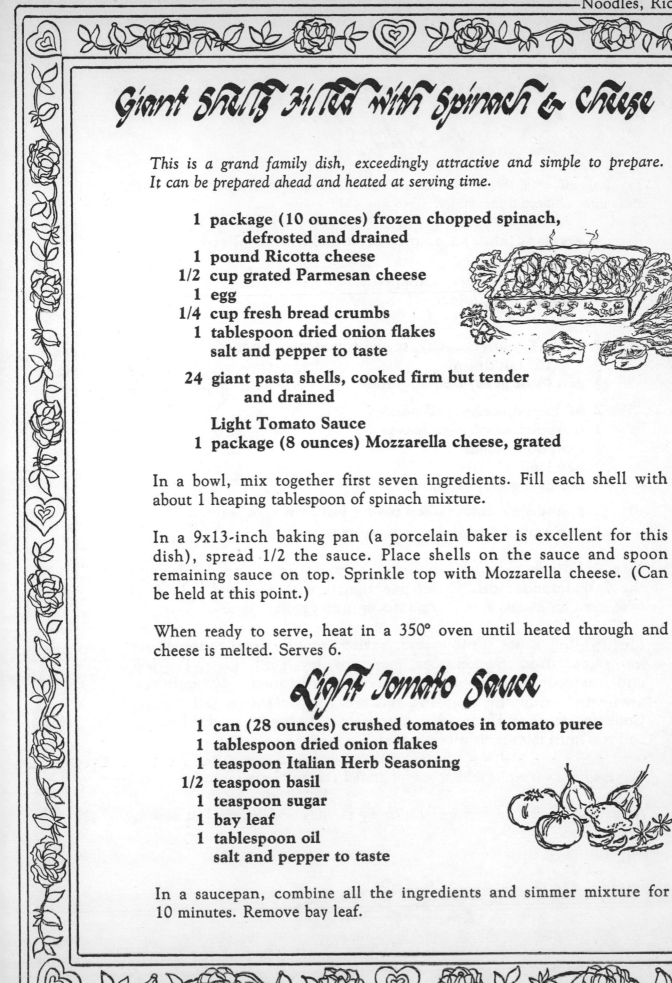

- 1 package (10 ounces) frozen chopped spinach, defrosted and drained
- 1 pound Ricotta cheese
- 1/2 cup grated Parmesan cheese
- 1 egg
- 1/4 cup fresh bread crumbs
- 1 tablespoon dried onion flakes
  salt and pepper to taste

- 24 giant pasta shells, cooked firm but tender and drained

  Light Tomato Sauce
- 1 package (8 ounces) Mozzarella cheese, grated

In a bowl, mix together first seven ingredients. Fill each shell with about 1 heaping tablespoon of spinach mixture.

In a 9x13-inch baking pan (a porcelain baker is excellent for this dish), spread 1/2 the sauce. Place shells on the sauce and spoon remaining sauce on top. Sprinkle top with Mozzarella cheese. (Can be held at this point.)

When ready to serve, heat in a 350° oven until heated through and cheese is melted. Serves 6.

Light Tomato Sauce

- 1 can (28 ounces) crushed tomatoes in tomato puree
- 1 tablespoon dried onion flakes
- 1 teaspoon Italian Herb Seasoning
- 1/2 teaspoon basil
- 1 teaspoon sugar
- 1 bay leaf
- 1 tablespoon oil
  salt and pepper to taste

In a saucepan, combine all the ingredients and simmer mixture for 10 minutes. Remove bay leaf.

Linguini Provencal with Eggplant, Tomatoes & Onions

Try linguini with this very unusual sauce. It is a lovely vegetarian dish and quite substantial for dinner.

1 eggplant (about 1 pound) peeled and thinly sliced
2 tablespoons olive oil
1 large onion, finely chopped
3 cloves garlic, minced
2 tablespoons olive oil

2 cans (1 pound, each) stewed tomatoes, chopped.
    Do not drain.
1 can (8 ounces) tomato puree

2 tablespoons chopped parsley
1 teaspoon dried basil leaves
2 teaspoons sugar
1 bay leaf
   salt and pepper to taste

1 pound linguini, cooked tender but firm and drained
1/2 cup grated Parmesan cheese, or to taste

In a 9x13-inch roasting pan, place eggplant slices and drizzle with the 2 tablespoons oil. Cover pan tightly with foil and bake in a 400° oven for about 20 to 25 minutes or until eggplant is soft.

Meanwhile, saute onion and garlic in oil until onions are transparent. Add the tomatoes, puree, parsley, basil, sugar, bay leaf and seasonings and simmer mixture for about 20 minutes, uncovered. Add the eggplant and break it up into small pieces. Cook for another 10 or 15 minutes. Add the sauce to the linguini and toss until mixture is nicely mixed.

Serve with a generous tablespoon of grated cheese. Serves 6 to 8.

Note: - Sauce can be prepared earlier in the day and reheated at serving time.

The Easiest & Best Homemade Egg Pasta

Freshly made pasta is delectable. It has a character and a body and a depth all it's own. However, it's preparation does require a little extra time (which, I agree, is becoming more and more rare.) But on a day, when it's cold or rainy, and you find yourself with "nothing to do," you'll find making fresh pasta a good deal of fun. And the rewards! Fresh pasta is a treat, deeply satisfying and delicious. Of course, using a pasta machine is recommended to save time and muscle. But in absence of one, I have included my Mixer Method which vastly simplifies the old hand kneading method.

    1 egg
    1 teaspoon oil
2/3 cup flour
    pinch of salt
    1 tablespoon flour

In the large bowl of an electric mixer, and with the paddle beater, beat egg and oil for 2 or 3 seconds or until egg is roughly blended. Add the flour and salt and beat for 1 minute. If the dough is sticky, add the additional flour and continue beating until blended.

If you are using a Pasta Machine: Divide dough into fourths and sprinkle a little flour over each piece of dough. Run each piece of dough (cover the remaining dough with plastic wrap to prevent drying) through the machine, with the rollers set at the widest distance. Fold dough into thirds, set rollers at the next narrow notch, and run it through again. Continue rolling and narrowing the rollers until pasta is about 1/16-inch thick. (No need to fold dough again.) Sprinkle dough with a little flour, if ever it feels sticky.

Now run the pasta through the desired cutting attachment, (wide, narrow, lasagna, etc.) Place noodles on a dry towel and let them dry for about 10 to 15 minutes. Noodles can be dried overnight and will keep for a month. They do not need to be refrigerated.

The Easiest & Best Homemade Egg Pasta (continued)

If you are using the Mixer Method: Continue beating. Now the dough should have collected in a ball. Beat for about 2 minutes. Dough should now be soft and pliable and easily handled.

Divide dough into fourths. Roll out one fourth at a time on a lightly floured pastry cloth until dough is 1/16-inch thick. (Cover the remaining dough with plastic wrap to prevent drying.) Sprinkle dough lightly with flour if ever it feels sticky.

Roll dough up, jelly roll fashion, and cut it into the desired width. Unravel the noodles and let them dry on a towel for 10 to 15 minutes. Noodles can be dried overnight and will keep for a month. They do not need to be refrigerated.

How to Cook Fresh Egg Pasta:

In a large pot (a spaghetti cooker is excellent for this), bring to a rapid boil, 4 quarts water and 1 tablespoon each of salt and oil. Stir in pasta, all at once. It will amaze you how quickly it will cook.

After pasta rises to the top (this will occur in about 1 minute), continue boiling rapidly for another minute or until pasta is firm, yet tender. Drain the pasta. Pasta is now ready to be used in the various recipes.

Note: - Triple the recipe to yield about 8 ounces of noodles.

"Eat your Vegetables...."

Acorn Squash with Pineapple, Cinnamon & Spiced Honey

3 medium acorn squash, cut into halves. Remove strings and seeds.
  hot water

1 can (8 ounces) crushed pineapple, drained
1/4 cup honey
1/4 cup brown sugar
1/4 cup butter, melted
2 tablespoons grated orange (use fruit, juice and peel)
1 tablespoon grated lemon (use fruit, juice and peel)
1/4 teaspoon cinnamon
  pinch of nutmeg
  pinch of powdered cloves
  salt to taste

Place acorn squash, cut side down in a baking pan. Add about 1/4-inch hot water to pan. Bake squash in a 350° oven for about 40 minutes or until squash is tender.

Into a large bowl, scoop out the pulp and mash it. Add the remaining ingredients and stir until thoroughly blended. Spoon mixture into a greased porcelain baker and bake in a 350° oven for 20 minutes or until casserole is heated through. Sprinkle a little cinnamon sugar on top when serving. Serves 6.

Asparagus with Lemon Cream Hollandaise

1 1/2 pounds asparagus, remove tough ends. Steam in
        a large, covered skillet with 1/2-inch water,
        until tender. Drain.
     2 tablespoons melted butter

Lemon Cream Hollandaise:
     3 egg yolks
     2 tablespoons lemon juice
   1/4 teaspoon finely grated lemon peel
     1 tablespoon chopped chives or green onions

   3/4 cup butter (1 1/2 sticks)
   1/4 cup sour cream, at room temperature

Lay asparagus in a shallow porcelain baker. Brush with melted
butter and keep warm in a 300° oven.

In a blender container, place yolks, lemon juice, peel and chives
and blend for 10 seconds, at high speed.

Heat butter until it is sizzling hot and bubbly, but be careful not
to brown it. Add the hot, sizzling butter very slowly, in a steady
stream, while the blender continues running. When the butter is
completely incorporated, blend in the sour cream.

Spoon sauce over the asparagus and heat in oven for 1 to 2
minutes, no more, or sauce will curdle. Serve at once. Serves 6.

Note: - If you are planning to start this earlier in the day, then you
        must adhere to the following considerations. Asparagus can be
        cooked and placed in shallow baker. Brush with butter and then
        refrigerate. Before serving, heat in a 300° oven. When asparagus
        is heated through, then spoon the sauce on top and heat for 1 or
        2 minutes.
      - Sauce can be prepared earlier in the day and stored in the
        refrigerator. It can be reheated in the top of a double boiler over
        hot, not boiling water and stirred carefully. I have done this
        before, but it is tricky. So, handle carefully, or your sauce will
        be "done in."

Broccoli with Tomatoes, Onions & Cheese

2 packages (10 ounces, each) broccoli spears,
   cut into 1-inch pieces and cooked for about
   5 minutes in 1/2 cup cream or until almost
   tender. Sprinkle with salt and pepper.
3 tomatoes, peeled, seeded and chopped
1/3 cup chopped green onions
2 tablespoons melted butter
1 tablespoon lemon juice
1 tablespoon chopped parsley

1/3 cup fresh bread crumbs
1/3 cup grated Swiss cheese

Combine first 6 ingredients in a buttered porcelain baker and toss until mixture is even. Sprinkle bread crumbs and cheese evenly over the top.

Bake in a 350° oven for 20 to 25 minutes or until casserole is heated through and top is nicely browned. Serve with broiled steak, broiled chicken or hamburgers. Serves 8.

Note: - Casserole can be assembled earlier in the day and stored in the refrigerator. Bake before serving.

Broccoli Frittata with Onions & Cheese

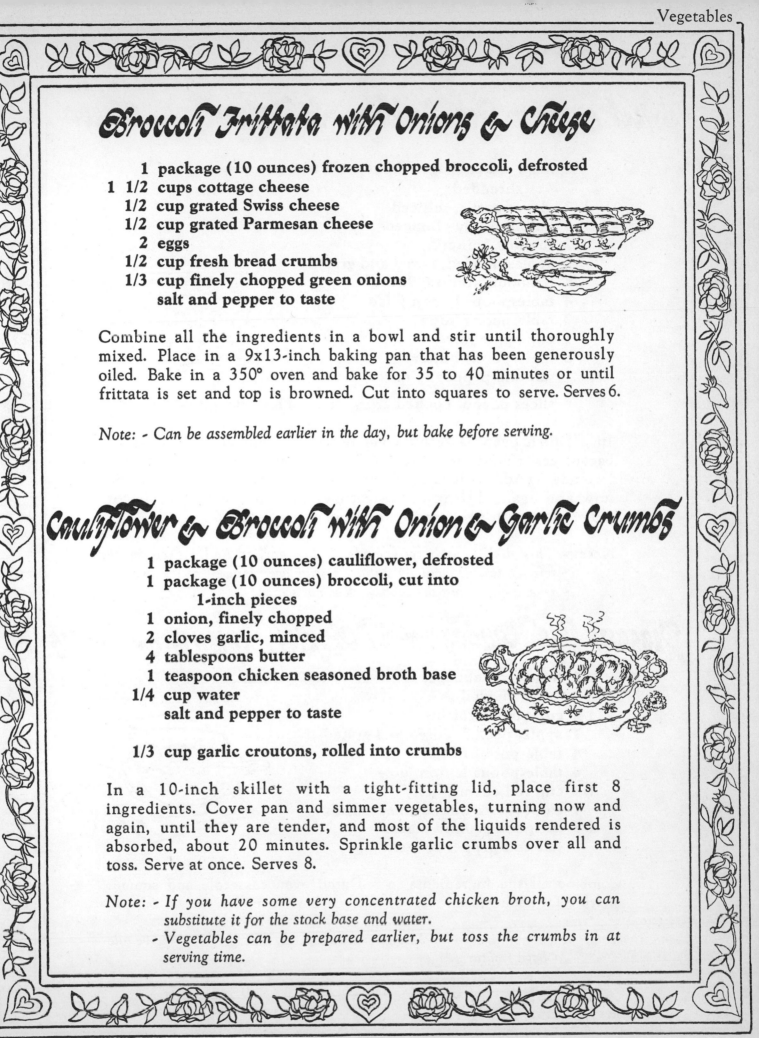

      1 package (10 ounces) frozen chopped broccoli, defrosted
 1 1/2 cups cottage cheese
   1/2 cup grated Swiss cheese
   1/2 cup grated Parmesan cheese
      2 eggs
   1/2 cup fresh bread crumbs
   1/3 cup finely chopped green onions
        salt and pepper to taste

Combine all the ingredients in a bowl and stir until thoroughly mixed. Place in a 9x13-inch baking pan that has been generously oiled. Bake in a 350° oven and bake for 35 to 40 minutes or until frittata is set and top is browned. Cut into squares to serve. Serves 6.

Note: - Can be assembled earlier in the day, but bake before serving.

Cauliflower & Broccoli with Onion & Garlic Crumbs

      1 package (10 ounces) cauliflower, defrosted
      1 package (10 ounces) broccoli, cut into
            1-inch pieces
      1 onion, finely chopped
      2 cloves garlic, minced
      4 tablespoons butter
      1 teaspoon chicken seasoned broth base
   1/4 cup water
        salt and pepper to taste

   1/3 cup garlic croutons, rolled into crumbs

In a 10-inch skillet with a tight-fitting lid, place first 8 ingredients. Cover pan and simmer vegetables, turning now and again, until they are tender, and most of the liquids rendered is absorbed, about 20 minutes. Sprinkle garlic crumbs over all and toss. Serve at once. Serves 8.

Note: - If you have some very concentrated chicken broth, you can substitute it for the stock base and water.
- Vegetables can be prepared earlier, but toss the crumbs in at serving time.

Sweet & Sour Red Cabbage with Apples & Bacon

    1 head red cabbage, about 1 1/2 to 2 pounds,
           shredded
    2 cloves garlic, minced
    1 onion, finely chopped
    2 shallots, minced
    2 apples, peeled, cored and grated
  1/8 teaspoon ground cloves
    4 tablespoons lemon juice
    2 tablespoons honey
    1 cup apple juice
    2 tablespoons butter
       salt and pepper to taste

    4 slices bacon, cooked crisp, drained and crumbled

In a Dutch oven casserole combine all the ingredients, except the bacon, and simmer mixture for about 45 minutes or until cabbage is tender. (Add a little apple juice if juices run a little dry.) Stir now and again during cooking time. Stir in the cooked bacon. Serve warm with sweet and sour beef or pork. Serves 6.

Note: - This dish is delicious made 1 day earlier and stored in the refrigerator. It actually improves with age. However, take care in reheating, so that the cabbage does not scorch.

Peasant Red Cabbage with Apples, Raisins & Cloves

    1 head red cabbage, about 1 1/2 to 2 pounds,
           shredded
  1/2 cup yellow raisins
    1 apple, peeled, cored and grated
    4 tablespoons butter
    4 tablespoons lemon juice
  1/3 cup red currant jelly
    1 can (10 1/2 ounces) beef broth
  1/8 teaspoon ground cloves
       salt and pepper to taste

Combine all the ingredients in a Dutch oven casserole and simmer mixture for about 45 minutes or until cabbage is tender. Serves 6.

Note: - I do not like to thicken gravy with flour, but prefer to serve the cabbage "natural."

Lemon Carrots with Butter & Honey

Even if you are so-so about carrots, you will enjoy the delicate flavor of this dish. It is also pretty to look at, glazed and flecked with parsley.

- 1 bag (1 pound) baby carrots
- 1/2 cup water

- 2 tablespoons butter
- 3 tablespoons honey

- 1 tablespoon lemon juice
- 2 tablespoons chopped parsley
- salt and pepper to taste

Cook carrots in boiling water for about 5 minutes and drain. In a large skillet, melt butter with honey. Add drained carrots and cook and stir until carrots are glazed. Add the remaining ingredients and cook for another minute or two, stirring. Serves 4.

Carrots & Onions in Cream Sauce

- 1 package (1 pound) baby carrots
- 1 package (1 pound) frozen baby onions
- 1/2 cup water

- 2 tablespoons butter
- 1/2 cup cream
- 2 tablespoons chopped parsley
- 1 teaspoon sugar
- salt and pepper to taste

Cook carrots in boiling water for about 5 minutes. Add onions and cook an additional 5 minutes. Drain. In a large skillet, add the remaining ingredients with the carrots and cook at a simmer, uncovered, until cream is almost evaporated and thickened into a sauce. Serves 8.

Note: - Both dishes can be prepared earlier in the day and stored in the refrigerator. Reheat carefully before serving.

Glazed Carrots with Butter & Cinnamon

1 pound carrots, peeled and seeded. Cook in
     1-inch water until tender and drain. Sprinkle with
     1 tablespoon lemon juice.
3 tablespoons butter
1/4 cup brown sugar
1/4 teaspoon cinnamon
     salt to taste

In a large skillet, combine all the ingredients and cook, tossing and turning until carrots are nicely glazed and butter and sugar are syrupy. Sprinkle with 1 teaspoon parsley flakes and cook for another minute. Serves 4 to 6.

Note: - Carrots can be prepared earlier in the day and reheated carefully at time of serving.

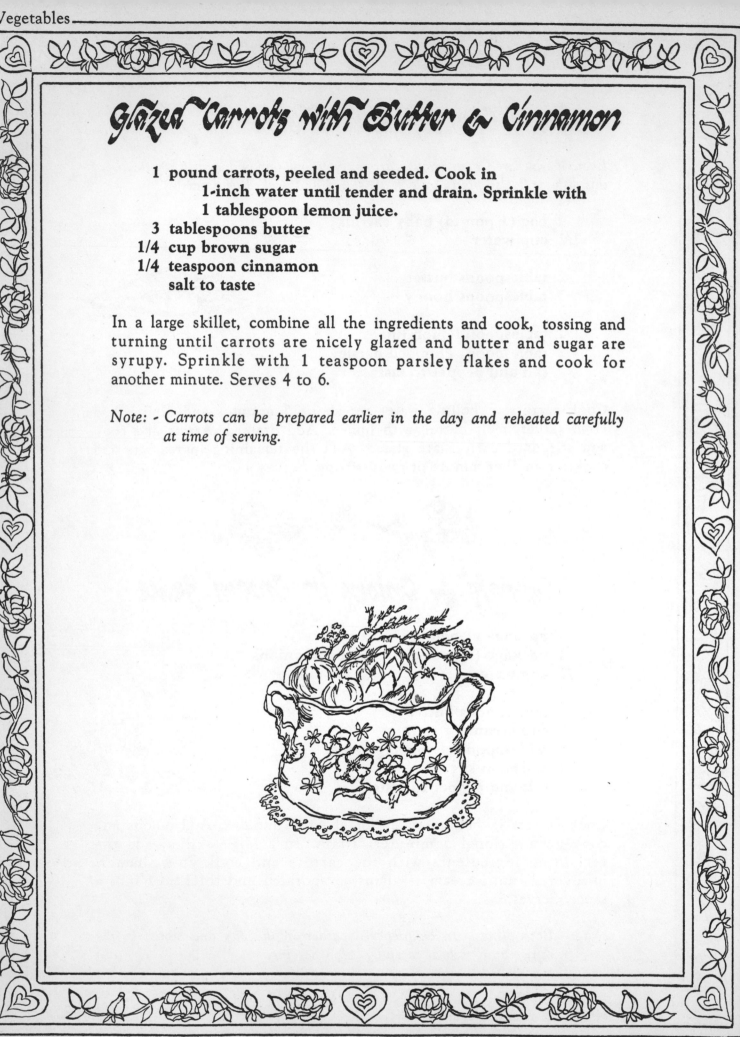

Cauliflower Casserole with Tomatoes, Onions & Cheese

2 packages frozen cauliflower, separated into
   small florets
2 tablespoons lemon juice

3 medium tomatoes, peeled, seeded and chopped.
   Drain.
3 green onions, chopped
1 cup grated Swiss cheese
1/4 cup grated Parmesan cheese
   salt and pepper to taste

4 tablespoons melted butter
4 tablespoons bread crumbs
4 tablespoons grated Parmesan cheese

In a large bowl place cauliflower and toss with the lemon juice.
Add the tomatoes, onions, cheeses and seasonings and toss until
mixture is nicely blended.

Place vegetable mixture into a shallow buttered porcelain baker.
Combine butter, crumbs and cheese and sprinkle mixture over the
vegetables. Bake in a 350° oven for 20 to 25 minutes or until
cheese is melted and crumbs are beginning to brown. Serve at
once. Serves 6 to 8.

Note: - Entire casserole can be assembled earlier in the day but should be
         baked before serving.
      - Make certain that the cauliflower is patted dry with paper
         towelling. Drain tomatoes and use juice for another use. This
         will prevent casserole from getting soupy.

Cauliflower & Tomatoes in Creamy Dijon Cheese Sauce

2 packages (10 ounces, each) frozen cauliflower,
    broken into florets
2 tomatoes, peeled, chopped and drained
2 green onions, chopped

1/4 cup mayonnaise
1/4 cup sour cream
1 teaspoon Dijon mustard
1 cup grated Swiss cheese
2 tablespoons grated Parmesan cheese
    salt and pepper to taste

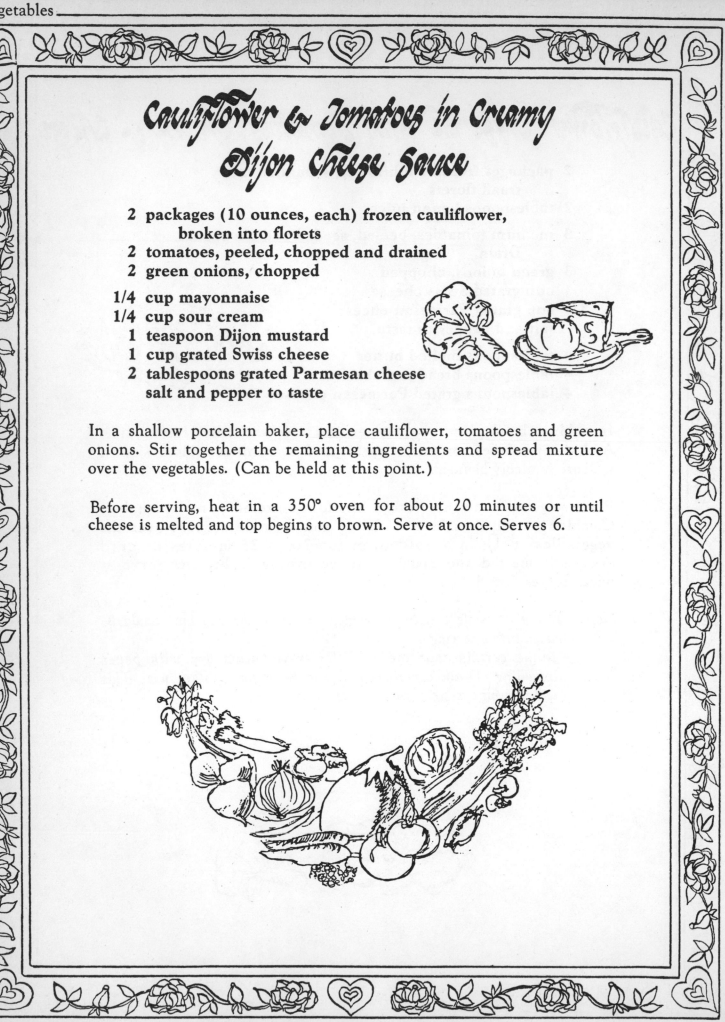

In a shallow porcelain baker, place cauliflower, tomatoes and green onions. Stir together the remaining ingredients and spread mixture over the vegetables. (Can be held at this point.)

Before serving, heat in a 350° oven for about 20 minutes or until cheese is melted and top begins to brown. Serve at once. Serves 6.

Herbed Eggplant with Tomatoes & Onions & Lemon Vinaigrette

This is excellent served hot as an accompaniment to dinner, or served cold as an antipasto or salad. It can be prepared several days earlier and stores well in the refrigerator.

1 eggplant (about 1 pound). Remove peel, cut in half, lengthwise, and cut into 1/4-inch thick slices
2 tablespoons oil
2 tablespoons lemon juice
4 cloves garlic, finely minced

1 can (1 pound) stewed tomatoes, drained and chopped
1 tablespoon sweet basil flakes
2 tablespoons chopped parsley
1 onion, grated
3 tablespoons lemon juice
1 tablespoon oil
salt and pepper to taste

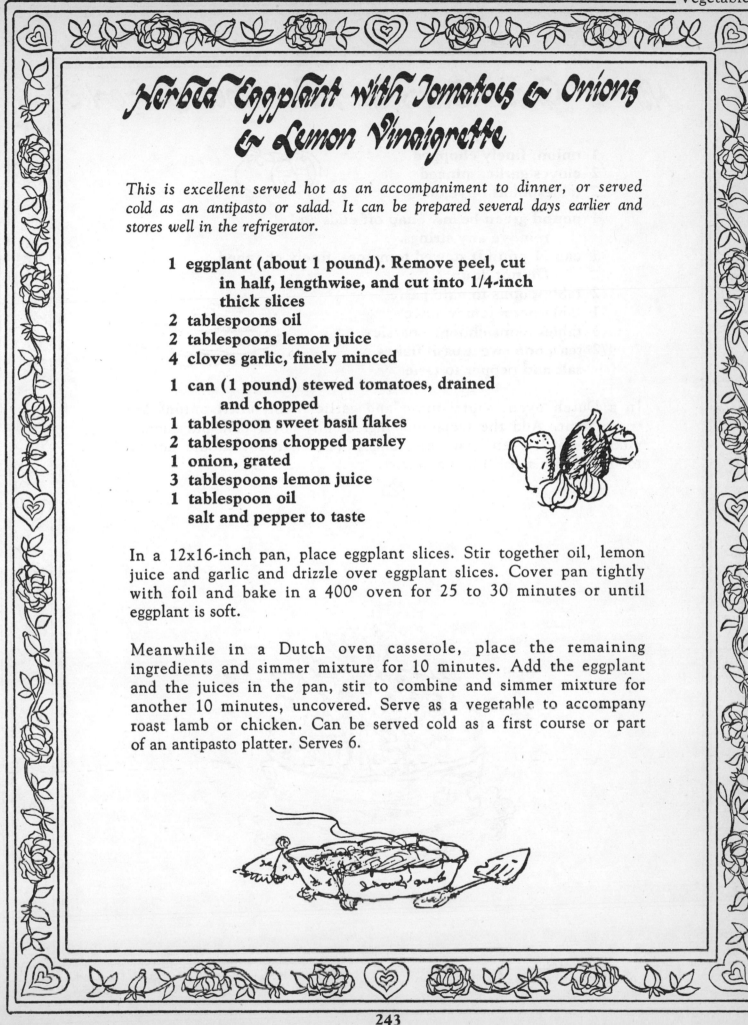

In a 12x16-inch pan, place eggplant slices. Stir together oil, lemon juice and garlic and drizzle over eggplant slices. Cover pan tightly with foil and bake in a 400° oven for 25 to 30 minutes or until eggplant is soft.

Meanwhile in a Dutch oven casserole, place the remaining ingredients and simmer mixture for 10 minutes. Add the eggplant and the juices in the pan, stir to combine and simmer mixture for another 10 minutes, uncovered. Serve as a vegetable to accompany roast lamb or chicken. Can be served cold as a first course or part of an antipasto platter. Serves 6.

Herbed Green Beans with Tomatoes & Garlic

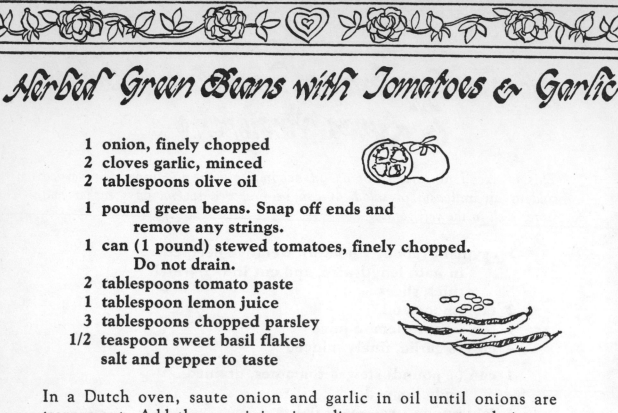

1 onion, finely chopped
2 cloves garlic, minced
2 tablespoons olive oil

1 pound green beans. Snap off ends and
    remove any strings.
1 can (1 pound) stewed tomatoes, finely chopped.
    Do not drain.
2 tablespoons tomato paste
1 tablespoon lemon juice
3 tablespoons chopped parsley
1/2 teaspoon sweet basil flakes
    salt and pepper to taste

In a Dutch oven, saute onion and garlic in oil until onions are transparent. Add the remaining ingredients, cover pan and simmer mixture until green beans are tender. (Green beans should not be too firm for this dish.) Serves 6.

French-Style Buttered Peas & Onions

1/4 cup butter (1/2 stick)
1/2 cup sliced green onions (use just the
 bulbs)
 2 packages (10 ounces, each) baby peas
 1 cup finely shredded Boston lettuce (sometimes
 called "butter")
 pinch of salt
 1 tablespoon parsley
1/4 cup rich chicken broth
 salt and pepper to taste

 1 tablespoon lemon juice

In a saucepan, simmer together first 8 ingredients until peas are tender. Stir in the lemon juice. Serve with roast chicken, veal or turkey. Serves 8.

Scalloped Potato Casserole with Onions & Cream

    4 tablespoons butter
    1 onion, chopped
    1 clove garlic, put through a press

    2 teaspoons paprika

    1 can (10 1/2 ounces) chicken broth
    1 cup cream

    2 pounds potatoes, peeled and cut into 3/4-inch
        thick slices
      salt and pepper to taste

In a saucepan, saute onion and garlic in butter until onions are soft. Add paprika and stir to combine. Add broth and cream and stir until blended. Add potatoes and seasonings. Cover saucepan and simmer mixture for 30 to 40 minutes or until potatoes are tender. Serves 6.

Note: - Can be made earlier in the day and heated before serving.

Parsleyed Potato Pancakes with Chives

    6 medium-sized potatoes, peeled and grated
    1 small onion, grated

    3 eggs, beaten
    1/2 cup cracker crumbs
    1/4 cup chopped parsley (or 1 tablespoon dried
        parsley flakes)
    1/4 cup chopped chives (or 2 tablespoons dried
        chive flakes)
      salt and pepper to taste

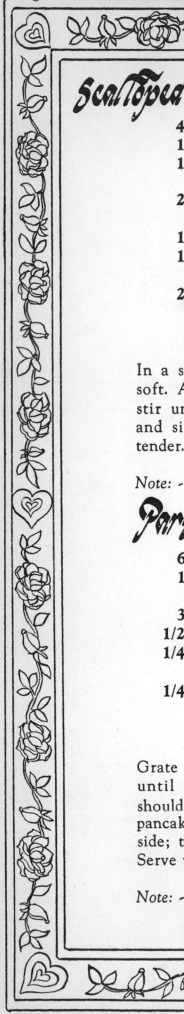

Grate potatoes and onions. Add the remaining ingredients and stir until blended. Heat a 12-inch skillet with 1/2-inch of oil. Oil should be very hot, but not smoking. Pour 1/4 cup batter for each pancake, but do not crowd the pan. Fry until golden brown on one side; turn and brown other side. Keep warm in a low oven (250°). Serve warm with a dollup of sour cream. Serves 6.

Note: - Potato pancakes can be made up earlier in the day and reheated. Place them in a shallow pan, cover with foil and heat in a 300° oven until heated through.

Creamed Potato Casserole with Chives & Bacon

This is a lovely, homey dish to serve with roast chicken or veal. It is like a giant baked potato, served with sour cream, bacon and chives.

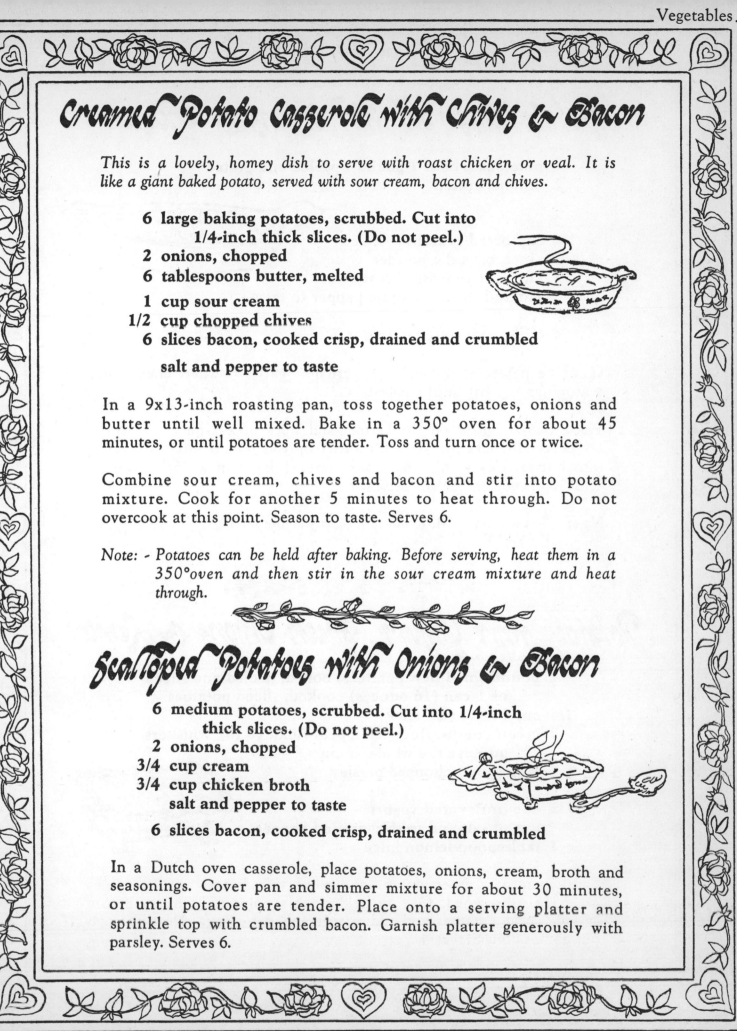

6 large baking potatoes, scrubbed. Cut into 1/4-inch thick slices. (Do not peel.)
2 onions, chopped
6 tablespoons butter, melted

1 cup sour cream
1/2 cup chopped chives
6 slices bacon, cooked crisp, drained and crumbled

salt and pepper to taste

In a 9x13-inch roasting pan, toss together potatoes, onions and butter until well mixed. Bake in a 350° oven for about 45 minutes, or until potatoes are tender. Toss and turn once or twice.

Combine sour cream, chives and bacon and stir into potato mixture. Cook for another 5 minutes to heat through. Do not overcook at this point. Season to taste. Serves 6.

Note: - Potatoes can be held after baking. Before serving, heat them in a 350°oven and then stir in the sour cream mixture and heat through.

Scalloped Potatoes with Onions & Bacon

6 medium potatoes, scrubbed. Cut into 1/4-inch thick slices. (Do not peel.)
2 onions, chopped
3/4 cup cream
3/4 cup chicken broth
salt and pepper to taste

6 slices bacon, cooked crisp, drained and crumbled

In a Dutch oven casserole, place potatoes, onions, cream, broth and seasonings. Cover pan and simmer mixture for about 30 minutes, or until potatoes are tender. Place onto a serving platter and sprinkle top with crumbled bacon. Garnish platter generously with parsley. Serves 6.

Potato Casserole with Onions & Cheese

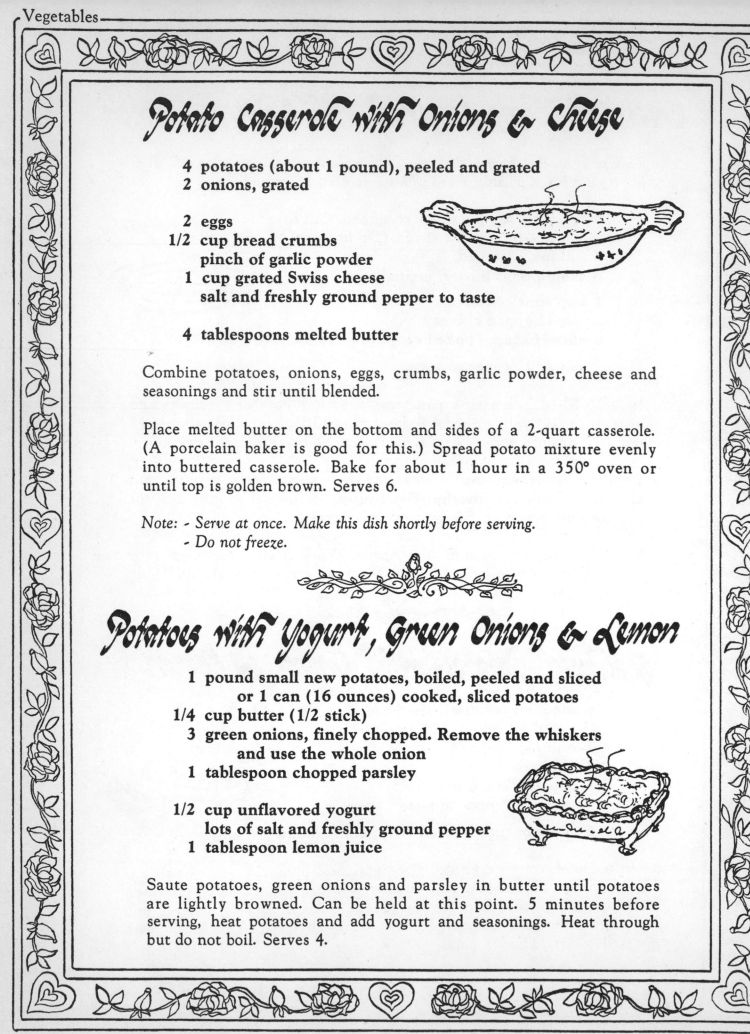

4 potatoes (about 1 pound), peeled and grated
2 onions, grated

2 eggs
1/2 cup bread crumbs
    pinch of garlic powder
1 cup grated Swiss cheese
    salt and freshly ground pepper to taste

4 tablespoons melted butter

Combine potatoes, onions, eggs, crumbs, garlic powder, cheese and seasonings and stir until blended.

Place melted butter on the bottom and sides of a 2-quart casserole. (A porcelain baker is good for this.) Spread potato mixture evenly into buttered casserole. Bake for about 1 hour in a 350° oven or until top is golden brown. Serves 6.

Note: - Serve at once. Make this dish shortly before serving.
      - Do not freeze.

Potatoes with Yogurt, Green Onions & Lemon

1 pound small new potatoes, boiled, peeled and sliced
    or 1 can (16 ounces) cooked, sliced potatoes
1/4 cup butter (1/2 stick)
3 green onions, finely chopped. Remove the whiskers
    and use the whole onion
1 tablespoon chopped parsley

1/2 cup unflavored yogurt
    lots of salt and freshly ground pepper
1 tablespoon lemon juice

Saute potatoes, green onions and parsley in butter until potatoes are lightly browned. Can be held at this point. 5 minutes before serving, heat potatoes and add yogurt and seasonings. Heat through but do not boil. Serves 4.

Potatoes & Onions Baked in Broth

This is a delicious way to serve potatoes and is so good with chicken or veal. It can be prepared ahead and heated before serving . . . and assembling couldn't be easier.

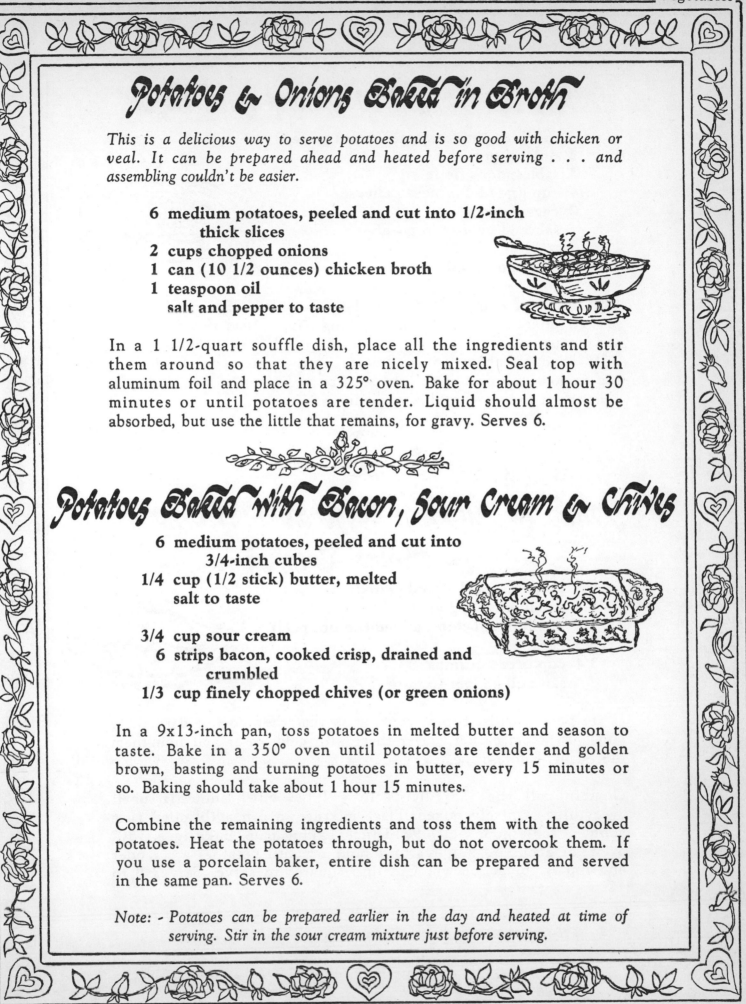

- **6 medium potatoes, peeled and cut into 1/2-inch thick slices**
- **2 cups chopped onions**
- **1 can (10 1/2 ounces) chicken broth**
- **1 teaspoon oil**
- **salt and pepper to taste**

In a 1 1/2-quart souffle dish, place all the ingredients and stir them around so that they are nicely mixed. Seal top with aluminum foil and place in a 325° oven. Bake for about 1 hour 30 minutes or until potatoes are tender. Liquid should almost be absorbed, but use the little that remains, for gravy. Serves 6.

Potatoes Baked with Bacon, Sour Cream & Chives

- **6 medium potatoes, peeled and cut into 3/4-inch cubes**
- **1/4 cup (1/2 stick) butter, melted**
- **salt to taste**

- **3/4 cup sour cream**
- **6 strips bacon, cooked crisp, drained and crumbled**
- **1/3 cup finely chopped chives (or green onions)**

In a 9x13-inch pan, toss potatoes in melted butter and season to taste. Bake in a 350° oven until potatoes are tender and golden brown, basting and turning potatoes in butter, every 15 minutes or so. Baking should take about 1 hour 15 minutes.

Combine the remaining ingredients and toss them with the cooked potatoes. Heat the potatoes through, but do not overcook them. If you use a porcelain baker, entire dish can be prepared and served in the same pan. Serves 6.

Note: - Potatoes can be prepared earlier in the day and heated at time of serving. Stir in the sour cream mixture just before serving.

Potato Frittata with Onions & Cheese

- **6 medium potatoes, peeled and grated**
- **2 onions, grated**
- **3 tablespoons flour**
- **3/4 cup grated Parmesan cheese**
- **2 eggs, beaten**
  salt and pepper to taste

- **2 tablespoons oil**

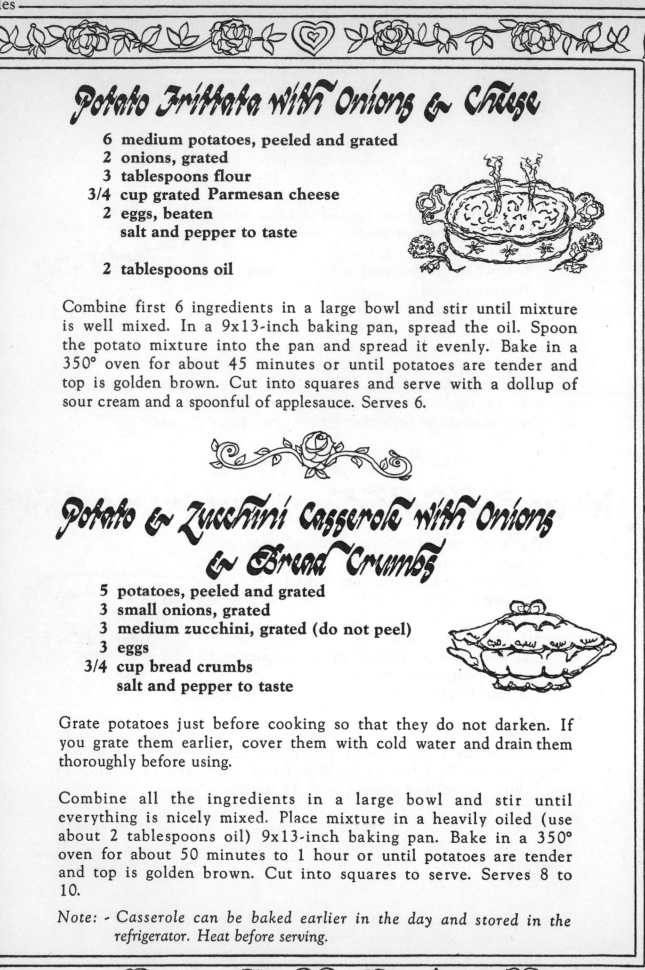

Combine first 6 ingredients in a large bowl and stir until mixture is well mixed. In a 9x13-inch baking pan, spread the oil. Spoon the potato mixture into the pan and spread it evenly. Bake in a 350° oven for about 45 minutes or until potatoes are tender and top is golden brown. Cut into squares and serve with a dollup of sour cream and a spoonful of applesauce. Serves 6.

Potato & Zucchini Casserole with Onions & Bread Crumbs

- **5 potatoes, peeled and grated**
- **3 small onions, grated**
- **3 medium zucchini, grated (do not peel)**
- **3 eggs**
- **3/4 cup bread crumbs**
  salt and pepper to taste

Grate potatoes just before cooking so that they do not darken. If you grate them earlier, cover them with cold water and drain them thoroughly before using.

Combine all the ingredients in a large bowl and stir until everything is nicely mixed. Place mixture in a heavily oiled (use about 2 tablespoons oil) 9x13-inch baking pan. Bake in a 350° oven for about 50 minutes to 1 hour or until potatoes are tender and top is golden brown. Cut into squares to serve. Serves 8 to 10.

Note: - Casserole can be baked earlier in the day and stored in the refrigerator. Heat before serving.

Florentine Pancakes with Swiss Cheese & Sour Cream

1   cup flour
1   cup milk
2   teaspoons baking powder
4   tablespoons melted butter
3   eggs, beaten
1   package (10 ounces) chopped spinach, drained
1/8 teaspoon nutmeg, salt and pepper to taste
1/4 cup grated Parmesan cheese

1   cup sour cream
1   cup grated Swiss cheese
1/3 cup grated Parmesan cheese

Combine first 8 ingredients in a bowl and beat until blended. Heat a heavily buttered skillet. (Use about 2 tablespoons butter.) Use about one-third cup of batter for each pancake. Cook until bottoms are lightly browned. Turn and brown other side. Continue with remaining batter. You should have 12 pancakes.

In a 9x13-inch porcelain baker, place 6 pancakes in one layer. Combine sour cream, Swiss cheese and Parmesan cheese until blended. Spread 1/2 of the sour cream mixture over the pancakes Top this with 6 more pancakes, and spread remaining sour cream mixture on top.

Bake in a 350° oven until heated through and cheese is melted. Serves 6.

Note: - This is a very different and lovely lunch dish. It can be assembled earlier in the day and heated at time of serving.

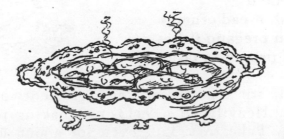

Creamed Spinach Casserole with Bacon, Chives & Cheese

This is a lovely way to serve spinach, sparkled with nutmeg, bacon and cheese. Entire casserole can be assembled earlier in the day and heated at time of serving.

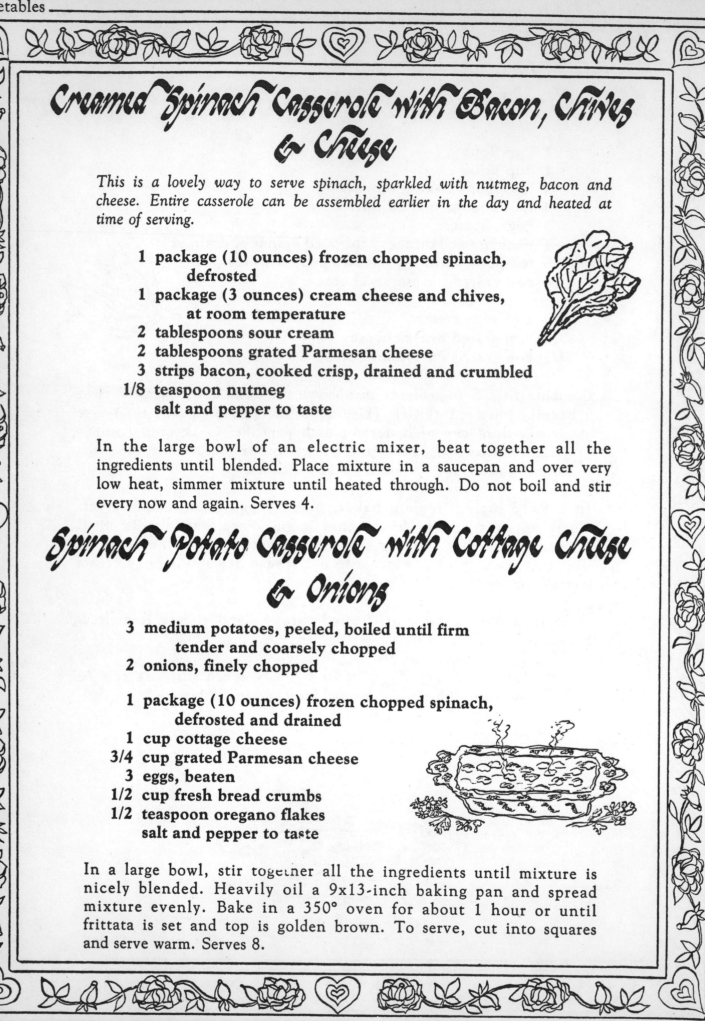

- 1 package (10 ounces) frozen chopped spinach, defrosted
- 1 package (3 ounces) cream cheese and chives, at room temperature
- 2 tablespoons sour cream
- 2 tablespoons grated Parmesan cheese
- 3 strips bacon, cooked crisp, drained and crumbled
- 1/8 teaspoon nutmeg
  salt and pepper to taste

In the large bowl of an electric mixer, beat together all the ingredients until blended. Place mixture in a saucepan and over very low heat, simmer mixture until heated through. Do not boil and stir every now and again. Serves 4.

Spinach Potato Casserole with Cottage Cheese & Onions

- 3 medium potatoes, peeled, boiled until firm tender and coarsely chopped
- 2 onions, finely chopped

- 1 package (10 ounces) frozen chopped spinach, defrosted and drained
- 1 cup cottage cheese
- 3/4 cup grated Parmesan cheese
- 3 eggs, beaten
- 1/2 cup fresh bread crumbs
- 1/2 teaspoon oregano flakes
  salt and pepper to taste

In a large bowl, stir together all the ingredients until mixture is nicely blended. Heavily oil a 9x13-inch baking pan and spread mixture evenly. Bake in a 350° oven for about 1 hour or until frittata is set and top is golden brown. To serve, cut into squares and serve warm. Serves 8.

Spinach Frittata with Onions & Cheese

This is like a crustless quiche and serves well as a dinner vegetable side dish or a main course for lunch. It is filled with good things that are "good" for you, too.

> 1 package (10 ounces) frozen chopped spinach, defrosted. Do not drain.
> 1 pint lo-fat cottage cheese
> 2 eggs
> 1/2 cup fresh bread crumbs
> 1/2 cup grated Parmesan cheese
> 6 tablespoons finely chopped green onions
> salt and pepper to taste
>
> 1 tablespoon oil

Combine first 7 ingredients in a mixing bowl and stir until mixture is blended. Spread oil into an 8x12-inch baking dish and spread spinach mixture evenly in pan.

Bake in a 350° oven for about 40 minutes or until top is golden brown. Cut into squares and serve warm. Serves 6.

Note: - Entire dish can be baked earlier in the day and stored in the refrigerator. Reheat in a 350° oven until heated through, about 15 minutes.

Eggplant Frittata with Onions & Cheese

Instead of the spinach, use 1 medium eggplant. Peel it and cut it into 1/4-inch thick slices. Place eggplant in a 12x16-inch pan, brush it with a little oil, cover pan tightly with foil, and bake eggplant in a 400° oven for 20 minutes or until it is very soft. Proceed with the remaining ingredients and bake as described above. This is a delicious and very unusual frittata.

Broiled Tomatoes with Herbed Crumbs, Lemon & Cheese

12 tomato slices, cut 1-inch thick
4 tablespoons mayonnaise

1/2 cup fresh bread crumbs
1/2 cup grated Parmesan cheese
2 tablespoons grated onion
1 tablespoon lemon juice
1 tablespoon chopped parsley
1/2 teaspoon basil
1 egg, beaten
salt and pepper to taste

Place tomato slices on a cookie sheet. Brush 1 teaspoon mayonnaise on the top of each slice. Combine the remaining ingredients in a bowl and mix until blended. Divide mixture between the tomato slices and pat it down, covering the tops. Broil 6-inches from the heat until lightly browned on top and heated through. Serves 6.

Fried Tomatoes with Seasoned Cracker Crumbs

12 tomato slices, cut 1-inch thick
2 eggs
2 tablespoons cream

1/2 cup green onion cracker crumbs
1/4 cup grated Parmesan cheese
1/4 teaspoon garlic powder
2 teaspoons paprika
1 tablespoon dried chopped chives
salt and pepper to taste

Beat eggs with cream and dip tomato slices in egg mixture. Combine the remaining ingredients and coat tomato slices on both sides with crumb mixture.

In a skillet, heat 2 tablespoons of butter until it is sizzling hot, but not brown. Fry tomato slices for about 3 minutes on each side, or until coating is lightly browned. Do this over moderately high heat so that the tomatoes do not get too soft. Serve with steak or roasted meat or chicken. Serves 6.

Gingersnap Yam Pudding with Honey & Raisins

1 can (1 pound) yams,, drained. Discard liquid.
3 eggs
1 1/2 cups half and half
2/3 cup honey
1/2 cup yellow raisins
1/2 cup gingersnap cookie crumbs
1 teaspoon cinnamon
1/4 teaspoon nutmeg

Combine all the ingredients in the large bowl of an electric mixer and beat for about 1 minute or until mixture is thoroughly blended. Pour mixture into a buttered 2-quart souffle dish and bake in a 350° oven for about 30 minutes. Combine Cinnamon Sugar Topping and sprinkle on top.

Continue baking for about 15 or 20 minutes or until casserole is puffed and set. Serve with roast chicken or turkey. Serves 6.

Cinnamon Sugar Topping: Combine 1 tablespoon cinnamon sugar with 1/4 cup chopped walnuts and mix until blended.

Yam Casserole with Apples, Prunes & Pecans

2 apples, peeled, cored and sliced
1 cup pitted prunes
1/2 cup raisins
1/4 cup butter (1/2 stick)
1/2 cup honey or to taste
2 slices of lemon
1 can (1 pound) yams, drained. Discard liquid.
1/3 cup chopped pecans

Combine first 6 ingredients in a saucepan and cook over low heat for about 15 minutes or until apples are almost tender. In a buttered porcelain casserole, slice yams and spread apple mixture evenly over them. Sprinkle top with chopped pecans. Bake in a 350° oven for about 15 minutes or until casserole is heated through. Serves 6.

Zucchini Frittata with Onions & Cheese Italienne

         5 medium zucchini, grated. Do not peel.
         1 onion, grated. (About 1/2 cup)
     1 1/2 cups small-curd cottage cheese
       1/2 cup grated Parmesan cheese
         4 eggs
       3/4 cup fresh bread crumbs. (Use 1 cup if
               cottage cheese is watery.)
       1/2 teaspoon Italian Herb Seasoning
       1/8 teaspoon garlic powder
           salt and pepper to taste

Combine all the ingredients in a large bowl and stir until blended. Place 2 tablespoons oil in a 9x13-inch baking pan. Spread zucchini mixture evenly in pan. Bake in a 350° oven for about 45 minutes or until frittata is set and top is golden brown. Cut into squares to serve. Yields 6 servings.

Note: - Frittata can be prepared earlier in the day and heated at time of serving.

Zucchini with Onion, Garlic & Lemon

         6 medium zucchini, cut into very thin slices.
               Do not peel.
         4 cloves finely minced garlic
         2 tablespoons finely minced onion
         2 tablespoons olive oil

         1 tablespoon lemon juice
         1 teaspoon Italian Herb Seasoning
         1 tablespoon minced parsley
           salt and pepper to taste

In a large skillet, saute together first 4 ingredients until zucchini are tender. Stir in the remaining ingredients and continue cooking for 1 or 2 minutes or until heated through. Can be served hot as a vegetable accompaniment or cold as part of an antipasto platter. Serves 6.

Zucchini Stuffed with Meat, Onions, Tomatoes & Cheese

This is a very tasty dish and filled with all kinds of good things. It serves well as a main course for lunch or dinner.

6 medium zucchini, cut in half lengthwise. With a spoon, scrape out the seeds. Simmer zucchini in 1 cup chicken broth for about 5 minutes or until zucchini are partially tender. Drain zucchini and reserve broth for another use.

1 pound ground beef
1 small onion, very finely chopped
1 clove garlic, minced
1 tablespoon oil

1/2 package (10 ounces) frozen chopped spinach, drained
1/2 cup grated Parmesan cheese
2 eggs, beaten
1 tablespoon chopped parsley
1 teaspoon Italian Herb Seasoning
salt and pepper to taste

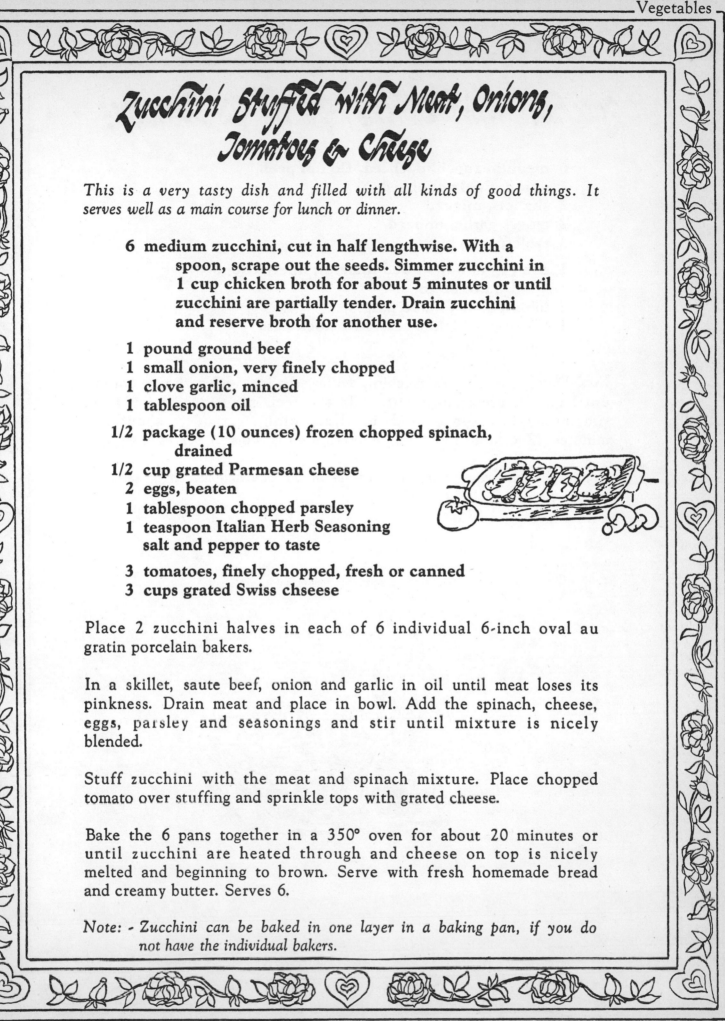

3 tomatoes, finely chopped, fresh or canned
3 cups grated Swiss chseese

Place 2 zucchini halves in each of 6 individual 6-inch oval au gratin porcelain bakers.

In a skillet, saute beef, onion and garlic in oil until meat loses its pinkness. Drain meat and place in bowl. Add the spinach, cheese, eggs, parsley and seasonings and stir until mixture is nicely blended.

Stuff zucchini with the meat and spinach mixture. Place chopped tomato over stuffing and sprinkle tops with grated cheese.

Bake the 6 pans together in a 350° oven for about 20 minutes or until zucchini are heated through and cheese on top is nicely melted and beginning to brown. Serve with fresh homemade bread and creamy butter. Serves 6.

Note: - Zucchini can be baked in one layer in a baking pan, if you do not have the individual bakers.

Zucchini with Onions, Garlic & Tomatoes

6 medium zucchini, sliced. Do not peel.
1 onion, finely chopped
2 shallots, minced
2 cloves garlic, minced
3 tablespoons butter

1 can (1 pound) stewed tomatoes, finely chopped.
  Do not drain.
2 tablespoons tomato paste
1 teaspoon chicken seasoned stock base
  salt to taste

In a Dutch oven, saute zucchini, onion, shallots and garlic in butter until onions are transparent. Add the remaining ingredients and simmer mixture, uncovered, until zucchini are tender, about 20 minutes. (Zucchini should not be too firm for this dish.) Serves 6.

Note: - Zucchini can be prepared earlier in the day and heated at serving
   time.

Sweet Dreams

Of course, you know, I love desserts. I am inviting you into my fantasyland . . . my dreamland of delights. Some people dream in black and white and some people dream in color. But I . . . I dream in chocolate. When visions of sugar plums dance in my head, they are nestled in a buttery crust, glistening with brandied glaze, and hopefully a little Creme Fraiche is very close by. When I think of all the recipes that follow, I literally ripple with delight. How I hope I could detail each one for you . . . but the limitations of space prevent this, so I must be satisfied with a general introduction.

You will notice some of the recipes are noted with "Minute Magic." They are grand and glorious confections that can be prepared in one minute. No way, you say. But it's true, I promise you. A Fudge Gateau, deep, dark, dense and delicious; an Imperial Chocolate Torte, tender and light as air; a Royal Apple and Orange Pecan Torte, tart, moist and fruity; and many more. You will feel like a wizard with a magic wand, transforming a few humble ingredients into these regal desserts. There are several 2-minute tortes that are really worth the "extra time."

Cakes, tortes, gateaus, glorious fruitcakes and cheesecakes, all made quickly and easily. They will add grace and style to the most fastidious dessert table.

Creamy cheesecakes with the texture of velvet and satin . . . a Pecan Meringue Torte with a thin layer of Chocolate Fudge Mousse, garnished with Grand Marnier Cream and plump strawberries dipped in chocolate, all devilishly delicious.

And crunchy nut cakes of every variety; a Hazlenut Roulage, enhanced with Chocolate Chestnut Cream is really fit for a Czar. Apple cakes and pumpkin cakes and tipsy sherry cakes. I could go on and on, but I mustn't forget the candies and cookies and the old-fashioned pies.

What can I say about the Royal White Chocolate Mousse with Raspberries, to urge you to try it soon. It is luxurious and extravagant and so decadently delicious, it will make you a star. And please try the Compote of Mixed Berries for your next buffet (brunch, lunch or dinner.) It is beautiful and very unusual.

How I hope these will bring you a measure of pleasure and build joyous memories for you, as they have done for me.

And for those who are watching calories, a small sliver of dessert will bring more pleasure and satisfaction than a carload of carrots. Keep the portions small and relish every bite.

Enjoy!

Royal Chocolate Fudge Gateau with Chocolate Rum Buttercream

Looking for a deep, dark, dense chocolate cake that is assembled in minutes? Well, this marvelous cake is just that. You will feel like a magician in the kitchen when you serve this little treasure.

- 1/2 cup (1 stick) butter, melted
- 4 tablespoons cocoa
- 4 eggs
- 1 1/4 cups sugar
- 1 cup chopped walnuts
- 1/2 cup flour
- 1/2 teaspoon baking powder
- 1 teaspoon vanilla

Combine all the ingredients in a food processor and blend for 30 seconds. Scrape down the sides and blend for another 30 seconds.

Pour batter into a buttered 10-inch springform pan and bake at 350° for 25 minutes or until a cake tester, inserted in center, comes out clean. Do not overbake. Allow cake to cool in pan.

Swirl Chocolate Rum Buttercream on the top and sides in a decorative fashion. Cut into wedges and serve with pride. Serves 8.

Chocolate Rum Buttercream

- 1/2 cup butter, softened
- 1/2 cup semi-sweet chocolate chips, melted
- 1 tablespoon rum
- 1/2 teaspoon vanilla

Beat butter until light and creamy. Beat in the melted chocolate, rum and vanilla until blended.

Note: - Cake can be prepared 1 day earlier and stored in the refrigerator. However, serve at room temperature.

- If you like a bittersweet taste, add 1 tablespoon cocoa to the batter.

Double Chocolate Fantasy with Sour Cream & Chocolate Chips

3/4 cup butter
2 cups sugar
3/4 cup water
2/3 cup cocoa

3 eggs
1 cup sour cream
2 teaspoons vanilla

2 cups flour
1 1/2 teaspoons baking soda
2/3 cup semi-sweet chocolate chips

In a saucepan, heat together butter, sugar, water and cocoa, until butter is melted and mixture is blended. Pour into the large bowl of an electric mixer, and allow to cool to warm. Beat for about 30 seconds.

Beat in eggs, sour cream and vanilla until blended. Beat in flour, soda and chocolate until blended. Divide batter between 2 10-inch springform pans that have been lightly buttered. Bake in a 350° oven for about 35 minutes, or until a cake tester, inserted in center, comes out clean. Allow to cool in pan.

Remove layers from pans and fill and frost with Chocolate Buttercream Frosting. Keep the portions small and serve 12.

Chocolate Buttercream Frosting

1 cup semi-sweet chocolate chips
1/3 cup butter
2/3 cup cream
1 teaspoon vanilla

Place chocolate chips in blender container. Heat together the butter and cream until it comes to a boil. Pour hot mixture into blender container and whip for 30 seconds or until frosting is smooth and chocolate is melted. Allow to cool and spread on cake. Will fill and frost 1 10-inch layer cake.

Note: - This will produce a thin layer of frosting which is just enough for this rich cake.

Chocolate Torte Royale with White Chocolate & Raspberry Frosting

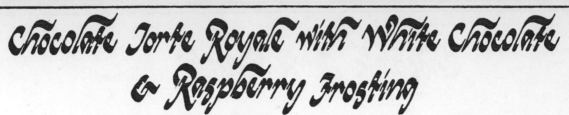

This dessert is so recklessly delicious and so beautiful to behold, you will enjoy the cries of "bravo." Tender chocolate layers, filled with white chocolate mousse and raspberries is literally, fit for a czar. Serve on your most beautiful platter and get ready to be swept off your feet.

- **6 egg whites**
- **1/2 cup sugar**

- **6 egg yolks**
- **1/2 cup sugar**

- **2 tablespoons flour**
- **5 tablespoons sifted cocoa**
- **1 teaspoon baking powder**
- **1 1/2 cups grated walnuts**

- **1 package (10 ounces) frozen raspberries in syrup, defrosted**

Preheat oven to 350°. Grease a 10x15-inch jelly roll pan. Line it with waxed paper extending 4-inches beyond the ends of the pan. Grease the wax paper and set aside.

Beat whites until foamy. Slowly add the sugar and continue beating until whites are stiff and glossy. Beat the yolks (not necessary to clean the beaters) with 1/2 cup sugar until very thick and pale. Beat in the flour, cocoa, baking powder and walnuts until blended. Fold in the beaten egg whites until blended. Do not overmix.

Pour batter into prepared pan and bake at 350° for about 20 minutes or until a cake tester, inserted in the center, comes out clean. Remove cake from oven and immediately cover with a damp towel. When cool, refrigerate cake until ready to frost. Cake may be baked 2 days before serving.

One day before serving, turn cake out on 2 overlapping strips of wax paper. Remove baking paper and trim edges. Cut cake into 3 strips, each measuring 3x15-inches. Place first layer on serving dish and sprinkle with 1/3 raspberry syrup. Spread with White Chocolate Mousse Frosting. Spoon 1/2 the raspberries over the frosting. Repeat with second layer. On third layer, just sprinkle 1/3 the raspberry juice. Cover tops and sides with White Chocolate Mousse Frosting. Decorate with chocolate leaves and finely grated chocolate. Store in the refrigerator and remove 10 minutes before serving. Serves 12.

Chocolate Torte Royale (continued)

White Chocolate Mousse Frosting: Place 3/4 pound finely chopped white chocolate in blender container. Pour in 3/4 cup of boiling cream and blend until white chocolate is melted. Add 1 teaspoon vanilla and blend. Allow to cool to thicken. Will fill and frost 1 15-inch layered cake.

Imperial Chocolate Torte with Strawberries & Chocolate Buttercream

Light as air and smooth as velvet, this cake is so delicate, you will enjoy serving it with pride. It is especially easy to assemble and a grand choice for an evening when you are running late. No one could ever guess that this joyously delicious cake took 1 minute to assemble.

- 4 eggs
- 1 cup sugar
- 1 cup chopped walnuts
- 1 teaspoon vanilla
- 3 tablespoons flour
- 3 tablespoons cocoa
- 1 teaspoon baking powder

1/2 cup strawberry jam, heated

Combine first 7 ingredients in food processor and blend for 30 seconds. Scrape down the sides and blend for another 30 seconds. Pour batter into a greased 10-inch springform pan and bake at 350° for 25 minutes, or until a cake tester, inserted in center, comes out clean. Do not overbake. Allow to cool in pan.

Spread warmed strawberry jam evenly over cake. Swirl Chocolate Buttercream decoratively over the cake, allowing some of the jam to show. Spread frosting on the sides. Serves 8.

Chocolate Buttercream Frosting

1/2 cup butter, at room temperature
1/2 cup semi-sweet chocolate chips, melted
1/2 teaspoon vanilla

Beat butter until light and creamy. Beat in the chocolate and vanilla until blended.

Note: - *Chocolate can be melted in microwave oven for 1 1/2 minutes on High.*
- *Cake can be prepared 1 day earlier and stored in the refrigerator. Allow to come to room temperature to serve.*

2-Minute Chocolate Torte with Cacao Whipped Cream

No one will ever guess that this incredible chocolate cake is assembled in minutes. It has humble beginnings, starting as it does with cookie crumbs, but the results will truly amaze you.

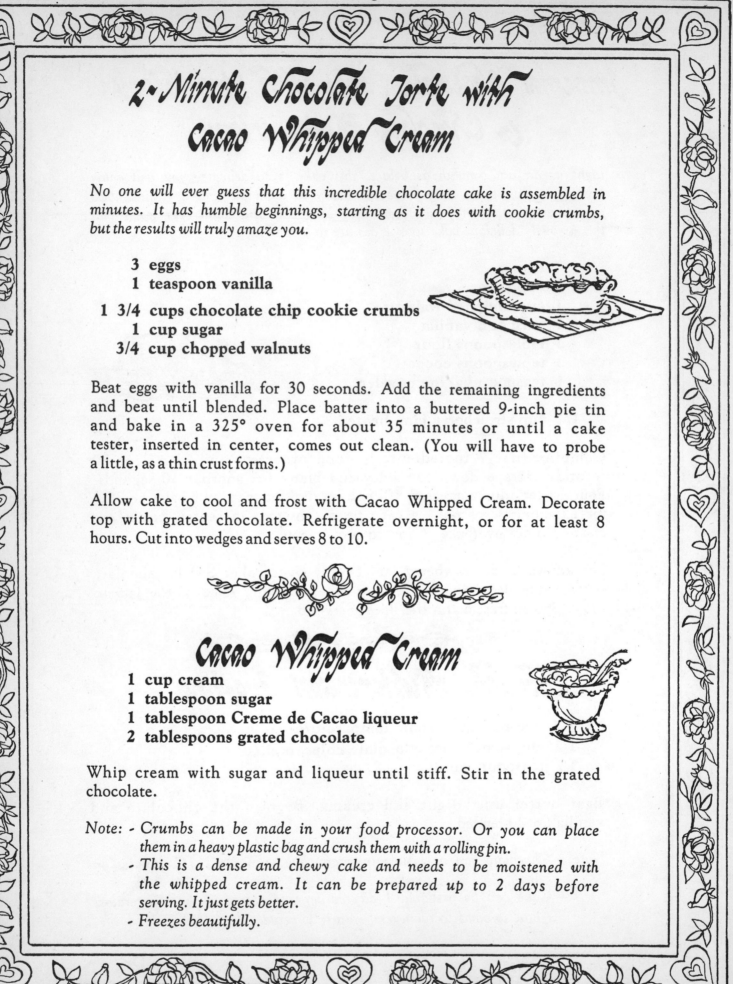

    3   eggs
    1   teaspoon vanilla

1 3/4   cups chocolate chip cookie crumbs
    1   cup sugar
  3/4   cup chopped walnuts

Beat eggs with vanilla for 30 seconds. Add the remaining ingredients and beat until blended. Place batter into a buttered 9-inch pie tin and bake in a 325° oven for about 35 minutes or until a cake tester, inserted in center, comes out clean. (You will have to probe a little, as a thin crust forms.)

Allow cake to cool and frost with Cacao Whipped Cream. Decorate top with grated chocolate. Refrigerate overnight, or for at least 8 hours. Cut into wedges and serves 8 to 10.

Cacao Whipped Cream

    1   cup cream
    1   tablespoon sugar
    1   tablespoon Creme de Cacao liqueur
    2   tablespoons grated chocolate

Whip cream with sugar and liqueur until stiff. Stir in the grated chocolate.

Note: - Crumbs can be made in your food processor. Or you can place them in a heavy plastic bag and crush them with a rolling pin.
- This is a dense and chewy cake and needs to be moistened with the whipped cream. It can be prepared up to 2 days before serving. It just gets better.
- Freezes beautifully.

Pecan Meringue Torte with Chocolate Strawberries & Leaves

Plump, juicy strawberries, dipped in chocolate are just beautiful on this spectacular dessert. A pecan meringue layer, topped with chocolate mousse and swirls of whipped cream. Topped with chocolate dipped strawberries and chocolate leaves makes it an ultimate dessert.

Meringue Layer:
- 4 egg whites
- 3/4 cup sugar
- 1 teaspoon vanilla

- 3/4 cup vanilla wafer crumbs
- 1 cup chopped pecans
- 1/2 cup chopped chocolate chips

Beat egg whites until foamy. Add 1/2 the sugar and vanilla and continue beating until whites are stiff and glossy. Beat in remaining sugar and rest of the ingredients, on very low speed and just until blended.

Scrape the meringue mixture into a greased 10-inch springform pan and spread to even. Bake meringue in a 350° oven for about 25 minutes or until top is dry and beginning to color. Allow to cool. Pour Chocolate Fudge Mousse Frosting over the layer. Allow to cool. Decorate with swirls of Grand Marnier Whipped Cream and Chocolate Dipped Strawberries and Chocolate Leaves. Serves 10.

Chocolate Fudge Mousse Frosting: Place 3/4 cup semi-sweet chocolate chips in blender container. Heat 1/2 cup cream to boiling point and pour into blender. Blend for 1 minute or until chocolate is melted. Beat in 1 tablespoon Grand Marnier Liqueur.

Grand Marnier Whipped Cream: Beat 1 cup cream with 1 tablespoon sugar and 1 tablespoon Grand Marnier until cream is stiff.

Pecan Meringue Torte (continued)

Chocolate Dipped Strawberries: Clean and pat dry, 1 pint strawberries. In the top of a double boiler, over hot, not boiling water, melt 1 cup semi-sweet chocolate chips. Holding on to the green leaves, or piercing hull with a toothpick, dip strawberries into chocolate, covering half the fruit. Place on wax paper to cool and then refrigerate, to firm up. (Chocolate can be melted in a microwave oven for 1 1/2 minutes on high.)

Chocolate Leaves: Spread about 2 teaspoons of melted chocolate on the back of scrubbed and dried camellia leaves. Place on wax paper and refrigerate until firm. Peel off the leaves and Voila! Beautiful chocolate leaves to decorate this masterpiece.

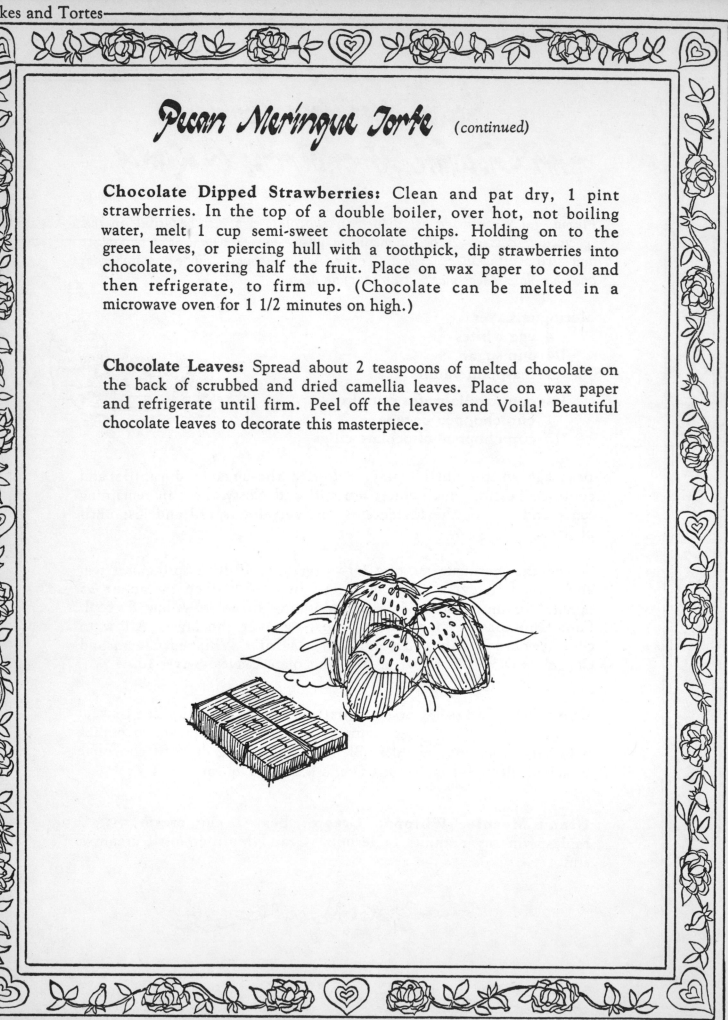

Royal Walnut Torte with Chocolate Chip Cream & Raspberries

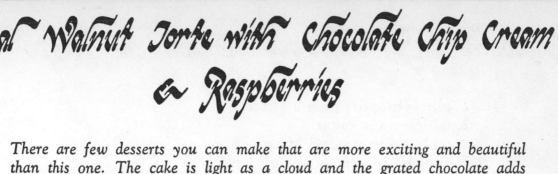

There are few desserts you can make that are more exciting and beautiful than this one. The cake is light as a cloud and the grated chocolate adds the perfect texture to the frosting. Add the raspberries . . . heavenly!

        6 egg whites, at room temperature
    1/2 cup sugar

        6 egg yolks, at room temperature
    1/2 cup sugar

    1 1/2 cups finely grated walnuts
        1 teaspoon baking powder
        1 teaspoon vanilla

Preheat oven to 350°. Butter a 10x15-inch jelly roll pan. Line it with waxed paper extending 4-inches beyond the ends of the pan. Butter the waxed paper. Set aside. Wet a towel and squeeze it until it is damp-dry.

Beat whites until foamy. Gradually add 1/2 cup sugar and continue beating until whites are stiff and glossy. Beat yolks with 1/2 cup sugar until mixture is very thick. Fold in nuts, baking powder and vanilla. Fold in egg whites. (This can be done on low speed of mixer).

Pour batter into prepared pan and bake at 350° for about 25 minutes or until top is golden and a cake tester, inserted in center comes out clean. Immediately cover cake with dampened towel. Allow cake to cool and refrigerate. This can be done 2 days ahead.

The day before serving, turn cake out on 2 overlapping strips of wax paper that have been sprinkled with sifted powdered sugar. Remove baking paper and trim edges. Cut cake into thirds, yielding 3 strips measuring 14x3-inches. Fill and frost with Chocolate Chip Whipped Cream and Raspberries. Sprinkle top with grated chocolate and decorate with whole raspberries. Refrigerate overnight. Serves 12.

Chocolate Chip Whipped Cream & Raspberries

1 pint whipping cream
2 tablespoons sugar
2 tablespoons Grand Marnier
1/2 cup semi-sweet grated chocolate
1 package (10 ounces) frozen raspberries, drained

Beat cream with sugar and liqueur until stiff. Beat in chocolate. Fill and frost with raspberries and whipped cream.

Nut Lovers' Greatest Walnut Cake with Raspberries & Lemon Drizzle

Nut Lovers Rejoice! If nut cakes are your fancy, this is a little "treasure" you will enjoy often. The nut crust is like an old-fashioned cookie crust, topped with raspberry jam and covered with a tender nut layer. The Lemon Drizzle adds the perfect tartness.

        3   eggs
        1/2 cup sugar
    1   1/2 cups walnuts, chopped
        2   tablespoons flour
        1/4 teaspoon baking powder
        1   teaspoon vanilla

Beat eggs with sugar for about 3 minutes or until eggs are light and fluffy. Stir in the walnuts, flour, baking powder and vanilla until blended.

Pour mixture into prepared Nut Cookie Crust and bake in a 350° oven for 40 minutes, or until top is browned and a cake tester, inserted in center, comes out clean. Allow to cool in pan.

When cool, spoon Lemon Drizzle on top in a circular and decorative fashion. To serve, cut into small wedges and be ready for a standing ovation. Serves 12.

Nut Cookie Crust:
        3   ounces butter (3/4 stick) softened
        1/2 cup sugar
        1   egg
        1   cup flour
        1   teaspoon vanilla

        1   cup chopped walnuts
        1/2 cup seedless red raspberry jam, heated

Cream butter and sugar until butter is light. Beat in egg, flour and vanilla until mixture is blended. Beat in chopped walnuts. Spread mixture on the bottom and 1/2-inch up the sides of a buttered 10-inch springform pan. Spread heated raspberry jam on top.

Lemon Drizzle: Stir together 1/2 cup sifted powdered sugar with 2 teaspoons lemon juice until blended. Add a little sugar or lemon juice until glaze is a drizzling consistency.

Walnut Raspberry Torte on Old-Fashioned Cookie Crust

This incredibly delicious torte is just bursting with plain old-fashioned goodness. The cookie crust is very versatile and can be used for fruit tarts and nut pies. I know it will become one of your favorites, because it can be easily prepared in a mixer and simply patted into the pan. The Walnut Raspberry Filling adds the perfect balance of flavors.

Old-Fashioned Cookie Crust :
- 2 cups flour
- 1 cup sugar
- 1 cup butter (2 sticks)

- 1 egg

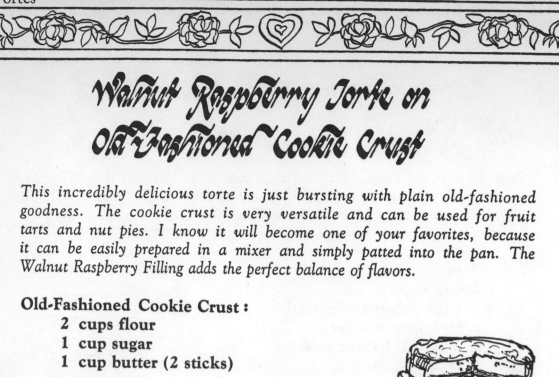

In the large bowl of an electric mixer, beat together flour, sugar and butter until mixture resembles coarse meal. Add the egg and beat until mixture is blended and forms a dough, about 1 minute. Do not overbeat. Pat 2/3 of the dough on the bottom and 1/2-inch up the sides of a 10-inch springform pan.

Spread Walnut Raspberry Filling over the dough. Pinch off pieces of the remaining dough, roll it into 1/4-inch ropes and lay them over the walnut filling, lattice-fashioned. Bake in a 325° oven for about 40 minutes or until top is golden brown. Allow to cool in pan. To serve, cut into 1-inch diamonds, and sprinkle with a faint hint of sifted powdered sugar.

Walnut Raspberry Filling :
- 1 cup grated walnuts
- 1/2 cup sugar
- 1/3 cup seedless raspberry jam
- 1 egg, beaten

In a bowl, combine all the ingredients and stir until thoroughly blended.

Note: - Can be frozen. Wrap carefully for freezing and remove wrappers while defrosting.

Royal Walnut Torte with Raspberry Jam & Brown Sugar Nut Topping

This is one of the best nut tortes I have ever created. It's as simple as that. I made it for a ladies luncheon and everyone screamed with delight. It is excellent and the excitement it generated was overwhelming. Actually, it is a buttery cookie nut crust, topped with raspberry jam and a nut topping.

1 1/2 **cups finely grated walnuts**
1/3 **cup flour**
1/4 **cup sugar**
3/4 **stick butter (3 ounces), at room temperature**

3/4 **cup raspberry jam**

3 **eggs**
1 1/4 **cups brown sugar**
1/2 **cup flour**
1 **teaspoon baking powder**
1 **teaspoon vanilla**
1 **cup chopped walnuts**

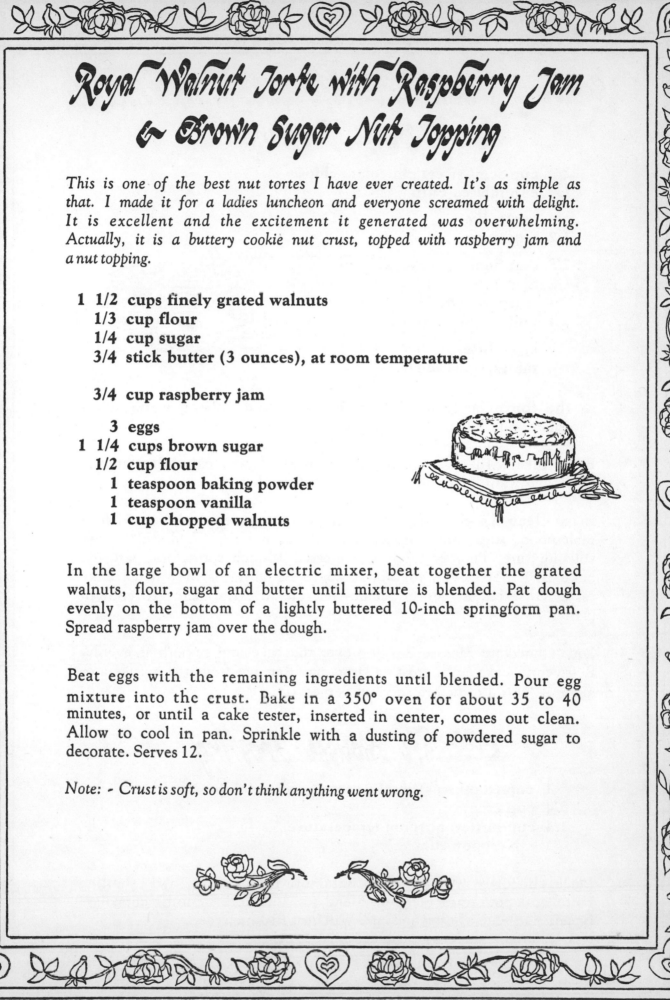

In the large bowl of an electric mixer, beat together the grated walnuts, flour, sugar and butter until mixture is blended. Pat dough evenly on the bottom of a lightly buttered 10-inch springform pan. Spread raspberry jam over the dough.

Beat eggs with the remaining ingredients until blended. Pour egg mixture into the crust. Bake in a 350° oven for about 35 to 40 minutes, or until a cake tester, inserted in center, comes out clean. Allow to cool in pan. Sprinkle with a dusting of powdered sugar to decorate. Serves 12.

Note: - Crust is soft, so don't think anything went wrong.

Company Fudge Chocolate Cake with Chocolate Mousse Frosting

2/3 cup semi-sweet chocolate chips
1/3 cup melted butter

4 egg yolks
1/2 cup sugar

7/8 cup finely ground walnuts
1/2 cup flour
1 teaspoon vanilla
1 tablespoon rum

4 egg whites
4 tablespoons sugar

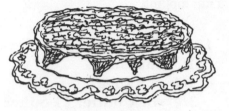

In the top of a double boiler, over hot not boiling water, melt chocolate and stir in the melted butter.

Beat yolks with sugar until mixture is thick and pale. Beat in the nuts, flour, vanilla, rum and chocolate until blended.

In a clean bowl, with clean beaters, beat egg whites with 4 tablespoons sugar until whites are stiff but not dry. Fold whites into yolk mixture. Pour batter into a greased 10-inch springform pan and bake in a 350° oven for about 25 to 30 minutes or until a cake tester, inserted in center, comes out clean. Allow cake to cool in pan.

Pour Chocolate Mousse Frosting over the cake and smooth it evenly. Refrigerate cake until frosting firms up. Remove from the refrigerator about 10 minutes before serving. Serves 10.

Chocolate Mousse Frosting

1 cup (6 ounces) semi-sweet chocolate chips
3/4 cup cream
1/4 cup butter, at room temperature
1 tablespoon rum

Place chocolate in a blender container. Heat cream to the boiling point and pour into blender. Blend for 1 minute or until chocolate is melted. Blend in butter and rum. Will frost 1 10-inch cake.

Holiday Hazelnut Roulage with Chocolate Chestnut Cream

This cake is indecently delicious. The sponge roll is sheer heaven and the whipped cream, delicately flavored with chestnuts and chocolate is awesome.

6 egg yolks
1/2 cup sugar
1 1/2 teaspoons baking powder
1 1/2 cups ground hazelnuts
1 teaspoon vanilla

6 egg whites
1/2 cup sugar

In the large bowl of an electric mixer, beat yolks with sugar until thick and lemon colored, about 5 minutes. Combine baking powder with hazelnuts and beat in with the vanilla, until blended.

With clean beaters and bowl, beat egg whites until foamy. Gradually add the sugar, beating until whites are stiff. Fold 1/4 of the whites into the nut mixture to lighten it. Fold in the remaining whites until blended. Do not overmix.

Oil a 10x15-inch jelly roll pan, line it with waxed paper extending 4-inches at each end, and oil the waxed paper. Spread batter evenly into the pan and bake in a 350° oven for about 25 minutes or until a cake tester, inserted in center, comes out clean. Remove from oven and cover hot cake with a slightly dampened towel. Allow cake to cool. Dust cake with sifted powdered sugar.

Turn cake out on 2 overlapping strips of waxed paper. Remove lining of waxed paper and trim edges of cake. Spread top with 2/3 of the Chocolate Chestnut Cream. Using the waxed paper to help you, roll cake up from long end, ending seam side down. Frost top with remaining frosting and sprinkle faintly with sifted cocoa. Serves 12.

Chocolate Chestnut Cream: Beat together 1 1/2 cups cream with 2 tablespoons brown sugar and 1 teaspoon vanilla until cream is stiff. Beat in 1/2 cup sweetened chestnut puree until blended. Beat in 1/3 cup finely grated chocolate.

Note: - Cake can be prepared 2 days before serving and refrigerated.
  - Cake can be frosted 1 day before serving and refrigerated.

Pecan Velvet Cake with Pecan Praline Cream

        5 egg yolks
    1/2 cup sugar

        1 cup grated pecans
    1/2 cup flour
        1 teaspoon baking powder
        1 teaspoon maple flavoring

        5 egg whites
    1/2 cup sugar

Preheat oven to 350°. Butter a 10x15-inch jelly roll pan. Line it with waxed paper extending 4-inches beyond the ends of the pan. Butter the waxed paper and set it aside. Wet a towel, and squeeze it until it is damp-dry.

Beat yolks with 1/2 cup sugar until mixture is very thick. Beat in the pecans, flour, baking powder and maple flavoring. Beat egg whites, in a clean bowl with clean beaters, until it is foamy. Continue beating, adding the sugar slowly, until whites are stiff and glossy. Fold whites into egg yolk mixture.

Pour batter into prepared pan and spread evenly. Bake at 350° for about 25 minutes or until top is golden and a cake tester, inserted in center, comes out clean. Immediately cover cake with slightly dampened towel. Allow cake to cool and then refrigerate. Leave towel on cake. This can be done 2 days ahead.

The day before serving, turn cake out on 2 overlapping strips of waxed paper and trim edges of cake. Cut cake into 3 sections, cross-wise, yielding 3 layers, 5x10-inches.

Fill and frost with Pecan Praline Cream. Pipe a few decorative rosettes on top and sprinkle with a hint of ground pecans.

Pecan Praline Cream:
    1 1/2 cups cream
      1/3 cup brown sugar (sift if necessary)
          1 teaspoon maple flavoring
      1/2 cup finely chopped pecans

Beat cream with brown sugar and maple flavoring until stiff. Beat in pecans.

Fresh Apple Sour Cream Cake on Brown Sugar Walnut Crust

Oh! what an apple cake. If you love fresh apple desserts, this one is a gem that you will treasure. A brown sugar cookie crust, topped with apples and sour cream and a hint of lemon is so joyously good, you will make it often.

- 1/4 cup flour
- 1/4 cup sugar
- 1/2 teaspoon baking soda
- 1/2 teaspoon cinnamon
- 1 egg
- 1 cup sour cream
- 1/4 cup apricot jam
- 2 tablespoons lemon juice
- 1 tablespoon butter

- 2 large apples, peeled, cored and very thinly sliced
- 1/2 cup yellow raisins

Beat together first 9 ingredients until blended, about 1 minute. Stir in the apples and raisins. Pour mixture evenly into Brown Sugar Walnut Crust and bake in a 350° oven for 40 minutes or until top is lightly browned. Allow to cool in pan.

Decorate with a faint sprinkling of powdered sugar and cut into wedges to serve. Serves 10.

Brown Sugar Walnut Crust

- 1 cup flour
- 1 cup brown sugar
- 1/2 cup (1 stick) butter

- 1/2 cup chopped walnuts

In the large bowl of an electric mixer, beat together flour, sugar and butter until mixture resembles coarse meal. Stir in the walnuts. Pat mixture evenly on the bottom of a 10-inch springform pan and bake in a 350° oven for 8 minutes. Allow to cool for 5 minutes before filling.

Easiest & Best Spiced Pumpkin Cake

1 package (18 1/2 ounces) yellow cake mix (use the
  regular cake mix and not the pudding cake mix)
1 1/4 cups canned pumpkin
2 eggs
1/4 cup orange juice
1/2 orange, grated (remove any large pieces of membrane)
3 teaspoons pumpkin pie spice
2 teaspoons baking soda

1 cup chopped walnuts
1 cup yellow raisins, plumped in orange juice
  and drained

Beat together first 7 ingredients for 4 minutes at medium speed. Stir in raisins and walnuts. Pour into a 10-inch tube pan that has been been buttered and lightly floured. Bake in a 350° oven for about 40 to 45 minutes or until a cake tester, inserted in center comes out clean. Cool in pan.

Turn cake out onto a footed platter and spread Orange Walnut Glaze over the top. Serve with a cup of hot cider with cinnamon. Serves 10.

Orange Walnut Glaze

1/2 orange, grated (remove any large pieces
  of membrane)
1 1/4 cups (about) sifted powdered sugar
1/3 cup chopped walnuts

Combine all the ingredients until blended. Amount of sugar will vary depending on the size of the orange. Glaze should be on the thicker side and not runny.

Note: - This is probably one of the most delicious glazes. Use it on spongecake or pound cake.

Spiced Sour Cream Pumpkin Cake with Walnuts & Raisins

This moist, spicy, fragrant cake is a delight served with hot, fruity cider. Serve with a dollup of whipped cream or frost with Cream Cheese Frosting.

        2 cups flour
        1 teaspoon baking powder
        1 teaspoon baking soda
      1/4 teaspoon salt
    1 1/2 teaspoons pumpkin pie spice (or 2 teaspoons if
              you like it spicier)

      1/2 cup butter, at room temperature
    1 1/2 cups sugar
        2 eggs
        1 cup sour cream
        1 cup canned pumpkin
        1 teaspoon vanilla

      1/2 cup yellow raisins
        1 cup chopped walnuts

Combine flour, baking powder, soda, salt and pumpkin pie spice and set aside.

Beat butter with sugar until light. Beat in eggs, sour cream, pumpkin and vanilla. Beat in the flour mixture until blended. Stir in the raisins and nuts. Pour batter into a 9x13-inch buttered pan. Bake at 350° for 40 to 45 minutes or until a cake tester inserted in center comes out clean. Serve with a spoonful of whipped cream or frost cake with Cream Cheese Frosting.

Cream Cheese Frosting

      1/4 cup butter (1/2 stick)
        4 ounces cream cheese
      1/2 teaspoon vanilla
    1 1/2 cups sifted powdered sugar
        1 tablespoon grated orange peel

Beat butter and cream cheese together until light and fluffy. Add vanilla, sugar and orange peel and beat until smooth.

Tipsy Sherry Cake with Orange, Walnuts

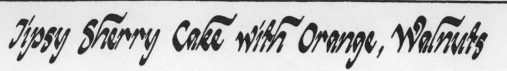

1 package (18 1/2 ounces) yellow cake mix. (Do not use the Super Moist or Pudding mixes. Duncan Hines makes the regular cake mix.)
1/4 cup sherry
1/4 cup water
1 cup sour cream
2 eggs
2 tablespoons grated orange peel
1 cup finely chopped walnuts or pecans
2 tablespoons cinnamon sugar
2 tablespoons Nestle's Quik Chocolate Flavored

In an electric mixer, beat together cake mix, sherry, water, sour cream and eggs. Beat at medium speed for 4 minutes. Beat in 1/2 cup of chopped nuts and orange peel until blended.

Pour 1/2 of the batter into a greased and floured 9-inch tube pan. Sprinkle the remaining 1/2 cup nuts, cinnamon sugar and Nestle's Quik over the batter. Drizzle the remaining batter over the filling, covering all the nuts. With your scraper, cut into the batter at 2-inch intervals to marble the filling.

Bake in a 325° oven for about 50 minutes or until a cake tester inserted in center comes out clean. When cool, drizzle top with Vanilla Glaze with Orange. Serves 8 to 10.

Vanilla Glaze with Orange

1/4 cup butter, at room temperature
2 tablespoons orange juice
1 tablespoon finely grated orange peel
1 teaspoon vanilla
1 cup powdered sugar, sifted

Beat together first 4 ingredients until blended. Add enough powdered sugar to make glaze a drizzling consistency.

Country Sour Cream Coffee Cake with Chocolate, Cinnamon Walnut Filling

    1/2 cup butter
      1 cup sugar

      3 eggs

      1 cup sour cream
      1 teaspoon vanilla

      2 cups flour
      1 teaspoon baking powder
      1 teaspoon baking soda
    1/3 cup semi-sweet chocolate chips

Cream butter with sugar. Add eggs, one at a time, beating well after each addition. Beat in sour cream and vanilla. Beat in flour, baking powder and baking soda until nicely blended.

Pour 1/3 of the batter into a 10-inch tube pan that has been buttered and lightly floured. Sprinkle with 1/2 of the Chocolate, Cinnamon, Walnut Filling. Repeat for next layer ending with batter layer on top. Bake in a 350° oven for 55 to 60 minutes or until a cake tester, inserted in center, comes out clean. Scatter chocolate chips on top and return to oven for 1 minute. Swirl melted chocolate in a decorative fashion, allowing some of the cake to show. Allow to cool. Serves 10.

Chocolate, Cinnamon, Walnut Filling:
    1/2 cup brown sugar
    1/4 teaspoon cinnamon
    1/2 cup crushed chocolate chips
    1/2 cup finely chopped walnuts

Combine all the ingredients and stir until blended.

Sour Cream Coffee Cake with Cinnamon & Chocolate

This simple little cake is a favorite at our house. Children and grownups enjoy the velvety cake with the crunchy filling.

- 1 package (8 1/2 ounces) yellow cake mix (not the supermoist but the old fashioned cake mix)
- 1 cup sour cream
- 1/2 cup water
- 2 eggs

- 1/3 cup sugar
- 2 tablespoons sifted cocoa
- 1 tablespoon brown sugar
- 1/3 teaspoon cinnamon
- 1/2 cup crushed chocolate chips, semi-sweet

Beat together cake mix, sour cream, water and eggs at medium speed for about 4 minutes.

Toss together the remaining ingredients until blended.

Place half the batter in a greased and lightly floured 10-inch tube pan. Sprinkle the sugar mixture evenly over the batter. Pour the remaining batter evenly over all. With your scraper, cut into the batter at 2-inch intervals. (This will marble the finished cake.)

Bake in a 325° oven for about 50 minutes or until a cake tester inserted in center comes out clean. Dust lightly with sifted powdered sugar when cool. If you like, decorate top with Chocolate Cinnamon Glaze. Serves 10.

Chocolate Cinnamon Glaze

- 2/3 cup semi-sweet chocolate chips
- 1/2 cup whipping cream
- 1/2 teaspoon vanilla
- 1/2 teaspoon cinnamon

Place chocolate chips in blender container. Heat cream just to boiling point and pour into blender. Blend for about 1 minute at high speed or until chocolate is melted. Add vanilla and cinnamon and blend for another 30 seconds. Drizzle glaze over cooled cake, swirling it in a decorative fashion to resemble a lacy pattern.

Royal Sour Cream Babka with Chocolate, Almonds & Raisins

This is the queen of coffee cakes. Usually rolled into a towering loaf, I have adjusted the recipe so that the Babka can be made in a mixer, without kneading, and can rise in the same pan in which it will be baked.

- 1 cup (2 sticks) butter
- 1/2 cup milk
- 1/2 cup sour cream
- 1 cup sugar
- 1 teaspoon vanilla

- 3 cups flour
- 3/4 teaspoon salt
- 2 packages dry yeast

- 4 eggs

- 1 to 1 1/2 cups additional flour

- 1 cup chocolate chips
- 1 cup toasted slivered almonds
- 1 cup yellow raisins

In a saucepan, heat together butter, milk, sour cream and sugar only until butter is melted. Stir in vanilla. Allow to cool until mixture is lukewarm.

In the large bowl of electric mixer, place flour, salt and yeast. Add the lukewarm butter mixture and beat until blended. Beat in the remaining flour to form a soft dough. Beat in the chocolate chips, almonds and raisins.

Grease a 10-inch tube pan and scrape dough into pan. Cover pan with plastic wrap and place dough in a warm place until it has risen to about 1/2-inch from the top of the pan. Sprinkle Streusel Topping on top of Babka and bake in a 350° oven for about 45 minutes to 1 hour or until a cake tester inserted in center comes out clean. Cool in pan and serve in slices. Serves 12.

Streusel Topping: Combine 5 tablespoons softened butter, 5 tablespoons flour, 1/2 cup sugar, 3 tablespoons brown sugar, 1/2 teaspoon cinnamon, 1 teaspoon cocoa and mix until blended. Sprinkle on top of risen Babka.

Sherry Spiced Fruit & Nut Cake

This is a variation of my 2-minute cake that will surprise you . . . and impress you, too. It is a good choice around holiday time, but very good for a winter dessert. Use the diced mixed fruit for a fruitcake or only chopped glaceed cherries if that is your preference. It is a delight either way.

- 3 eggs
- 1 tablespoon sherry

- 1 1/3 cups vanilla wafer crumbs
- 1 cup diced glaceed fruit
- 1 cup chopped walnuts
- 1 teaspoon cinnamon
- 1/4 teaspoon nutmeg
- 1 cup sugar

Beat eggs with sherry for 30 seconds or until blended nicely. Beat in the remaining ingredients until blended. (If your mixer does not have a paddle, do this by hand. A whip does not do well here.) Place batter into a buttered 9-inch pie pan and bake in a 325° oven for about 35 minutes or until a cake tester, inserted in center, comes out clean. (You will have to probe a little, as a thin crust forms.)

Allow cake to cool and frost with Cointreau Whipped Cream. Refrigerate overnight or for at least 8 hours. Decorate top with whole glaceed cherries and a light sifting of cinnamon. Cut into wedges to serve. Serves 8 to 10.

Cointreau Whipped Cream

- 1 cup cream
- 1 tablespoon Cointreau or other orange liqueur
- 1 tablespoon sugar

Beat cream with liqueur and sugar until stiff.

Note: - This cake can be prepared 2 days before serving.
- It can also be frozen, frosted and decorated.

Best Golden Fruitcake with Cherries & Walnuts

*This cake is so delicious, it will become a tradition at your celebrations.
Chop the glaceed fruit, so cutting is easier.*

1/2 cup (1 stick) butter
1 cup sugar

3 eggs
1/4 cup Cognac or brandy
1/2 cup orange juice
2 teaspoons vanilla

2 cups chopped walnuts
1/2 cup coconut flakes
1 cup chopped yellow raisins
1/2 cup chopped glaceed orange peel
1/2 cup chopped glaceed lemon peel
1/2 cup chopped glaceed cherries
1/2 cup chopped glaceed pineapple
2 1/2 cups flour
1 1/2 teaspoons baking powder

Cream together butter and sugar. Beat in eggs, until blended. Beat in brandy, orange juice and vanilla until blended.

In a large bowl, place the remaining ingredients and toss until fruit is nicely coated with flour. Pour batter into fruit mixture and stir until blended. Place batter into a greased and floured 10-inch tube pan and bake in a 275° oven for about 1 1/2 hours or until a cake tester, inserted in center, comes out clean. Allow cake to cool in pan. Remove cake from pan and brush on all sides with Orange Brandy Glaze. Cover securely with plastic wrap and store in the refrigerator. Brush with glaze, every now and again, if you are planning to age the cake for more than 1 week. Cut into thin slices to serve.

Orange Brandy Glaze

2 tablespoons orange juice
2 tablespoons Cognac or brandy
2/3 cup sifted powdered sugar

Stir together all the ingredients until blended.

Note: - Chopping can be done in a food processor, in batches. Add some of the flour to the bowl to prevent fruit from sticking.

Royal Sour Cream Brandied Fruit & Nut Cake

        1/2 cup butter (1 stick)
          1 cup sugar

          3 eggs

        1/4 cup brandy or Cognac
        1/4 cup orange juice
        1/2 orange, grated. Use fruit, juice and peel.
        1/2 cup sour cream

      2 1/4 cups flour
          1 teaspoon baking powder
          2 teaspoons cinnamon
        1/2 teaspoon salt
          1 cup chopped walnuts
          1 cup chopped almonds
          1 cup yellow raisins
          1 cup chopped glaceed cherries
          1 cup mixed glaceed fruit
        1/2 cup coconut flakes

Cream together butter and sugar until mixture is light and fluffy. Beat in eggs, one at a time, beating well after each addition. Beat in the brandy, orange juice, grated orange and sour cream.

Combine the remaining ingredients in a bowl and toss together so that the fruit and nuts are nicely coated with flour. Add this to the butter mixture and beat until blended. (Batter is very thick so you may want to do this by hand.)

Place batter in a heavily greased and lightly floured 10-inch angel tube pan and bake in a 275° oven for 1 1/2 to 2 hours, or until a cake tester, inserted in center, comes out clean. Remove cake from oven and allow to cool in pan. When cool, drizzle top with Orange Brandy Glaze. Serves 12.

Orange Brandy Glaze

          1 tablespoon brandy or Cognac
          1 tablespoon orange juice
          1 tablespoon finely chopped glaceed cherries
          2 tablespoons finely chopped walnuts
        3/4 cup sifted powdered sugar

Stir together all the ingredients, adding a little sugar or orange juice until glaze is a drizzling consistency.

Royal Apple & Orange Pecan Torte with Pecan Orange Glaze

Particularly moist and fruity, there are few cakes that you can serve that are more delicious than this one. Using the food processor brings preparation time to 1 minute, but no one could guess, unless you tell.

        6 eggs
        1 cup sugar
    1 3/4 cups chopped pecans
        1 cup vanilla wafer crumbs
        1 teaspoon baking powder
        1 teaspoon vanilla

        1 large apple, peeled, cored and grated
      1/2 medium orange, grated (about 4 tablespoons
              peel, fruit and juice)
      1/3 cup yellow raisins

Combine first 6 ingredients in food processor and blend for 30 seconds. Scrape down the sides and blend for another 30 seconds. Stir in the apple, orange and raisins until blended.

Pour batter into a buttered 10-inch springform pan and bake at 350° for 40 to 45 minutes or until a cake tester, inserted in center, comes out clean. Allow cake to cool and then drizzle with Pecan Orange Glaze. Serves 8.

Pecan Orange Glaze

        1 cup sifted powdered sugar
    1 1/2 tablespoons orange juice
        1 tablespoon grated orange peel
        3 tablespoons chopped pecans

Stir together all the ingredients until blended. Add a little orange juice or powdered sugar to make glaze a drizzling consistency.

Note: - This recipe was tested in the Cuisinart with the large bowl. It can be prepared in your mixer, but then you will have to grate the pecans before beating them in.

No-Cook Chocolate & Cream Cheese Fudge Truffles

1 package (8 ounces) cream cheese, at
    room temperature
1 package (6 ounces) semi-sweet chocolate chips
1 teaspoon vanilla
    pinch of salt
1 cup chopped toasted walnuts

Beat cream cheese until light and fluffy. Melt chocolate in the top of a double boiler over hot, not boiling water and add it to the cream cheese. Beat until blended. Add the remaining ingredients and beat until blended.

Line a shallow 6x10-inch pan with plastic wrap. Spread the fudge in the pan. Cover with another sheet of plastic wrap and press down to make fudge even thickness. Refrigerate until firm. Cut into squares and place in individual bon bon liners. Yields a little over 1 pound of fudge.

Note: - This is not a very sweet fudge, but very creamy. It has a rather
    interesting taste.
    - You can add a thin layer of chopped nuts on top as a variation.
    - If you like a bittersweet taste, then dust the fudge with
    unsweetened cocoa.

Pecan Turtles with Caramel & Chocolate

30 vanilla caramels
1 cup toasted pecans, coarsely broken (not chopped)
1/2 cup semi-sweet chocolate chips, melted

In a double boiler, over hot, not boiling water, melt the caramels. Stir in the pecans. Drop mixture, by the tablespoon, onto a parchment-lined cookie sheet. Allow to cool. Drizzle melted chocolate over the tops and allow to cool again. Easy, but delicious. Yields about 30 turtles.

Note: - If the chocolate needs firming up, then refrigerate candies for a
    few minutes. If the candies become too cold, they will "sweat
    up" when served.

Candied Pecans with Sour Cream Praline

These are simply delicious for snacking and are a welcomed gift from your kitchen around holiday time. Candied nuts are rather undistinguished, but coating them with a sour cream praline will definitely pamper the most discriminating taste buds.

- **1 cup brown sugar**
- **1/2 cup sugar**
- **2/3 cup sour cream**
- **2 cups pecan halves, lightly toasted in a 350° oven for 6 minutes**
- **1 teaspoon vanilla (or maple extract)**

In a saucepan, stir together sugars and sour cream and bring mixture to a boil. Lower heat and simmer syrup until it reaches 240° on a candy thermometer. Stir in the pecans and vanilla and stir until pecans are nicely coated.

Spread mixture out on waxed paper and with 2 forks, separate the nuts. Allow to dry. Place in a jar with a tight-fitting lid and store in a cool, dry place. Do not refrigerate. Yields about 1 pound.

Spiced Pumpkin Cheesecake with Rummy Cream

Crust:
- 1 1/2 cups graham cracker crumbs
- 3 ounces butter (3/4 stick), melted
- 1/2 cup coarsely chopped walnuts
- 4 tablespoons cinnamon sugar

Filling:
- 2 pounds cream cheese, at room temperature
- 1 1/2 cups sugar
- 5 eggs
- 1 cup sour cream
- 1 can (1 pound) pumpkin
- 2 teaspoons pumpkin pie spice
- 2 teaspoons vanilla
- 1/4 cup flour
- 1 tablespoon grated orange peel

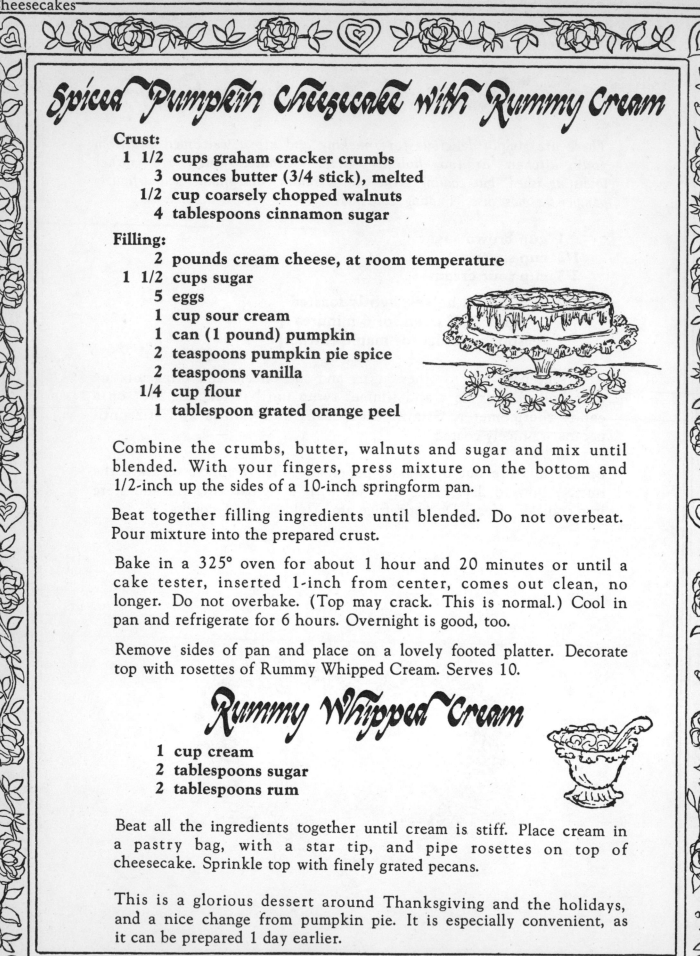

Combine the crumbs, butter, walnuts and sugar and mix until blended. With your fingers, press mixture on the bottom and 1/2-inch up the sides of a 10-inch springform pan.

Beat together filling ingredients until blended. Do not overbeat. Pour mixture into the prepared crust.

Bake in a 325° oven for about 1 hour and 20 minutes or until a cake tester, inserted 1-inch from center, comes out clean, no longer. Do not overbake. (Top may crack. This is normal.) Cool in pan and refrigerate for 6 hours. Overnight is good, too.

Remove sides of pan and place on a lovely footed platter. Decorate top with rosettes of Rummy Whipped Cream. Serves 10.

Rummy Whipped Cream

- 1 cup cream
- 2 tablespoons sugar
- 2 tablespoons rum

Beat all the ingredients together until cream is stiff. Place cream in a pastry bag, with a star tip, and pipe rosettes on top of cheesecake. Sprinkle top with finely grated pecans.

This is a glorious dessert around Thanksgiving and the holidays, and a nice change from pumpkin pie. It is especially convenient, as it can be prepared 1 day earlier.

Royal Velvet Lemon Cheesecake with Raspberry Sauce

This is an incredible cheesecake, velvety smooth, and with the faint hint of lemon. It is a compact cheesecake, so do not overbeat it. It is a light and refreshing dessert and just bursting with good taste.

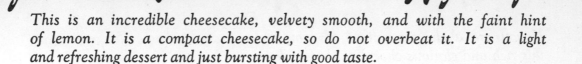

- 1 cup sour cream
- 1 cup cream
- 2 packages (8 ounces, each) cream cheese, at room temperature
- 1 1/4 cups sugar
- 4 eggs
- 1 1/2 teaspoons vanilla
- 3 tablespoons lemon juice
- 1 package (10 ounces) frozen raspberries in syrup, defrosted

In a bowl, stir together sour cream and cream and stir until blended. Allow to stand at room temperature for 1 hour.

Beat cream cheese and sugar until blended. Beat in eggs, one at a time, and at low speed, until blended. Beat in vanilla, lemon juice and sour cream mixture until blended. Do not overbeat and keep the beating at low speed. Pour mixture into Lemon Vanilla Crust and bake in a 325° oven for about 1 hour and 10 minutes, or until top is beginning to color. Turn oven off, open oven door, and allow cake to cool in oven for 1 hour. Refrigerate until chilled.

When ready to serve, cut into wedges and spoon a tablespoon of raspberry sauce on top. Serves 12.

Lemon Vanilla Crust

- 1 1/2 cups vanilla wafer crumbs
- 3 ounces butter (3/4 stick), melted
- 1/2 cup coarsely chopped walnuts
- 1 tablespoon grated lemon peel
- 2 tablespoons sugar

Combine all the ingredients and mix until blended. Pat the mixture on the bottom and 1-inch up the sides of a 10-inch springform pan.

Heavenly Chocolate Ricotta Cheesecake

If you are a chocolate fiend, as you know I am, I know you will enjoy this rich and glorious chocolate cheesecake.

Crust:
- 1 cup chocolate wafer crumbs
- 1/3 cup butter, melted
- 1/2 cup finely chopped walnuts

Combine crumbs, butter and walnuts and mix until blended. Press the mixture on the bottom of a 9-inch springform pan.

Filling:
- 1/4 cup cream
- 8 ounces semi-sweet chocolate chips

- 1 1/2 pounds Ricotta cheese, at room temperature
- 1 cup sugar
- 3 eggs, at room temperature
- 1 cup sour cream, at room temperature
- 2 teaspoons vanilla

In a small saucepan heat the cream. Add the chocolate chips and stir until chocolate is melted. Do this over low heat so that you do not scorch the chocolate. Set aside.

Beat together the Ricotta, sugar, eggs, sour cream and vanilla until the mixture is thoroughly blended. Beat in the melted chocolate. Pour cheese mixture into the prepared pan and bake in a 350° oven for about 55 minutes, or until a cake tester inserted in center comes out clean. Do not overbake. Allow to cool in pan and then refrigerate for 4 to 6 hours. Overnight is good too. Garnish top with lots of chocolate curls. Serves 12.

Note: - *To make chocolate curls, take a vegetable peeler and run it down the sides of a chocolate bar that is at room temperature.*
- *Get ready for a standing ovation.*

Chocolate Amaretto Cheesecake with Chocolate Almond Crust

If you love almonds, you will find this cheesecake totally irresistible. There's a hint of almonds in the crust, in the filling and sprinkling on top. Do not overbeat this cheesecake to maintain its dense texture.

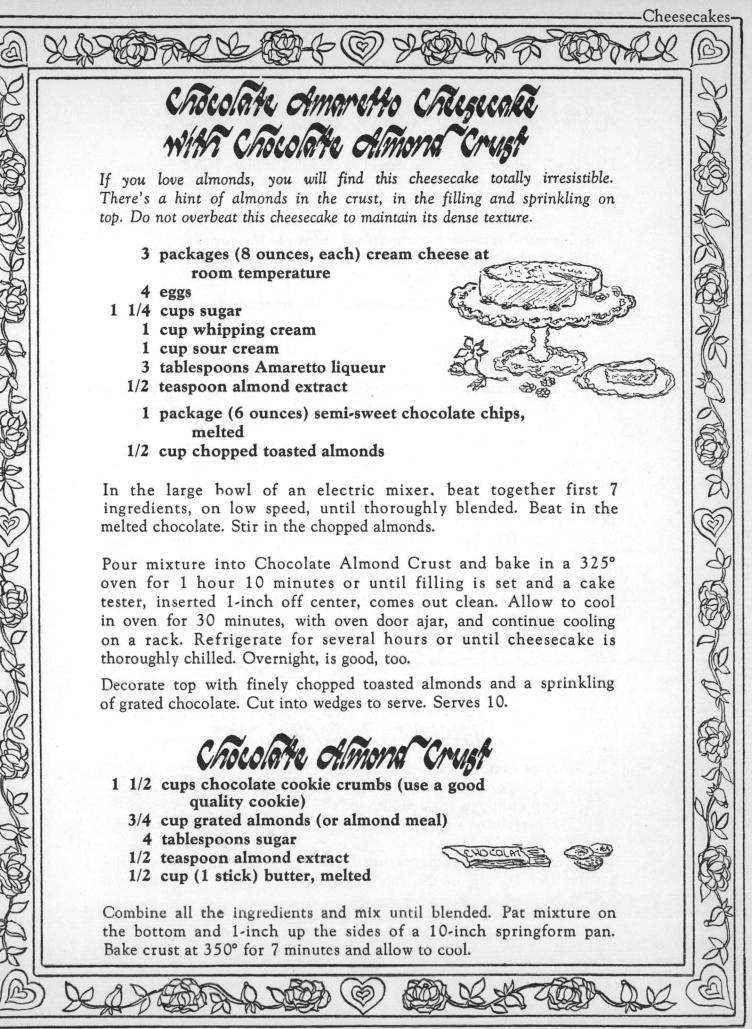

      3 packages (8 ounces, each) cream cheese at
           room temperature
      4 eggs
 1 1/4 cups sugar
      1 cup whipping cream
      1 cup sour cream
      3 tablespoons Amaretto liqueur
   1/2 teaspoon almond extract

      1 package (6 ounces) semi-sweet chocolate chips,
           melted
   1/2 cup chopped toasted almonds

In the large bowl of an electric mixer, beat together first 7 ingredients, on low speed, until thoroughly blended. Beat in the melted chocolate. Stir in the chopped almonds.

Pour mixture into Chocolate Almond Crust and bake in a 325° oven for 1 hour 10 minutes or until filling is set and a cake tester, inserted 1-inch off center, comes out clean. Allow to cool in oven for 30 minutes, with oven door ajar, and continue cooling on a rack. Refrigerate for several hours or until cheesecake is thoroughly chilled. Overnight, is good, too.

Decorate top with finely chopped toasted almonds and a sprinkling of grated chocolate. Cut into wedges to serve. Serves 10.

Chocolate Almond Crust

 1 1/2 cups chocolate cookie crumbs (use a good
           quality cookie)
   3/4 cup grated almonds (or almond meal)
      4 tablespoons sugar
   1/2 teaspoon almond extract
   1/2 cup (1 stick) butter, melted

Combine all the ingredients and mix until blended. Pat mixture on the bottom and 1-inch up the sides of a 10-inch springform pan. Bake crust at 350° for 7 minutes and allow to cool.

Royal Satin No~Bake Chocolate Cheesecake

This lovely dessert can be assembled in literally, minutes, and produces a satin-smooth, velvety cheesecake. It does not need to be baked and firms up very quickly in the refrigerator.

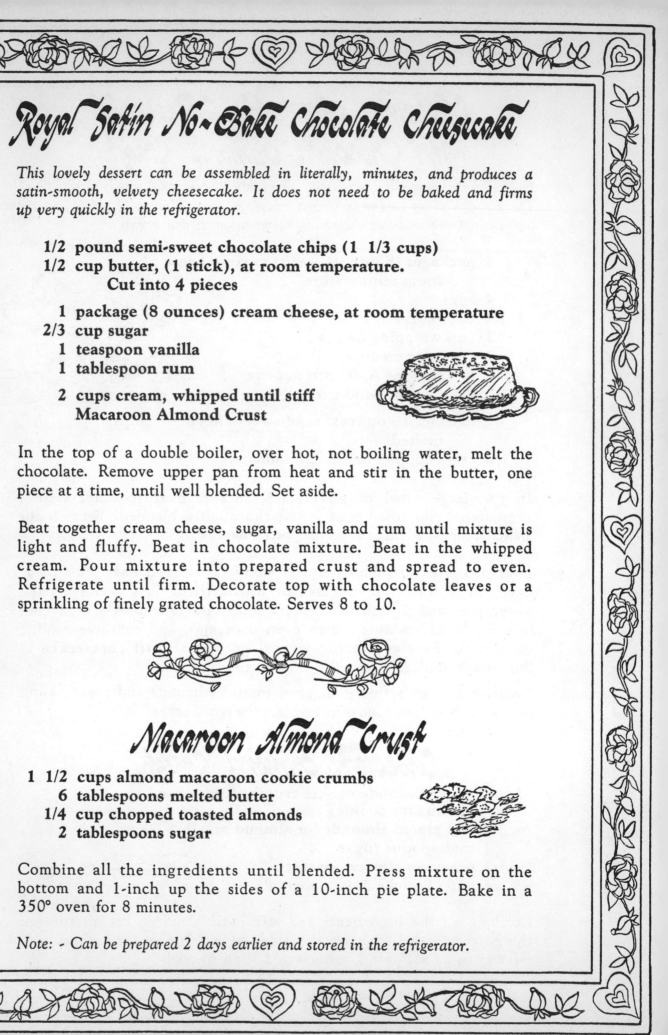

- 1/2 **pound semi-sweet chocolate chips (1 1/3 cups)**
- 1/2 **cup butter, (1 stick), at room temperature.**
  Cut into 4 pieces

- 1 **package (8 ounces) cream cheese, at room temperature**
- 2/3 **cup sugar**
- 1 **teaspoon vanilla**
- 1 **tablespoon rum**

- 2 **cups cream, whipped until stiff**
  Macaroon Almond Crust

In the top of a double boiler, over hot, not boiling water, melt the chocolate. Remove upper pan from heat and stir in the butter, one piece at a time, until well blended. Set aside.

Beat together cream cheese, sugar, vanilla and rum until mixture is light and fluffy. Beat in chocolate mixture. Beat in the whipped cream. Pour mixture into prepared crust and spread to even. Refrigerate until firm. Decorate top with chocolate leaves or a sprinkling of finely grated chocolate. Serves 8 to 10.

Macaroon Almond Crust

- 1 1/2 **cups almond macaroon cookie crumbs**
- 6 **tablespoons melted butter**
- 1/4 **cup chopped toasted almonds**
- 2 **tablespoons sugar**

Combine all the ingredients until blended. Press mixture on the bottom and 1-inch up the sides of a 10-inch pie plate. Bake in a 350° oven for 8 minutes.

Note: - Can be prepared 2 days earlier and stored in the refrigerator.

World's Best Southern Pecan & Coconut Cookies

These cookies received the most votes in a recent tasting at my home and I couldn't wait to share these with you. Each little square is like a miniature pecan pie. The taste is deep and delicious.

1 1/2 cups flour
3/4 cup brown sugar
3/4 cup butter softened

3 eggs
3/8 cup flour
6 tablespoons brown sugar
6 tablespoons sugar
3/4 cup dark Karo syrup
1/4 teaspoon salt

2 cups coarsely chopped pecans
1/2 cup coconut flakes

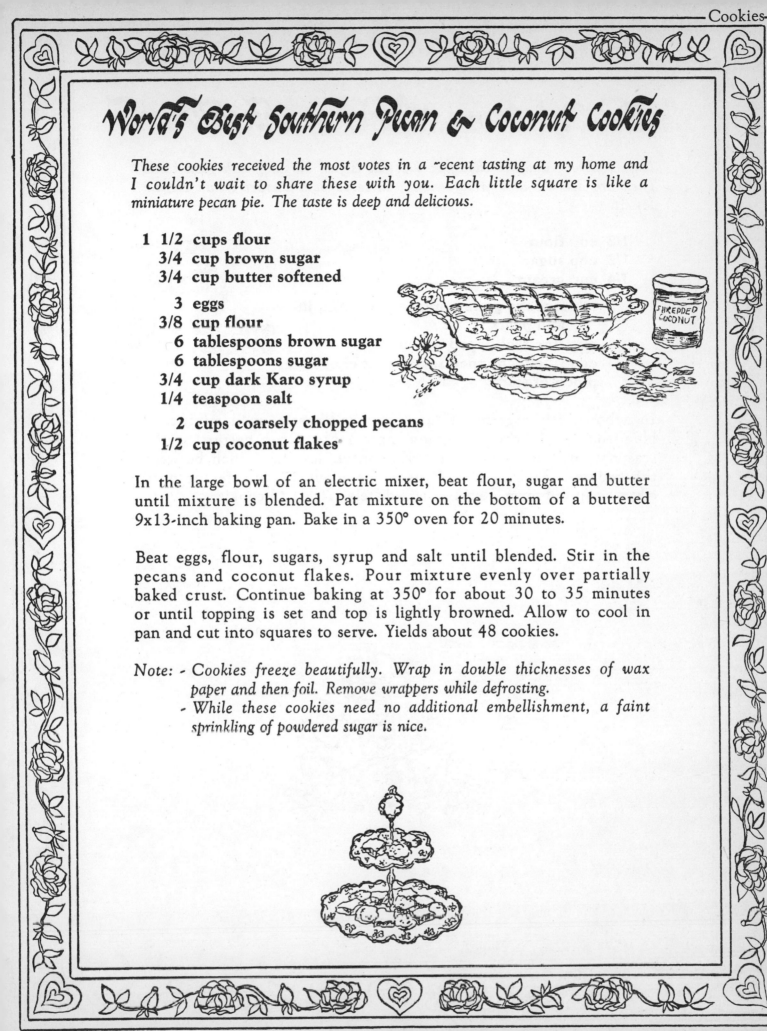

In the large bowl of an electric mixer, beat flour, sugar and butter until mixture is blended. Pat mixture on the bottom of a buttered 9x13-inch baking pan. Bake in a 350° oven for 20 minutes.

Beat eggs, flour, sugars, syrup and salt until blended. Stir in the pecans and coconut flakes. Pour mixture evenly over partially baked crust. Continue baking at 350° for about 30 to 35 minutes or until topping is set and top is lightly browned. Allow to cool in pan and cut into squares to serve. Yields about 48 cookies.

Note: - Cookies freeze beautifully. Wrap in double thicknesses of wax paper and then foil. Remove wrappers while defrosting.
- While these cookies need no additional embellishment, a faint sprinkling of powdered sugar is nice.

World's Best Orange, Walnut & Chocolate Cookie

This is a very unusual chewy cookie that is just bursting with good taste.
They are delicate and pretty enough to serve with sherbet as an elegant
dessert.

1/2 cup flour
1/2 cup sugar
3/4 cup cream

2 tablespoons grated orange (use fruit, juice
        and peel)
1 cup finely chopped walnuts
2/3 cup finely chopped semi-sweet chocolate
        pinch of salt

In a bowl, stir together flour, sugar and cream until mixture is
blended. Stir in the remaining ingredients. Drop batter, by the
teaspoonful, onto a greased cookie sheet, leaving 1-inch between
the cookies. Bake in a 350° oven for about 12 minutes or until
edges begin to brown. Remove immediately. Yields 36 cookies.

Giant Oatmeal Raisin Walnut Cookies

Oh! what a cookie. Large, moist and superbly delicious, these marvelous cookies are a treat to have on hand. Children love these with milk and grown-ups love them with anything.

       3/4 cup margarine
    1 1/4 cups sugar
          1 egg
       1/4 cup orange juice
    1 1/2 teaspoons vanilla

         3 cups quick oats
         1 cup flour
       1/2 teaspoon baking soda

         1 cup chopped walnuts
         1 cup yellow raisins

In the large bowl of an electric mixer, beat together margarine and sugar until creamy, about 2 minutes. Beat in egg, orange juice and vanilla. Beat in oats, flour and baking soda, until well blended. Stir in walnuts and raisins.

Drop mixture by the heaping tablespoon onto a greased 12x16-inch pan, leaving 2-inches between each cookie. (Cookie sheet will only hold 12 cookies.) Bake in a 350° oven for about 12 or 13 minutes or until edges are just beginning to color and cookies look set. Remove from pan and cool on brown paper. Yields 24 cookies.

Note: - Cookies freeze beautifully. Wrap in double thicknesses of plastic wrap, then foil. Remove wrappers while defrosting.
- "Can I substitute chocolate chips for the raisins?" you might ask. Oh yes, and these are very good indeed.
- The glory of these cookies are in their moist, chewy texture. Do not overcook or they will become crisp.

Old-Fashioned Honey Spiced Prune & Walnut Cookies

Children will love these delicious cookies, filled with prunes and nuts and honey spiced.

- 1/2 cup butter (1 stick), softened
- 1 1/2 cups flour
- 1/2 cup sugar
- 1/2 cup brown sugar
- 1/2 teaspoon baking powder
- 1 teaspoon cinnamon
- 1/2 teaspoon nutmeg

- 3/4 cup pitted prunes, chopped and soaked in a bowl with 1/2 cup warm water and 1/2 teaspoon baking soda

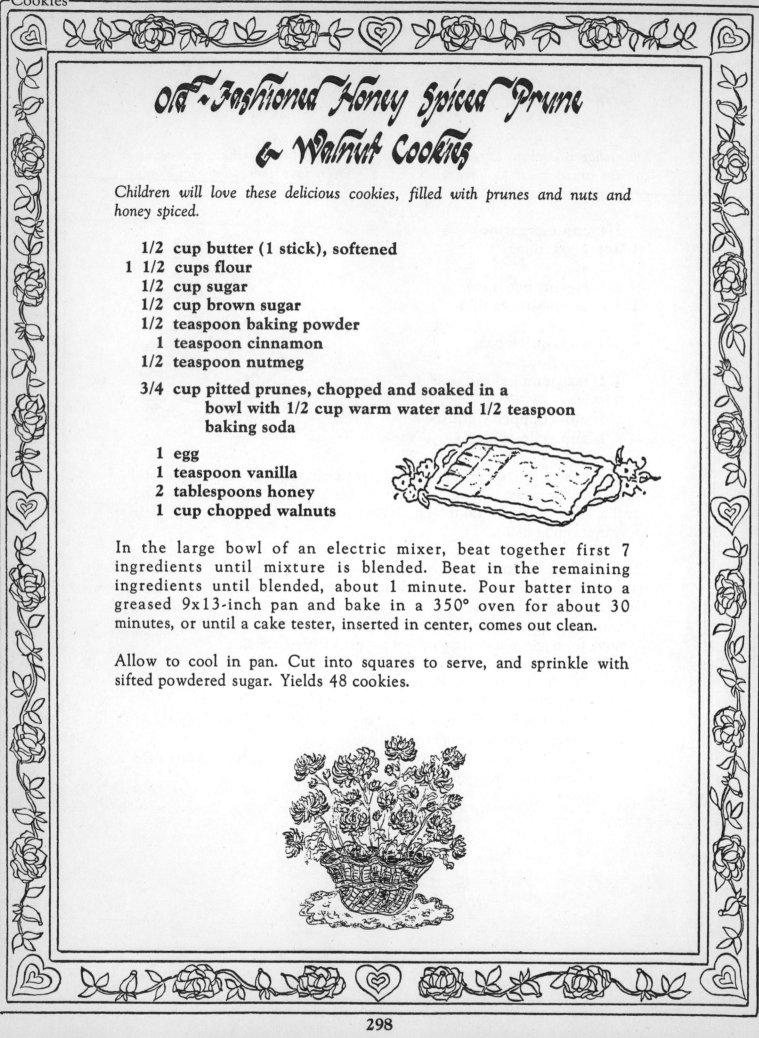

- 1 egg
- 1 teaspoon vanilla
- 2 tablespoons honey
- 1 cup chopped walnuts

In the large bowl of an electric mixer, beat together first 7 ingredients until mixture is blended. Beat in the remaining ingredients until blended, about 1 minute. Pour batter into a greased 9x13-inch pan and bake in a 350° oven for about 30 minutes, or until a cake tester, inserted in center, comes out clean.

Allow to cool in pan. Cut into squares to serve, and sprinkle with sifted powdered sugar. Yields 48 cookies.

The Best Chocolate Chip Oatmeal Cookies with Coconut & Raisins

1   cup butter
1   cup brown sugar
1   cup granulated sugar
2   eggs
1   teaspoon vanilla

1 1/2   cups quick oats (oatmeal)
1 1/2   cups flour
1   teaspoon baking soda
1/2   teaspoon baking powder
1   cup yellow raisins
1   cup chopped walnuts
1   package (6 ounces) chocolate chips, semi-sweet
1/2   cup flaked coconut

In the large bowl of an electric mixer, beat together butter, sugar, eggs and vanilla until mixture is light, about 2 minutes. Stir in the remaining ingredients until blended.

Drop batter by the heaping tablespoonful, on a greased cookie sheet. Bake at 350° for about 15 minutes or until cookies are very lightly browned. (It is important for this recipe not to overbake.) Yields about 48 giant cookies.

Note: - These cookies are soft but chewy. They are filled with all kinds of good things and are totally irresistible.

Dainty Little Walnut Cookies with Cinnamon & Orange

This is a delicate little cookie to accompany ice cream or sherbert. It can be prepared in minutes and has a rather unusual texture.

- 1 egg
- 1 1/2 cups finely grated walnuts
- 1/2 cup sugar
- 1/2 teaspoon cinnamon
- 1 tablespoon finely grated orange peel

In the large bowl of an electric mixer, beat egg for 1 minute. Add the remaining ingredients and beat until blended. Batter will be thick. Place batter, by the teaspoonful, on a teflon-lined cookie sheet. (Pat dough with your fingertips to shape into rounds.) Bake in a 350° oven for 10 minutes or until tops are just beginning to take on color. Do not overbake. Remove immediately from pan and cool on brown paper. When cool, sprinkle top with sifted powdered sugar. Yields 20 cookies.

Note: - Recipe can be doubled.
- Please note that these cookies contain no flour or butter.

Grandma's Best Mandelbread with Chocolate & Walnuts

- 1/2 cup butter, at room temperature
- 1/2 cup sugar
- 2 eggs
- 1 teaspoon vanilla

- 1 1/2 cups flour
- 1 teaspoon baking powder
  pinch of salt

- 1 cup chopped walnuts
- 1 cup semi-sweet chocolate chips

Beat butter and sugar until creamy. Beat in the eggs and vanilla until blended. Add flour, baking powder and salt and beat until blended. Stir in walnuts and chocolate chips. Divide batter between 3 heavily greased 8x4-inch foil loaf pans and bake in a 350° oven for 20 minutes or until tops are browned. Allow to cool for 5 minutes, remove cookies from pan, and carefully cut into 3/4-inch thick slices. Place cookies on cookie sheet, return to oven and lightly toast on both sides, about 3 minutes. Yields 36 cookies.

Almond Meringue Cookies with Chocolate Fudge Frosting

What a delicious chewy cookie, covered with a thin layer of chocolate fudge. Children and grown-ups love the unusual texture.

- 3 egg whites
- 3/4 cup sugar
- 1 teaspoon vanilla

- 3/4 cup vanilla wafer crumbs
- 1 cup chopped toasted almonds
- 1/2 cup chocolate chips

Beat egg whites until foamy. Add 1/2 the sugar and vanilla and continue beating until whites are stiff and glossy. Beat in the remaining sugar, crumbs, almonds and chocolate chips until blended.

Scrape batter into a heavily greased 9-inch square baking pan and bake in a 350° oven for about 25 minutes or until top is dry and a cake tester inserted in center comes out clean. (Important! Do not overbake as meringue will become too crisp.) Allow to cool a little and spread Chocolate Fudge Frosting evenly over the top. Continue cooling in pan.

To serve, loosen sides, cut into squares and serve with a cold glass of milk or hot cocoa. Yields 36 cookies.

Chocolate Fudge Frosting

- 1 cup semi-sweet chocolate chips
- 1/2 cup cream
- 1/2 teaspoon vanilla

Place chocolate chips in blender container. Heat cream to boiling and pour into blender. Blend for about 1 minute or until chocolate is melted. Beat in vanilla. Pour frosting over cookies and spread to even.

Note: - These cookies are best when made 1 day before serving to allow flavors to blend.

Cinnamon Mandlebread Cookies with Toasted Almonds & Orange

It is a delight to share this variation of an old, old family recipe. Originally made with candied cherries and walnuts, it is truly delicious with toasted almonds and the fragrance of orange peel. The cinnamon topping is the perfect balance. These are great for dunking in milk or coffee.

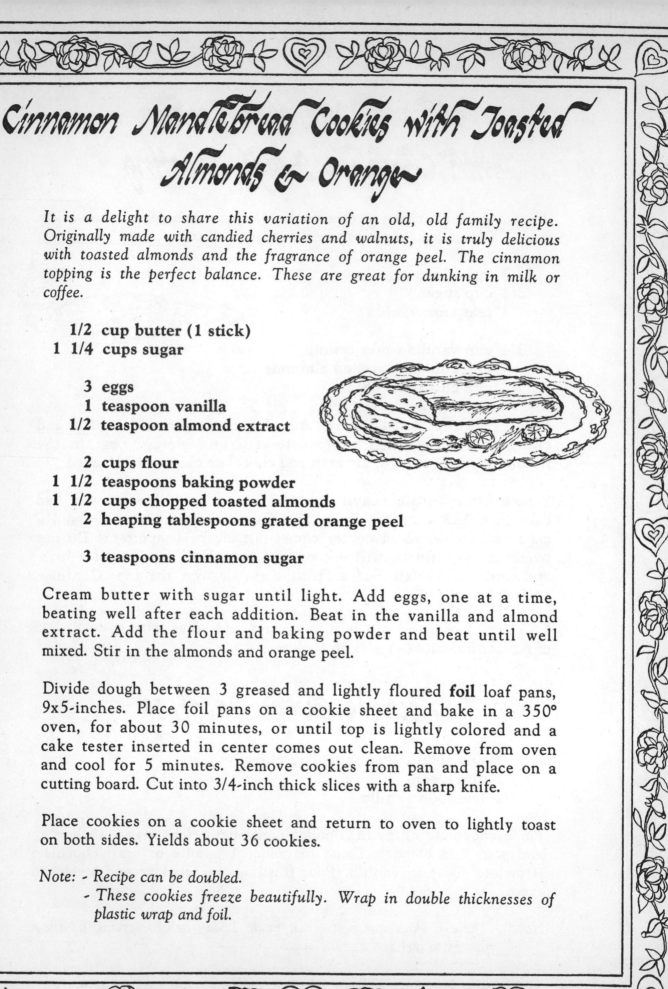

  1/2 **cup butter (1 stick)**
1 1/4 **cups sugar**

    3 **eggs**
    1 **teaspoon vanilla**
  1/2 **teaspoon almond extract**

    2 **cups flour**
1 1/2 **teaspoons baking powder**
1 1/2 **cups chopped toasted almonds**
    2 **heaping tablespoons grated orange peel**

    3 **teaspoons cinnamon sugar**

Cream butter with sugar until light. Add eggs, one at a time, beating well after each addition. Beat in the vanilla and almond extract. Add the flour and baking powder and beat until well mixed. Stir in the almonds and orange peel.

Divide dough between 3 greased and lightly floured **foil** loaf pans, 9x5-inches. Place foil pans on a cookie sheet and bake in a 350° oven, for about 30 minutes, or until top is lightly colored and a cake tester inserted in center comes out clean. Remove from oven and cool for 5 minutes. Remove cookies from pan and place on a cutting board. Cut into 3/4-inch thick slices with a sharp knife.

Place cookies on a cookie sheet and return to oven to lightly toast on both sides. Yields about 36 cookies.

Note: - Recipe can be doubled.
     - These cookies freeze beautifully. Wrap in double thicknesses of plastic wrap and foil.

Easiest & Best Oatmeal Bars with Chocolate & Walnuts

The children will run home from school for this one. What a delicious cookie for "kids" of all ages.

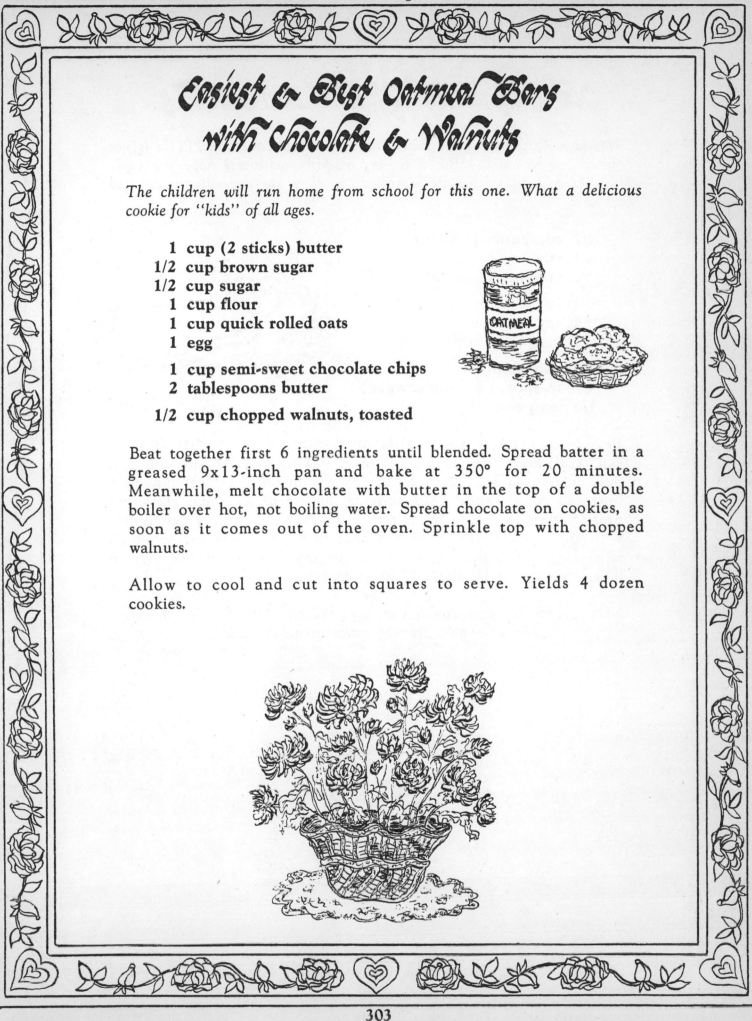

        1 cup (2 sticks) butter
    1/2 cup brown sugar
    1/2 cup sugar
        1 cup flour
        1 cup quick rolled oats
        1 egg

        1 cup semi-sweet chocolate chips
        2 tablespoons butter

    1/2 cup chopped walnuts, toasted

Beat together first 6 ingredients until blended. Spread batter in a greased 9x13-inch pan and bake at 350° for 20 minutes. Meanwhile, melt chocolate with butter in the top of a double boiler over hot, not boiling water. Spread chocolate on cookies, as soon as it comes out of the oven. Sprinkle top with chopped walnuts.

Allow to cool and cut into squares to serve. Yields 4 dozen cookies.

Old-Fashioned Giant Sugar Cookies

This is a delicious sugar cookie. It's big and pale and soft. (This is not the crisp type cookie.) But it is very old-fashioned and I hope you enjoy it. These do not have to be rolled, so they are exceedingly easy to prepare.

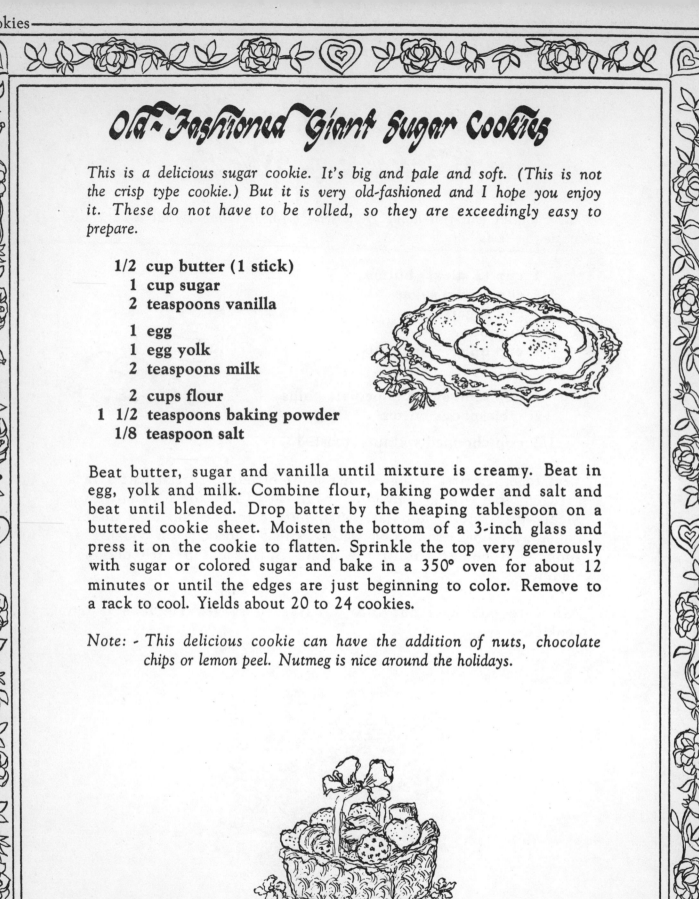

    1/2 cup butter (1 stick)
      1 cup sugar
      2 teaspoons vanilla

      1 egg
      1 egg yolk
      2 teaspoons milk

      2 cups flour
    1 1/2 teaspoons baking powder
    1/8 teaspoon salt

Beat butter, sugar and vanilla until mixture is creamy. Beat in egg, yolk and milk. Combine flour, baking powder and salt and beat until blended. Drop batter by the heaping tablespoon on a buttered cookie sheet. Moisten the bottom of a 3-inch glass and press it on the cookie to flatten. Sprinkle the top very generously with sugar or colored sugar and bake in a 350° oven for about 12 minutes or until the edges are just beginning to color. Remove to a rack to cool. Yields about 20 to 24 cookies.

Note: - This delicious cookie can have the addition of nuts, chocolate chips or lemon peel. Nutmeg is nice around the holidays.

Chewy Granola Cookies with Chocolate Chips & Raisins

1/2 cup butter (1 stick)
1/2 cup brown sugar
1/2 cup granulated sugar
1 egg
1 teaspoon vanilla

1 1/4 cups granola mix
1 1/4 cups flour
1/2 teaspoon baking soda
1/4 teaspoon salt

1 cup semi-sweet chocolate chips
3/4 cup yellow raisins

In the large bowl of an electric mixer, beat together butter, sugars, egg and vanilla until mixture is light, about 2 minutes. Stir in the remaining ingredients until blended.

Drop batter, by the tablespoonful, on a greased cookie sheet. Bake at 350° for about 15 minutes or until cookies are lightly browned. Yields about 48 cookies.

Note: - To make Chocolate Granola Cookies, use only 1 cup flour and add 1/4 cup cocoa.
- Add 1/2 cup chopped nuts or 1/2 cup coconut flakes for another variation.
- 1/2 cup chopped dates or apricots are also delicious substitutions.

Butter Pecan Tassies - Miniature Pecan Pies

These little morsels are always a joy to serve. They are lovely for a luncheon buffet.

Dough:
- 1 cup butter (2 sticks) softened
- 1 package (8 ounces) cream cheese
- 2 cups flour

Beat together butter and cream cheese until blended. Beat in flour until blended. Wrap dough in floured wax paper and shape into a 6-inch circle. Refrigerate for several hours or until firm.

Pinch off small pieces of dough and shape them into 1 1/2-inch balls. Place each ball in a muffin cup and press dough on the bottom and sides, lining cup evenly. (Use hors d'oeuvre size muffin pans.) Spoon 1 teaspoon Butter Pecan Filling into each tassie, filling them almost to the top.

Bake at 350° for about 20 minutes or until filling is set and edges are beginning to brown. Yields 4 dozen tassies.

Butter Pecan Filling:

- 2 eggs, beaten
- 2 tablespoons melted butter
- 1 1/2 cups brown sugar
- 1 cup chopped pecans

Beat eggs, butter and sugar until blended. Beat in the chopped pecans.

Note: - These freeze well. Wrap in double plastic bags and remove wrappers while defrosting.

Easy Tart Lemon Chewies with Raisins & Walnuts

If you are looking for a tart lemon cookie, this little gem will surprise you. No one will guess how simple it is . . . unless you tell.

1/2 cup butter (1 stick)
2 1/2 cups lemon cake mix (not the pudding variety)

1 1/2 cups yellow raisins
1 1/2 cups chopped walnuts

1 can (14 ounces) condensed milk
**1/2 lemon grated (Use fruit and peel, but discard
        any large pieces of membrane.)**

In a 9x13-inch baking pan, melt butter and tilt pan to spread it evenly. Sprinkle the cake mix evenly over the butter and pat it down gently with a fork. Scatter the raisins and nuts evenly over the cake mix.

Stir together milk and lemon and drizzle mixture evenly over the nuts and raisins. Bake in a 350° oven for about 25 to 30 minutes or until top is golden brown. Allow to cool in pan. Cut into squares and sprinkle top faintly with sifted powdered sugar. Yields 48 cookies.

Orange Spiced Peaches with Cinnamon & Cloves

This is a lovely accompaniment to roast turkey, chicken or veal. Everyone loves it. It is admirably simple to prepare and the flavor of fruit and spices is simply delicious. The chopped walnuts add a marvellous contrast in texture.

1/2 cup sugar
1/4 cup butter (1/2 stick)
1/4 cup orange juice
1/4 teaspoon cinnamon
1/8 teaspoon nutmeg
1/8 teaspoon powdered cloves

1/2 cup chopped walnuts

1 can (1 pound 12 ounces) spiced peaches. Drain and
reserve syrup for another use.

In a skillet, combine first 6 ingredients and cook syrup at a low bubble for about 2 to 3 minutes or until the sugar is totally dissolved. Add the nuts and cook for 1 minute more.

Place drained peaches in one layer, and close together, in an 8-inch shallow baker. Pour syrup and nuts evenly over the fruit. Refrigerate until ready to serve.

About 20 minutes before serving, heat in a 350° oven until heated through. Serve peaches warm, not hot. Yields about 8 or 9 peaches and will serve 4. I recommend you make extras as these invite seconds.

Note: - *Drain peaches thoroughly. They will still render some syrup as they heat. This is okay.*
- *Dish can be assembled 1 day earlier and stored in the refrigerator. Heat before serving.*
- *Spiced apricots is a nice substitution.*

Wine Poached Pears with Almonds & Apricot Glaze

This is a light dessert and remarkably easy to prepare. Pears, poached in a butter wine sauce, glazed with apricot jam, and sprinkled with macaroons and almonds, is just heavenly.

6 **large bartlett pears, peeled, cored and cut into halves**

2 **tablespoons melted butter**
2 **tablespoons sugar**
1/2 **cup dry white wine**
3 **tablespoons lemon juice**
1/4 **cup apricot jam**
1/4 **teaspoon cinnamon**
1/8 **teaspoon nutmeg**
1/8 **teaspoon powdered cloves**

1/4 **cup almond macaroon cookie crumbs**
1/2 **cup chopped almonds**

Place pears in a 9x13-inch porcelain baker, cut side down. Stir together the next 8 ingredients until blended and drizzle mixture evenly over the pears. Bake in a 350° oven for 20 minutes, basting now and again.

Sprinkle crumbs and almonds over the pears and continue baking for 10 minutes or until pears are tender and almonds are toasted. Serves 6.

Note: - *If you are making this for company, then serve with a dollup of Creme Fraiche Vanilla.*
- *Pears can be prepared earlier in the day and warmed at serving time.*

Creme Fraiche Vanilla

1/2 **cup sour cream**
1/2 **cup cream**
2 **tablespoons sugar**
1/2 **teaspoon vanilla**

In a jar, stir together all the ingredients until blended. Allow to stand at room temperature for 3 hours and then refrigerate until serving time. This can be prepared 2 days before serving.

Warm Fruit Salad with Honey Wine Sauce & Cinnamon Yogurt

1/2 cup orange juice
1/2 cup white wine
1 tablespoon butter
1/4 cup sugar
1/4 cup honey
2 thin slices lemon

1 package (6 ounces) dried apricots
2 red Delicious apples, cored and cut into
    thin slices (1/4-inch thick)
2 Bartlett pears, cored and cut into
    thin slices (1/4-inch thick)

1/2 cup pitted dates
1/2 cup yellow raisins
1/2 cup coarsely broken toasted walnuts

In a saucepan, place first 6 ingredients and simmer mixture for 3 minutes. Add the apricots, apples and pears and continue to simmer until fruits are tender, about 10 minutes. Add the remaining ingredients and simmer for another 3 or 4 minutes.

Place salad in a lovely porcelain baker and refrigerate. To serve, heat in a 325° oven until warmed through. Serve warm, not hot. Serve with a spoonful of Cinnamon Yogurt and a faint sprinkling of cinnamon. Serves 6.

Note: - Grapefruit, orange or tangerine sections can be added to the above at the last addition.

Cinnamon Yogurt:
1 cup unflavored yogurt
1 tablespoon frozen concentrated orange juice
1 tablespoon cinnamon sugar

In a glass jar, stir together all the ingredients until blended. Refrigerate until ready to use. Yields 1 1/4 cups sauce.

Note: - Fruit salad and yogurt dressing can be prepared 1 day earlier and stored in the refrigerator.

Compote of Mixed Berries, Bananas & Peaches in Orange Wine Sauce & Honey Cream

The lovely aspect of this compote, is that, with the aid of frozen berries, it can be enjoyed all year round. Of course, if the fruit is in season, fresh fruit can (and should) be substituted.

   1/2 **cup orange juice**
   1/2 **cup white wine (Chablis or Chenin Blanc)**
   3/4 **cup sugar**
     1 **thin slice lemon (about 1/8-inch thick)**

     2 **cups frozen strawberries**
     2 **cups frozen raspberries**
     1 **cup frozen blackberries**
     1 **cup frozen sliced peaches**
     1 **cup frozen blueberries or frozen pitted bing**
           cherries (optional)
     2 **bananas, cut on the diagonal into**
           1/2-inch thick slices

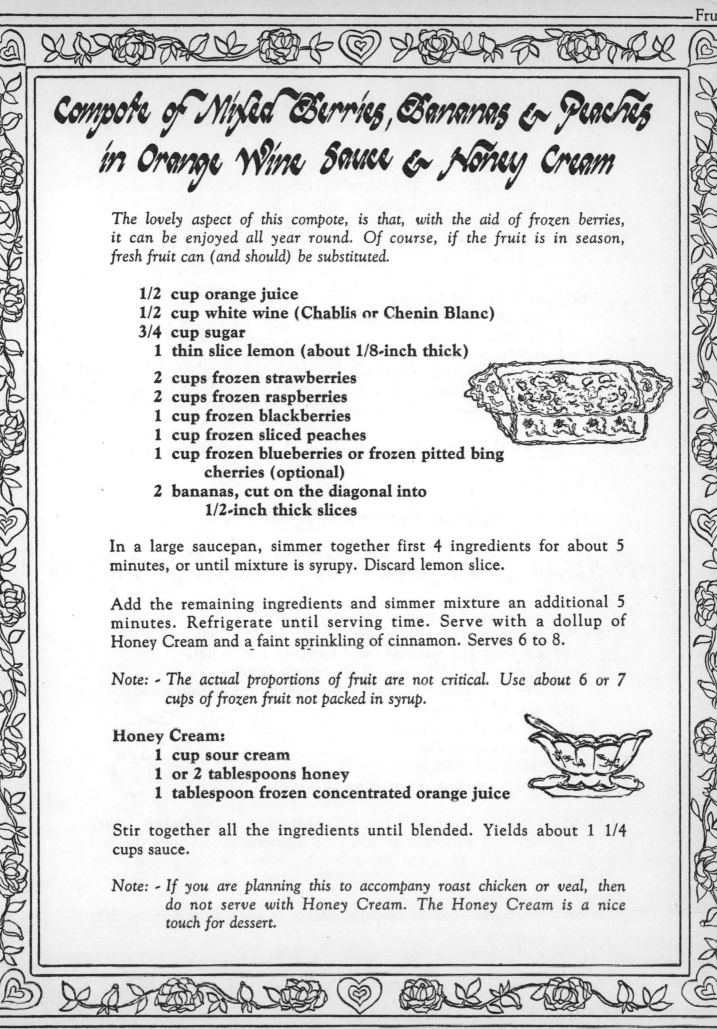

In a large saucepan, simmer together first 4 ingredients for about 5 minutes, or until mixture is syrupy. Discard lemon slice.

Add the remaining ingredients and simmer mixture an additional 5 minutes. Refrigerate until serving time. Serve with a dollup of Honey Cream and a faint sprinkling of cinnamon. Serves 6 to 8.

Note: - The actual proportions of fruit are not critical. Use about 6 or 7 cups of frozen fruit not packed in syrup.

Honey Cream:
     1 **cup sour cream**
   1 or 2 **tablespoons honey**
     1 **tablespoon frozen concentrated orange juice**

Stir together all the ingredients until blended. Yields about 1 1/4 cups sauce.

Note: - If you are planning this to accompany roast chicken or veal, then do not serve with Honey Cream. The Honey Cream is a nice touch for dessert.

Fresh Fruit Platter with Strawberry Almond Cream

Arrange a platter of fresh fruit in a decorative fashion. Cut fruit in slices, wedges, balls, etc. Use different melons, strawberries, peaches or any fruit that is in season. Place a bowl of Strawberry Almond Cream in the center. Either dip the fruit in the sauce or spoon some sauce over the fruit at serving.

Strawberry Almond Cream:
- 1 cup cream, whipped stiff
- 1/2 cup sour cream
- 1/2 cup frozen strawberries in heavy syrup, defrosted and drained
- 1/2 teaspoon almond extract
- 1/2 cup chopped toasted almonds

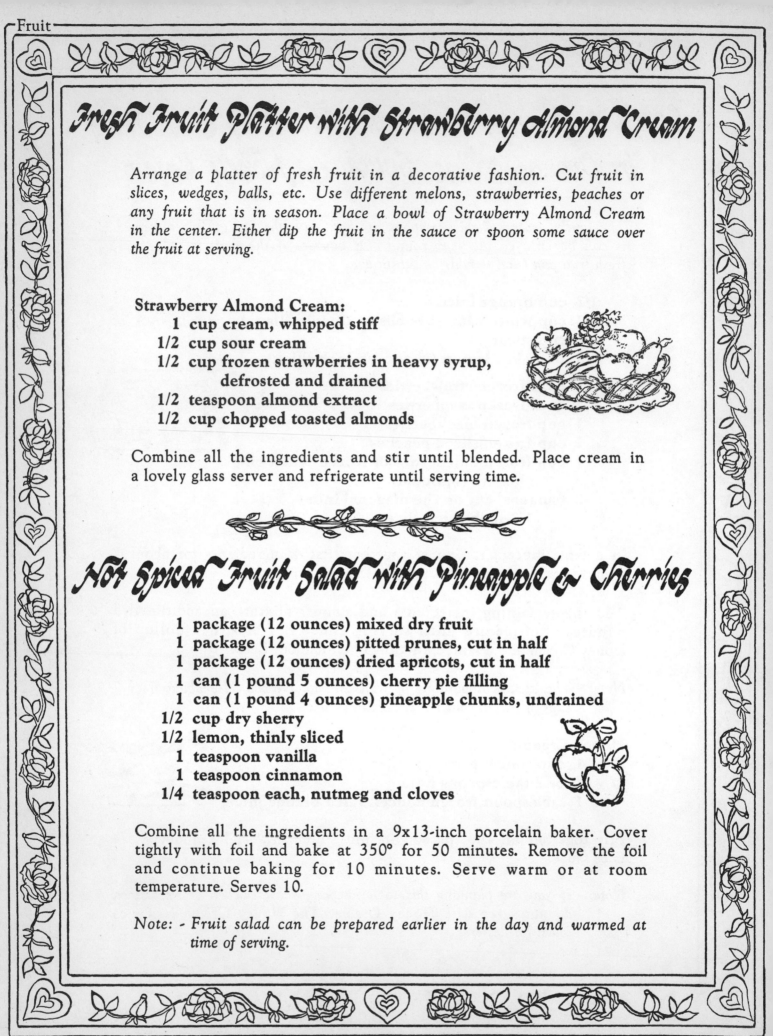

Combine all the ingredients and stir until blended. Place cream in a lovely glass server and refrigerate until serving time.

Hot Spiced Fruit Salad with Pineapple & Cherries

- 1 package (12 ounces) mixed dry fruit
- 1 package (12 ounces) pitted prunes, cut in half
- 1 package (12 ounces) dried apricots, cut in half
- 1 can (1 pound 5 ounces) cherry pie filling
- 1 can (1 pound 4 ounces) pineapple chunks, undrained
- 1/2 cup dry sherry
- 1/2 lemon, thinly sliced
- 1 teaspoon vanilla
- 1 teaspoon cinnamon
- 1/4 teaspoon each, nutmeg and cloves

Combine all the ingredients in a 9x13-inch porcelain baker. Cover tightly with foil and bake at 350° for 50 minutes. Remove the foil and continue baking for 10 minutes. Serve warm or at room temperature. Serves 10.

Note: - Fruit salad can be prepared earlier in the day and warmed at time of serving.

Strawberry & Vanilla Bombe with Chocolate & Grand Marnier

1 1/2 quarts strawberry sherbert, softened

1 1/2 quarts vanilla ice cream, softened
   3 tablespoons Grand Marnier liqueur
   1 cup almond macaroons, rolled into crumbs
 3/4 cup chopped semi-sweet chocolate
 1/4 cup chopped toasted almonds

Line a 3-quart bombe mold or bowl with strawberry sherbert and freeze until firm. Beat the softened vanilla ice cream with the remaining ingredients until blended. Place vanilla ice-cream mixture into the sherbert-lined bowl and pack down to even. Cover top and freeze until firm.

To unmold, place mold in hot water for a second or 2 and invert onto a platter that can be placed in the freezer. Decorate with large rosettes of whipped cream and sprinkle top and sides with shaved chocolate and finely chopped toasted almonds. Return to freezer and freeze until firm. Cover bombe with double thicknesses of plastic wrap and then foil.

To serve, remove wrappings and leave at room temperature for about 5 to 10 minutes. Serves 8.

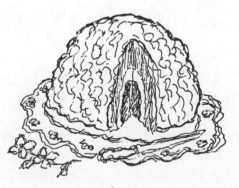

Chocolate Sherbert alla Ire Scallini with Chocolate Cherry Sauce

2/3 cup sifted cocoa
3/4 cup sugar
2 cups half and half

2 teaspoons vanilla
4 tablespoons Cheri-Suisse Liqueur (Chocolate
Cherry Liqueur)

In a saucepan, combine cocoa, sugar and half and half. Cook mixture, over low heat, stirring constantly, until sugar is dissolved and mixture is smooth, about 5 minutes. Stir in vanilla and Chocolate Cherry Liqueur until blended. Pour into a wide-mouth plastic jar, with a tight-fitting lid, cover and freeze until firm.

Remove from the freezer and allow to stand for 10 minutes, or until slightly softened. Spoon into food processor and beat until creamy. Divide between 6 paper-lined muffin cups and freeze until firm. When frozen, remove from pan and store in freezer in double plastic bags.

Remove from freezer about 5 minutes before serving. To serve, remove paper liners and place chocolate ice in a lovely stemmed glass. Spoon a little Chocolate Cherry Sauce on top and garnish with a long-stemmed maraschino cherry. A dollup of whipped cream can be substituted for the chocolate sauce. Serves 6.

Note: - Be certain to sift the cocoa, or you will grow old waiting for the lumps to disappear.

Chocolate Cherry Sauce

3/4 cup semi-sweet chocolate chips
3/4 cup cream
4 tablespoons Chocolate Cherry Liqueur

Place chocolate in blender container. Heat cream to boiling point and pour into blender. Beat for 30 seconds. Add liqueur and beat until blended. Serve sauce warm, or at room temperature. Yields about 1 cup sauce.

Note: - If you refrigerate sauce, it will firm up. In this case, heat in the top of a double boiler over hot water. Unused sauce can be stored in the refrigerator.

Cappuccino Ice Cream with Brandy Kahlua Sauce

3 egg whites
4 tablespoons sugar

1 cup cream
4 tablespoons sugar
1 tablespoon Cognac (or brandy)
1 tablespoon Kahlua liqueur
2 teaspoons powdered instant coffee

Beat egg whites until foamy. Gradually add the sugar and continue beating until whites are stiff and glossy.

In another bowl, whip the cream with the sugar until stiff. Add the Cognac, Kahlua and instant coffee and beat until blended.

Combine beaten egg whites and whipped cream mixture and beat together on low speed of your mixer until thoroughly combined. Divide mixture between 12 paper-lined muffin cups. Place in the freezer until firm. When frozen firm, store in double plastic bags.

To serve, remove the paper liners and place ice cream in a lovely stemmed glass or glass dessert dish. Spoon a little Brandy Kahlua Sauce over the top and sprinkle with chopped toasted almonds. Serves 12.

Brandy Kahlua Sauce

1 cup sugar
3/4 cup water

1 tablespoon Cognac or brandy
1 tablespoon Kahlua liqueur
2 teaspoons instant powdered coffee

In a saucepan, heat together the sugar and water. Cook mixture over medium heat for about 7 minutes or until mixture is syrupy. Stir in the remaining ingredients until blended. Allow mixture to cool. Serve over ice cream. Yields about 1 cup sauce.

Spiced Pumpkin Ice Cream with Gingersnap Crumb Crust

This little dessert is creamy and refreshing, if you are looking for a "light" finale to a sumptuous dinner. It is easy to prepare and can be made a week earlier.

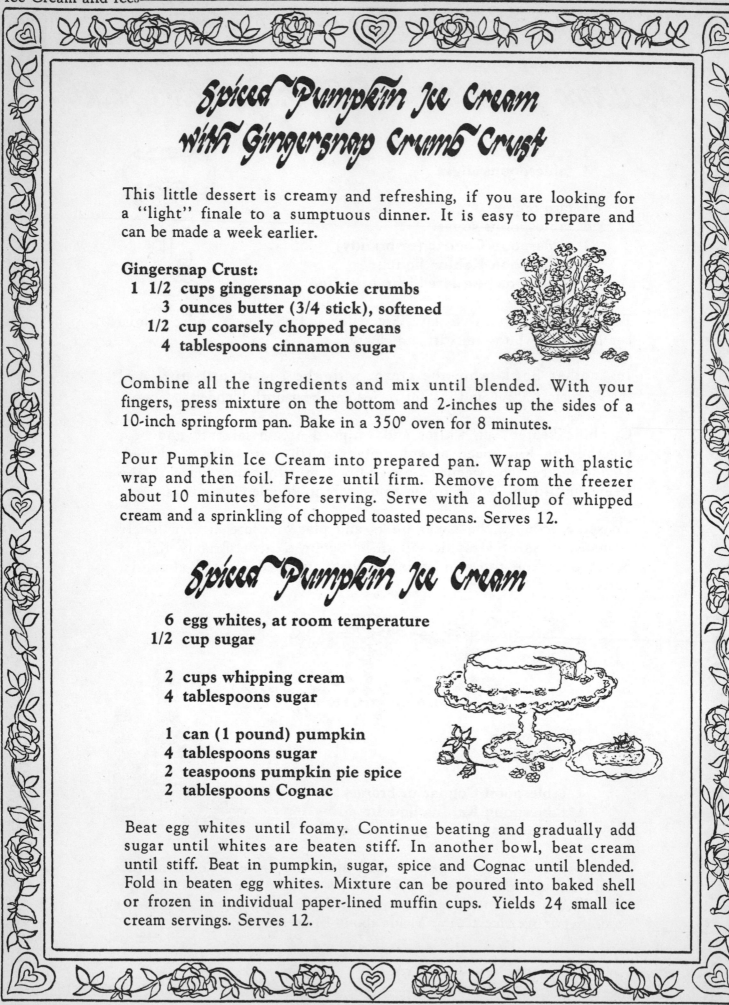

Gingersnap Crust:

1 1/2	cups gingersnap cookie crumbs
3	ounces butter (3/4 stick), softened
1/2	cup coarsely chopped pecans
4	tablespoons cinnamon sugar

Combine all the ingredients and mix until blended. With your fingers, press mixture on the bottom and 2-inches up the sides of a 10-inch springform pan. Bake in a 350° oven for 8 minutes.

Pour Pumpkin Ice Cream into prepared pan. Wrap with plastic wrap and then foil. Freeze until firm. Remove from the freezer about 10 minutes before serving. Serve with a dollup of whipped cream and a sprinkling of chopped toasted pecans. Serves 12.

Spiced Pumpkin Ice Cream

6	egg whites, at room temperature
1/2	cup sugar
2	cups whipping cream
4	tablespoons sugar
1	can (1 pound) pumpkin
4	tablespoons sugar
2	teaspoons pumpkin pie spice
2	tablespoons Cognac

Beat egg whites until foamy. Continue beating and gradually add sugar until whites are beaten stiff. In another bowl, beat cream until stiff. Beat in pumpkin, sugar, spice and Cognac until blended. Fold in beaten egg whites. Mixture can be poured into baked shell or frozen in individual paper-lined muffin cups. Yields 24 small ice cream servings. Serves 12.

Amaretto Ice Cream Pie with Macaroons & Almonds

If a glamorous dessert is your fancy, then this is an impressive choice. It is light and refreshing and a good choice after an Italian dinner.

6 egg whites
1/2 cup sugar

2 cups cream
4 tablespoons sugar
2 tablespoons Amaretto liqueur
1 teaspoon almond extract
1/2 teaspoon vanilla extract

1/2 cup chopped toasted almonds
1/4 cup maraschino cherries, drained and finely chopped

1/4 cup finely chopped toasted almonds

Beat egg whites until foamy. Gradually add the sugar and continue beating until egg whites are stiff.

Beat cream with 4 tablespoons sugar, liqueur and extracts until stiff. Add whites to cream, and on low speed, gently beat together until blended. Beat in almonds and cherries until blended. Pour mixture into Almond Macaroon Crust and sprinkle top with finely chopped almonds. Freeze until firm. Remove from freezer about 10 minutes before slicing to serve. Serves 8 to 10.

Almond Macaroon Crust

2 cups good quality macaroon crumbs
6 tablespoons (3/4 stick) melted butter
1/2 cup chopped toasted almonds

Combine all the ingredients and press on the bottom and 1-inch up the sides of a 10-inch springform pan. Bake in a 350° oven for 8 minutes. Allow to cool.

Note: - At serving time, and if dinner was light, serve with 1 teaspoon hot chocolate sauce.

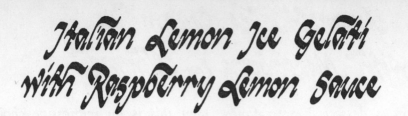

Italian Lemon Ice Gelati with Raspberry Lemon Sauce

This is a light, refreshing dessert that is a perfect finale to a hearty meal. Serve it with a cookie or a biscuit. Preparing it with milk, keeps the calories lower than with cream.

- **2 cups milk**
- **1/3 cup lemon juice**
- **1/2 lemon, finely grated. Use peel, fruit and juice. Remove any large pieces of membrane.**
- **3/4 cup sugar**

In a 1-quart wide-mouth plastic jar, with a tight-fitting lid, place all the ingredients and stir until sugar is dissolved. Cover and freeze until firm. Remove from freezer and allow to stand for 10 minutes or until slightly softened.

Spoon lemon ice into food processor and beat until creamy. Divide mixture between 6 paper-lined muffin cups and place in freezer until firm. When frozen, remove from pan and store in freezer in double plastic bags.

Remove from freezer about 5 minutes before serving. To serve, remove the paper liners and place lemon gelati in a lovely stemmed glass or pretty glass dessert dish. Spoon a little Raspberry Lemon Sauce on top. Serves 6.

Raspberry Lemon Sauce

- **1 package (10 ounces) frozen raspberries in syrup, defrosted**
- **2 tablespoons lemon juice**
- **1 teaspoon grated lemon peel**

Stir together all the ingredients and place mixture in a sauce boat. Serve on lemon ice. Yields about 1 1/4 cups sauce.

Note: - Raspberry Lemon Sauce can be prepared earlier in the day and stored in the refrigerator.
- Lemon Ice can be prepared 4 or 5 days earlier, providing it is stored, well-wrapped, in the freezer.

Old-Fashioned Mud Pie with Double Coffee Ice Cream & Hot Fudge Sauce

This is an updated version of an old classic. The combination of chocolate and coffee, sparkled with almonds is totally irresistible. The Hot Fudge Sauce is one of the easiest and a little "treasure" for last minute preparation.

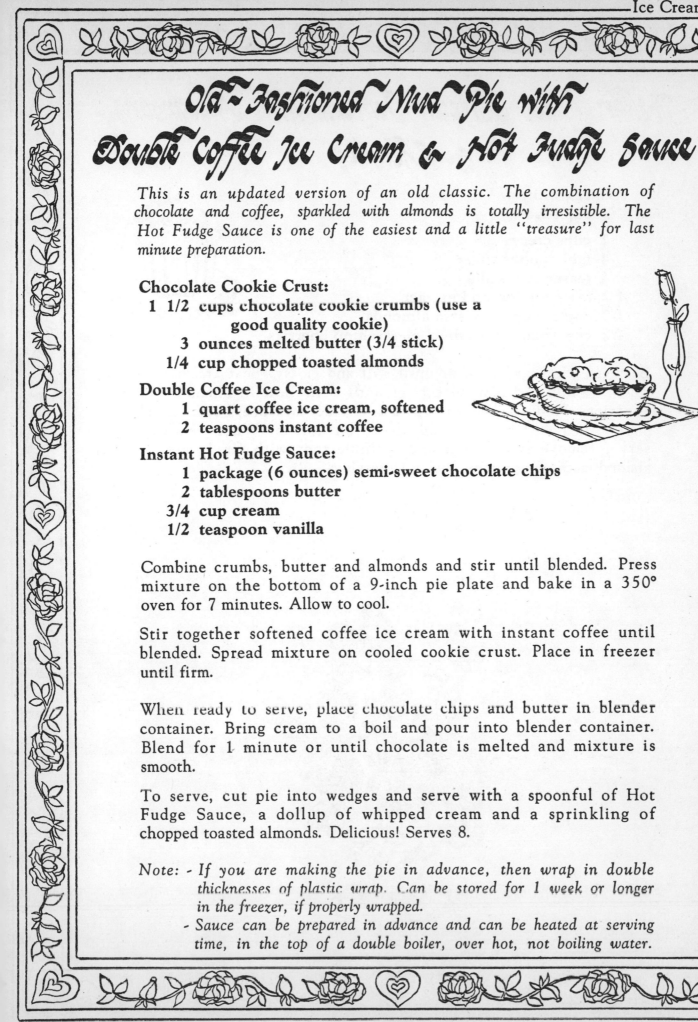

Chocolate Cookie Crust:
- 1 1/2 cups chocolate cookie crumbs (use a good quality cookie)
- 3 ounces melted butter (3/4 stick)
- 1/4 cup chopped toasted almonds

Double Coffee Ice Cream:
- 1 quart coffee ice cream, softened
- 2 teaspoons instant coffee

Instant Hot Fudge Sauce:
- 1 package (6 ounces) semi-sweet chocolate chips
- 2 tablespoons butter
- 3/4 cup cream
- 1/2 teaspoon vanilla

Combine crumbs, butter and almonds and stir until blended. Press mixture on the bottom of a 9-inch pie plate and bake in a 350° oven for 7 minutes. Allow to cool.

Stir together softened coffee ice cream with instant coffee until blended. Spread mixture on cooled cookie crust. Place in freezer until firm.

When ready to serve, place chocolate chips and butter in blender container. Bring cream to a boil and pour into blender container. Blend for 1 minute or until chocolate is melted and mixture is smooth.

To serve, cut pie into wedges and serve with a spoonful of Hot Fudge Sauce, a dollup of whipped cream and a sprinkling of chopped toasted almonds. Delicious! Serves 8.

Note: - If you are making the pie in advance, then wrap in double thicknesses of plastic wrap. Can be stored for 1 week or longer in the freezer, if properly wrapped.
- Sauce can be prepared in advance and can be heated at serving time, in the top of a double boiler, over hot, not boiling water.

Italian Glacé Biscuit Tortoni with Macaroons & Cherries

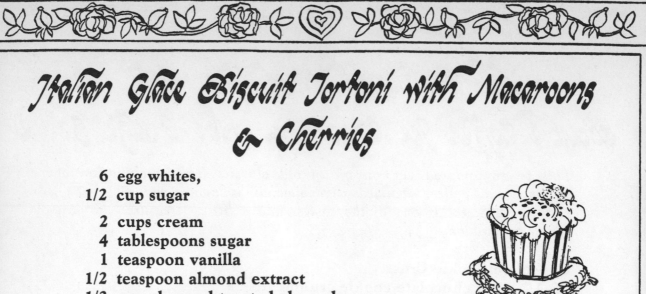

6 egg whites,
1/2 cup sugar

2 cups cream
4 tablespoons sugar
1 teaspoon vanilla
1/2 teaspoon almond extract
1/2 cup chopped toasted almonds
1/2 cup chopped, drained maraschino cherries

Beat egg whites with sugar until stiff and glossy. Beat cream with sugar, vanilla and almond extract until stiff. Beat in almonds and cherries. Fold in beaten whites. Divide mixture between 18 paper-lined muffin cups and freeze until firm. When ready to serve, remove paper liner and sprinkle tops with finely ground almond macaroon crumbs. Yields 18 servings.

Royal White Chocolate Mousse with Raspberries

This is one of the most delicious, exciting and impressive desserts I have ever created. It is a majestic dessert fit for an emperor. Decorated with chocolate leaves and fresh raspberries, it is a glory to behold. Use the best quality white chocolate for best results. I used Lindt chocolate.

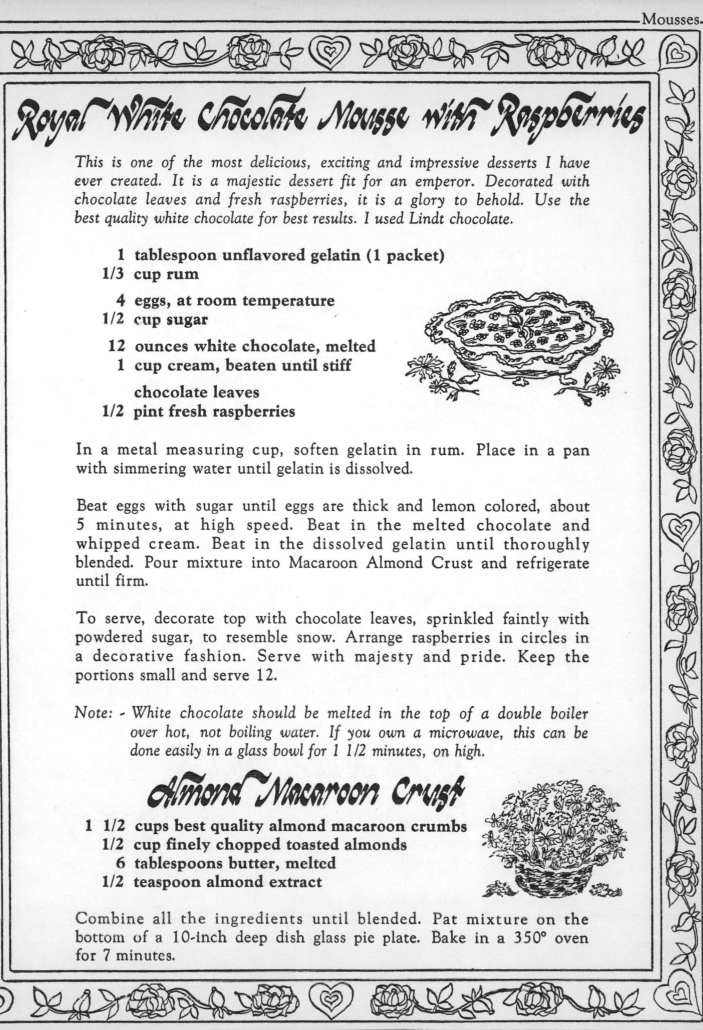

- 1 tablespoon unflavored gelatin (1 packet)
- 1/3 cup rum

- 4 eggs, at room temperature
- 1/2 cup sugar

- 12 ounces white chocolate, melted
- 1 cup cream, beaten until stiff

- chocolate leaves
- 1/2 pint fresh raspberries

In a metal measuring cup, soften gelatin in rum. Place in a pan with simmering water until gelatin is dissolved.

Beat eggs with sugar until eggs are thick and lemon colored, about 5 minutes, at high speed. Beat in the melted chocolate and whipped cream. Beat in the dissolved gelatin until thoroughly blended. Pour mixture into Macaroon Almond Crust and refrigerate until firm.

To serve, decorate top with chocolate leaves, sprinkled faintly with powdered sugar, to resemble snow. Arrange raspberries in circles in a decorative fashion. Serve with majesty and pride. Keep the portions small and serve 12.

Note: - White chocolate should be melted in the top of a double boiler over hot, not boiling water. If you own a microwave, this can be done easily in a glass bowl for 1 1/2 minutes, on high.

Almond Macaroon Crust

- 1 1/2 cups best quality almond macaroon crumbs
- 1/2 cup finely chopped toasted almonds
- 6 tablespoons butter, melted
- 1/2 teaspoon almond extract

Combine all the ingredients until blended. Pat mixture on the bottom of a 10-inch deep dish glass pie plate. Bake in a 350° oven for 7 minutes.

Spiced Pumpkin Cream Mousse with Walnuts

When it's pumpkin time, it usually means dinners, with many courses and a light-as-air dessert is very welcome. This pumpkin mousse is perfect around holiday time, when we do munch a little more than usual.

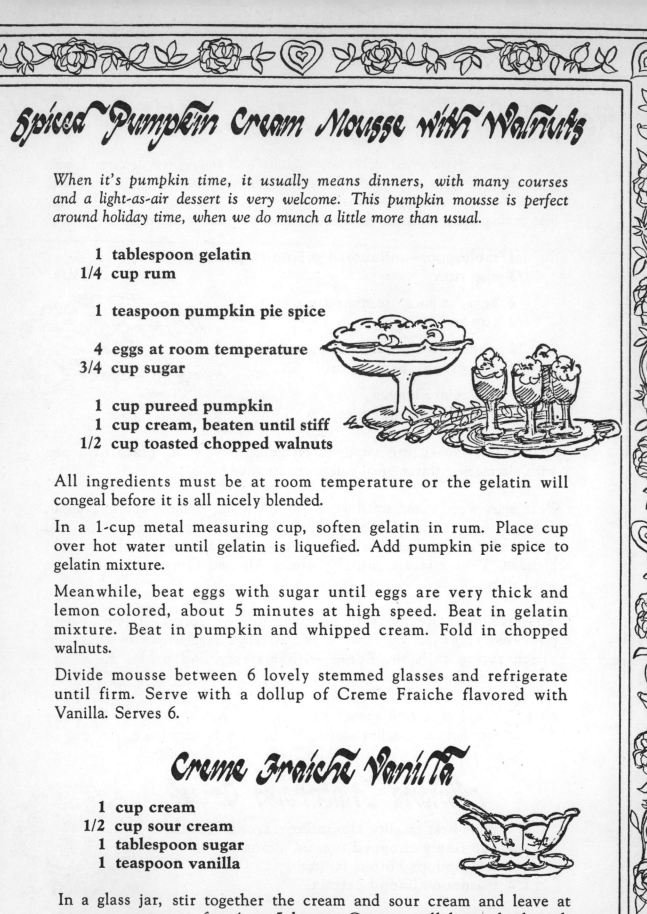

    1   tablespoon gelatin
    1/4 cup rum

    1   teaspoon pumpkin pie spice

    4   eggs at room temperature
    3/4 cup sugar

    1   cup pureed pumpkin
    1   cup cream, beaten until stiff
    1/2 cup toasted chopped walnuts

All ingredients must be at room temperature or the gelatin will congeal before it is all nicely blended.

In a 1-cup metal measuring cup, soften gelatin in rum. Place cup over hot water until gelatin is liquefied. Add pumpkin pie spice to gelatin mixture.

Meanwhile, beat eggs with sugar until eggs are very thick and lemon colored, about 5 minutes at high speed. Beat in gelatin mixture. Beat in pumpkin and whipped cream. Fold in chopped walnuts.

Divide mousse between 6 lovely stemmed glasses and refrigerate until firm. Serve with a dollup of Creme Fraiche flavored with Vanilla. Serves 6.

Creme Fraiche Vanilla

    1   cup cream
    1/2 cup sour cream
    1   tablespoon sugar
    1   teaspoon vanilla

In a glass jar, stir together the cream and sour cream and leave at room temperature for 4 to 5 hours. Creams will have thickened. Stir in sugar and vanilla and refrigerate until serving time. Yields 1 cup.

Imperial Cheesecake Mousse with Raspberries & Chocolate

This is a splendid dessert to serve for the finest occasion. The combination of raspberries and chocolate in a whipped cream cheese mousse is heavenly. As it does not have to be cooked, it is rather easy to prepare. If you are planning to serve this for a small group, this recipe can be halved.

- 1 tablespoon butter
- 3/4 cup vanilla wafer crumbs

- 1 1/2 tablespoons unflavored gelatin
- 1/3 cup water

- 2 packages (8 ounces, each) cream cheese, at room temperature
- 1/2 cup sugar
- 1 teaspoon vanilla

- 2 cups cream, whipped

- 2 packages (10 ounces, each) frozen raspberries in syrup, defrosted
- 4 ounces semi-sweet chocolate, chopped into small chunks

In a 10-inch springform pan, spread butter and sprinkle crumbs evenly. In a metal measuring cup, soften gelatin in water. Place cup in a larger pan with simmering water and stir until gelatin is dissolved. Set aside.

Beat cream cheese with sugar and vanilla until cream cheese is smooth and fluffy. Fold in the whipped cream, raspberries, chocolate and dissolved gelatin until blended. Pour mousse into the prepared crumbed pan and spread to even. Refrigerate until firm.

To serve, decorate top with raspberries and grated chocolate. Serves 8 to 10.

Note: - Do not drain the raspberries. Use the syrup and fruit for this recipe.

Old-Fashioned Honey Apple Pie with Walnut Streusel Topping

The aroma of this pie, baking in your kitchen, will virtually bring the neighborhood to your door. So, if you are feeling magnanimous, I recommend you bake 2.

1 frozen 9-inch deep dish frozen pie shell.
  Brush bottom with 3 tablespoons apricot jam.

3 tablespoons butter, melted
3 tablespoons flour
1/4 cup honey
1/4 cup apricot jam
1 tablespoon grated orange peel
1/2 cup brown sugar
1 teaspoon cinnamon
1/8 teaspoon nutmeg
1/2 cup yellow raisins
2 pounds apples, peeled, cored and thinly sliced

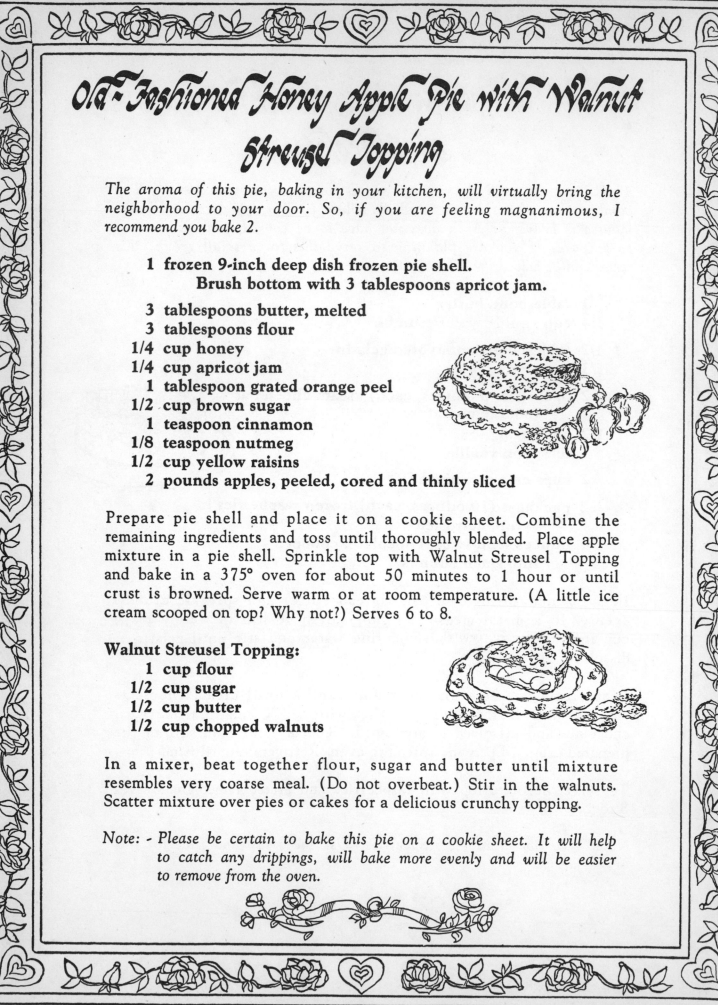

Prepare pie shell and place it on a cookie sheet. Combine the remaining ingredients and toss until thoroughly blended. Place apple mixture in a pie shell. Sprinkle top with Walnut Streusel Topping and bake in a 375° oven for about 50 minutes to 1 hour or until crust is browned. Serve warm or at room temperature. (A little ice cream scooped on top? Why not?) Serves 6 to 8.

Walnut Streusel Topping:
    1 cup flour
    1/2 cup sugar
    1/2 cup butter
    1/2 cup chopped walnuts

In a mixer, beat together flour, sugar and butter until mixture resembles very coarse meal. (Do not overbeat.) Stir in the walnuts. Scatter mixture over pies or cakes for a delicious crunchy topping.

Note: - Please be certain to bake this pie on a cookie sheet. It will help to catch any drippings, will bake more evenly and will be easier to remove from the oven.

The Best Old-Fashioned Apple Pie with Walnuts & Raisins

Joyously delicious, remarkably easy, you will be singing songs and sonnets in praise of this delightful pie. The cookie crust is sparkled with walnuts and the apples are combined with a grand mixture of sour cream, lemon and raisins.

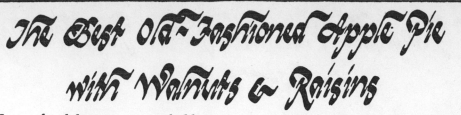

2	eggs
1	cup sour cream
2/3	cup sugar
1	teaspoon vanilla
1/2	cup yellow raisins
3	apples, peeled, cored and very thinly sliced
2	tablespoons lemon juice
2	tablespoons cinnamon sugar

Beat together eggs, sour cream, sugar and vanilla until blended. Stir in the raisins, apples and lemon juice until blended. Pour mixture into prepared Butter Cookie Crust and sprinkle top with cinnamon sugar.

Bake in a 350° oven for 50 minutes or until top is golden brown. Allow to cool in pan. Cut into wedges and ENJOY! Serves 8.

Butter Cookie Crust

1 1/2	cups flour
1/2	cup butter
6	tablespoons sugar
1	egg
3/4	cup sour cream
1/2	cup chopped walnuts

In the large bowl of an electric mixer, beat together flour, butter and sugar until mixture resembles coarse meal. Beat in egg and sour cream until mixture forms a dough. Do not overbeat. Press dough on the bottom and 1/2-inch up the sides of a 10-inch springform pan. Sprinkle walnuts evenly on the bottom and press them into the dough.

Bake in a 350° oven for 30 minutes or until dough is set and just beginning to color. Yields 1 10-inch pie shell.

Brandy Pumpkin Pie with Pecan Praline Topping & Cognac Cream

1 9-inch frozen deep-dish pie shell, baked in a 400°
    oven for 8 minutes

1 can (1 pound) pumpkin
2 eggs
1 1/2 cups cream
3/4 cup sugar
1/4 cup brown sugar
3 teaspoons pumpkin pie spice
1 tablespoon Cognac or brandy

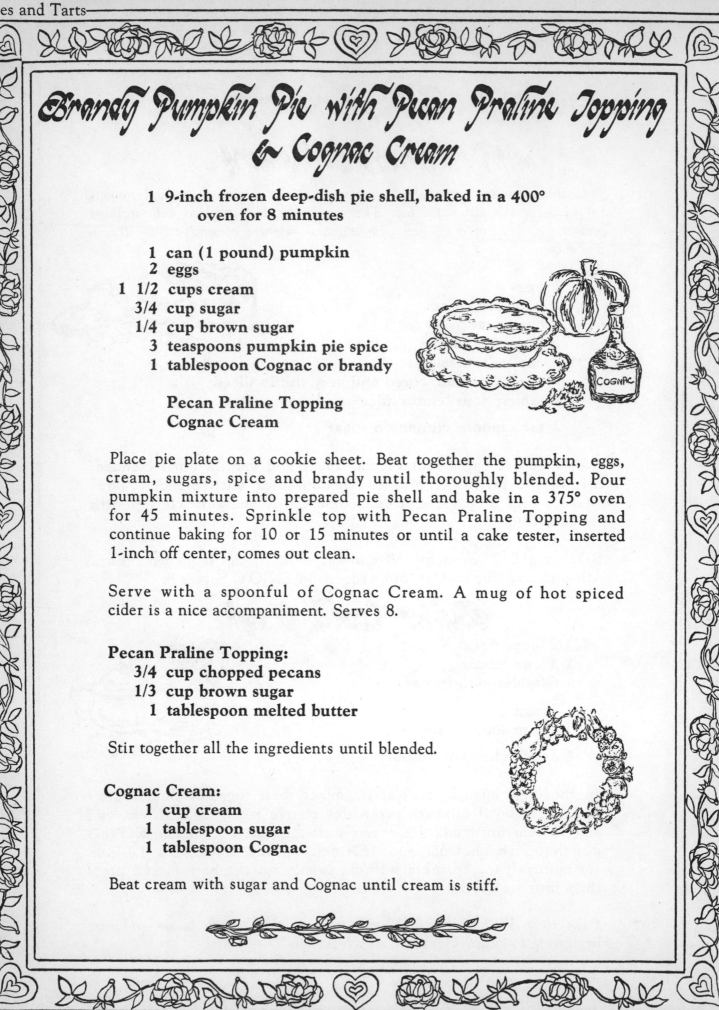

Pecan Praline Topping
Cognac Cream

Place pie plate on a cookie sheet. Beat together the pumpkin, eggs, cream, sugars, spice and brandy until thoroughly blended. Pour pumpkin mixture into prepared pie shell and bake in a 375° oven for 45 minutes. Sprinkle top with Pecan Praline Topping and continue baking for 10 or 15 minutes or until a cake tester, inserted 1-inch off center, comes out clean.

Serve with a spoonful of Cognac Cream. A mug of hot spiced cider is a nice accompaniment. Serves 8.

Pecan Praline Topping:
3/4 cup chopped pecans
1/3 cup brown sugar
1 tablespoon melted butter

Stir together all the ingredients until blended.

Cognac Cream:
1 cup cream
1 tablespoon sugar
1 tablespoon Cognac

Beat cream with sugar and Cognac until cream is stiff.

Viennese Linzer Tart with Brandied Apricots Almond Cookie Crust

Almond Cookie Crust:

        2   cups flour mixed with 1/4 teaspoon cinnamon
        1   cup sugar
        1   cup (2 sticks) butter

        1   egg
    3/4   cup chopped toasted almonds
        1   teaspoon vanilla

In the large bowl of an electric mixer, beat together flour, sugar and butter, until mixture resembles coarse meal. Beat in the egg, almonds and vanilla until dough forms a ball. Do not overbeat.

Pat 2/3 the dough on the bottom and 1/2-inch up the sides of a 10-inch springform pan. Spread Brandied Apricots over the dough. Pinch off pieces of the remaining dough, roll it into 1/4-inch ropes and lay them over the apricot filling, lattice-fashioned. Bake in a 325° oven for about 40 minutes or until top is golden brown. To serve, cut into 1-inch diamonds and sprinkle with a faint hint of sifted powdered sugar. Serves 8.

Brandied Apricots:

        1   pound dried apricots
        1   cup apricot nectar
    1/2   cup sugar

        1   tablespoon brandy

In a saucepan, combine apricots, apricot nectar and sugar and simmer mixture, until apricots are tender, and liquid syrupy. Stir now and again while cooking. Stir in the brandy.

Note: - Apricots can be left whole, chopped or pureed. Taste is still magnifique.

Heavenly Chocolate Almond Pie with Chocolate Almond Crust

This is a variation of a torte given to me by a very special lady, Emita Armi. The original recipe called for 4 1/2 dozen ladyfingers, which are grand in this dessert. But in deference to keeping the cost down, I have used the cookie crust, sparkled with almonds and chocolate.

Chocolate Almond Crust:
- 1 1/2 cups chocolate cookie crumbs
- 1/2 cup chopped almonds
- 1/3 cup butter, melted
- 2 tablespoons grated semi-sweet chocolate
- 1/2 teaspoon almond extract

Combine all the ingredients and mix until blended. Press mixture on the bottom of a 9-inch pie pan. Bake in a 350° oven for 6 minutes. Cool before filling.

Chocolate Almond Filling:
- 1/2 cup (1 stick) butter, at room temperature
- 2/3 cup sugar
- 3 tablespoons sifted cocoa
- 3 egg yolks
- 1 1/4 cups grated almonds
- 1 teaspoon vanilla
- 3 tablespoons Creme de Cacao liqueur
- 1/2 cup milk, at room temperature

- 1 cup cream, whipped

In the large bowl of an electric mixer, beat butter and sugar until light and creamy. Beat in cocoa, yolks, almonds, vanilla, liqueur, and milk, beating well after each addition. Beat in the whipped cream.

Spread filling evenly in prepared crust and refrigerate for several hours. Decorate top with a sprinkling of grated chocolate and chocolate leaves. Sprinkle a hint of sifted powdered sugar on the leaves to resemble snow. Serves 10.

Note: - Pie can be prepared 1 day earlier and stored in the refrigerator.
- Do not freeze.

Glazed Strawberry Tart with Almond Malakov Cream

There are few desserts you can make, that are more glamorous or exciting than this one. An almond macaroon crust, topped with an incredible creamy filling and plump glazed strawberries, is literally fit for a czar. It is a royal dessert and a magnificent finale to dinner.

    3/4 cup butter (1 1/2 sticks) at room temperature
    3/4 cup sugar
      1 egg, at room temperature
    3/4 teaspoon almond extract
  2 1/2 tablespoons Amaretto liqueur
      3 tablespoons half and half, at room temperature

      2 pints strawberries, hulled
    3/4 cup currant jelly, heated

Beat butter and sugar until mixture is very light and creamy. Beat in the egg, almond extract, Amaretto and half and half, beating well after each addition.

Spread mixture on Macaroon Almond Crust and refrigerate for 30 minutes. Set whole strawberries upright on filling, in a circular pattern. Brush melted currant jelly generously over the strawberries, and fill in any gaps. Refrigerate until serving time. Serves 10.

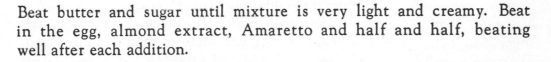

Macaroon Almond Crust

      2 cups almond macaroon cookie crumbs
      6 tablespoons melted butter (3/4 stick)
    1/2 cup chopped toasted almonds

Combine all the ingredients until blended. Press mixture on the bottom of a 10-inch springform pan. Bake in a 350° oven for 7 minutes. Allow to cool.

Note: - If strawberries are very expensive, then cut them in half and lay them, cut-side down, on the cream. In this case, you would need 1 pint of strawberries.
- Raspberries may be substituted.

Holiday Spiced Pumpkin Pie with Praline & Cream

What a divine way to end a Thanksgiving feast. The Praline Pecan Topping adds a delightful touch.

1 deep dish frozen pie shell (9-inch). Prebake in a 350° oven for 8 minutes.

3 eggs, beaten
3/4 cup brown sugar
1/4 teaspoon salt
3 teaspoons pumpkin pie spice (or to taste)
1 1/2 cups half and half (can use 1/2 cream for a richer taste)
1 can (1 pound) pumpkin

Prepare pie shell. Combine the remaining ingredients and beat until blended. Pour mixture into prepared pie shell. Place pie on a cookie sheet and bake in a 350° oven for 40 minutes. Spread Praline Pecan Topping carefully on the top and continue baking for about 10 or 15 minutes, or until a knife, inserted in center comes out clean. Serves 8.

Praline Pecan Topping:
Stir together 1/4 cup melted butter, 1/2 cup brown sugar and 3/4 cup chopped pecans.

How to Make Successful Meringues

Making meringues that aren't "weeping" or "beading" or generally unsightly is one of the sensitive techniques in working with egg whites. The following are a few points to keep in mind to help you produce successful meringues.

1. Egg whites should be at room temperature to assure greater volume. Start beating them slowly and then gradually pick up speed. If you start beating too quickly, you will weaken the air cells that form.

2. When the whites are foamy, add cream of tartar and salt. The cream of tartar will help stabilize the foam. If you do not use the cream of tartar, the air bubbles formed will be thin and weak and the egg whites will collapse and lose volume. Use about 1/8 teaspoon cream of tartar and a pinch of salt for every 3 egg whites.

3. Add the sugar gradually, beating, but make certain that all the sugar is added before whites are too stiff. Sugar should be completely dissolved and when you touch the meringue with your fingers, it should feel perfectly smooth without a trace of graininess. If sugar is not dissolved completely, meringue can "bead" which is actually undissolved sugar forming a syrup.

4. To avoid "beading" 1. make certain sugar is dissolved in the beating or 2. use sifted powdered sugar (this has a small quantity of cornstarch and will help stabilize the meringue.

5. Whites should be beaten just until stiff peaks form when beaters are lifted. If you overbeat, meringue can "weep" which is the accumulation of moisture (tears) between the meringue and the filling. To avoid "weeping" do not overbeat the meringue and of course, don't underbeat either. Beat just until stiff peaks are formed when the beater is lifted. The addition of 1 teaspoon cornstarch to each 3 whites can help stabilize the meringue.

6. "Weeping" can also occur if the meringue is not baked long enough. This can be avoided by spreading meringue on hot lemon filling. If the filling is hot, the bottom of the meringue will bake longer. Bake for 12 to 15 minutes in a 350° oven.

Meringues (continued)

7. Spread the finished meringue over the warm filling in decorative swirls, and be certain that the meringue covers every bit of crust.

8. Bowls and beaters should be scrupulously clean without a trace of grease or yolk.

9. If a bit of the yolk happens to get into the whites, pick it out with a piece of shell. If any yolk is in the egg whites, they will not beat to proper volume. Separate one egg at a time in a cup and then transfer yolks and whites to separate bowls.

Old-Fashioned Lemon Meringue Pie on Lemon Cookie Crust

When we were growing up, this was one of our favorite pies. Visions of this tart and tangy pie on a delicious lemon cookie base, with mountains of meringue piled on top, fill me with a wonderful nostalgia.

Lemon Cookie Crust:

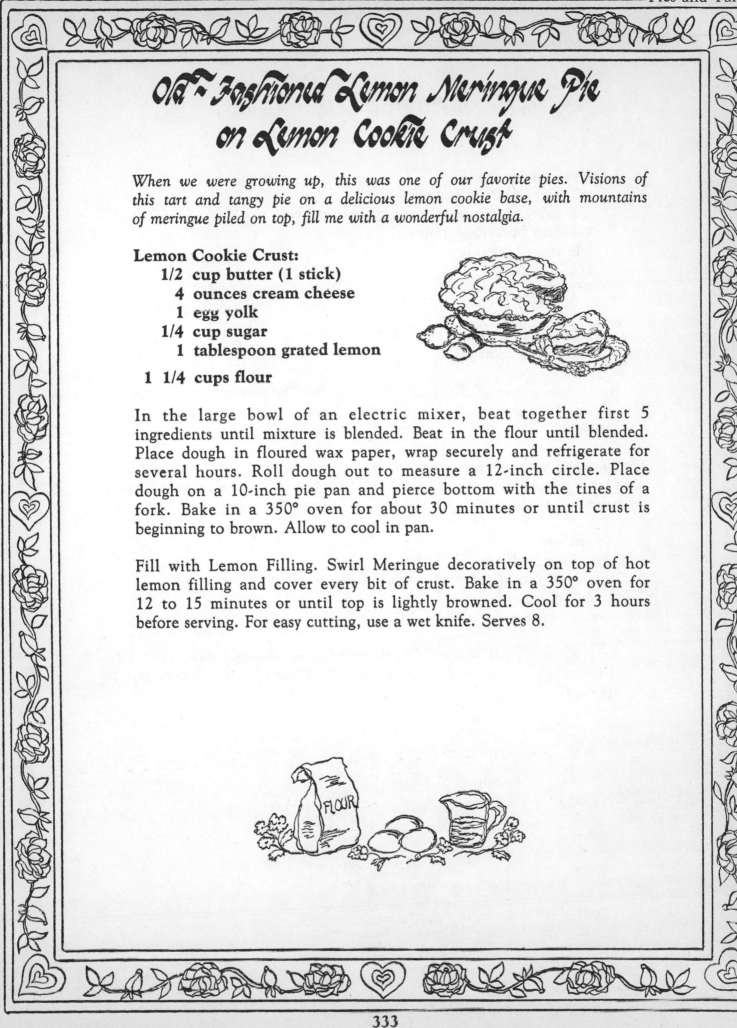

- 1/2 cup butter (1 stick)
- 4 ounces cream cheese
- 1 egg yolk
- 1/4 cup sugar
- 1 tablespoon grated lemon

1 1/4 cups flour

In the large bowl of an electric mixer, beat together first 5 ingredients until mixture is blended. Beat in the flour until blended. Place dough in floured wax paper, wrap securely and refrigerate for several hours. Roll dough out to measure a 12-inch circle. Place dough on a 10-inch pie pan and pierce bottom with the tines of a fork. Bake in a 350° oven for about 30 minutes or until crust is beginning to brown. Allow to cool in pan.

Fill with Lemon Filling. Swirl Meringue decoratively on top of hot lemon filling and cover every bit of crust. Bake in a 350° oven for 12 to 15 minutes or until top is lightly browned. Cool for 3 hours before serving. For easy cutting, use a wet knife. Serves 8.

Lemon Meringue Pie (continued)

Lemon Filling:
  2 cups boiling water
  2 tablespoons finely grated lemon peel
1/4 cup butter, softened
1/8 teaspoon salt
1/2 cup sugar

  4 egg yolks
  1 cup sugar
1/2 cup cornstarch
2/3 cup lemon juice

In a saucepan, off the heat, stir together hot water, peel, butter, salt and sugar. In a large mixer bowl, beat the yolks, sugar, cornstarch and lemon juice until thoroughly blended.

Pour egg yolk mixture into hot water mixture and stir until blended. Place saucepan on low heat and cook and stir constantly until mixture has thickened. Do not boil or filling will curdle.

Meringue:
  5 egg whites
    pinch of salt and cream of tartar
2/3 cup sugar
  1 teaspoon vanilla

Beat whites until foamy. Continue beating and add salt, cream of tartar, sugar (1 tablespoon at a time) and vanilla, until meringue is very stiff.

Grandma's Old-Fashioned Southern Pecan Pie

Absolutely delicious and gorgeous, this lovely creation is recklessly rich. Serve it "natural" for any addition would be gilding the lily.

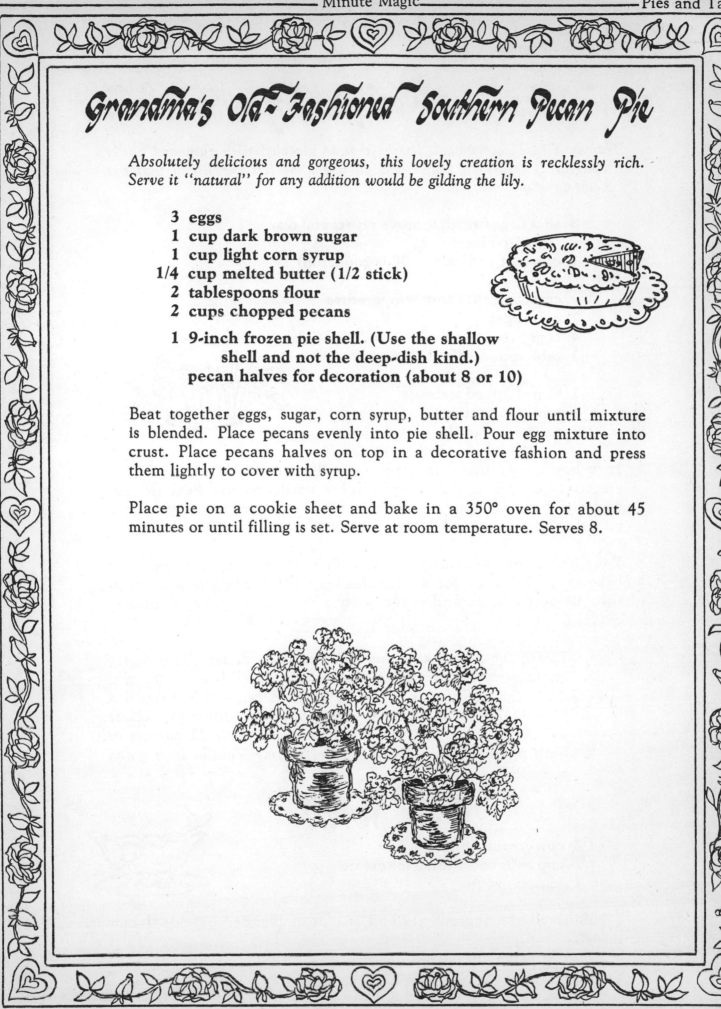

- 3 eggs
- 1 cup dark brown sugar
- 1 cup light corn syrup
- 1/4 cup melted butter (1/2 stick)
- 2 tablespoons flour
- 2 cups chopped pecans

- 1 9-inch frozen pie shell. (Use the shallow shell and not the deep-dish kind.)
  pecan halves for decoration (about 8 or 10)

Beat together eggs, sugar, corn syrup, butter and flour until mixture is blended. Place pecans evenly into pie shell. Pour egg mixture into crust. Place pecans halves on top in a decorative fashion and press them lightly to cover with syrup.

Place pie on a cookie sheet and bake in a 350° oven for about 45 minutes or until filling is set. Serve at room temperature. Serves 8.

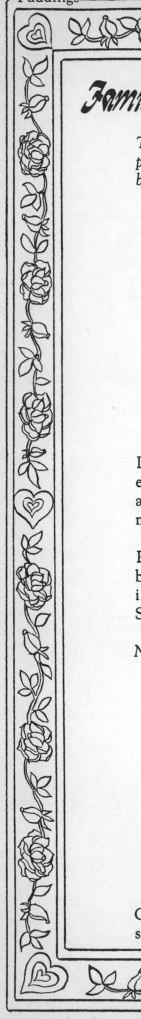

Family Chocolate Bread Pudding with Walnuts

This is a nice economical dessert that is sparkled with rum and easily prepared. It is also a grand way to use some leftover bread that has become day-old.

8   slices egg bread, remove crusts and tear
      into pieces
1   cup half and half (milk is good, too)

1/4   cup butter at room temperature
1   cup sugar
4   eggs
3   tablespoons sifted cocoa

1   cup chopped walnuts
1   tablespoon rum
1/2   teaspoon vanilla

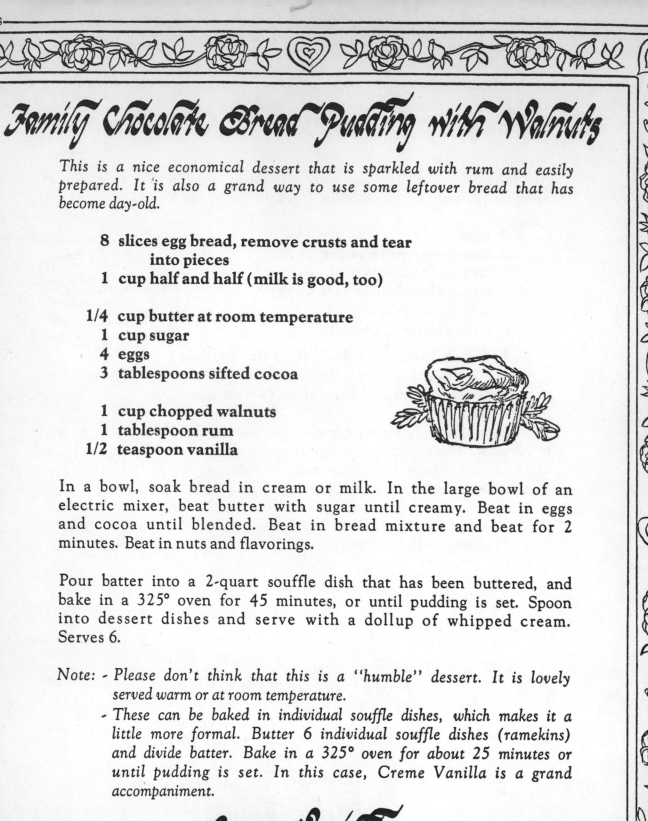

In a bowl, soak bread in cream or milk. In the large bowl of an electric mixer, beat butter with sugar until creamy. Beat in eggs and cocoa until blended. Beat in bread mixture and beat for 2 minutes. Beat in nuts and flavorings.

Pour batter into a 2-quart souffle dish that has been buttered, and bake in a 325° oven for 45 minutes, or until pudding is set. Spoon into dessert dishes and serve with a dollup of whipped cream. Serves 6.

Note: - Please don't think that this is a ''humble'' dessert. It is lovely served warm or at room temperature.
- These can be baked in individual souffle dishes, which makes it a little more formal. Butter 6 individual souffle dishes (ramekins) and divide batter. Bake in a 325° oven for about 25 minutes or until pudding is set. In this case, Creme Vanilla is a grand accompaniment.

Creme Vanilla

1/2   cup cream, whipped
1/2   cup softened vanilla ice cream
1   teaspoon rum

Combine all the ingredients and stir until blended. Yields 1 cup sauce.

Old-Fashioned Raisin Bread Pudding with Strawberries & Bananas

1 quart milk
4 eggs
3/4 cup sugar
1 teaspoon vanilla

6 slices egg bread, crusts removed and diced
1/2 cup yellow raisins

1 package (10 ounces) frozen strawberries in
    syrup, defrosted
2 medium bananas, coarsely chopped
1 tablespoon lemon juice

In a large bowl, beat together milk, eggs, sugar and vanilla until blended. Beat in the bread and raisins. Allow mixture to stand for 20 minutes.

Divide mixture between 8 buttered ramekins (individual souffle dishes) and place in a baking pan. Pour boiling water into pan to reach 1-inch up the sides of the souffle dishes. Bake in a 300° oven for about 45 minutes or until a cake tester, inserted 1/2-inch off center, comes out clean. Do not overbake. Allow custard to cool and then refrigerate.

Meanwhile, stir together the strawberries in syrup, bananas and lemon juice and refrigerate. At serving time, spoon a tablespoon or two of fruit on the top of the custard. Serves 8.

Old-Fashioned Apple Pudding with Dates

This is a homey dessert just filled with flavor and goodness. It should be served warm with a spoonful of whipped cream or Creme Vanilla. A small scoop of ice cream is also lovely.

1 egg
1/2 cup sugar
1 teaspoon vanilla

1/3 cup flour
1 teaspoon baking powder

1 medium apple, cored, peeled and very thinly sliced
1 tablespoon lemon juice
1 teaspoon grated lemon peel
1/2 cup chopped toasted walnuts
1/3 cup chopped dates (can substitute yellow raisins)

1 tablespoon cinnamon sugar

Beat together egg, sugar and vanilla until mixture is light and fluffy. Beat in the flour and baking powder just until blended. Stir in the apple, lemon juice, peel, walnuts and dates.

Place mixture in a buttered 1-quart souffle dish and sprinkle top with cinnamon sugar. Bake in a 350° oven for about 35 minutes or until batter is set and top is lightly browned. Spoon into dessert dishes and serve warm with a dollup of whipped cream or Creme Vanilla. Serves 4.

Note: - This is a very easy recipe, except it is hard to test for doneness. A thin crust forms on top which does not allow a cake tester to do its job. So, you must pierce the center with a sharp knife, and then test.
- This can be prepared earlier in the day, and reheated at time of serving.

Creme Vanilla

1/4 cup sour cream
1/4 cup cream
2 teaspoons sugar
1/2 teaspoon vanilla

Combine all the ingredients in a jar with a tight-fitting lid and stir to blend. Refrigerate for 4 hours before serving.

Apple Pudding with Dates, Walnuts & Raisins

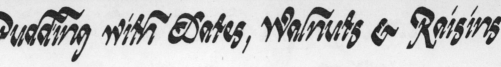

    3 egg whites
  1/2 cup sugar

    3 egg yolks

  1/2 cup vanilla wafer crumbs
  1/2 cup (1 stick) melted butter
  1/2 cup chopped walnuts, toasted
    2 apples, peeled, cored and grated
    4 tablespoons lemon juice
  1/2 cup raisins
  1/2 cup chopped dates
    1 teaspoon vanilla
    2 teaspoons grated orange peel

Beat egg whites until foamy. Gradually add the sugar and continue beating until whites are stiff. Continue beating, adding the egg yolks.

In a bowl, combine the remaining ingredients and toss until blended. Fold in the beaten egg whites. Place mixture into a greased, shallow, 10-inch porcelain baker and spread evenly. Bake at 350° for about 40 minutes or until top is golden brown. To serve, spoon into dessert dishes and top with a dollup of Orange Whipped Cream. Serves 6.

Orange Whipped Cream

    1 cup cream
    2 tablespoons sugar
    2 tablespoons grated orange (use fruit, juice and peel)
    2 tablespoons finely chopped toasted walnuts

Beat cream with sugar until stiff. Beat in the remaining ingredients until blended.

Note: - The pudding is very delicious without the whipped cream and can be served "natural" as well.
      - Pudding can be made earlier in the day and heated at time of serving. Serve warm, not hot.

Country-Kitchen Bread Pudding with Bananas, Apples & Raisins

3 slices of stale bread, remove crusts and cube

1 banana, sliced (can use 2 bananas)
1/3 cup orange juice
2/3 cup golden raisins
1 orange, peeled and chopped
1 teaspoon orange zest
1 apple, peeled and grated
1/3 cup sugar
1/2 teaspoon vanilla

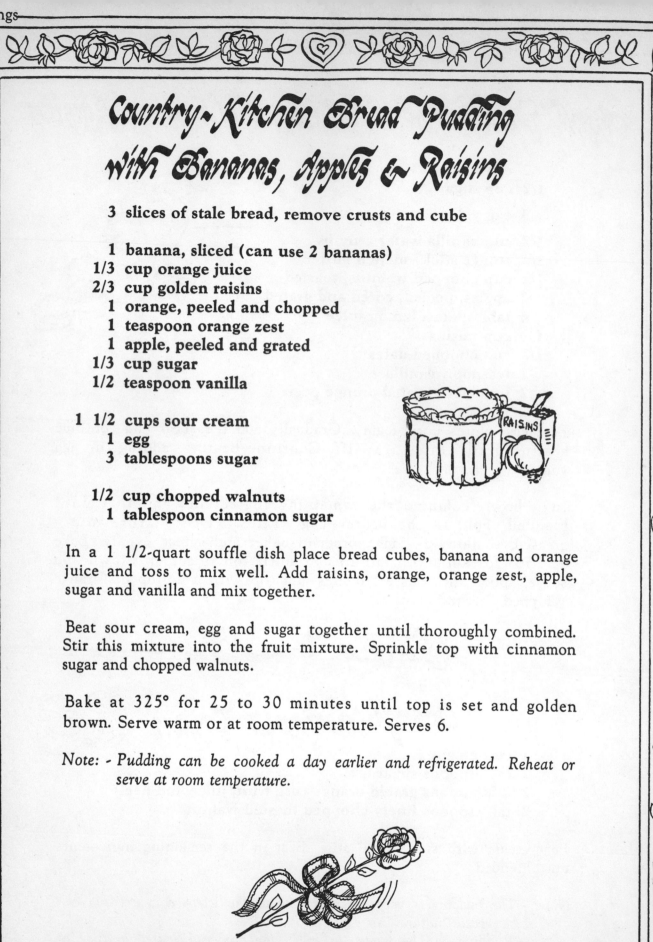

1 1/2 cups sour cream
1 egg
3 tablespoons sugar

1/2 cup chopped walnuts
1 tablespoon cinnamon sugar

In a 1 1/2-quart souffle dish place bread cubes, banana and orange juice and toss to mix well. Add raisins, orange, orange zest, apple, sugar and vanilla and mix together.

Beat sour cream, egg and sugar together until thoroughly combined. Stir this mixture into the fruit mixture. Sprinkle top with cinnamon sugar and chopped walnuts.

Bake at 325° for 25 to 30 minutes until top is set and golden brown. Serve warm or at room temperature. Serves 6.

Note: - Pudding can be cooked a day earlier and refrigerated. Reheat or serve at room temperature.

Chocolate Fudge Pudding Cake with Cocoa Cream

This simple little cake forms its own pudding sauce and can be assembled and baked AND served in the same dish.

        1/2 cup milk
          4 tablespoons butter, melted
          1 teaspoon vanilla

          1 cup flour
        1/2 cup sugar
          3 tablespoons cocoa, sifted
          2 teaspoons baking powder
        1/2 teaspoon salt

          5 tablespoons cocoa, sifted
        1/2 cup sugar
      1 1/2 cups hot water

In a 2-quart oven-proof bowl or souffle dish, place milk, melted butter and vanilla. Stir in the flour, sugar, cocoa, baking powder and salt and stir until batter is blended and smooth. Spread batter evenly in bowl. Sprinkle cocoa and sugar evenly over the batter. Pour the hot water over all.

Place bowl in a 350° oven and bake for 40 minutes or until a cake tester inserted in center comes out clean. Cool. Frost with Cocoa Whipped Cream. When serving spoon a little sauce that formed on the bottom, over the whipped cream. Serves 6.

Cocoa Whipped Cream

        3/4 cup cream
          3 tablespoons sugar
          4 teaspoons sifted cocoa
        1/2 teaspoon vanilla

Combine all the ingredients and beat until cream is stiff. Spread over pudding cake. Refrigerate cake until ready to serve.

Note: - If you are planning to serve the pudding cake warm, then serve with a dollup of whipped cream. Do not frost.
*   - Cake is fudgy and very much like a brownie. Kids love it. However, it can be glamorized with the addition of 1 or 2 tablespoons of rum to the batter. Whipped cream can be enhanced with the addition of 1/2 tablespoon rum.*

Danish Pastry Croissants
with Lemon Cream Cheese Filling & Lemon Glaze

These wonderful melt-in-your-mouth croissants are delightful for breakfast or brunch. The dough handles very easily and produces an exquisite pastry.

- 1/2 cup butter (1 stick), softened
- 1 cup small curd cottage cheese
- 1 cup flour

Lemon Cream Cheese Filling:
- 4 ounces cream cheese
- 1/4 cup sugar
- 1 tablespoon grated lemon peel

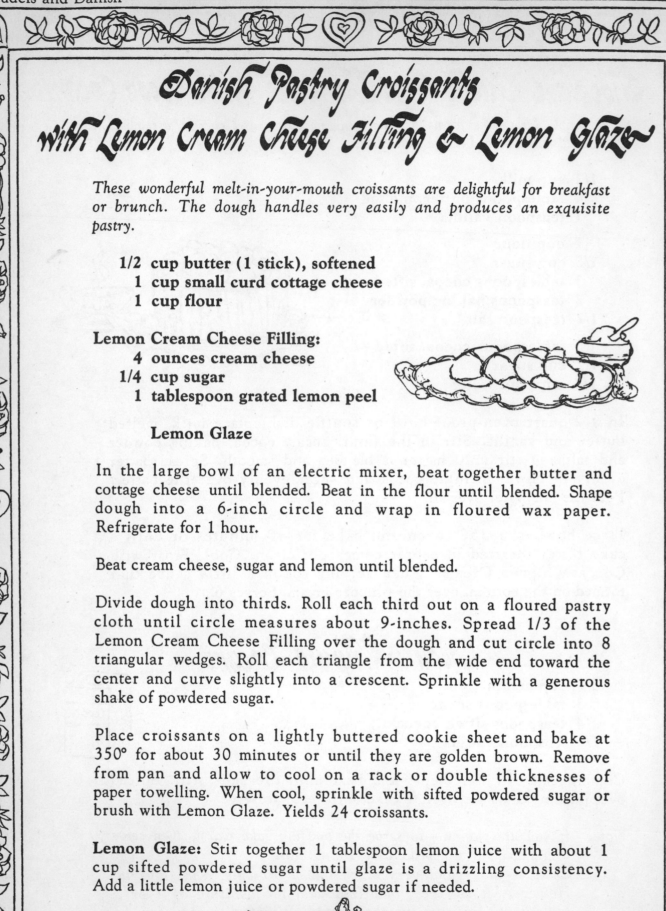

Lemon Glaze

In the large bowl of an electric mixer, beat together butter and cottage cheese until blended. Beat in the flour until blended. Shape dough into a 6-inch circle and wrap in floured wax paper. Refrigerate for 1 hour.

Beat cream cheese, sugar and lemon until blended.

Divide dough into thirds. Roll each third out on a floured pastry cloth until circle measures about 9-inches. Spread 1/3 of the Lemon Cream Cheese Filling over the dough and cut circle into 8 triangular wedges. Roll each triangle from the wide end toward the center and curve slightly into a crescent. Sprinkle with a generous shake of powdered sugar.

Place croissants on a lightly buttered cookie sheet and bake at 350° for about 30 minutes or until they are golden brown. Remove from pan and allow to cool on a rack or double thicknesses of paper towelling. When cool, sprinkle with sifted powdered sugar or brush with Lemon Glaze. Yields 24 croissants.

Lemon Glaze: Stir together 1 tablespoon lemon juice with about 1 cup sifted powdered sugar until glaze is a drizzling consistency. Add a little lemon juice or powdered sugar if needed.

The Rest of the Best

Helpful Hints

How often we find ourselves without an ingredient for a special recipe and we feel grumbly about a trip to the market. The following are a list of substitutions that could help in just such an emergency. One word of caution, however. Sensitive and delicate recipes should not be attempted because of their precise balance.

Vanilla Wafer Crumbs:

If you need crumbs of the cookie type for a crust, this is a lovely substitution. In a skillet, melt 5 tablespoons butter. Add 3/4 cup flour, 3 tablespoons sugar and 1/2 teaspoon vanilla. Cook and stir mixture constantly until crumbs are a golden brown. Use for a crust or to sprinkle on top of fruit or puddings. Yields enough crumbs for an 8-inch pie shell.

Buttermilk or Sour Milk:

Buttermilk can be substituted in certain recipes by stirring together 1 1/2 cups milk with 2 tablespoons lemon juice. Let it stand for 5 minutes.

Honey:

For 1 cup of honey you can substitute 1 1/3 cups sugar stirred with 1/3 cup liquid.

Unsweetened Chocolate:

You can substitute 3 tablespoons cocoa with 1 tablespoon butter for 1 ounce of unsweetened chocolate.

Self-Rising Flour:

1 cup self-rising flour can be substituted with 1 cup all-purpose flour mixed with 1 1/3 teaspoons baking powder and a pinch of salt.

Whole Milk:

To make 1 cup whole milk you can stir together 1/2 cup evaporated milk and 1/2 cup water.

To make 1 cup whole milk (for baking) you can substitute 7 ounces skim milk with 2 tablespoons butter.

Sour Cream:

Sour cream can be substituted by stirring together 1 cup cream with 1 tablespoon lemon juice. Allow to stand until thickened.

Holiday Eggnog with Cognac & Creme de Kahlua

1 quart prepared eggnog (from the refrigerated
    section in your market)
1 cup Kahlua liqueur
1/2 cup Cognac
1 cup cream, whipped until stiff

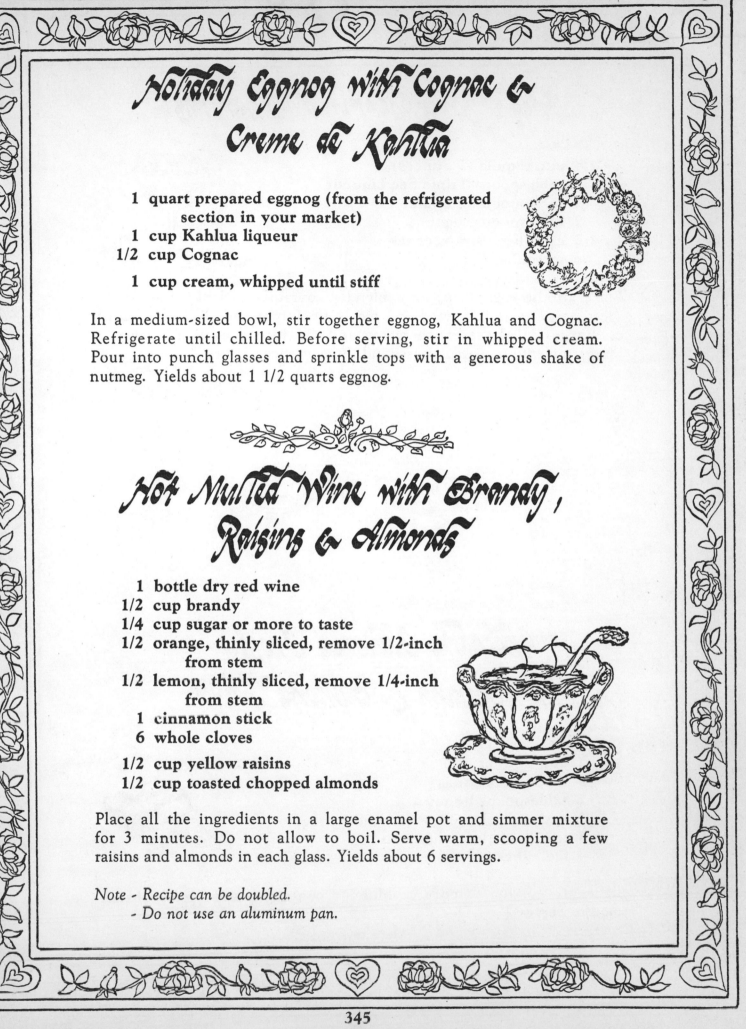

In a medium-sized bowl, stir together eggnog, Kahlua and Cognac.
Refrigerate until chilled. Before serving, stir in whipped cream.
Pour into punch glasses and sprinkle tops with a generous shake of
nutmeg. Yields about 1 1/2 quarts eggnog.

Hot Mulled Wine with Brandy, Raisins & Almonds

1 bottle dry red wine
1/2 cup brandy
1/4 cup sugar or more to taste
1/2 orange, thinly sliced, remove 1/2-inch
    from stem
1/2 lemon, thinly sliced, remove 1/4-inch
    from stem
1 cinnamon stick
6 whole cloves

1/2 cup yellow raisins
1/2 cup toasted chopped almonds

Place all the ingredients in a large enamel pot and simmer mixture
for 3 minutes. Do not allow to boil. Serve warm, scooping a few
raisins and almonds in each glass. Yields about 6 servings.

Note - Recipe can be doubled.
    - Do not use an aluminum pan.

Fresh Strawberry Margaritas

1/4 cup tequila (2 ounces)
2 tablespoons Triple Sec Liqueur
1 tablespoon lime juice
2 tablespoons sugar
1/2 cup sliced strawberries
6 ice cubes

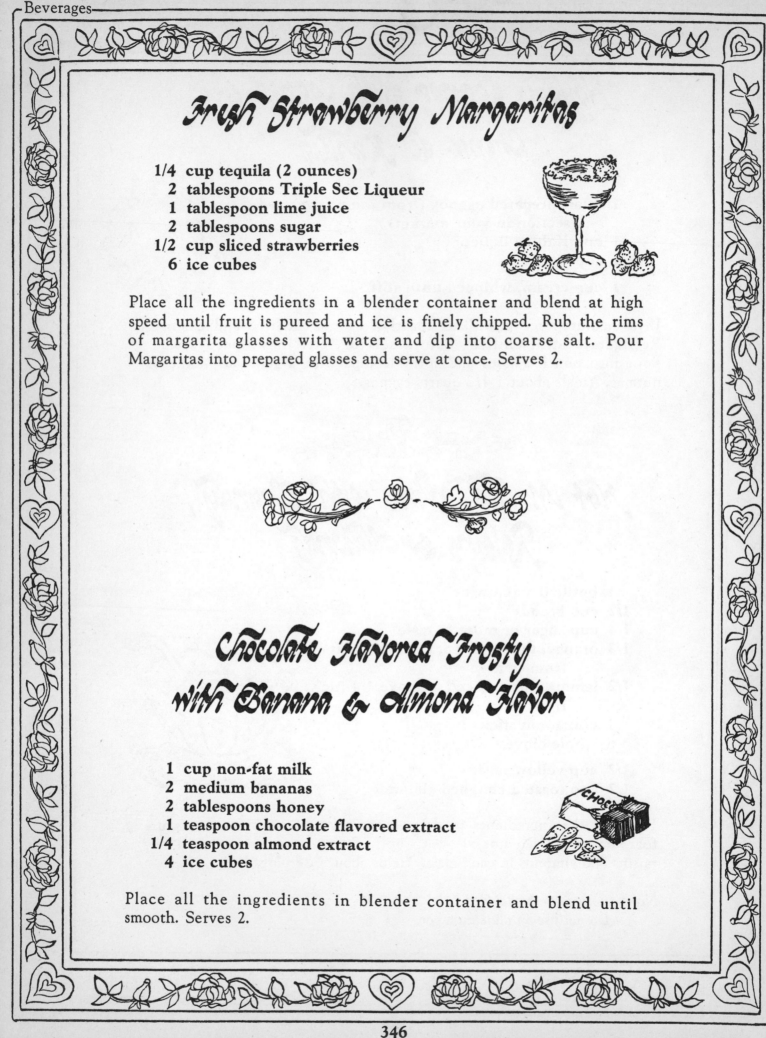

Place all the ingredients in a blender container and blend at high speed until fruit is pureed and ice is finely chipped. Rub the rims of margarita glasses with water and dip into coarse salt. Pour Margaritas into prepared glasses and serve at once. Serves 2.

Chocolate Flavored Frosty with Banana & Almond Flavor

1 cup non-fat milk
2 medium bananas
2 tablespoons honey
1 teaspoon chocolate flavored extract
1/4 teaspoon almond extract
4 ice cubes

Place all the ingredients in blender container and blend until smooth. Serves 2.

Strawberry Frosty with Banana & Yogurt

1 cup unflavored yogurt
1/2 cup sliced strawberries
1 medium banana
4 ice cubes
2 tablespoons honey
1 egg
1/4 teaspoon vanilla

Place all the ingredients in blender container and blend until smooth. Serves 2.

Vanilla Shake with Peaches & Banana

1 cup non-fat milk
1 cup fresh peaches, peeled and sliced
1 medium banana
2 tablespoons honey
1/2 teaspoon vanilla
4 ice cubes

Place all the ingredients in blender container and blend until smooth. Serves 2.

Pineapple Shake with Banana & Orange

1 cup unflavored yogurt
1/2 cup crushed pineapple
1 medium banana
2 tablespoons frozen orange juice concentrate
2 tablespoons honey
1 egg
1/4 cup coconut flakes
4 ice cubes

Place all the ingredients in blender container and blend until smooth. Serves 2.

Instant Sun Tea Concentrate for a Crowd

Keep this recipe handy for those times when you expect a large group and are crunched for space. One quart of this concentrate will serve 16 iced teas and 32 hot teas.

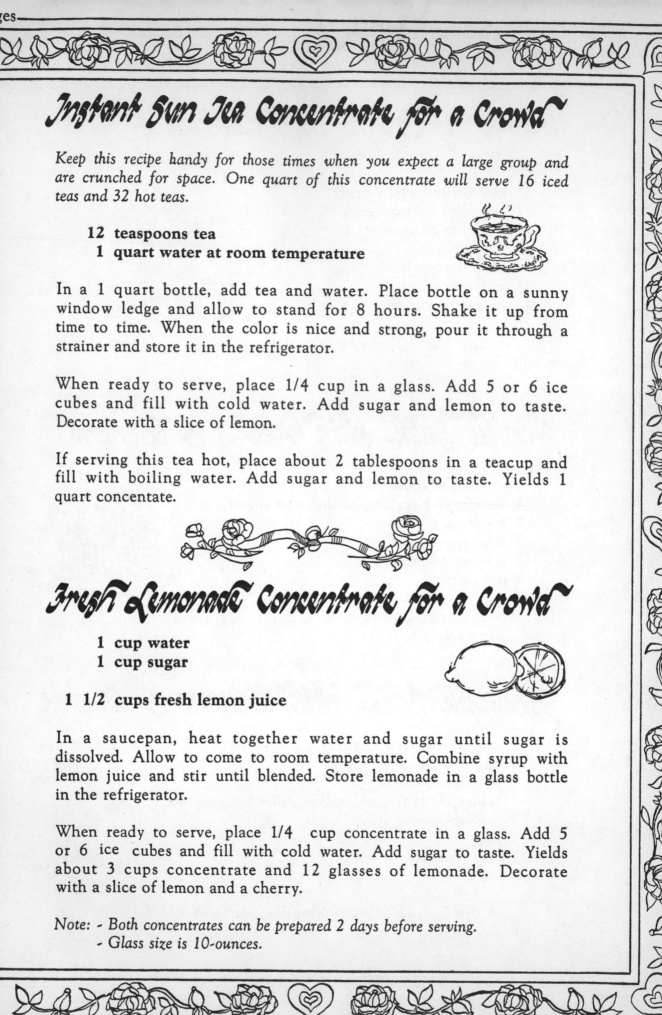

12 teaspoons tea
1 quart water at room temperature

In a 1 quart bottle, add tea and water. Place bottle on a sunny window ledge and allow to stand for 8 hours. Shake it up from time to time. When the color is nice and strong, pour it through a strainer and store it in the refrigerator.

When ready to serve, place 1/4 cup in a glass. Add 5 or 6 ice cubes and fill with cold water. Add sugar and lemon to taste. Decorate with a slice of lemon.

If serving this tea hot, place about 2 tablespoons in a teacup and fill with boiling water. Add sugar and lemon to taste. Yields 1 quart concentate.

Fresh Lemonade Concentrate for a Crowd

1 cup water
1 cup sugar

1 1/2 cups fresh lemon juice

In a saucepan, heat together water and sugar until sugar is dissolved. Allow to come to room temperature. Combine syrup with lemon juice and stir until blended. Store lemonade in a glass bottle in the refrigerator.

When ready to serve, place 1/4 cup concentrate in a glass. Add 5 or 6 ice cubes and fill with cold water. Add sugar to taste. Yields about 3 cups concentrate and 12 glasses of lemonade. Decorate with a slice of lemon and a cherry.

Note: - Both concentrates can be prepared 2 days before serving.
      - Glass size is 10-ounces.

Dutch Babies - Popover Pancakes

Try this delightful dish some Sunday morning for an exciting and fun breakfast. This beautiful puffy pancake looks and serves so well and it really is so very easy.

- 1/2 **cup butter (1 stick)**
- 1 **cup flour**
- 1 **cup milk**
- 1/4 **teaspoon salt**
- 4 **eggs**

Melt butter in a 9x13-inch pan and spread evenly. Beat together the flour, milk, salt and eggs until thoroughly blended. Pour batter into prepared pan.

Bake in a 400° oven for about 30 minutes or until pancake is puffed and golden. Sprinkle generously with sifted powdered sugar and serve with one of the following toppings. Serves 5 or 6.

Honey Orange - Heat together 1 cup honey and 3 ounces concentrated orange juice until blended. Spoon over pancake to taste. Unused honey can be stored in the refrigerator.

Yogurt and Strawberries - Serve pancake with a dollup of yogurt and sliced strawberries, sweetened with a little sugar.

Cinnamon Sugar - Sprinkle top with cinnamon sugar to taste and serve with a dollup of sour cream and strawberry jam.

Apples and Raisins - Cook together 3 cups sliced apples, 1/2 cup yellow raisins, 1/2 cup sugar, 1/4 cup apple juice, 1/4 cup butter, 2 tablespoons grated lemon peel and 1 teaspoon vanilla until apples are soft. Sprinkle top of pancake with cinnamon sugar and serve with cooked apples.

Sour Cream and Strawberry Orange Topping - In a bowl, combine 1 package (10 ounces) frozen strawberries in syrup with 3 ounces concentrated frozen orange juice. Serve pancake with a dollup of sour cream and a few tablespoons of Strawberry Orange Topping.

Note: - Sour Cream can be flavored with a little brown sugar and cinnamon to taste.

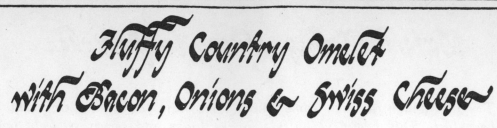

Fluffy Country Omelet
with Bacon, Onions & Swiss Cheese

6 eggs

1 onion, finely chopped
1 potato, grated

4 tablespoons oil (do not substitute butter or margarine)

6 slices bacon, cooked crisp, drained and crumbled
   salt and pepper to taste

1 cup grated Swiss cheese

Place eggs in the large bowl of an electric mixer and beat for 3 to 4 minutes at high speed.

Meanwhile, in a 10 or 12-inch skillet, saute onions and potatoes in oil, until potatoes are tender. Stir in the cooked bacon. Pour the beaten eggs over the onion mixture and stir and turn gently, allowing uncooked egg to run to the bottom. When top is still soft, but not runny, sprinkle cheese on top and cook until cheese is melted. Serve omelet open. Serves 3 or 4.

Fluffy Country Omelet
with Tomatoes, Chiles & Cheese

6 eggs
1 can (2 ounces) diced green chiles
1/3 cup chopped green onions
2 cups grated Jack cheese
1 package (8 ounces) cream cheese
6 thin slices tomato
  salt and pepper to taste
4 tablespoons oil

Place eggs in the large bowl of an electric mixer and beat for 3 to 4 minutes at high speed.

Meanwhile, stir together chiles, green onions, Jack cheese and cream cheese until blended.

In a 10 or 12-inch skillet, heat oil. Pour beaten eggs into the pan and stir gently, allowing uncooked egg to run to the bottom. Spoon cheese mixture over the eggs and place sliced tomatoes over all. Cook until top is still a little soft but not runny and cheese is melted. Serve omelet open. Serves 3 or 4.

Note: - It is important that you use oil. If you use butter or margarine, eggs will not stay fluffy.
  - This is an extraordinary omelet technique for the eggs retain a fluffy and marvellous texture.

Royal French Toast

3 eggs
1/2 cup milk
1/2 cup sour cream
3 tablespoons cinnamon sugar
8 slices cinnamon bread

Beat eggs with milk, sour cream and cinnamon sugar. Dip bread slices in egg and saute them in a skillet with a small amount of butter until they are golden brown. Turn and brown other side. Serve warm with syrup, honey or cinnamon sugar. Serves 4.

French Raisin Toast with Cinnamon & Orange Honey

3 eggs
1/2 cup cream
3 tablespoons cinnamon sugar
1/2 teaspoon vanilla

8 slices raisin bread

Beat eggs with cream, cinnamon sugar and vanilla until eggs are light, about 1 minute.

Dip bread into egg mixture and let it soak up the egg. In a skillet or griddle, cook the bread slices in a small amount of butter until golden brown. Turn and brown other side. Keep warm in a low oven until all the bread is sauteed. Serve warm with Orange Honey. Serves 4.

Orange Honey

1 cup honey
2 teaspoons grated orange peel
1/4 cup orange juice concentrate

In a saucepan, heat together all the ingredients until they are well blended.

French Orange Toast with Country Orange Marmalade

8   slices French bread, cut into 1-inch slices

3   eggs
1/2 cup orange juice
1/2 cup cream
1/4 cup cinnamon sugar

Butter
Country Orange Marmalade

In a 9x13-inch pan, place bread slices in one layer. Beat together eggs, orange juice, cream and cinnamon sugar until blended. Pour egg mixture evenly over the bread. Allow bread to soak up egg, turning now and again until evenly moistened.

In a large skillet, heat 1 tablespoon butter until sizzling hot. Saute bread slices until golden brown on both sides. Use more butter as needed. Serve with Country Orange Marmalade or your favorite syrup. Serves 4.

Note: - *The French toast can be baked in the oven for a slightly different effect. After the eggs are nicely soaked up, place pan in a 350° oven and bake until bread is golden and puffed.*

Country Orange Marmalade

1 cup orange marmalade
1 tablespoon lemon juice
4 tablespoons chopped walnuts
3 tablespoons yellow raisins
2 tablespoons chopped Maraschino cherries

Combine all the ingredients and stir until blended. Store in the refrigerator until ready to use.

Honey Granola with Dates, Nuts & Wheat Germ

There is so much talk nowadays about the "healthy" breakfast cereals and some of them are also really very good tasting. Here is a rather delicious one that is filled with good things and makes for a good breakfast or snack.

Dry Ingredients:
- 6 cups quick-cooking oats
- 3 cups assorted chopped nuts (choose from almonds, walnuts, pecans, cashews, sunflower seeds, peanuts, soy nuts, etc.)
- 3/4 cup powdered milk
- 1 cup wheat germ
- 1/2 cup sesame seeds
- 1/2 cup brown sugar
- 1 cup coconut flakes

Liquid Ingredients:
- 1 cup honey
- 1 cup orange juice
- 1 cup butter, melted
- 1 teaspoon vanilla

- 1 cup raisins
- 1 cup chopped dates
- 1/2 cup chopped apricots

Combine dry ingredients in a large bowl and toss to mix. Combine liquid ingredients and stir until blended. Combine the two mixtures and toss and turn until mixture is thoroughly mixed.

Spread it out on a 12x16-inch pan and bake in a 300° oven, turning now and again until mixture is dry. Do not allow to get too brown. About 45 minutes should do it. When cool enough to handle, break up the clumps and add the raisins, dates and apricots. Store in an air-tight container in the refrigerator. Serve with milk or as a dry snack. Yields about 16 cups cereal or 32 servings.

Note: - This is just a very rough indication of quantities. Roughly speaking, you can use about 12 cups of dry ingredients to 3 cups of liquid ingredients. You can substitute other fruit juices for the orange juice and you can also substitute oil for butter.

German Apple Pancake with Sour Cream & Lingonberries

2 apples, peeled and grated and tossed
    with 2 tablespoons lemon juice
4 tablespoons butter
1/2 cup yellow raisins
1/2 cup chopped walnuts
1/4 cup sugar
1/4 teaspoon cinnamon

3 eggs
1 cup flour
1 cup milk
2 tablespoons melted butter
2 tablespoons sugar
1/2 teaspoon vanilla

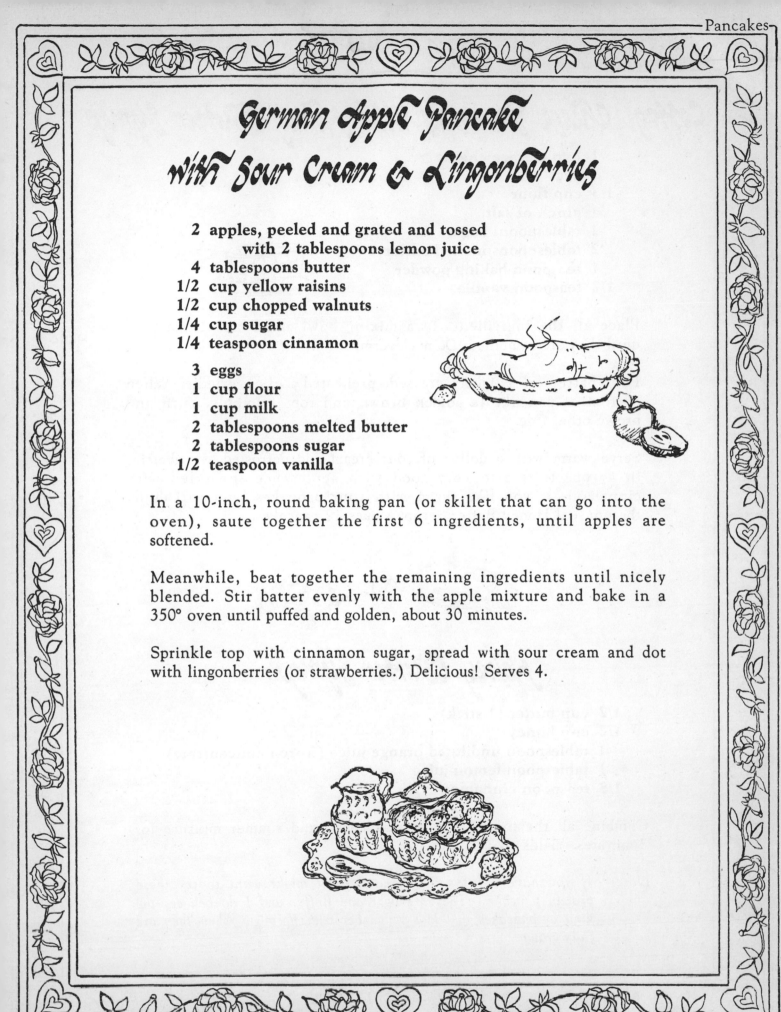

In a 10-inch, round baking pan (or skillet that can go into the oven), saute together the first 6 ingredients, until apples are softened.

Meanwhile, beat together the remaining ingredients until nicely blended. Stir batter evenly with the apple mixture and bake in a 350° oven until puffed and golden, about 30 minutes.

Sprinkle top with cinnamon sugar, spread with sour cream and dot with lingonberries (or strawberries.) Delicious! Serves 4.

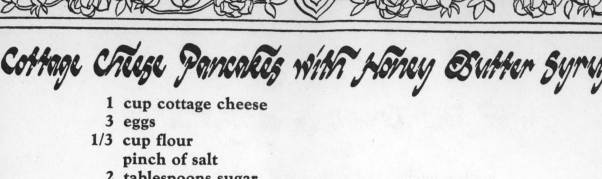

Cottage Cheese Pancakes with Honey Butter Syrup

1 cup cottage cheese
3 eggs
1/3 cup flour
   pinch of salt
2 tablespoons sugar
2 tablespoons melted butter
1 teaspoon baking powder
1/2 teaspoon vanilla

Place all the ingredients in a mixing bowl and beat with a fork until they are combined. Do not overmix.

Pour batter on a lightly greased, preheated Teflon griddle. When bottom of pancake is golden brown and top is bubbly, turn and brown other side.

Serve warm with a dollup of sour cream and defrosted strawberries in syrup. It is also very good with applesauce sprinkled with cinnamon. If you like syrup with your pancakes, you will enjoy the unusual Honey Butter Syrup. Makes 12 pancakes.

Honey Butter Syrup

1/2 cup butter (1 stick)
1/2 cup honey
1 tablespoon undiluted orange juice (frozen concentrate)
1 tablespoon lemon juice
1/8 teaspoon cinnamon

Combine all the ingredients in a saucepan and simmer mixture for 2 minutes. Yields about 1 cup.

Note: - *If you have a fussy, picky eater, you might want to try these protein pancakes. They are light and fluffy, and I do believe, the kind of pancakes that kids remember with nostalgia when they are fully grown.*

Here are two versions of a simply delicious relish. The addition of apples and cinnamon gives it a totally different character. One recipe starts with prepared ingredients and the other starts from scratch. They are both very good, indeed.

Orange Cranberry Relish with Apples & Cinnamon

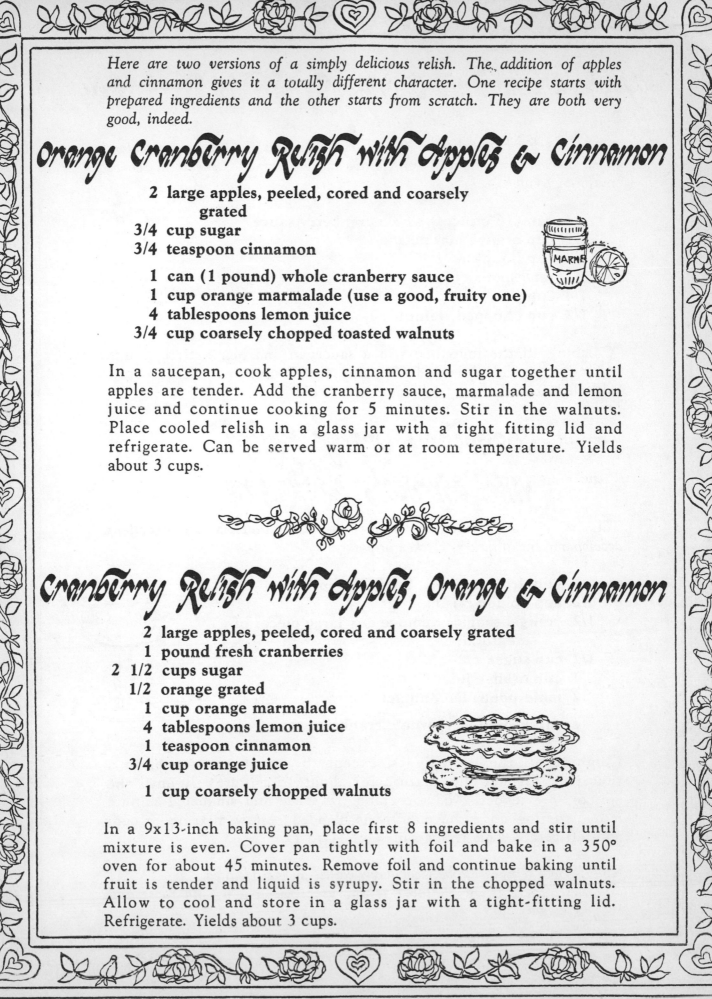

    2 large apples, peeled, cored and coarsely
       grated
  3/4 cup sugar
  3/4 teaspoon cinnamon

    1 can (1 pound) whole cranberry sauce
    1 cup orange marmalade (use a good, fruity one)
    4 tablespoons lemon juice
  3/4 cup coarsely chopped toasted walnuts

In a saucepan, cook apples, cinnamon and sugar together until apples are tender. Add the cranberry sauce, marmalade and lemon juice and continue cooking for 5 minutes. Stir in the walnuts. Place cooled relish in a glass jar with a tight fitting lid and refrigerate. Can be served warm or at room temperature. Yields about 3 cups.

Cranberry Relish with Apples, Orange & Cinnamon

      2 large apples, peeled, cored and coarsely grated
      1 pound fresh cranberries
  2 1/2 cups sugar
    1/2 orange grated
      1 cup orange marmalade
      4 tablespoons lemon juice
      1 teaspoon cinnamon
    3/4 cup orange juice

      1 cup coarsely chopped walnuts

In a 9x13-inch baking pan, place first 8 ingredients and stir until mixture is even. Cover pan tightly with foil and bake in a 350° oven for about 45 minutes. Remove foil and continue baking until fruit is tender and liquid is syrupy. Stir in the chopped walnuts. Allow to cool and store in a glass jar with a tight-fitting lid. Refrigerate. Yields about 3 cups.

Hot Cranberry Orange Relish in Port Wine

Serve this lovely relish with turkey or chicken. It is also very good with ham. If you're planning a very festive holiday dinner, serve it in scooped out orange cups.

- 1 **can (16 ounces) whole cranberry sauce**
- 1/2 **cup orange marmalade**
- 1/4 **cup honey**
- 2 **tablespoons lemon juice**
- 1/4 **cup port wine**
- 1/2 **cup chopped walnuts**

Combine all the ingredients in a saucepan and heat, stirring, until mixture is well blended. Simmer for 2 minutes. Serve warm, although it is also very delicious served cold.

Cranberry Orange Relish with Apricots & Raisins

This is a very delicious cranberry relish that is an excellent accompaniment to turkey, chicken or pork.

- 1 **cup dried apricots, finely chopped**
- 1/2 **cup golden raisins**
- 1/2 **orange, grated. Remove any large pieces of membrane**
- 1/2 **cup sugar**
- 1 **cup orange juice**
- 2 **tablespoons lemon juice**
- 1 **can (16 ounces) whole cranberry sauce**

Combine all the ingredients, except the cranberry sauce, in a saucepan. Simmer the mixture for about 15 minutes or until the apricots are tender. Add the cranberry sauce and simmer 1 minute more, stirring until the mixture is blended. Allow mixture to cool and refrigerate. This recipe will serve 10 to 12.

Note: - Both relishes can be made a day earlier and refrigerated.
- If there is any leftover relish, use it as a jam with toast and creamy butter.

Fresh Cranberry Relish with Apricots, Currants & Walnuts

        1   pound fresh cranberries
        1   cup chopped dried apricots
    1/2   cup yellow raisins
    1/4   cup black currants
        1   cup sugar
    3/4   cup orange juice
        2   tablespoons lemon juice

    3/4   cup chopped toasted walnuts
    1/2   teaspoon vanilla

Combine first 7 ingredients in a saucepan and simmer mixture for about 20 minutes or until apricots are tender and liquid is syrupy. Stir in the walnuts and vanilla.

Yields about 3 cups relish. Delicious served with turkey, chicken or Cornish hens.

Easiest & Best Cranberry Orange Relish

        1   can (16 ounces) whole cranberry sauce
    1/2   cup orange marmalade
    1/2   cup yellow raisins
        2   tablespoons lemon juice
        2   tablespoons orange honey

    1/2   cup coarsely chopped walnuts, toasted

Combine first 5 ingredients in a saucepan and simmer mixture for about 2 minutes or until cranberry sauce is well blended with the other ingredients. Add the chopped walnuts and stir until they are combined. Serve this relish warm or at room temperature.

Yields about 3 cups relish. Serve with roast chicken or roast turkey.

Fresh Cranberry Relish with Apples, Orange & Cinnamon

This relish will add a joyous touch to roast turkey, chicken or veal. It is fragrant with orange and lemon.

1 cup orange juice
1 cup sugar
1 medium orange, grated. Use fruit, juice and peel.
2 tablespoons lemon juice

1 pound fresh cranberries
2 apples, peeled, cored and grated
3/4 cup chopped walnuts
1/4 teaspoon cinnamon

In a saucepan, cook together orange juice, sugar, orange and lemon juice for about 5 minutes. Add the cranberries and apples and continue cooking for 10 minutes or until cranberries are popped and very soft. Add the walnuts and cook for an additional minute. Allow relish to cool. Place in a glass bowl, cover securely and refrigerate until ready to use. Yields about 3 cups relish.

Note: - *This relish is on the tart side. Add a little sugar if you like it sweeter.*

Honey Spiced Apples with Orange & Walnuts

1/3 cup butter
3 apples, peeled, cored and sliced
2 tablespoons grated orange (use fruit, juice and peel)
1/2 cup honey
1 teaspoon pumpkin pie spice
1/2 cup chopped walnuts

In a skillet, saute apples and orange in butter until apples are softened. Add the remaining ingredients and cook mixture for about 2 minutes or until mixture is nicely blended. Serve warm as an accompaniment to chicken or turkey.

The Index

Additional Copies of
WITH LOVE FROM DARLING'S KITCHEN
can be purchased at your local bookstore or
directly from:

RECIPES-OF-THE-MONTH CLUB
P.O. Box 5027   Beverly Hills, CA 90210